Danielle Larocca

W9-AAI-729

SAMS
Teach Yourself
SAP R/3
in 24 Hours

SAMS

800 East 96th St., Indianapolis, Indiana, 46240 USA

Sams Teach Yourself SAP™ R/3 in 24 Hours

Copyright © 1999 by Sams Publishing

International Standard Book Number: 0-672-31624-2

Library of Congress Catalog Card Number: 99-61493

Printed in the United States of America

First Printing: June 1999

05   04   12   11   10   9

Trademarks

Warning and Disclaimer

Bulk Sales

Sams Publishing offers excellent discounts on this book when ordered in quantity for bulk purchases or special sales. For more information, please contact

U.S. Corporate and Government Sales
1-800-382-3419
corpsales@pearsontechgroup.com

For sales outside of the U.S., please contact

International Sales

1-317-428-3341

international@pearsontechgroup.com

ASSOCIATE PUBLISHER
Bradley L Jones

ACQUISITIONS EDITOR
Chris Webb

DEVELOPMENT EDITOR
Thomas Cirtin

MANAGING EDITOR
Jodi Jensen

PROJECT EDITOR
Dawn Pearson

COPY EDITOR
Rhonda Tinch-Mize

INDEXER
Rebecca Salerno

PROOFREADER
Linda D. Morris

TECHNICAL EDITOR
Brian Bokanyi

INTERIOR DESIGN
Gary Adair

COVER DESIGN
Aren Howell

COPY WRITER
Eric Borgert

LAYOUT TECHNICIAN
Louis Porter, Jr.

Overview

Contents

About the Author

DANIELLE LAROCCA currently resides in Massapequa on New York's Long Island. Danielle has earned a bachelor of science degree in Psychology and holds certificates for many of SAP's courses. She is a SAP ABAP programmer as well as a SAP Human Resources Functional Specialist. Danielle has documented and instructed multiple computer languages and applications, including ABAP, Visual Basic, Electronic Data Interchange (EDI), and Oracle. Danielle is an avid technical reader and perpetual student, and is currently working for Bertelsmann's Doubleday Direct in New York.

Dedication

To my best friend Jimmy.

Acknowledgments

Special thanks to my family, especially my overworked *pro bono* attorney Cathy Larocca, and to my lifelong companion and future husband, James Signorile. Warm thanks and appreciation to the Doubleday Direct Project Team and consultants—with a special thanks to Dinesh Bakhru, Elizabeth Heilig, and Carol Maake.

Tell Us What You Think!

As the reader of this book, *you* are our most important critic and commentator. We value your opinion and want to know what we're doing right, what we could do better, what areas you'd like to see us publish in, and any other words of wisdom you're willing to pass our way.

As an associate publisher for Sams, I welcome your comments. You can email or write me directly to let me know what you did or didn't like about this book—as well as what we can do to make our books stronger.

Please note that I cannot help you with technical problems related to the topic of this book, and that due to the high volume of mail I receive, I might not be able to reply to every message.

When you write, please be sure to include this book's title and author, as well as your name and phone or fax number. I will carefully review your comments and share them with the author and editors who worked on the book.

Fax: (317) 581-4770

Email: feedback@samspublishing.com

Mail: Associate Publisher
            Sams Publishing
            800 East 96th Street
            Indianapolis, IN 46240 USA

Introduction

Welcome to *Sams Teach Yourself SAP R/3 in 24 Hours,* your teach-yourself guide to learning one of the most sophisticated enterprise solutions available on the market today. This book is divided into 24 chapters that can each be completed in about an hour.

SAP is the market and technology leader in client/server enterprise application software. SAP is the number one vendor of standard business-application software and is the fourth-largest independent software supplier in the world. SAP is also the undisputed leader in providing comprehensive solutions for companies of all sizes and all industry sectors.

This book covers everything you will need to become acquainted with the SAP system, from basic navigation through creating your own reports. *Sams Teach Yourself SAP R/3 in 24 Hours* begins with the very basics of SAP and slowly develops building on the items that you have learned. The pace of the book is designed to begin with the very basics and to move forward to cover the topics necessary to unleash the power of SAP.

This book is ideal for people just getting started with SAP because it begins with the very basics that teach you how to navigate and perform tasks in SAP. This book is also well suited for people who are already familiar with SAP, but who want to learn more about the software package and what it has to offer.

The examples used in this book, including tables, fields, and reports, are all taken from the SAP pre-delivered system. There is no additional disk required for installation, and readers can follow along with their own systems. Each chapter concludes with a *Summary, Workshop, Q&A* and *Quiz* section. These sections give you a comprehensive reference to the material you learned in the hour, and the opportunity to apply it through the quiz questions.

I hope you enjoy *Sams Teach Yourself SAP R/3 in 24 Hours* and learning the new world of SAP. Good luck.

Conventions Used in This Book

Text that you type and text that should appear on your screen is presented in `monospace` type.

```
It will look like this to mimic the way text looks on your screen.
```

In addition to this, the following icons are used to introduce other pertinent information used in this book.

A Note presents interesting pieces of information related to the surrounding discussion.

A Tip offers advice or teaches an easier way to do something.

A Caution advises you about potential problems and helps you steer clear of disaster.

New Term icons provide clear definitions of new, essential terms. The term appears in italic.

PART I

SAP R/3 Introduction

Hour

HOUR 1

Introduction to SAP

Congratulations. You have taken advantage of the opportunity to learn a software package that is truly revolutionary. All the "buzz" that you have heard about SAP is true: Its design, philosophy, and architecture are truly unrivaled, and it seems that there is virtually nothing this software solution cannot do. As a result, you will possess the knowledge that will make you a valuable asset to your corporation and the envy of your co-workers. The skills, tips, and knowledge you will learn from this book will empower you with an insight and security that you will truly appreciate for many years to come.

The first hour gives you an overview of the SAP structure and philosophy. It includes the background information on SAP as well as information about SAP's structure and three-tier architecture.

The highlights of this hour include

- An overview of SAP
- An introduction to SAP's architecture
- Investigating the client/server environment

- Discover a logical unit of work (LUW)
- Review of the dialog dispatch and dataflow in SAP

Overview of SAP

SAP is based in Walldorf, Germany and is the world's largest enterprise software company. SAP's foundation is built upon the concept of integration. The SAP family of products and services unite an organization from Financials and Human Resources to Manufacturing and Sales and Distribution. These different modules are explained in subsequent hours. Individually, each of these modules effectively manages an area of the organization. Each module contains business processes that are based on the industry's best practices in that area.

Development of SAP

SAP was founded in 1972 in Mannheim, Germany. The five original engineers who developed the concept of SAP originally named the company Systemanalyse und Programmentwicklung. Their goal was to develop a package that could integrate business solutions to get a better return on information. Their small company grew into Systems, Applications, and Products in Data Processing (SAP).

From day one, SAP was designed to be a global software product engineered on a multilingual and multinational platform. The revolutionary and innovative design of SAP made it Germany's top software vendor.

SAP Today

Today SAP reigns as the fourth largest software vendor in the world and is the market leader in Enterprise applications software. SAP is listed on the New York Stock Exchange (NYSE) under the symbol SAP. SAP offers comprehensive industry solutions including SAP Aerospace & Defense, SAP Automotive, SAP Banking, SAP Chemicals, SAP Consumer Products, SAP Engineering & Construction, SAP Healthcare, SAP High Tech, SAP Insurance, SAP Media, SAP Mill Products, SAP Oil & Gas, SAP Pharmaceuticals, SAP Public Sector Real Estate, SAP Retail, SAP Service Provider, SAP Telecommunications & Transportation, and SAP Utilities. The following are the SAP operating regions:

The Americas

Argentina	Mexico
Brazil	Peru
Canada	USA
Chile	Venezuela
Columbia	

Europe/Africa/Middle East

Austria	Norway
Belgium	Poland
Bulgaria (through partners)	Portugal
Croatia (through partners)	Romania (through partners)
Czech Republic	Russian Federation
Denmark	Saudi Arabia (through partners)
Finland	Slovak republic
France	Slovenia
Germany	South Africa
Greece (through partners)	Spain
Hungary	Sweden
Italy	Switzerland
Ireland	Turkey (through partners)
Israel (through partners)	U.K.
Kazakhstan	Ukraine
Netherlands	United Arab Emirates (through partners)

Asia Pacific

China	India
Hong Kong	Indonesia
Japan	Malaysia
Korea	New Zealand
Taiwan	Philippines
Australia	Thailand

R/3 System Architecture

The term *R/3* stands for *runtime system three*, and provides a set of business applications designed for the client/server environment. R/3 has evolved from SAP's original SAP R/2 system, which is based on a mainframe. R/3 architecture allows for the distribution of the workload to multiple PCs linked together through a network. The SAP R/3 system is designed in a fashion that distributes the presentation, application logic, and data management to different computers. See Figure 1.1 for an example.

FIGURE 1.1

The R/3 system architecture contains the database servers, application servers, and presentation systems.

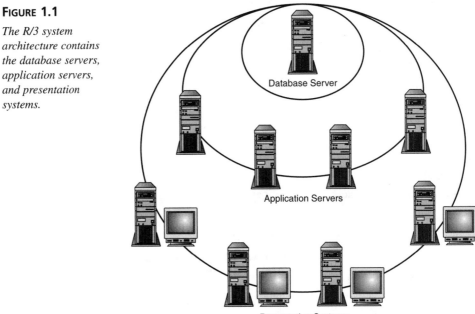

Database Server

Application Servers

Presentation Systems

Client/Server Environment

The concept of client/server has become very popular and is essentially a standard in building any type of computer communication architecture (see Figure 1.2).

A *client/server environment* is one in which the *client* (an individual PC or workstation) is requesting information (via a connection) of the supplying machine, known as the *server*. The communication and interchange of data between the requesting and supplying machine is known as a *client/server relationship*.

FIGURE 1.2

A standard client/server architecture connects workstations and printers to a server.

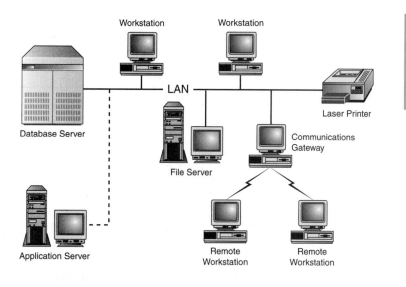

Three-Tier Hierarchy

The R/3 system architecture is constructed as a *three-tier hierarchy*, which is a client/server architecture in which software systems are structured into three layers:

- The user interface layer
- The business logic layer
- The database layer

The configuration shown in Figure 1.3 is a good example of a three-tier architecture structure as it applies to SAP.

In this example, a central computer houses the database, known as the *database server*. In terms of a distributed R/3 system, it is enough to understand that a database is the place where the data is stored. I will get into more detail about a database in the upcoming Hour 3, "Database Basics."

The *application server* is responsible for the administrative functions of the system. This includes background processing, printing (spool requests), and process request management. Multiple application servers can exist in this R/3 design. Additional computers are used as the presentation systems (see Table 1.1). These computers, or *clients* as they are called, display the software and screens that you will use when working with SAP. This is what is referred to as the *graphical user interface (GUI)*.

FIGURE 1.3

The three-tier archi-
tecture has become
the most popular
architectural design
for SAP R/3 installa-
tions.

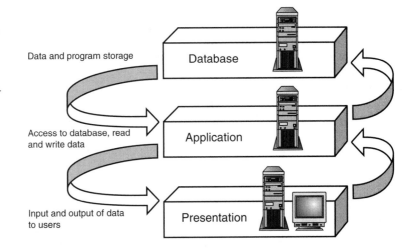

Data and program storage

Access to database, read
and write data

Input and output of data
to users

NEW TERM   *Graphical user interface*: The first user interfaces to computers were text-and-key-
board oriented. The command-line interface of the MS-DOS operating system (the
black screen, which you can still get to from your Windows operating system and that
first appears when you turn on your computer) is an example of the typical text-based
computer interface. In contrast, a *graphical user interface* consists of graphic images
called *icons* that include buttons, pull-down menus, dialog boxes, and scroll bars, and are
manipulated with a mouse. It was developed to make computers *user friendly*.

TABLE 1.1   R/3 SYSTEM ARCHITECTURE

Server	Server Name	Server Description
🖥	Presentation server	Displays the SAP R/3 window, also known as the SAPGUI or interface
🖥	Application server	Manages SAP administrative functions process request management
🖥	Database server	Collective storage of all data in the form of database tables and structures.

SAP Integration

One of the key elements of SAP that separates it from other enterprise applications is its
true sense of integration. This integration allows for a more connected business environment from Financials and Human Resources to Manufacturing and Sales and
Distribution.

Integration in SAP means that all your company's business processes are related and interspersed with each other so that a change in one area of your business will reflect on another area of your business, as shown in Figure 1.4. An example is payroll monies from your Human Resources module would also be linked to the General Ledger monies in your Financials module.

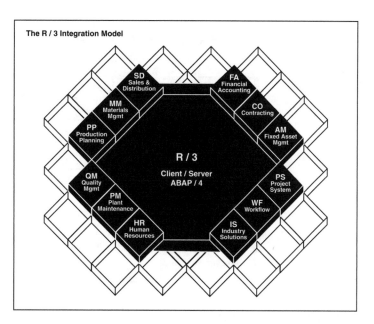

SAP Transactions

An SAP R/3 transaction is any logical process in the R/3 System. A simpler way to define this is to say a transaction is a self-contained unit. Creating a new customer, generating a list of existing customers, processing an order, and executing a program are all examples of SAP transactions.

NEW TERM   An R/3 *logical unit of work (LUW)* contains all the dialog steps of a transaction, concluding with the update to the SAP database.

Suppose that you are adding a new employee in the SAP Human Resources module. To complete this employee hiring, you will need to go through several screens to add that new employee to the system. Adding the employee's name and address on one screen would be considered a dialog step within the process. Adding that new employee's salary and paycheck information on another screen would be an additional dialog step. At the end of an employee hiring, after you have gone through all the necessary screens (or dialogs) in the process, the data would be updated in the SAP database, thus completing your LUW (see Figure 1.5).

FIGURE 1.5

A logical unit of work concludes with an update to the database.

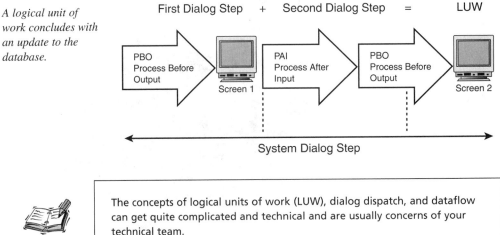

The concepts of logical units of work (LUW), dialog dispatch, and dataflow can get quite complicated and technical and are usually concerns of your technical team.

Dialog Dispatch and Dataflow

Dialog dispatch and *dataflow* refer to the information entered on a screen (dialog), the transference of the data to the database (dispatch), and the update to the database and movement to the next process (dataflow). The information typed into a screen by the user is at the Presentation or SAPGUI level. In order for this information to make its way to eventually update the database, it needs to be manipulated and managed by a dispatcher.

NEW TERM A *dispatcher* enables SAP to communicate with the presentation server by managing the information exchange between the SAPGUI and the work processes.

In simpler terms, the dispatcher really serves as the go-to-guy. Its role is to get things done. You learned about a logical unit of work, the steps performed to complete a task. It is the responsibility of the dispatcher to assure that complete processing of these steps occurs. The dispatcher evenly distributes the work it receives and organizes the communication activities so that, in the end, the database is updated and the transaction is complete (see Figure 1.6).

FIGURE 1.6

The SAP R/3 Dispatcher is responsible for controlling which processes run on which servers.

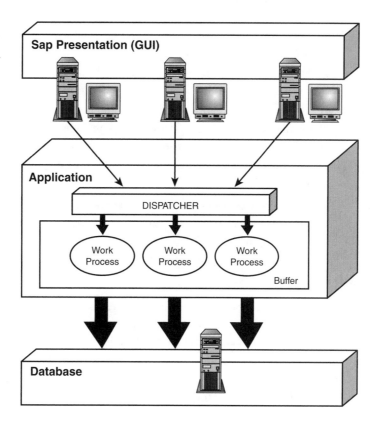

Summary

This hour provides you with an introduction to the world of SAP. You have gained an understanding of SAP's R/3 architecture and design, and you should be more familiar with some SAP catch phrases and terms (such as client/server, logical unit of work, dialog, dispatch, and dataflow). You are now in an ideal position to jump right into the SAP world as you progress into Hour 2, "SAP Basics," where you log in and begin to explore SAP.

Q&A

Q Are you required to use a three-tier architecture for your SAP implementation?

A Although a popular standard, the three-tier architecture design is not required for the implementation of SAP.

Q Is there a limit to the number of presentation systems that you have in your SAP design?

A Depending on the size of your SAP implementation, you may have hundreds, even thousands, of presentation systems. Although there is not a limit, there are some concerns with regard to licensing of your SAP software.

Q Can you use your SAP system to support multiple languages within a single client?

A The way that SAP is designed, each time you log on to a client you are prompted to enter a logon language. You can enter in to the same client in all of the different languages available in SAP.

Workshop

The workshop is designed to help you anticipate possible questions, review what you've learned, and begin thinking ahead to putting your knowledge into practice. The answers to the quiz that follows can be found in Appendix A, "Answers."

Quiz

1. What does SAP stand for?
2. Name a few of the industries that SAP offers comprehensive solutions for.
3. Describe a client/server environment.
4. Define the SAP term *dispatcher*.
5. What are the three distinct servers that comprise the R/3 system architecture?
6. What is the main benefit of SAP's integration?
7. Describe an important benefit to the design of a relational database management system (RDBMS).
8. A logical unit of work (LUW) is not complete until what action is accomplished?

Hour **2**

SAP Basics

Now you are ready to actually dive into the SAP world. If SAP is installed on your system, you can follow along as you progress through this hour. If your SAP connection is not yet available, you can follow along in the book, so when your connection becomes available, you will be more prepared to jump right in. Let's get started.

This highlights of this hour include

- Logging on and off
- Session management and multitasking
- R/3 Window Basics
- User snooping

Session Basics

Each instance that you connect to SAP is referred to as a session. The number of the current session is displayed in the status bar, which you will see in a few minutes.

NEW TERM An *SAP session* is the window where the user can process a certain task in the SAPGUI window (the user interface). When a user logs on to the R/3 system, the system opens the first session.

One of the benefits from this multiple session option is that you can multitask. Assume that you are processing a new customer order and your boss calls asking you to generate a report. There is no need to stop the processing of the order. You can leave that session (screen) open on your computer and begin a new session. With this new session, you can request and generate your boss's report. You can open up to nine sessions at the same time (as I explain later in the section "Session Management"). Think of how much more efficient you will become because of this important multitasking feature!

Start Up of the R/3 System

The SAP R/3 system is designed as a client system. What this means is that you have the freedom to operate the system from any computer that has the SAPGUI (presentation software that you see on your screen) installed and that is connected to your SAP database. In other words, you are not required to be at your desk to perform tasks. If you happen to be visiting your distribution plant and realize that you forgot to perform a task back at your office, you could perform it at the plant. SAP recognizes who you are and what activities you are allowed to process through your SAP username.

All SAP users are assigned a username. In most cases, it is your own name or initials. You are also assigned an initial password, which you will need to connect to the SAP system.

The Client Concept

Your organization will likely have multiple clients. *Clients* as described here are self-contained units within the R/3 system with separate master records and their own set of tables. Here is a general example. When you are first installing SAP and configuring the system, you will likely have a Development as well as a Production client. These two distinct environments within your database allow you to segregate your actual data (production client) from your test and configuration data (development client). Each client is assigned a three-digit number, which you will be required to enter at login time.

 Within the SAP world, the term client can be used to describe two distinctly different things. In certain situations, a client can represent an individual PC or workstation. In other instances, it is used to describe a logical environment with the database.

Initial Log On

The initial screen that you will see when connecting to SAP is the SAP R/3 Log On
Screen. See Figure 2.1.

FIGURE 2.1

*The first screen you
will see when logging
on to your SAP sys-
tem is the Client
Login Screen.*

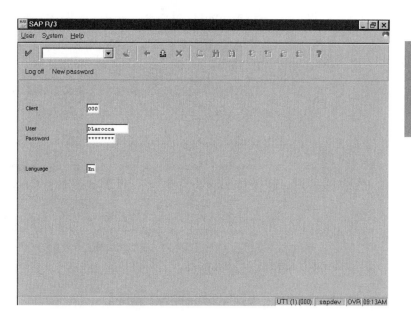

On this screen, you will need to provide the client number, username, and initial password that were assigned to you. Enter the information on this screen and select the green
check mark (or hit the Enter key on your keyboard) to continue.

It is not necessary for you to enter your logon language on this initial login
screen (see Figure 2.1). Your system will likely be configured to default to a
standard language for your organization. If your organization requires a
global (multilingual) login, you can specify the two-digit language code in
the language box.

Changing Your Password

On your first log in to SAP, you will be prompted to change your password. You must use the following five rules to create your password:

Rule 1   A password must consist of at least three characters.

Rule 2   The first character can not be ! or ?.

Rule 3   The first three characters must be unique.

Rule 4   The first three characters might not be contained in the username.

Rule 5   The password might not be SAP* or PASS.

> In addition to the standard rules for governing passwords, your company can also define a set of rules that pertains to its own operation.

On the Change Password screen, as shown in Figure 2.2, enter your new password, following the preceding rules, on both lines and select the green check mark (or press Enter) to continue.

FIGURE 2.2

Upon your first connection to SAP, you will be required to change your password.

SAP R/3	✕
New password	╟********
Repeat password	╟********
Transfer	Cancel

Logging Off of SAP

To terminate your SAP session or connection, you can select the System, Logoff option from the main menu or select the Windows 95 ✕ key in the top right-hand corner of your window. SAP will prompt you with a box confirming the shutdown of SAP.

Session Management

As mentioned at the beginning of this hour, you can create up to nine sessions. Each session you create is as if you logged on to the system again. Consequently, the system has more work to do, which can affect how fast it responds to your requests. Your company can set limits to the number of sessions that you can create.

Creating a New Session

In SAP you can create a session at any time and from any screen in the system. You do not lose any data in the sessions that are already open with each new session you create. Create a new session by following the menu path System, Create Session. You will now have two sessions open on your computer. If you want to determine which session you are currently in, you can check the status bar on the bottom right of your screen (see Figure 2.3).

FIGURE 2.3

The R/3 window displays the current session number in the bottom right hand side of the screen in each R/3 window.

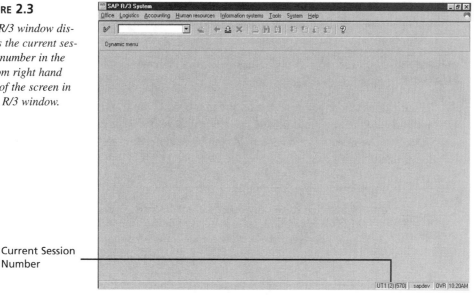

Current Session
Number

Creating a New Session With the Command Prompt

You can also create a new session by typing in an /0 (*O* for open) in the command field on the top left-hand side of your R/3 window, and pressing Enter. You will be prompted with a window like the one shown in Figure 2.4.

FIGURE 2.4

The Overview of Sessions window displays the number of open sessions and allows you to create or end sessions.

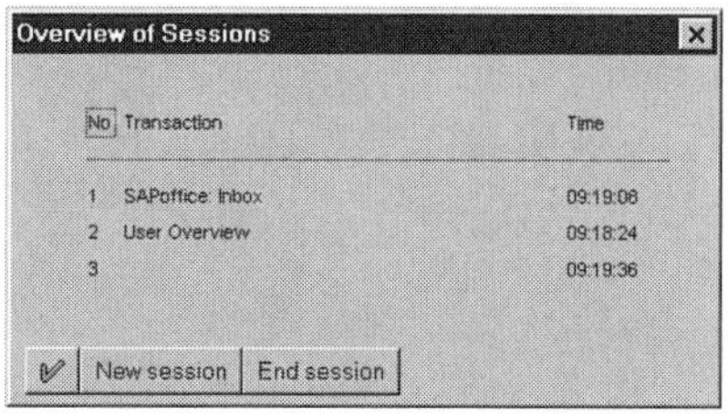

From this box, you can create a new session by selecting the new session box or terminate an existing session by selecting the end session box. This box also gives you an overview of all the sessions that you currently have open.

When you open a session, the system displays the initial SAP R/3 system screen in the new session. But you can change this by changing what you enter in the command field.

Creating a New Session and Start a New Task At the Same Time

You can also create a new session and start a new task at the same time. Again, you use the command field. By entering transaction codes in the command field, you can call a task or proceed to a certain screen without having to choose menu options.

NEW TERM A *transaction code* is a sequence of four alphanumeric characters that identify a transaction in the R/3 system.

To call a transaction, you enter the transaction code in the command field on the top left-hand side of your R/3 window, and press Enter. Give it a try using the transaction code SE38. Type **se38** in the command field, and press Enter. You should arrive at the ABAP Editor Initial screen (see Figure 2.5).

Transaction codes are not case sensitive, which means that you can enter them in lower- or uppercase. For information on finding and using transaction codes, see Hour 5, "Navigation in the R/3 System."

Depending on your systems security authorization, you may not be able to enter certain transaction codes or navigate to certain screens.

If you want to create a new session and call a transaction at the same time, you would need to add the /O prefix to the transaction code. Try entering /OS000 and pressing Enter. This creates a new session that opens to the main SAP R/3 system screen. To use this method, you must know which transaction code to use for the task you want to perform. I will explore this concept more in Hour 5, "Navigation in the R/3 System."

Enter transaction code here

FIGURE 2.5

*Using a transaction
code, we immediately
jumped to the ABAP
Editor Initial Screen
without having to use
menu paths for navi-
gation.*

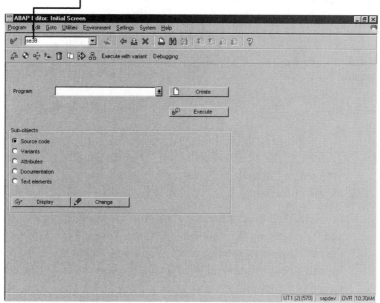

2

 It is important to note than when using Transaction codes from any screen
except the initial screen, you will need to add an /N prefix before the transaction code, or an /O to create a new session and start a new transaction.

End a Session

After you are done using a session, it is a good idea to end it. Each session uses system
resources that can affect how fast the R/3 system responds to your requests. Before you
end a session, it is important to note that you must save any data that you want to keep.
When you end a session, the system will NOT prompt you to save your data.

Ending a session is similar to creating a session. You follow the menu path System, End
session. If you have followed along, you should now have four open sessions. For each
open session, you will see a number indicating what session you are currently in listed in
the bottom right-hand side of the window (see Figure 2.3).

Next, go to the command field and type in /O like you did earlier in the section
"Creating A New Session With The Command Prompt" to retrieve the Overview of
Sessions box. It should appear similar to the window shown in Figure 2.6.

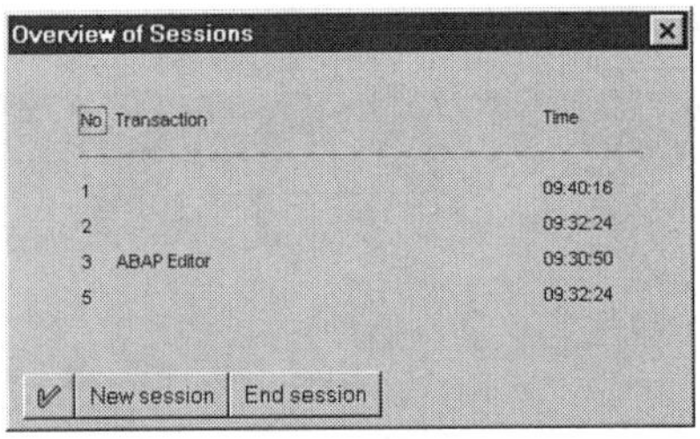

FIGURE 2.6

Your Overview of Sessions box will reflect your open sessions and transactions.

Overview of Sessions		☒
No. Transaction		Time
1		09:40:16
2		09:32:24
3	ABAP Editor	09:30:50
5		09:32:24

| ✔ | New session | End session |

This box lists all the sessions that you currently have open. In my example, numbers 1, 2, and 4 appear blank because I am not on a specific transaction and still on the main SAP screen. Transaction 3 corresponds to the name of the transaction that I called using a transaction code.

From the Overview of Sessions box, you can selectively close a session by selecting it and then selecting the End Session button. Give it a try. Select number 3, by single clicking on it and select the End Session button. It might not initially appear that anything has happened, but that session was closed. To check, return to the Session Overview box by typing in the transaction code /0 in the command field. Transactions 1,2, and 4 should still be listed, but number 3 is no longer open. Follow the same steps to end sessions 2 and 4, leaving only session 1 open.

Overview of Users

Have you ever been curious to see what your co-workers or your boss is working on? SAP has a snooping screen in which you can see a list of every user currently logged on to the SAP system. The Users Overview screen lists the client number they are logged in to, the number of sessions that they currently have open, and the transaction code that they are currently on in their first session.

Depending on your SAP system's configuration, your SAP system administrator might have blocked your access to this transaction.

To access this transaction, type /nSM04 in your command field and press Enter. The screen should appear similar to the one shown in Figure 2.7.

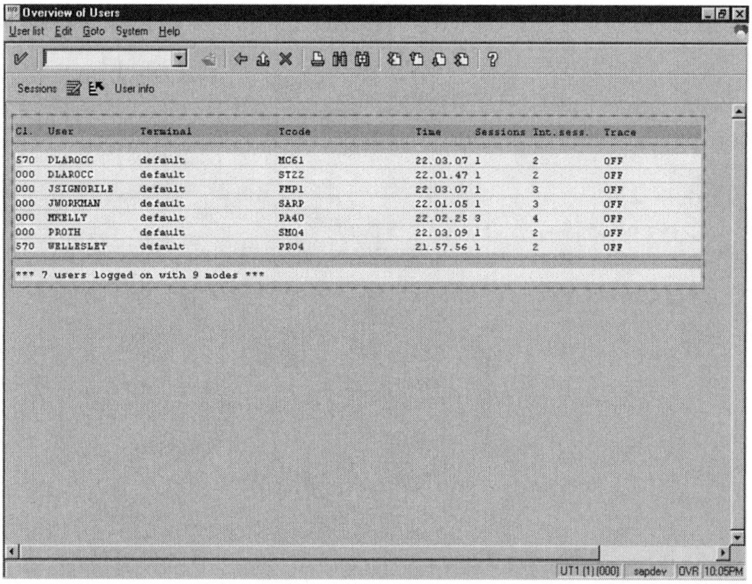
Overview of Users
User list Edit Goto System Help
Sessions User info
Cl. User Terminal Tcode Time Sessions Int.sess. Trace
570 DLAROCC default MC61 22.03.07 1 2 OFF
000 DLAROCC default ST22 22.01.47 1 2 OFF
000 JSIGNORILE default FMP1 22.03.07 1 3 OFF
000 JWORKMAN default SARP 22.01.05 1 3 OFF
000 MKELLY default PA40 22.02.25 3 4 OFF
000 PROTH default SM04 22.03.09 1 2 OFF
570 WELLESLEY default PR04 21.57.56 1 2 OFF
*** 7 users logged on with 9 modes ***
UT1 (1) (000) sapdev OVR 10:05PM

FIGURE 2.7

The Users Overview Screen allows you to see a list of all users currently logged in to SAP.

The Users Overview screen only shows you the transaction code of the first session that the user has logged on to. What if that user has multiple sessions open? To look at a list of all the transactions a user is currently processing, double-click on any user's name. An Overview of Sessions box like you saw in Figure 2.6 will appear, listing all the current transaction codes that the user is processing.

> Be careful when snooping with this transaction and never select the end session button for another user's session.

Window Basics

The R/3 window is the user interface to the R/3 system. At the very top of the window is the *Title bar*, which gives the screen (or transaction) description for the window that is displayed. The standard elements of an R/3 window are shown in Figure 2.8, and are explained in the following sections.

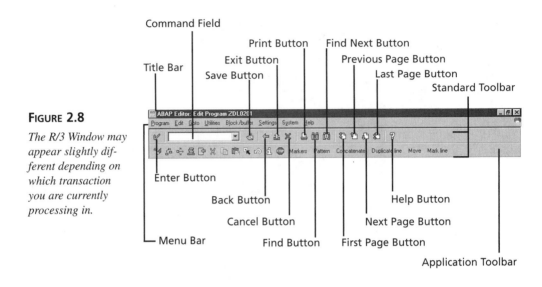

FIGURE 2.8

The R/3 Window may appear slightly different depending on which transaction you are currently processing in.

The Menu Bar

Under the Title bar is the *Menu bar*, which contains all the menu options available. The menu bar changes from screen to screen to be specific to the function module that you are currently processing in. The last two items on the menu bar, System and Help, remain constant on all SAP's screens and contain the same submenu options.

The Standard Toolbar

The *Standard toolbar* is easy to identify because of all the buttons. It varies slightly, but generally contains the same basic components on every screen. The main navigational, printing, page viewing, and help functions are all made available here. It contains the following elements:

- *Enter Button*: This button has the same function as the Enter key on your keyboard and is used to check your entry in a field or your work in a transaction when you have finished entering data on a screen. This button should not be confused with the Save button.

- *Command Field*: The command field is located to the right of the Enter button and is used to enter transaction codes to call a task without having to choose menu options for navigation.

- *Save Button*: The Save button saves your work and performs the same function as selecting Save in the Edit menu.

The Save button is the most misleading button on the toolbar if you are used to a Microsoft environment. In Microsoft applications, this same icon is used as the Open button.

2

- *Back Button*: The back button is quite similar to the back button used in most Web browsers, and it does just as its name implies. It will take you back to the previous screen. If you use this button to return to the previous screen, your data will not be saved unless you save it before hand using the Save button on the toolbar.
- *Exit Button*: The exit button is used to leave the current application. The system returns you to the previous application or to the main menu screen.
- *Cancel Button*: The cancel button is used to exit the current task without saving and performs the same function as selecting Cancel in the Edit menu.
- *Print Button*: The print button is used to print data from the screen in which you are currently working. (There are some advanced settings that the user should set up in order for the print setting to work more efficiently. These are covered in Hour 5, Navigation in the R/3 System.")
- *Find Button*: This button is used to perform a search for data on the screen in which you are currently working.
- *Find Next Button*: This button is used to perform an extended search for data on the screen in which you are currently working.
- *First Page Button*: This page navigation key is generally used in reports. It is used to travel to the top of a screen (or page) if the information on the screen is too long to fit on a single screen.
- *Previous Page (Page Up) Button*: This page navigation key is generally used in reports. It is used to travel up one screen (or page) if the information on the screen is too long to fit on a single screen. This button is equivalent to using the Page Up key on your keyboard.
- *Next Page (Page Down) Button*: This page navigation key is generally used in reports. It is used to travel down one screen when the information on the screen is too long to fit on a single screen. This button is equivalent to using the Page Down key on your keyboard.
- *Last Page Button*: This page navigation key is generally used in reports. It is used to travel to the end of a screen (or page) when the information on the screen is too long to fit on a single screen.

- *Help Button*: The Help button is used for context-sensitive help. That is, if you place your cursor on any object on the screen and select the Help button, you will receive specific help for that item. (You will learn more about the Help button and SAP's Help system in Hour 23, "SAP Help Overview.")

The Application Toolbar

The *Application toolbar* is located under the Standard toolbar (see Figure 2.8). This toolbar is application specific and varies depending on the screen (or transaction) that you are currently processing in and it offers additional function for that particular screen (or transaction).

For example, if you are in the Finance modules Create Rental Agreement Screen, your application toolbar will contain buttons allowing you to copy or retrieve master data from SAP. But if you are in the ABAP/4 Workbench Initial Editor screen, your application toolbar will contain buttons for the Dictionary, Repository Browser, and Screen Painter.

Summary

Hour 2 allows you to explore the SAP R/3 window, learn about its basic features, and get an introduction to the concept of session management and navigation. The basics that you have learned in this hour will be required skills for the remaining hours in this book.

Q&A

Q Can a user navigate to the same transaction code in more than one session?

A Using multiple sessions is like logging on to the system again and again, you can have all of your sessions on the same transaction at the same time if you wish.

Q If the Production and Development clients reside on different servers can they both be viewed on the Overview of Users (snooping screen)?

A Only the clients resident on the server that you are logged in to will be visible in the Overview of Users (snooping screen).

Q If your security access prevents a user from navigating to a particular screen using the menu paths can they jump there using a transaction code.

A All system security configurations are different but as a general rule, users who are not permitted to enter a particular SAP screen will not be able to access it via a menu path or a transaction code.

Workshop

The workshop is designed to help you anticipate possible questions, review what you've learned, and begin thinking ahead to putting your knowledge into practice. The answers to the quiz that follows can be found in Appendix A, "Answers."

Quiz

1. What is the maximum number of sessions that you can have open at one time in SAP?

2. What is the transaction code to the Users Overview screen?

3. If you are on any screen in the SAP system EXCEPT the main screen, what two-digit code must you enter before entering a transaction code so that you can navigate using the command field?

4. What two items on the Menu bar are constant on all SAP screens?

5. What is one of the most important benefits of using multiple sessions in SAP?

6. What three items are required in order for you to log on to the SAP system?

7. What is the menu path to create a new session in SAP (without using the command field)?

Exercises

1. Create a new session and navigate to the Overview Users Screen (snooping screen) and then view all of your open sessions.

2. You the transaction code /nFS10 to navigate to the GL account: initial screen balances display and then you the selection specific help to get help for the Company Code field.

HOUR 3

Database Basics

To understand the general concept of what SAP is, it is necessary to understand what a database is because SAP is based on a database. This hour I will explore the different features and structures in a database. Highlights of this hour include

- Discover what an RDBMS is
- Find out which databases are supported by SAP
- Learn the difference between a primary and foreign key
- See why indexes speed up data retrieval

Database Structure

A database is essentially an electronic filing system that houses a collection of information organized in such a way that allows a computer program to quickly select desired pieces of data.

 A *database* is a container to store, organize, retrieve, and present information.

In the simplest form, a database is composed of tables, columns (called *fields*), and rows (called *records* or *data*). A good example of a database is a telephone book in which the telephone book would be the table, a storage container for information (see Figure 3.1). There would be three columns (or fields): Name, address, and telephone number. Within these fields, there would be rows (or records).

FIGURE 3.1

One common use of a database program is to store names, addresses, and phone numbers—essentially an electronic version of a telephone book, which itself is a type of database.

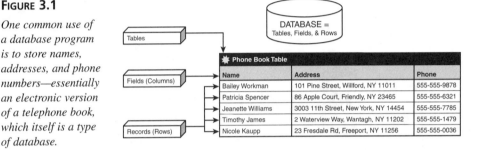

The basic structure of a database is quite similar to a Microsoft Excel spreadsheet wherein columns store rows and rows of data. The difference between a database and a spreadsheet is that databases can have multiple tables that are connected to each other through relationships.

The database plays a very central role to your SAP R/3 system. It is located on a central computer and houses all the data that is used by your SAP R/3 system. SAP can use different brand names databases to support the SAP system. A list of supported databases can be found in Table 3.1.

TABLE 3.1 SAP SUPPORTED DATABASES

Partner	Web site
Microsoft SQL Server	www.microsoft.com
DB2/CS	www.ibm.com
DB2/400	www.ibm.com
Informix	www.informix.com
Oracle	www.oracle.com
Dynamic Server	www.informix.com
DB2/UDB	www.ibm.com

Relational Database Management System (RDBMS)

The SAP database has over 12,000 tables that store information. These tables are connected to each other through relationships. This connection of multiple tables through relationships is known as a Relational Database Management System (RDBMS).

NEW TERM   A database system that stores data as well as the relationships between the data in two-dimensional tables is called a *Relational Database Management System (RDBMS)*.

An important benefit in the design of RDBMS is that it eliminates redundancy. To get an idea, you can look at the concept of RDBMS using the phonebook example. In this example, the phonebook is a table that stores the names, addresses, and phone numbers for everyone in your area. Say that you obtain a separate book, an Internet directory, that contains the names, Web site addresses, and email addresses of all the people in your area. You then have two separate tables that store information.

Say that you wanted to create a report listing Names and Phone numbers from the phonebook table and the email addresses from the Internet directory. This data is stored in two different tables. If you updated the phonebook table with all the information from the Internet directory, the same information would be stored in two tables.

Besides being redundant, this is more cumbersome from a maintenance perspective. Say that someone's email address changes, as they often do: You would then be required to change it in both tables. Using an RDBMS design, these problems are no longer a concern. Tables within an RDBMS are associated to each other through relationships. In the example, both the tables contain a column (or field) containing the person's name. In an RDBMS, these two tables could be linked by the name field (see Figure 3.2).

FIGURE 3.2

The phonebook example using RDBMS to link tables.

RELATIONSHIP

Phone Book Table

Name	Address	Phone
Bailey Workman	101 Pine Street, Willford, NY 11011	555-555-9878
Patricia Spencer	86 Apple Court, Friendly, NY 23465	555-555-6321
Jeanette Williams	3003 11th Street, New York, NY 14454	555-555-7785
Timothy James	2 Waterview Way, Wantagh, NY 11202	555-555-1479
Nicole Kaupp	23 Fresdale Rd, Freeport, NY 11256	555-555-0036

Internet Directory Table

Name	Email Address
Bailey Workman	Bworkman@Zucker.com
Patricia Spencer	Spenie@prodigy.inc
Jeanette Williams	LMT@Infotype.com
Timothy James	Tsig@Pat.com
Nicole Kaupp	Kaupp.Nicole@Airline.com

Both Tables Contain a *Name* Field.

Based on This Relationship, a Report Can Be Created with Output from both Tables

Report Based on Relationship Between 2 Tables

Name	Email Address	Phone
Bailey Workman	Bworkman@Zucker.com	555-555-9878
Patricia Spencer	Spenie@prodigy.inc	555-555-6321
Jeanette Williams	LMT@Infotype.com	555-555-7785
Timothy James	Tsig@Pat.com	555-555-1479
Nicole Kaupp	Kaupp.Nicole@Airline.com	555-555-0036

Primary Key

Database tables in an RDBMS are required to contain a unique field that individually distinguishes a record from all others. This unique field is called a primary key.

NEW TERM   A *primary key* is composed of one or more fields that make a record unique.

I'll use the SAP Human Resources module as an example of a primary key. The Human Resources module stores all your company's employees. Some of your employees will have the same department number, some will have the same job title, and some will even have the same salary. In order to uniquely distinguish each employee, a primary key could be used based on the employee's Social Security Number. Because a person's Social Security Number is truly unique, it would be a good candidate for a primary key in your employee's table. Figure 3.3 gives a good example of two different tables and their unique primary keys.

FIGURE 3.3

Primary keys in an Employee table and a Department table.

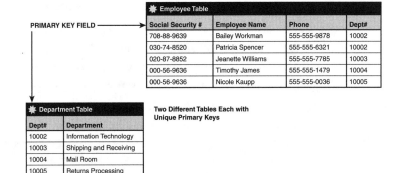

Foreign Key

You use the primary key field in one table to link it to another. The common link field in the other table is usually not the primary key in the other table: It is called a foreign key.

NEW TERM   The field or fields used to link a primary key field in another table is a *foreign key*.

Let's use the Human Resources employee example again. We have an employee table that stores the basic employee data with a primary key defined as the social security number, and we have a Department Table that stores all the department numbers and departments for employees with a department number as the primary key (see Figure 3.3). In these two tables, we have the same field, Department Number. In the Employees table, the department number is the foreign key linking it to the department table (see Figure 3.4).

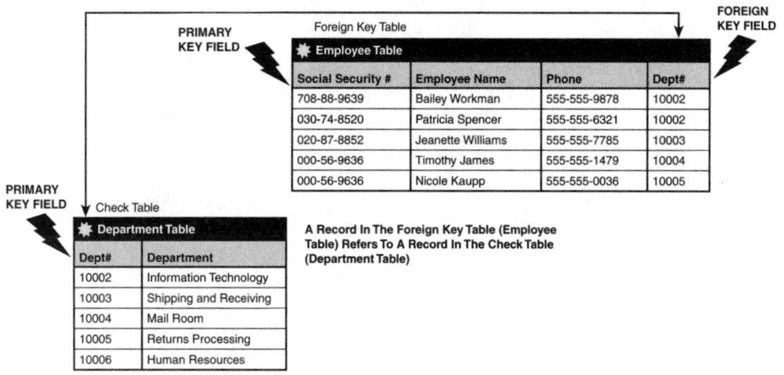

FIGURE 3.4

FIGURE 3.4

The department numbers in the Employee Table are checked against the Check table using a foreign key relationship.

The foreign key is used to establish consistency between tables. An example of consistency would be that you do not want an employee entered into the system with a department number that is not currently in the database table in which department numbers are stored. The use of a foreign key relationship is to check that the number entered exists in the department table, as shown in Figure 3.4, and rejects any numbers that do not. This way all the data is consistent in your tables.

Check Table Violation

Your SAP database will not accept data in any fields that contain a foreign key to a check table in which the data entered does not exist in the check table (see Figure 3.5).

In this example, you need to enter a Marital Status for the employee. The possible values in the check table are listed in the small window. If you enter a value that is not listed in the check table as a valid entry, you will receive a check violation error like the one shown in Figure 3.6.

Database Concepts

The SAP R/3 system contains many different types of concepts and structures within the R/3 data Dictionary. The majority of these concepts tend to get very technical. We do however get an overview of many of these concepts later in Hour 15 "R/3 Data Dictionary." The topics discussed below give you an idea of how different elements of the database are usually designed with the end result of increased performance in mind.

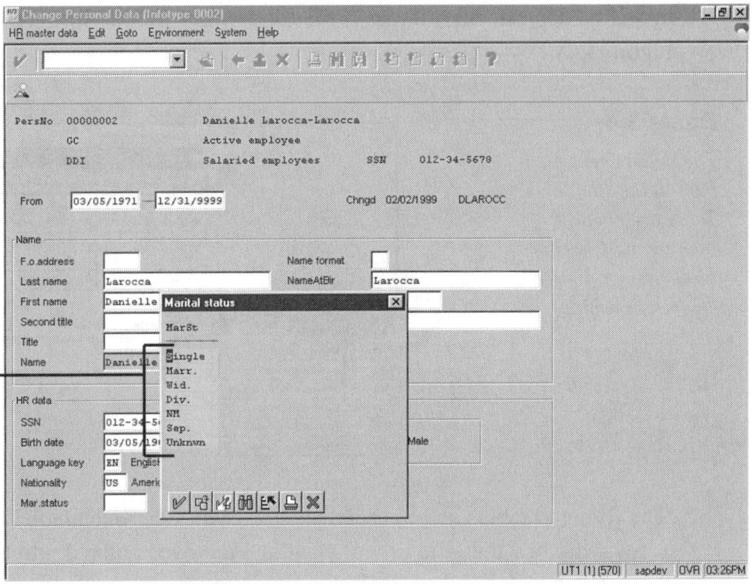

FIGURE 3.5

On the Employee Personnel Data screen the Mar. status field will only accept an entry from the check table.

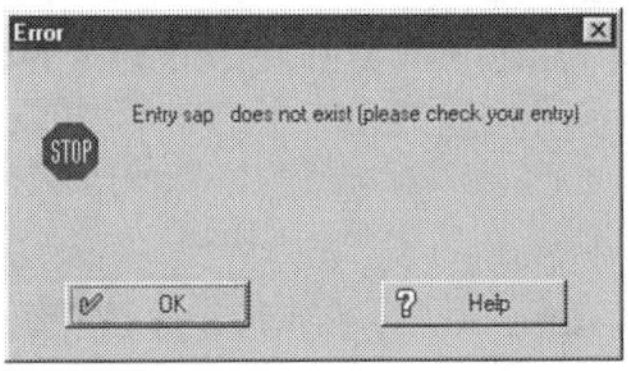

Valid Entries in Check Table for Marital Status

FIGURE 6

A Check violation message appears when you enter data in to a field that is not in the check table for that field.

Database Indexes

Database indexes are used to speed up the retrieval of data from tables (see Figure 3.7). An index might best be described as a copy of a database table reduced to only the key fields. The data in this reduced copy would be sorted, according to some pre-defined criteria, enabling rapid access to the data. Not all fields from the copied table would exist in the index, and the index would contain a pointer to the associated record of the actual table.

In Hour 15, "R/3 Data Dictionary," I will go into more detail about databases and tables when we take a more indepth look into the SAP Data Dictionary.

FIGURE 3.7

In SAP, database indexes are used to speed up the retrieval of data from tables in the database.

Index

Dept #	Pointer
10002	Record 101
10003	Record 273
10004	Record 33
10005	Record 5
10006	Record 576
10007	Record 11
10008	Record 460
10009	Record 33
1010	Record 411

Table

Employee Table

Record #	Social Security	Employee Name	Phone	Dept #
Record 1	708-88-9639	Bailey Workman	555-555-9878	10002
Record 2	030-74-8520	Patricia Spencer	555-555-6321	10002
Record 3	020-87-8852	Jeanette Williams	555-555-7785	10003
Record 4	000-56-9636	Timothy James	555-555-1479	10004
Record 5	000-56-9636	Nicole Kaupp	555-555-0036	10005

The Index is Accessed and the Pointer is Used
To Locate The Actual Record in the Table

Transparent Tables

SAP has another concept called transparent tables, which are SAP database tables that only contain data at runtime. A Transparent table is automatically created in the database when a table is activated in the ABAP/4 Dictionary. This transparent table contains the same name as your database table in the ABAP/4 Dictionary. Each of its fields also contain the same names as their database counterparts although the field sequence might change. The varying field sequence makes it possible to insert new fields into the table without having to convert it.

> The concept of Transparent tables can get quite technical and is more of a concern to your ABAP/4 programmers. The concept is only discussed here so that you can be familiar with the term.

Database Structures

Database structures is another technical term that you really do not need to concern yourself with too much. It would be enough to understand that database structures are a group of internal fields that logically belong together. Structures are activated and defined in the ABAP/4 Data Dictionary and only contain data temporarily during the execution of a program. Structures are differentiated from database tables based on the following three criteria:

- A structure does not contain an associated ABAP/4 Data Dictionary table.
- A structure does not contain a primary key.
- A structure does not have any technical properties like a class, size, category, or buffering specification.

Summary

The SAP R/3 system is based on an RDBMS Relational Database Management System. The database serves as the core to all your R/3 systems and modules. This hour you learned about the structure of a database and what it contains. The concepts covered in this hour are the key to understanding the behind the scenes functioning of your SAP system.

Q&A

Q **Will the R/3 system function the same regardless of the database used Oracle, UNIX, DB2, and so on?**

A The R/3 system functions the same regardless of the brand name of database used to store data.

Q **Will the R/3 system permit you to create a new record that has the same primary key as another record?**

A The R/3 system prevents you from being able to create new records with a primary key that already exists.

Workshop

The workshop is designed to help you anticipate possible questions, review what you've learned, and begin thinking ahead to putting your knowledge into practice. The answers to the quiz that follows can be found in Appendix A, "Answers."

Quiz

1. What is a database?

2. A database is composed of what three components?

3. What kind of database contains two-dimensional relationships between its tables?

4. What kind of key in a database table requires unique values in each field?

5. What is the field or fields used to link a primary key field in another table called?

6. What causes a check key violation?

7. What is used in a database to speed up the retrieval of records?

Hour **4**

Customizing Your R/3 Display

Now that you have the basics under your belt from Hours 1, 2, and 3, you are ready to customize the R/3 environment to your liking. In this hour, I will cover tasks that show you how to manipulate the R/3 window to your custom specifications.

The highlights of this hour include

- Customizing R/3 to your specifications
- Changing colors and fonts
- Changing the way SAP responds to you

Using the Options Panel

On the top right side of every SAP R/3 Window, you will see three inter-twined colored circles (see Figure 4.1). Some people refer to it as the "beach ball," others call it the "Mickey Mouse ears," but the SAP term is the *Interface menu*. Selecting the Interface menu allows you to access the R/3 Display Options.

FIGURE 4.1

You can change the appearance of your SAP screens using the SAP R/3 Interface Menu.

Interface Menu —

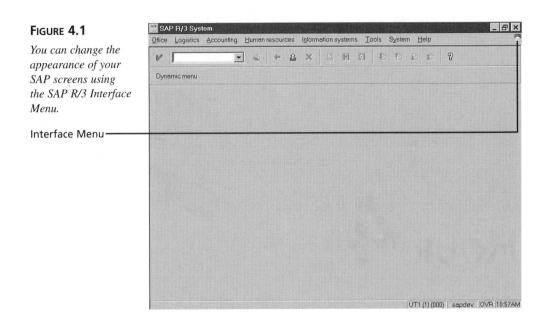

Using your mouse, click the Interface menu to access the customizing menu. From this menu, select Options. An Options window appears similar to the one shown in Figure 4.2.

FIGURE 4.2

The R/3 Options Window can be accessed from any SAP screen.

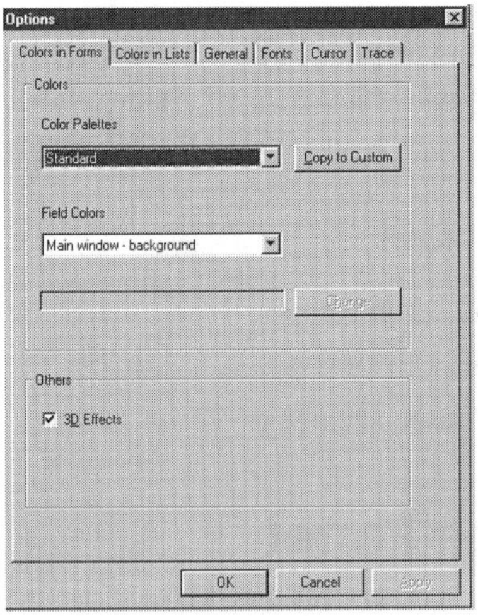

From this options window, you can

- Change the colors of various elements of the R/3 window

- Change the display font of text

- Customize the window (for example, hide the standard toolbar or return to the default window size)

- Display or hide grid lines in lists

- Enable or disable automatic tabbing between fields to determine where the cursor should appear when you click a field

General Look and Feel

I will start with the General tab in the Options window (see Figure 4.3). From this tab, you can make changes on how the system will notify you of certain events and the general screen settings of your R/3 system. In other words, the settings you define on the General tab will reflect how you receive information and in what form, as well as how the screen appears in general. It is important to note the default settings for this tab in case you are unhappy with any changes that you make, and you want to restore the defaults.

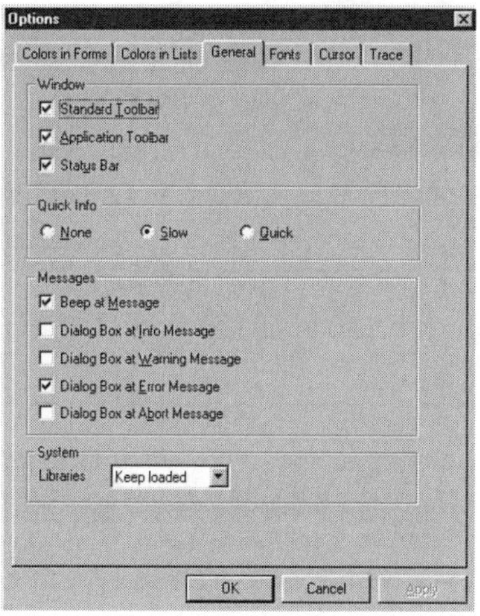

FIGURE 4.3

You can change your General tab options so that your system beeps with each new system message.

Window

The first three check boxes in the Window option apply to the SAP toolbars. From here, you can select whether or not you want to have the application toolbar and the standard menu bar visible on all screens. It also has a check box for the status bar that is on the

bottom left side of the window. I cannot think of any reason why you would not want
these three options checked.

Quick Info

The Quick Info option controls how quickly the help information (description) launches
whenever you place the pointer (cursor) over an item in the button bar.

Messages

These options allow you to configure how the SAP system presents you with information. The default setting is that any messages from the system appear in the status bar in
the bottom left side of your screen. By default, all messages pertaining to system output,
warning messages, and error messages all appear in the status bar. You can set these messages to appear in a pop-up box by selecting the appropriate box on this settings screen
(see Figure 4.4).

FIGURE 4.4

*R/3 Message boxes
are more noticeable
to report system
warnings and errors
than messages dis-
played in the status
bar.*

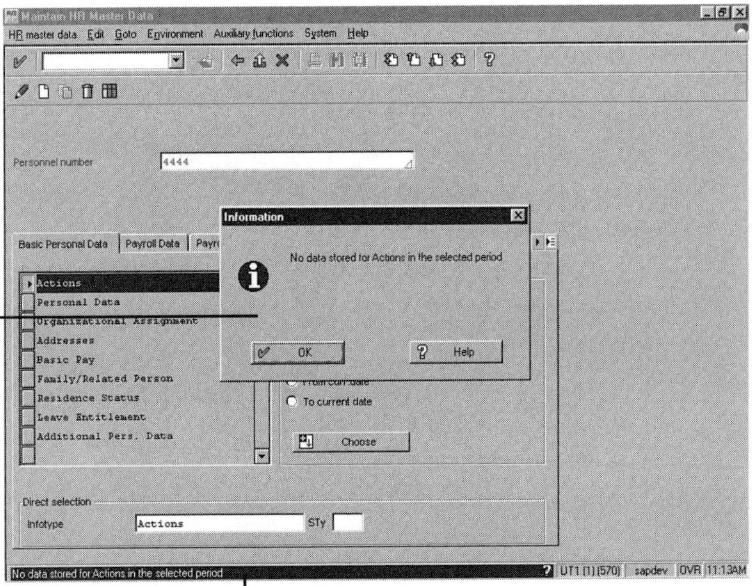

Message box will
appear

Message will also appear in status bar

System

This option refers to the location from which SAP is retrieving its help files. It is best to
leave this setting as it is; any changes should be made by your system administrator.

Changing Colors in Forms

Single-click on the Colors In Forms tab (refer to Figure 4.2). From this tab, you can change the color options on your SAP R/3 screens. You can change the colors of various elements of your R/3 window. You can choose from a number of predefined color palettes, or you can define your own (custom) colors.

Color Palettes

There are twelve different Color Palettes to choose from, as follows:

Standard	Orion
Andromeda	Venus
Crabs	Cassiopeia
Earth	Hercules
Scorpion	Mercury
Fishes	Jupiter

Field Colors

The following is a list of elements that you can change the color of:

Main Window—Background

Entry Field—Background

Entry Field—Background At Focus

Output Field—Background

Output Field—Background At Focus

Frame—Background

Entry Field—Text Normal

Entry Field—Text Intensive

Output Field—Text Normal

Output Field—Text Intensive

Text Field—Text Normal

Text Field—Text Intensive

Be careful when you change colors in forms. Only the default settings guarantee that all the information on a screen is legible.

To change the color of an SAP element, select the element and then select the color from the palette.

Changing Colors in Lists

Select the Colors In Lists tab to change the colors of items as they appear in lists (see Figure 4.5).

FIGURE 4.5

A large portion of data in SAP appears in Lists which you can customize.

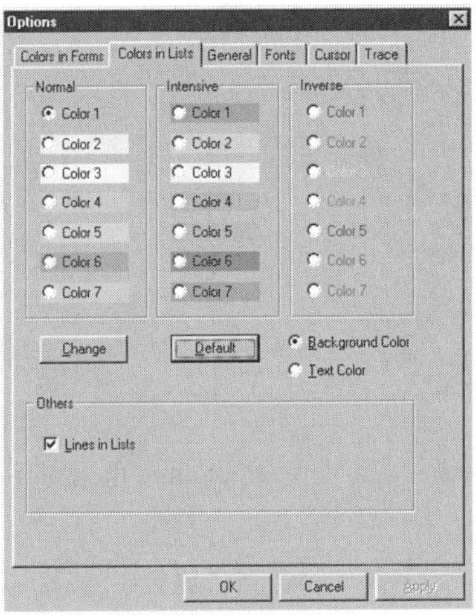

The List colors dialog box contains 21 selections. There are three categories of text display in lists: normal, intensive, and inverse. Normal appears as regular text, intensive appears bold, and inverse presents the opposite of Normal. For example if the background color blue with gray font is the normal setting, then the inverse would be blue font on a gray background. You assign a particular color and display category to specific text types in lists, as shown in Table 4.1.

TABLE 4.1 SAP Colors

Color Number	Intensive	Normal
1	headings	secondary headings
2	body of the list (1st row only)	body of the list
3	totals higher level subtotals	subtotals
4	key columns	highlighted lines/columns
5	positive threshold value	inserted lines
6	negative threshold value	
7	hierarchy heading	hierarchy information

Colors in Lists applies mainly to reporting output. When you create a report of all customer orders or a list of all employees' annual salaries subtotaled by department, you would see the benefits of these color changes. If your SAP system has existing reports that you know how to navigate to, you can do so and apply the color changes there to see the results. Most likely though, you are new to SAP and don't know where the reports are, or perhaps there is no data in the SAP system yet to generate a report.

> Be careful when you change colors in lists. Only the default settings guarantee that all the information on a screen is legible.

At the completion of Hour 19, "ABAP Query Reporting," you will be more familiar with reporting and list generation, and you might want to wait until then to test out the different possibilities of color changes in reports.

To change a color, perform the following steps:

1. Select the color you want to change (you should use Table 4.1 as a reference).
2. Click the Change button.
3. Click the Apply button.

To restore a color to its original settings, perform the following steps:

1. Select the color that you changed.
2. Click the Default button.
3. Click the Apply button.

The Lines in Lists button on the bottom of the screen allows separator lines to appear between line items in a list. By default, this setting is on.

Changing SAP Fonts

Select the Fonts tab in the Options window (see Figure 4.6). From this window, you can change the appearance and size of the fonts on your SAP R/3 window. The Fonts tab is the option most frequently employed by users because screen resolution varies from system to system.

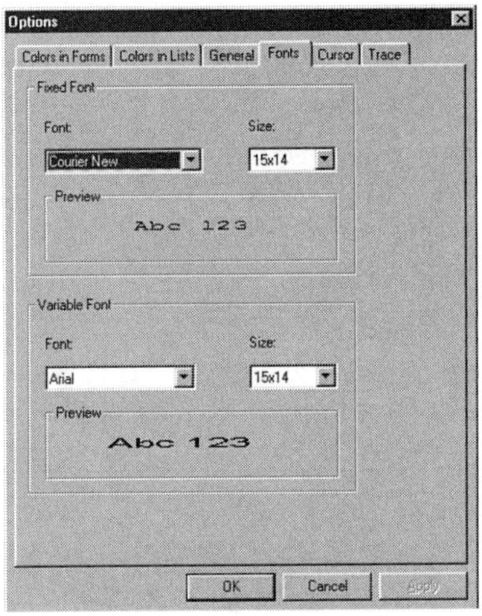

FIGURE 4.6

No standard Font setting exists because screen resolution varies between systems and monitors.

[Figure 4.6: Options dialog box showing the Fonts tab. Tabs across the top read: Colors in Forms, Colors in Lists, General, Fonts, Cursor, Trace. The Fixed Font section shows Font set to "Courier New" and Size "15x14", with a Preview displaying "Abc 123". The Variable Font section shows Font "Arial" and Size "15x14", with a Preview displaying "Abc 123". OK, Cancel, and Apply buttons at the bottom.]

Not every user has the same size monitor or the same settings for their screen resolution. Because of this, occasionally we need to tweak these settings so that the R/3 window looks right on our computers. The two different items to change on this screen are fixed fonts and variable fonts. Fixed fonts refer to fixed text elements in screens, such as text input (the data you enter in to fields). Variable fonts refer to variable text elements such as the field names that are listed next to the input fields.

> Before changing font settings, be sure to note the initial setting; just in case you cannot find a better alternative, you will want to remember your initial setting.

To change the font of fixed text elements in screens, such as text input, perform the following steps:

1. Display the list of available fonts in the Fixed font box by clicking the possible entries arrow to the right of the Font input field.

2. Choose one of the available fonts from the list. A sample of text in the font that you have chosen will appear in the Preview box display.

3. To get a true sense of the impact this will have on your screen, select the apply button.

Follow the same steps to alter the variable font setting. In most cases, these two settings will automatically conform to each other when you change one, maintaining an aspect ratio.

Cursor Placement

The Cursor tab allows you to make custom setting changes to the position and appearance of your cursor. The default setting is usually best, as shown in Figure 4.7.

FIGURE 4.7

Your R/3 Cursor placement has an impact when you are doing data entry in your R/3 system.

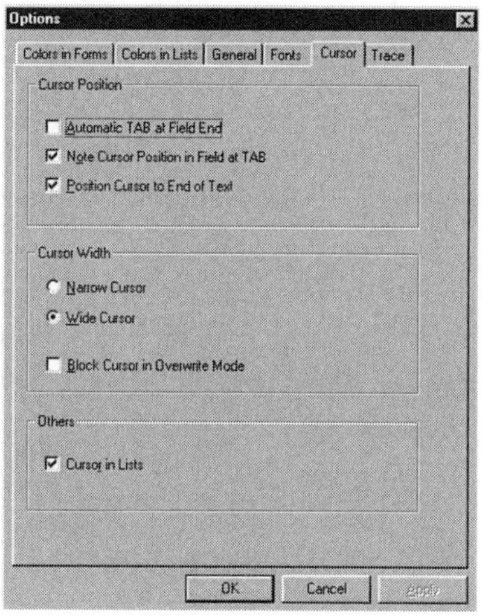

Cursor Position

With the Automatic TAB at Field End option, you can determine whether the system should automatically move the cursor to the next input field when the cursor reaches the end of the current input field.

> For data entry, Automatic tabbing (AutoTAB) is useful when you must enter data in many fields and you don't want to press the TAB key to move from field to field.

In the R/3 system, you can determine where you want the cursor to appear when you click in the blank area of an input field. The place where your cursor appears in an entry field is called the cursor position. You can change this setting so that your cursor automatically tabs to the end of a field (when you use the tab key on your keyboard to navigate between fields). You can also set the cursor to appear exactly where you place it in the field, whether there are blank spaces or not.

You can also set your cursor to note the cursor position in the field at Tab, or position the cursor to the end of the text. These options are designed to make your SAP environment more user-friendly and allow you to set the screen and placement of the cursor to your liking.

If you primarily work in tasks that require a great deal of data entry, it is helpful to have the cursor appear at the end of any text when you click anywhere behind the text. This is the SAP default setting. This way, when the input field is empty, the cursor will appear at the beginning, allowing you to freely enter data without worrying about extra spaces in front of the cursor.

Cursor Width

The cursor width is just as it sounds: You can set your cursor to be narrow or wide. The last option in this section is for block cursor in Overwrite mode that allows you to block out all the text when replacing data in a field.

By default, the SAP R/3 system is always in Overwrite mode. If you want to change this setting to Insert mode, select the Insert key on your keyboard. You will see the abbreviation in the bottom right corner of your SAP window change from OVR to INS (see Figure 4.8). With each new session you create, the system will default to Overwrite mode.

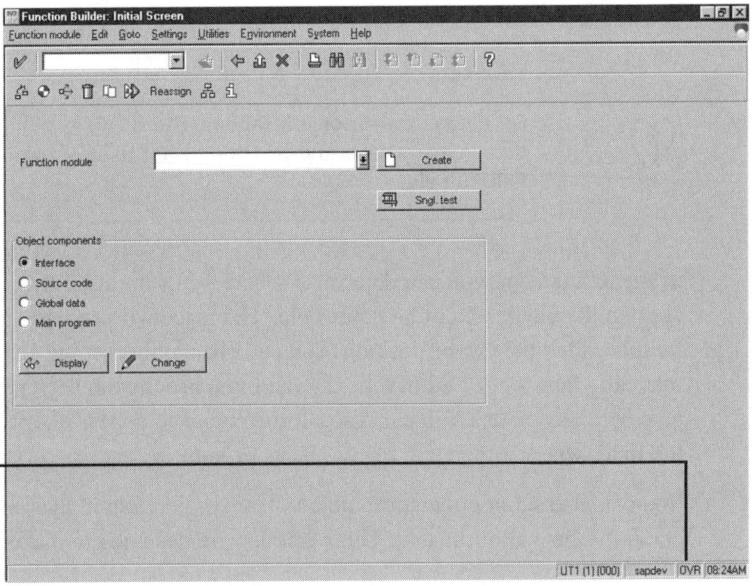

FIGURE 4.8

Insert and Overwrite mode determines how text entry functions in SAP.

OVR indicates Overwrite mode. INS indicates Insert mode.

Others

The last setting allows you to indicate whether or not you want your cursor to appear and function in lists.

Tracing System Activity

The Trace tab has options that allow you to create a file to trace activity in the system. The settings under the Trace tab are managed by your system administrator in an effort to monitor and diagnose system concerns. Traces can be set to keep a record of errors and warning messages a user receives. In addition, it can be used to monitor where a user has been by keeping a file of each transaction code for each screen visited by the user.

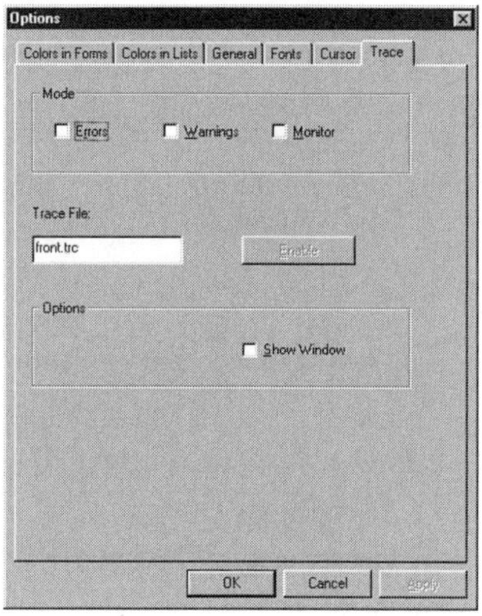

FIGURE 4.9

The Trace tab is a good tool for diagnosing system problems experienced by a user, but its use has a performance effect on the speed of the system.

Summary

In this hour, you learned how to customize the SAP R/3 environment to best suit your needs, including handy configuration methods for changing your system colors and fonts and customizing your SAP screens. The modification of how the screen presents information to you and the use of traces may also be valuable as you become a more advanced SAP user. These custom modifications will become handy once you have become a savvy SAP user or "Sapper," as some call it. As you become more accustomed to working in your SAP system and begin performing tasks in the system, you will be in a good position to determine which configuration changes will be ideal for you.

Q&A

Q When you make changes in the Interface menu, do they apply only for the current session?

A Changes made in the interface menu apply to any SAP system that you log on to through your machine, independent of the server or client you are processing in.

Q Is there any benefit to having warning and error messages set to appear in dialog boxes as opposed to appearing only in the status bar?

A The behavior of system messages is usually a matter of preference. There is some argument about this because many feel that error messages only should appear as dialog boxes, with all other messages appearing only in the status bar.

Workshop

The workshop is designed to help you anticipate possible questions, review what you've learned, and begin thinking ahead to putting your knowledge into practice. The answers to the quiz that follows can be found in Appendix A, "Answers."

Quiz

1. What is the name of the beach ball–looking item in the top right side of your SAP window?

2. What should you always do before changing a setting in the Customizing Display Window?

3. How do you change the SAP system setting from Overwrite mode to Insert mode?

4. How do you access the SAP R/3 Customize Display options window?

5. Where would you change the setting, if you would like your SAP error messages to display in a pop-up window (dialog box)?

6. How many different color choices do you have for changing the colors in lists?

Exercises

Navigate to the Overview of Users screen (using transaction code /nSM04) to see items displayed in a list, and then modify your Colors in Lists using the interface menu to test out the different color schemes.

From the main SAP screen, enter your name into the command field and select the Enter key. An error message should appear in the status bar. Change your settings in the general tab of the interface menu so that your error message appears as a dialog box.

Modify your Quick Info setting in the Interface menu to give you fast access to the help information (description) of fields.

4

Navigation in the R/3 System

This hour gives you an in-depth overview of navigation within the R/3 system. It goes into detail about how to navigate using menu paths and transaction codes. It also gives you some helpful hints on how to determine the transaction code for a screen that you reached using a menu path.

Highlights of this hour include

- Menu path navigation
- Transaction code navigation
- Using the SAP history list

Performing Tasks Using Menu Paths

Using the menus in the R/3 menu bar, you can navigate to the application and the task you want to begin, or you can choose the function to start the task. With menus, you can easily find your application and functions without having to memorize transaction codes.

Navigation Using the Mouse

To select a menu, single-click on the menu to display all the options listed under that menu. Menu entries that contain an additional list of objects (submenus) include an arrow (see Figure 5.1).

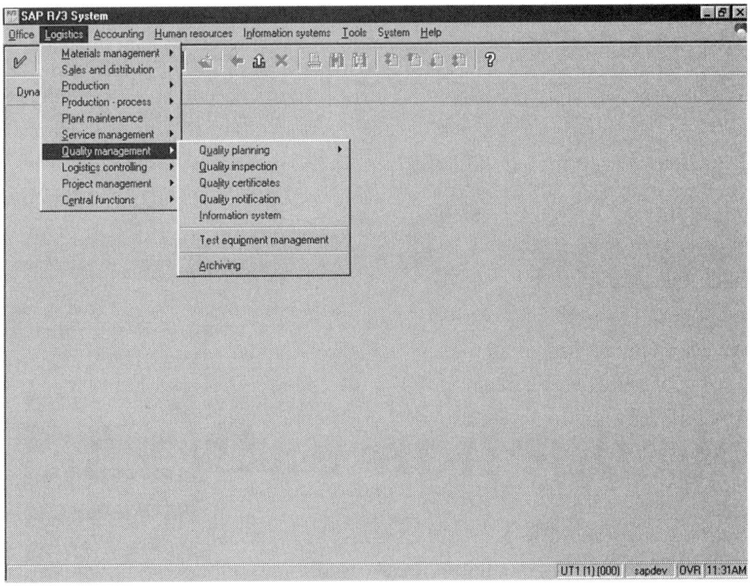

FIGURE 5.1

Menus and submenus can be selected using your mouse.

Navigation Using the Keyboard

Menus can be selected with the mouse or the keyboard. To select menu paths using your keyboard, press F10 (to activate the menu bar), and then use the navigational arrow keys on your keyboard to select and display the menu. You choose a function by highlighting it with the arrow keys and then pressing Enter.

Performing Tasks Using Transaction Codes

As you learned earlier, you can jump to any screen in the SAP system by entering a SAP transaction code into the command field on the standard toolbar. A transaction code is a four-character code that takes you directly to the screen for the task you want to perform.

From any SAP screen except the main screen, you need to enter /N before
the transaction code in the command field to execute a new transaction. To
open a new session and create a new task, use a /O plus the transaction
code.

Finding the Transaction Code For the Task You Want

To find a transaction code for a certain task, you begin by using the SAP Dynamic menu.
The Dynamic menu can be displayed from the main SAP screen by selecting the
Dynamic menu button on the application toolbar. A screen will appear similar to the one
shown in Figure 5.2.

FIGURE 5.2

*You can use the
Dynamic menu to
search for transaction
codes.*

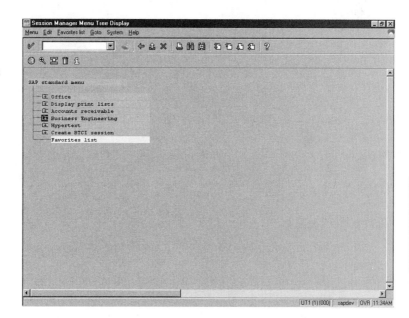

5

Depending on the SAP modules that you are using, the client that you are
logged into, and your systems configuration, your Session Manager Menu
Tree Display screen may be different. Another view of the Dynamic menu is
shown in Figure 5.3.

On the screen, you see a list of the R/3 application areas, with plus (+) signs to the left of every item that has sublists attached to it. On the menu bar, select Edit, Technical Name, Technical Name On. This turns on the feature allowing all transaction codes to be displayed next to the tasks. To display one of the application area sublists, double-click on it. The sublist appears, as shown in Figure 5.3, containing tasks, more sublists, or both. You can identify a task by the fact that no plus or minus sign appears to the left of it, and a transaction code is listed to the right of it.

FIGURE 5.3

Using the Dynamic menu, I was able to find the transaction code for entering Personnel actions in the Human Resources module.

Transaction Code

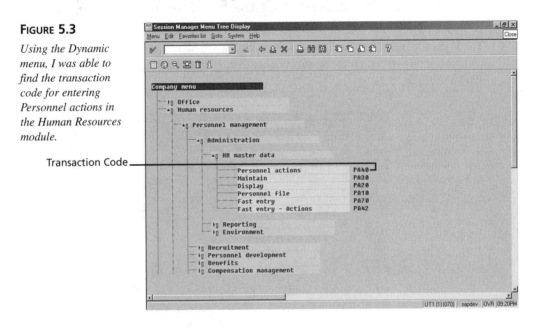

In Figure 5.3, continue to drill down until you see the task you want. You can start the function now by double-clicking on it. Otherwise, you can use this transaction code to start this task from any screen in the R/3 system. When you use a transaction code to start a task, the R/3 system closes, or ends, your current task and then displays the initial screen of the new task.

To me, this seems like the long way to find out the transaction code. I prefer to find the transaction code while I am already on the current task, as I explain in the following section.

Finding the Transaction Code for the Current Task

From every screen in SAP, the system allows you to determine the transaction code.
There is a shortcut way to do this. From any screen in SAP, select the menu path System,
Status. This displays the System Status screen that gives you the detail and technical
information about the screen you are on (see Figure 5.4).

FIGURE 5.4

The System: Status window provides useful information including the transaction code for the screen that you are currently on.

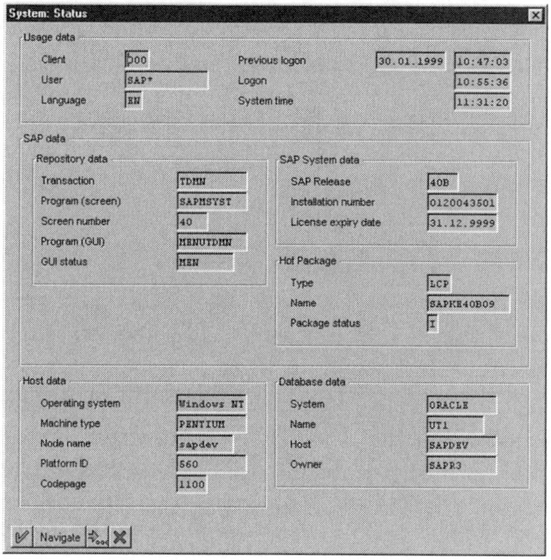

In addition to all the detailed and technical information, the System: Status screen gives
you the transaction code for the screen. Look in the field under the SAP Data heading
called transaction. This gives you the four-character transaction code for the current
screen. In the example shown in Figure 5.4, the transaction code is TDMN. You can use
this method from any screen in the system.

> In some instances, an SAP action or event contains a series of screens. Some
> of the screens within that action might contain the same transaction code
> as the first screen in the action, in essence, forcing you to begin at thebegin-
> ning of the action or event without being able to jump to steps mid way.

5

Using the History List to Find Transaction Codes

A list of all the transaction codes processed since you logged on is called a history list. To access the history list, use your mouse to select the down arrow to the right of the command field (see Figure 5.5).

FIGURE 5.5

The History list is useful for navigating back and forth to different transactions that you have visited within your session.

Down Arrow

From the history list, select the transaction code you want to execute by highlighting it and pressing the Enter key on your keyboard or clicking the green check mark on the toolbar. The initial screen of the task associated with that transaction code will appear.

SCROLLING TECHNIQUES

When you view information in reports or view the SAP R/3 online help, occasionally some of the information will not fit in your window. To see the additional information, you can use the scrollbars. Your window has a vertical and a horizontal scrollbar.

You use the vertical scrollbar to move, or scroll, up and down through the information in the window. You use the horizontal scrollbar to scroll left and right through the information in the window, as follows:

To Scroll	Do This
Up or down one line	Click on the up or down scroll arrow on the vertical scrollbar.
Left or right one character	Click on the left or right scroll arrow on the horizontal scrollbar.
Up or down one screen page	Click above or below the slider box on the vertical scrollbar.
Left or right the width of the screen page	Click to the right or left of the slider box on the horizontal scrollbar.

To Scroll	Do This
To a certain position in the information up or down	Drag the slider box on the vertical scrollbar to the approximate location of the desired information; then release the mouse button.
To a certain position in the information left or right	Drag the slider box on the horizontal scrollbar to the approximate location of the desired information; then release the mouse button.

You can also use the scroll (page up and down) buttons in the standard toolbar, to view information in windows, as follows:

Destination	Toolbar Button	Function Key Shortcut
First Screen Page	🔼	F21 Ctrl+PageUp
Last ScreenPage	🔽	F24 Ctrl+PageDown
Previous Screen Page	🔼	F22 PageUp
Next Screen Page	🔽	F23 PageDown

Using the Clipboard

You can transfer the contents of SAP fields onto your Windows clipboard and then paste the data into other fields of the R/3 System or into other applications.

Moving Data

To select a field or the text you want to move, perform the following steps:

1. Click and drag the pointer over the text you want to select. The selected text then appears highlighted.

2. To move the information in an input field onto the Windows Clipboard, use the keyboard combination Ctrl+X. The selected text no longer appears and is now stored in your Windows Clipboard.

3. To paste this information into another SAP screen or into a different application, go to the destination and use the keyboard combination Ctrl+V to paste the data.

The Cut (or Move) command is generally used on input fields.

5

Copying Data

To select a field or the text you want to copy, perform the following steps:

1. Click and drag the pointer over the text you want to select. The selected text then appears highlighted.

2. To move the information in an input field onto the Windows Clipboard, use the keyboard combination Ctrl+C. The selected text still appears and is also stored in your Windows Clipboard.

3. To paste this information into another SAP screen on your R/3 system or into a different application, go to the destination and use the keyboard combination Ctrl+V to paste the data.

The transferred data remains in the clipboard until you use Cut or Copy again to move or copy new texts onto the clipboard.

If you are viewing your Help via a browser like Netscape or Microsoft Internet Explorer, you can give this functionality a try using the following steps:

1. Begin with the menu path Help, R/3 Library from the menu bar. Your SAP help application launches and brings you to the R/3 library main screen.

2. Select the ABC Glossary button on the top right of the screen. This brings you to the R/3 Glossary main screen and a definition appears in the right of the screen. Depending on your version number, the definition that is displayed on your screen might appear different from the one shown in Figure 5.6.

FIGURE 5.6

If you are viewing your SAP Help application via a standard browser, your SAP Glossary main screen will appear like a Web page.

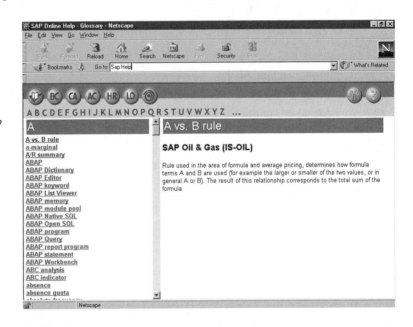

3. Next, select the text of this definition and copy it to the clipboard. Select the text by using your mouse to highlight it.

4. After all the text is selected, use the keyboard combination Ctrl+C to copy it to the clipboard.

5. You are going to paste this definition into the Windows Notepad. From your Windows 95 Start menu, select Start, Run. Type in the word notepad and press Enter (see Figure 5.7). The Window 95 Notepad launches.

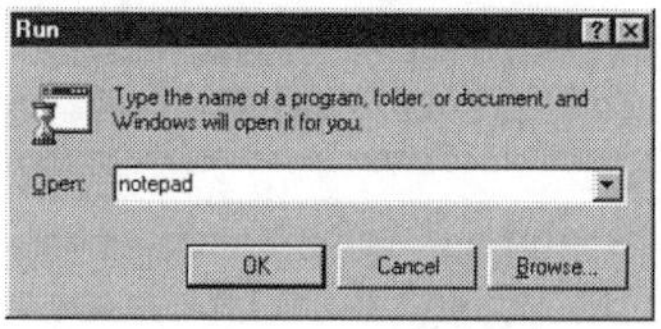

FIGURE 5.7

All Windows applications can be executed using the Windows 95 Run Window.

6. Place your cursor at the top of the blank notepad and use the keyboard combination Ctrl+V to paste the data. Your selected text now appears in the notepad application.

The formatting might appear a little strange, but this sometimes occurs when you copy and paste information across applications.

Copying Unselectable Data

You are not able to select certain data displayed on SAP screens using your mouse and the method previously described. To give you an example, return to your main SAP window and use the transaction code /NSE11 to travel to the SAP Data Dictionary Initial screen. Place your cursor in the Object Name field and select the F1 key to launch the field specific help, as shown in Figure 5.8. (If you do not have access to transaction code /NSE11, place your cursor in any SAP field and select the F1 button on your keyboard.) A window will appear giving detailed definitions and technical information for the field that you selected.

I will go into more detail about using the SAP Help system in Hour 23, "SAP Help Overview."

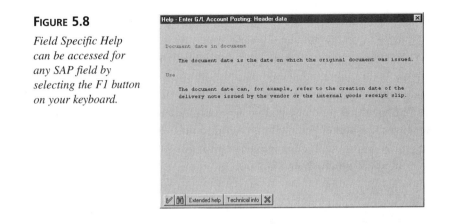

FIGURE 5.8

Field Specific Help can be accessed for any SAP field by selecting the F1 button on your keyboard.

Try to use the mouse to select the text displayed on this screen. You will see that you are unable to select the data. In cases like these, you will need to add one more keyboard combination. Use your mouse to tap once anywhere on the screen. Next use Ctrl+Y to change your mouse to a crosshair cursor. Use this cursor to select the desired text and follow the same steps as before: Ctrl+C to copy the text and Ctrl+V to paste the text.

Creating Screen Prints from SAP

There might be times when you want to obtain a print of an SAP screen. Although the Print function is available on most SAP screens, there might be an occasion when you want to print a copy of a status message (that appears on the bottom left-hand side of the window) that would not appear using the standard SAP print function.

To take a screen print of an SAP screen, perform the following steps:

1. Select the Print screen button on the upper right-hand side of your keyboard. This stores a snapshot of your current screen in the Windows clipboard.

2. Next, launch the Windows paintbrush application to paste the file for output. Follow the Windows menu path Start, Programs, Accessories, Paint to launch the Windows Paintbrush application.

3. On the Edit menu of the Paintbrush application, select the Paste option. (If you are prompted to enlarge the bitmap, select OK.)

Your screen print will now appear in the Windows paintbrush application. From here, you can print or save it to a bitmap file on your computer for later reference.

On the Interface menu, there is an option called Generate Graphic. The screen capture facility allows you to pick up table data from any screen in the SAP system and display it using SAP Business Graphics.

Printing in SAP

Printing enables you to make hard copies of lists, tables, and reports in the R/3 system. The SAP Print button is available on most SAP screens (see Figure 5.9).

FIGURE 5.9

The Print button allows you to create a hard copy of your SAP output.

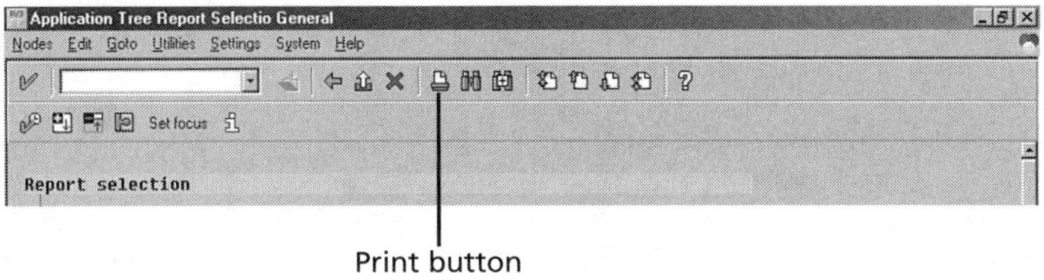

Print button

Let's take a look at the printing features in SAP. If you are not connected to a printer, you can still follow along.

In order to print from SAP, your workstation needs to be connected to a printer, via a network or directly plugged into your PC.

The SAP Print Screen List

Start with the SAP transaction code /nSM04, which you might recall is the SAP Overview of Users screen that you learned about earlier. If you do not have access to this screen, you can use any SAP screen where the Print button is available. Select the Print button on the standard toolbar. You will be prompted with the SAP Print List Output screen similar to the one shown in Figure 5.10. Select the Print button, and the data that you wanted to print is sent to the output device specified in your settings.

If you are not presented with this screen or if you receive a warning message saying your system is not connected to a printer, contact your system administrator for assistance in connecting to a printer. The SAP Print Screen List contains the necessary information on your connection to your printer, as well as information on spool control.

5

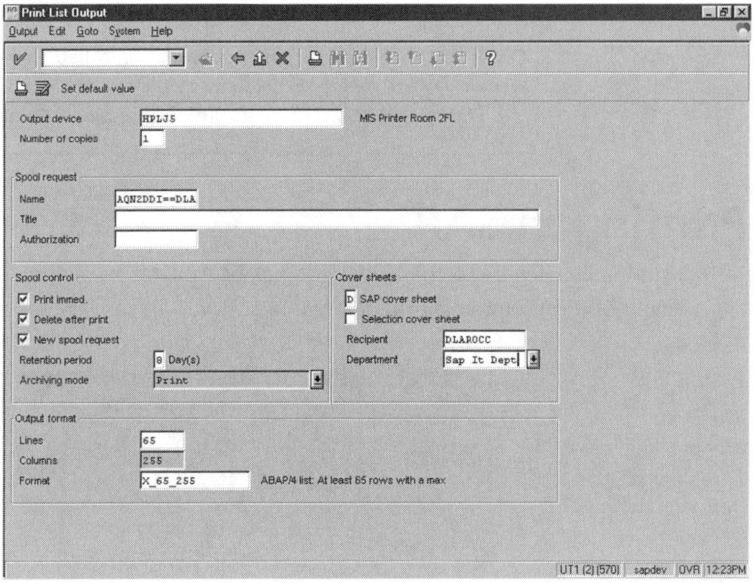

FIGURE **5.10**

The Print List Output screen allows you to customize your printer settings.

| Print List Output |
| Output Edit Goto System Help |

Set default value

| Output device | HPLJ5 | | MIS Printer Room 2FL |
| Number of copies | 1 | | |

Spool request
Name	AQN2DDI==DLA
Title	
Authorization	

Spool control
| ☑ Print immed. |
| ☑ Delete after print |
| ☑ New spool request |
| Retention period | 8 Day(s) |
| Archiving mode | Print |

Cover sheets
| D SAP cover sheet |
| ☐ Selection cover sheet |
| Recipient | DLAROCC |
| Department | Sap It Dept |

Output format
Lines	65
Columns	255
Format	X_65_255	ABAP/4 list: At least 65 rows with a max

UT1 (2) (570)   sapdev   OVR   12:23PM

Output Device

This field contains the name of the output device. This could be a printer, a fax machine, or some other hardware connected to the SAP system. In the example in Figure 5.10, it contains my printer name. To see a list of available output devices connected to your SAP system, select the down arrow to the right of this field.

Number of Copies

The Number of Copies field is where you would specify the number of copies of the document you want to print.

Sometimes in SAP, your reports may be lengthy. It is always a good idea to determine how many pages your output is going to be before printing one or multiple copies. Use your scrolling options on the toolbar, covered earlier in this chapter in "Scrolling Techniques," to navigate through your output to determine its length before printing.

Spool Request

The Name field contains the name of the spool request. As you will learn, everything in SAP is assigned a name or an identifier within the SAP system. This name designates the item, in this case, a print request to the system. For example, if you go to your printer and you do not find your output, you can search in the SAP system by this Spool Request Name and find out what happened to your output.

The spool request name might consist of letters, numerals, special characters, and blanks. The standard name proposed by the system for a spool request comprises the 8-character report name, the separator '_', and the first three characters of your user name. You can, however, add a description of your own in the Spool Request Title field, although it is usually a good idea to accept the name proposed by the system.

The Title field contains a description of the spool request. It might consist of any combination of letters, digits, special characters, and blanks. This field can help you to identify your spool request.

The Authorization field contains the authorization for the spool request. Say that a Human Resources Manager created a report of all employee salaries and sent it to the printer. As this item sits in the SAP spool waiting to be printed, only users with the correct authorization are allowed to display the contents of the spool request.

Spool Control

The Print Immed. option determines whether the spool request (that is the report output) should be sent to the output device immediately. This setting is usually marked at runtime if you are printing a small report. This designation will bypass the standard spool routing and get sent directly to the designated printer.

The Delete After Print option determines whether to delete the spool request immediately after it has been sent to the output device or only after the spool retention period has expired. The default setting for this option is blank, indicating that the spool requests are saved for the duration of the spool retention period set in the retention period box. This is helpful in the previous scenario I detailed. If the spool request was immediately deleted, you would not be able to go back and search for the item, in case the output had been misplaced.

Most users mark this box in an effort to conserve space by not saving a spool request for every item printed. The box is cleared only when the user feels it is necessary to retain the request for very important spool requests.

5

The New Spool Request option determines whether to append the current spool request to an existing request with similar attributes or whether to generate a new spool request. If left blank, this option allows users to add their spool request to an existing request.

To append the current spool request to an existing spool request, the values contained in the Name, Output device, Number of copies, and Format fields must be the same, and the existing spool request should not yet have been completed. This setting applies particularly when a spool request is released for output. If no suitable spool request is found, a new one is generated.

The Retention Period field determines how many days a spool request is to remain in the spool system before it is deleted.

Archiving Mode allows the user the option to send the file to Print, Archive, or Archive and Print. The default setting is for Print (so that the data would be output on paper). Sending output to an archive is a function managed by your system administrator.

Cover Sheets

The SAP Cover Sheet field determines whether to include a cover sheet with your output that is sent to the printer. Information such as recipient name, department name, format used, and so on can all be included on your SAP Cover Sheet. The permitted values for this field are

' ' : (left blank) No cover sheet

'X' : Output cover sheet

'D' : Cover sheet output depends on the setting of the output device (printer) being used.

The Recipient field contains the spool request recipient's name that appears on the cover sheet of hard copy printouts. The default value for the name of the recipient is the current user name.

The Department field contains the name of the department originating the spool request. On hard copy printouts, the name is displayed on the cover sheet.

Output Format

The Lines field determines the number of lines per list page. If this field contains a zero or is blank, the number of pages is unlimited, which is not permitted during printing. The length of the list is then determined by its content alone. When printing, the maximum number of lines per page depends on the formatting you choose. If you want to change the number of lines, you must use different formatting. It is a good idea to accept the default setting for this field.

The Columns field contains the current line width of the list; the maximum line width of a list is 255 characters. When printing, the maximum line width depends on the format. If you want to change the line width, you must also choose a different format. It is a good idea to accept the default setting for this field.

The Format field contains the spool request format for output. Selecting the down arrow to the right of this field brings you a list of available formats for your selected device. This setting defines the page format: that is, the maximum number of lines and columns that print per page. It would be a good idea to test the different formats listed to find one that is most acceptable for the output you are printing.

Setting Default Values for the Printer

Each time you select the Print button in the SAP system, you will be prompted with the Print Screen List. You can set a default value for each field in this screen so that you need not re-enter your settings each time you print. After you have entered all the settings to your specifications, select the Set Default Value button from the application toolbar. This brings up a Print List Output window like the one shown in Figure 5.11.

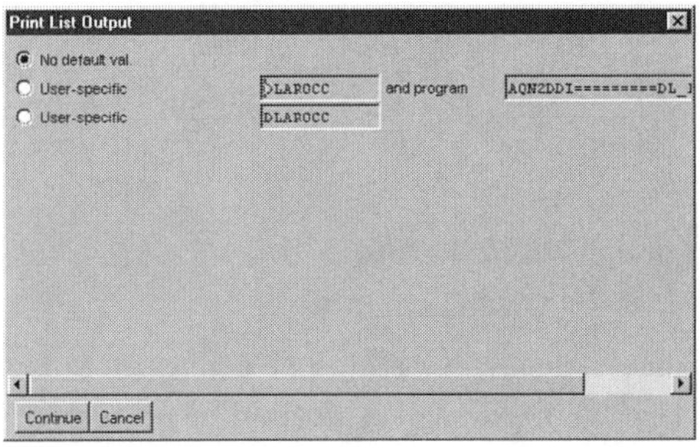

FIGURE 5.11

You can specify default settings for printing in SAP on your Print List Output window.

The following three options are listed on the Print Screen List window:

- Selecting the No Default Value option sets your system to not save any changes that you made to your settings. With this setting, you must enter your preferences each time you print.
- The second setting for User-Specific and Program allows you to save the settings for a particular program or report.
- The last setting for User-Specific allows you to save the current settings so that each time you select the Print button, you will be prompted with the Print List Output screen with all your preferences already filled in.

Don't forget when you select the Print button from the standard toolbar, you will always be prompted with the Print List Screen. You must select the Print button from this screen in order to send the output to your printer.

Summary

In this hour, you have learned about the different methods of navigation within SAP. You should now be more familiar with the concept of navigation using transaction codes and how to find a transaction code for any screen within the SAP system. You should also be comfortable with the scrolling concept in reports and screens, as well as how to use the Windows Clipboard to store data as you move between screens and applications.

A very important topic that I covered in this hour is the concept of retrieving print screens from the SAP system and of setting your preferences for printing using the SAP Print List screen.

Q&A

Q If you make your own screens, can you make your own transaction codes?

A Yes, when you create your own screens using the Screen Painter covered in Hour 17, "Designing Screens and Menus," you also create your own transaction codes for your screens.

Q Can you set up your SAP desktop to be connected to more than one printer at a time?

A You can configure your SAP system to be connected to multiple output devices including printers and fax machines. Each time you select the print button, you must specify the output device on the Print List Output screen.

Q If you are working in multiple clients, does your history reflect navigation in both clients?

A Your history list will save all transaction codes used on your system, at any given point, regardless of the client.

Workshop

The workshop is designed to help you anticipate possible questions, review what you've learned, and begin thinking ahead to putting your knowledge into practice. The answers to the quiz that follows can be found in Appendix A, "Answers."

Quiz

1. What is the transaction code for the main SAP screen?

2. What Windows application can you launch to paste and save SAP screen prints in?

3. What check box on the SAP Print List Screen would you select if you do not want your spool request saved in the SAP system for the duration of the retention period?

4. To select SAP menu paths using your keyboard instead of your mouse, you first need to select what function key?

5. How do you find the transaction code from any screen in the SAP system?

6. How do you access the history list?

7. What is the Retention Period used for on the Print Screen List window?

Exercises

1. Find the transaction code for the main SAP screen.

2. Place your cursor in the command field and then select the F1 key on your keyboard to select the field specific help. Copy this help and paste it in to your Windows Notepad application.

3. Print the Overview of Users screen to your local printer.

5

HOUR **6**

Screen Basics

This hour will help you begin to understand the fundamental elements of the SAP screens. This overview will familiarize you what the screens will look like and how you will interact with them. Highlights of this hour include

- Entering data in SAP screens
- Using the SAP Possible Entries Help function
- Saving your data
- SAP screen objects

Understanding and Using Fields

The SAP system houses a large database of information. This database is composed of tables that store data. The tables are composed of columns (called fields) and rows (called records or data). SAP screens display these database fields on their screens. Use your command field to navigate to transaction code /nFF7A. This transaction code will take you to the Cash Management Forecast screen in the Financial Accounting module (see Figure 6.1.) For help navigating in SAP please, refer to Hour 5, "Navigation in the R/3 System."

FIGURE 6.1

*The Cash
Management
Forecast screen gives
a good example of an
arrangement of fields
presented on an SAP
screen.*

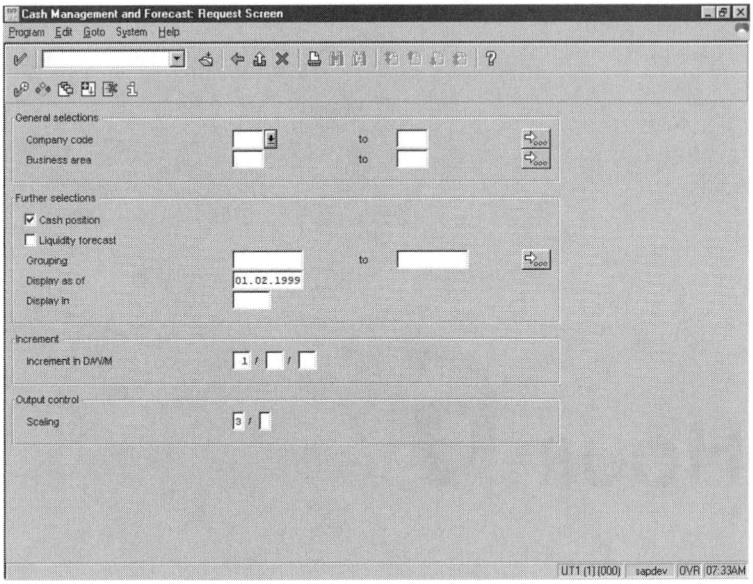

Input Fields

This screen displays a series of fields that are linked to database tables in the system.
Most screens in the R/3 system contain fields in which you enter data. These types of
fields are called input fields. An example of an input field is shown in Figure 6.2.

FIGURE 6.2

*SAP input fields
accept the entry of
the data and are tied
to fields in your R/3
Data Dictionary.*

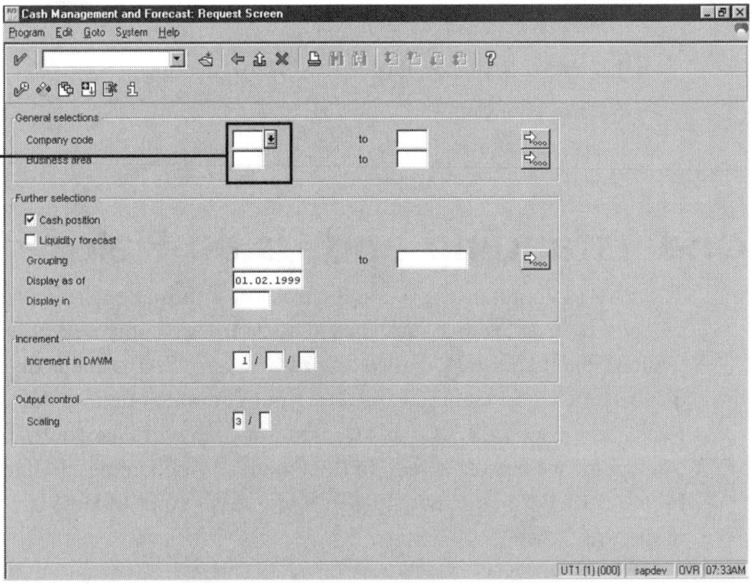

Input Fields

Input fields vary in size: The length of a field determines how many characters you can enter in the field. In the example shown in Figure 6.2, the Display As Of date input field is 10 characters long. The length of the rectangular box indicates the length of the longest valid data entry for that field.

NEW TERM The *active* field is the field that currently contains the cursor and is waiting for input.

When you place the cursor anywhere in an empty input field, the cursor appears at the beginning of the field, making data entry simple. Remember that the field can only hold data that fits into its rectangular box. After entry, the cursor remains in the input field until you press the Tab key to move it to the next field, press the Enter key to check your entry, or click on another input field.

> The initial placement of the cursor in a field is determined by your system settings, and can be modified. See the section "Cursor Position" in Hour 4, "Customizing Your R/3 Display," for more information.

Replace and Insert Modes

Your computer keyboard has a button called Insert on its top right side above the Delete button. This Insert key toggles your computer setting between two writing modes. The Insert mode allows you to insert data into an existing field without typing over it. The Overwrite mode allows you to type over existing data in a field. The Overwrite mode is the SAP default.

You can tell which setting your SAP system is set on by looking at the bottom right of your screen. In the box to the left of the system clock, you will see the abbreviation OVR for Overwrite mode or INS for Insert mode. This setting is usually user-specific, as indicated by the following:

- Most users familiar with the Microsoft family of products, such as Microsoft Word and Excel, are used to the Insert mode.
- Users familiar with WordPerfect and similar products prefer the Overwrite mode.

Either way, the system will adjust to your suiting; however, keep in mind that with each new session you create, the default Overwrite mode setting will be active unless you change it.

6

Possible Entries for an Input Field

As I explained at the beginning of this hour, each input field is linked to a database table. If you are unsure of a valid entry, meaning the exact name of a field that already exists in the table, you can use the Possible Entries button to select a valid entry from the list (see Figure 6.3).

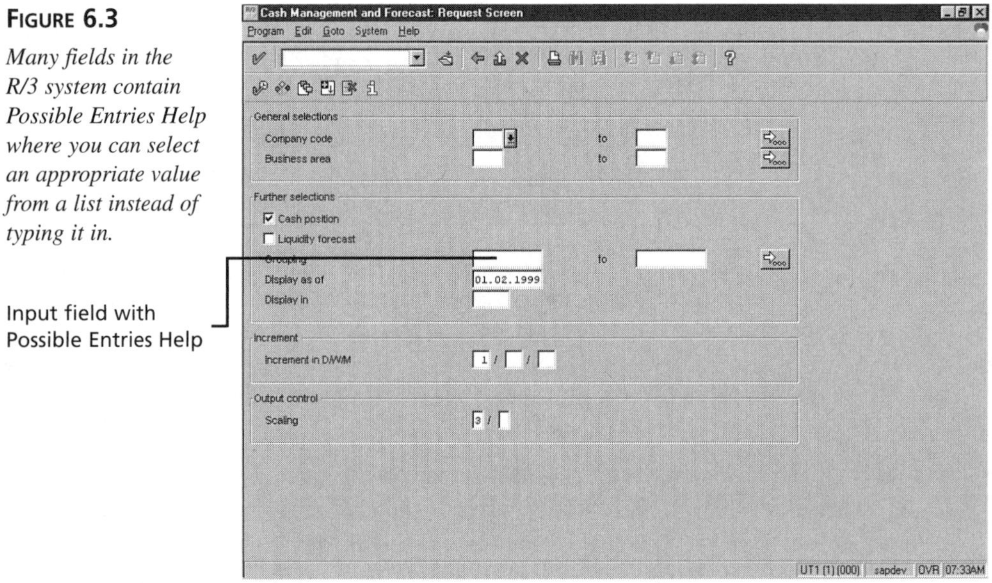

FIGURE 6.3

Many fields in the R/3 system contain Possible Entries Help where you can select an appropriate value from a list instead of typing it in.

Input field with Possible Entries Help

Any field containing a down arrow (like the one indicated in Figure 6.3) on the far right side has a Possible Entry function. Give one a try. Use the Transaction code /NFK10 to travel to the Vendor: Initial Screen Balances Display screen. This screen contains three input fields. Use your Tab key to navigate between the three fields. You will see that as you travel from one field to another, the Possible Entries down arrow appears only when the field is active. You will also see that the Possible Entries down arrow is not present on the Fiscal year field. Use your Tab key to return to the Company Code field. Use your mouse to select the Possible Entries arrow (see Figure 6.4). (The Possible Entries Help button down arrow disappears when the Possible Entries window opens.)

Not all input fields have lists of possible entries. You cannot determine if such a list is available for an input field until you place the cursor in the input field. Also, some fields that contain Possible Entries Help do not have a down arrow even when the field is active. You can select the F4 button on the top of your keyboard to retrieve the Possible Entries Help in any SAP field where it is available.

FIGURE 6.4

The Possible Entries Help window displaying available company codes appears after you select the down arrow in the Company Code field.

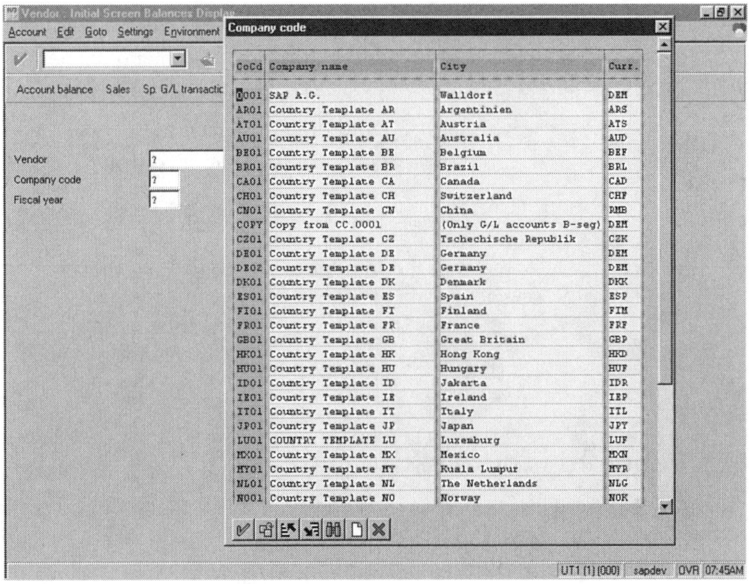

In this example, after selecting the Possible Entries down arrow for the Company Code field, you are presented with a list of Possible Entries that are acceptable and valid for that field.

Keep in mind, depending on your system's configuration, your possible entries list might appear slightly different from the one displayed in Figure 6.4.

To select an item from a Possible Entries list, you can double-click it or use your mouse to highlight it once, and then choose the green check mark Enter key. The list will disappear and the value selected will then be present in your Company Code field.

6

See what happens when you enter a value that is not an item listed in the Possible Entries Help. Return your cursor to the Company Code field, type in your initials, and press the Enter key. A warning appears in the Status bar saying something like "Invalid Entry." This warning indicates that initials are not a valid entry for this field, and the system will not let you proceed to additional screens until it is corrected.

Editing the Data in an Input Field

Now that you have an invalid entry in your Company Code field, you need to return to that field to correct the input. Place your cursor in the Company code box and then select the Possible Entries Help down arrow for the Company Code field. Select any item from the list of possible entries and press the green check mark. Now your invalid entry is replaced by a valid one. Press the Enter key, and SAP checks your entry to confirm that it is acceptable and removes your warning message from the status bar.

Sometimes the SAP system saves the last value entered in an input field into memory. Even when you replace it with a new value, it retains the old one. To clear the SAP memory for an input box, select the exclamation point key and press Enter; this clears the memory for that input field.

Required Input Fields

On SAP screens, some fields require you to fill them with data before proceeding. These are called *required fields* and usually contain a question mark , as shown in Figure 6.5. The following are examples of required fields:

- A purchase order number field on a Create Purchase Order screen in the Financials module
- An employee personnel number on a Change Basic Pay screen in the Human Resources module
- A date of accepted delivery field in a Inventory Management Control screen in the Logistics module

Generally, if a screen does not contain question marks in the input fields, you can navigate to the next screen without entering data in any fields. However, some screens that contain required fields are not marked with a question mark. This situation can occur when you enter data in an optional field that has required fields associated with it.

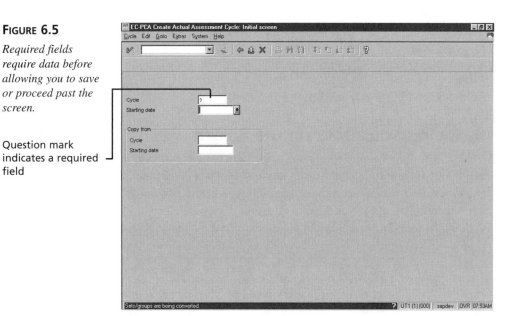

FIGURE 6.5

Required fields require data before allowing you to save or proceed past the screen.

Question mark indicates a required field

If you have not completed all the required fields on a screen and then try to proceed to another screen, the R/3 System displays an error message in the status bar. At the same time, it returns the cursor to the first required field that needs data entered so that you can make the necessary change.

Field Entry Validation

After entering data into input fields on the screen, use the Enter key or the green check mark on your SAP toolbar to check the validity of your entries. If your entries are valid, the system will proceed to the next screen in the task. If the system checks your entries and finds any errors—for example, entries in the wrong format—it displays a message in the status bar and positions the cursor in the field that you need to correct.

Canceling All the Data Entered on a Screen

To cancel all the data you just entered on a screen, use the menu path Edit, Cancel or use the red X Cancel button on the toolbar. In most instances, you will be prompted with an SAP window confirming that data will be lost if you proceed to exit the screen. See Figure 6.6.

6

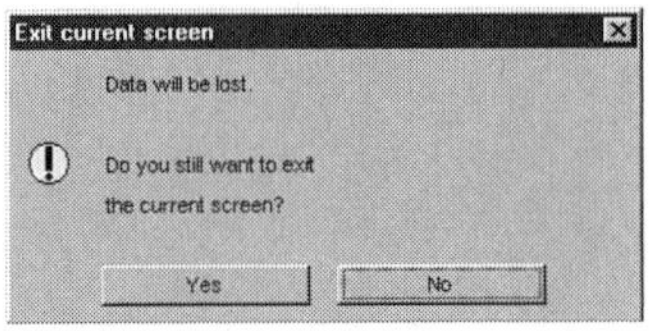

FIGURE 6.6

The Exit current screen box confirms that data will be lost if you choose to exit.

Exit current screen

Data will be lost.

Do you still want to exit the current screen?

Yes   No

Saving Your Data on the Screen

The SAP Save button appears on the standard toolbar and looks like an open folder. When you are working in a task that consists of several screens, the system temporarily stores the data that you enter on each screen. After you complete all the necessary screens in your task, you need to save your data by selecting the Save button. The Save button processes your data and sends your changes to the database.

If you are doing a task for the first time and you do not know which screen is the last screen, the system prompts you to save when you reach the last screen.

Printing Data On a Screen

Use the Print button on the standard toolbar for sending the information on your screen to the printer. Advanced printing options are covered in Hour 5, "Navigation in the R/3 System."

Replicating Data

No one likes entering data. However, SAP has a way to simplify the process. Say that you need to enter a handful of new employees into the SAP R/3 Human Resources module. All the employees have the same hire date. Using the Hold data or Set data SAP functions, you can set the hire date to automatically default to the date you set for each of the employees that you need to enter, without having to rekey it each time.

Hold Data

To use the Hold Data function on any SAP screen (except the log in screen), enter the data that you want to hold in an input field. While your cursor is still in the input field, navigate to the menu path System, User Profile, Hold Data, as shown in Figure 6.7.

FIGURE 6.7

Hold Data is a useful tool for entering data in SAP.

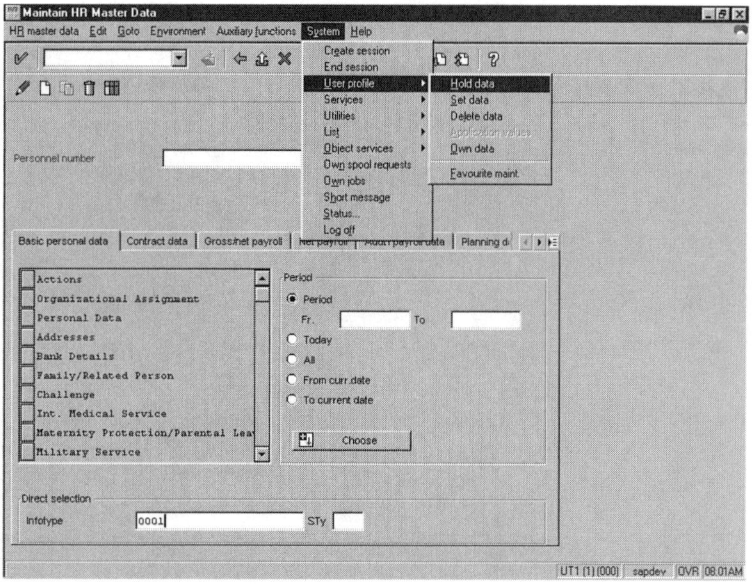

The data will be set in memory for that field for each new record you create until you turn the Hold Data setting off. The Hold Data feature also has another advantage: The input field will default to the data that you have set to hold, yet it will also allow you to override the data. If you want to hold data and not give the user the ability to change the default, you would use the Set Data setting.

Set Data

The Set Data feature works in the same fashion as the Hold Data setting, but it does not allow the user to override the default in the input field. The advantage to using the Set Data setting is that it gives you the ability to automatically skip fields with held data, so you do not need to tab from field to field during data entry.

To use the Set Data function on any SAP screen (except the login screen), enter the data in an input field that you want to set. While your cursor is still in the input field, go to the menu path System, User Profile, Set Data, as shown in Figure 6.8.

Deleting Data That Is Held or Set on a Screen

You can hold data for as many different screens as you like. The data you enter and hold on a screen is held for that screen until you delete it or until you log off the R/3 System. If you want to remove the setting without having to log off the system, place the cursor in the input field that you want to delete, and follow the menu path System, User Profile, Delete Data. The data will be deleted, and the next time you access the screen the data will not be displayed.

6

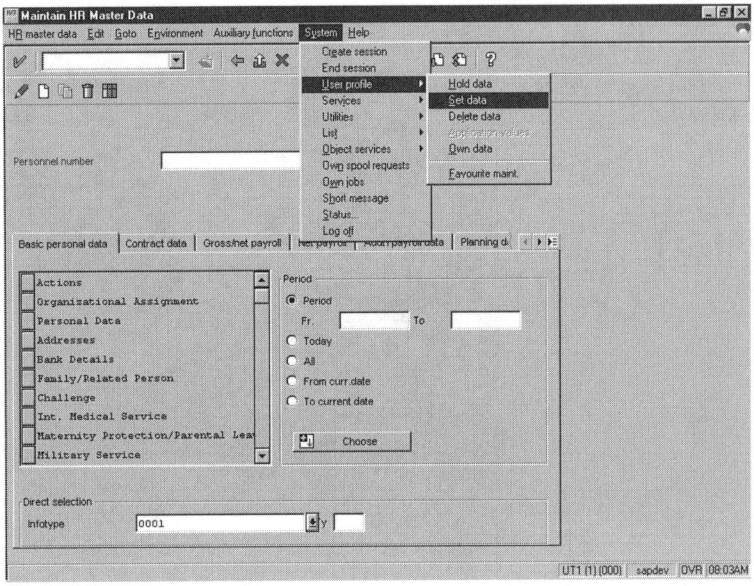

FIGURE 6.8

Using the Set Data option restricts users from changing the set value in the field.

You can also simplify the input of repeated data using parameters and variants. Parameters are a more advanced topic that is not within the scope of this book. For more information on parameters, search your R/3 Help for more information. Variants will be discussed in Hour 18, "R/3 Reporting Basics."

Display Fields

Another type of SAP field is a display field. This type of field is not used to enter, but only to display data. Display fields are always shaded with a gray background to indicate that the field can not be changed.

Display fields are often used for values that were set according to some configuration in the system or by previous steps in a process. What this translates to is fields are often assigned values based on configuration that occurs behind the scenes. For example if you add a new employee to your Human Resources Module, on their new hire screen, there will be a display field listing the employee's status as active. This value is assigned by the system and cannot be changed by the user.

By the same token, when system administrators run processes for maintaining the system, their screens often include date fields storing the current date, which are display only. The system does not allow you to change the value in these fields because in most cases the values are used by the SAP system for accurate processing. Using the Human Resources example, if we hired a new employee and were able to change his status from active to terminated, the new employee would not be recognized in SAP as an active employee. Therefore, he would not be paid or receive benefits as an active employee.

> Some fields come pre-delivered from SAP as display only, but you can also customize your system to change additional fields to display only so users cannot make changes to the data.

Screen Objects

This section covers the different types of items that you will see on the SAP screens. Regardless of the module that you are processing in, the same types of screen objects will appear on the different SAP screens.

SAP promotes itself as very logically designed so that a user can easily navigate through its system. The style of the R/3 system is much different than many popular applications available on the market today, including the Microsoft Windows and the Microsoft Office family of products. Absent in SAP are the friendly pictures, detailed formatted text, or elaborate design. Most screens in SAP are designed in tree structures through which the user navigates by drilling down in a tree.

SAP Trees

You will soon become accustomed to using SAP trees in navigating through the SAP R/3 system (see Figure 6.9). SAP's logically devised environment centers around a basic tree structure. The SAP trees appear similar to the Windows structure that you would see in your Windows 95 Explorer or File Manager. The tree structure is formulated so that you can drill down in the tree to get to deeper levels within a concept. To use a SAP tree for navigation, you need to select the sign to expand the tree to view more selections, and the (–) sign to compress SAP selections.

Check Boxes

When you are working in the R/3 System, entering information sometimes involves selecting options. These options can be in the form of check boxes like the one shown in Figure 6.10. A check mark placed in the check box indicates that the box is selected, and an empty box indicates that the box is not selected.

6

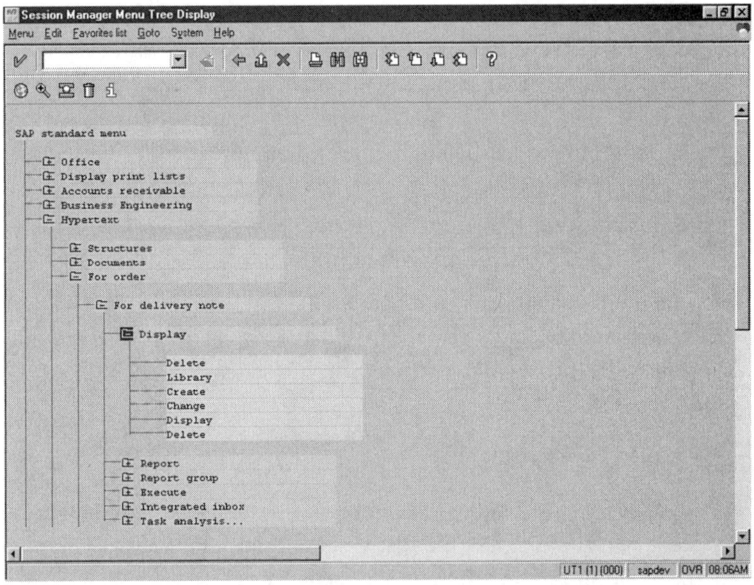

FIGURE 6.9

The SAP R/3 system is based on an elementary tree structure.

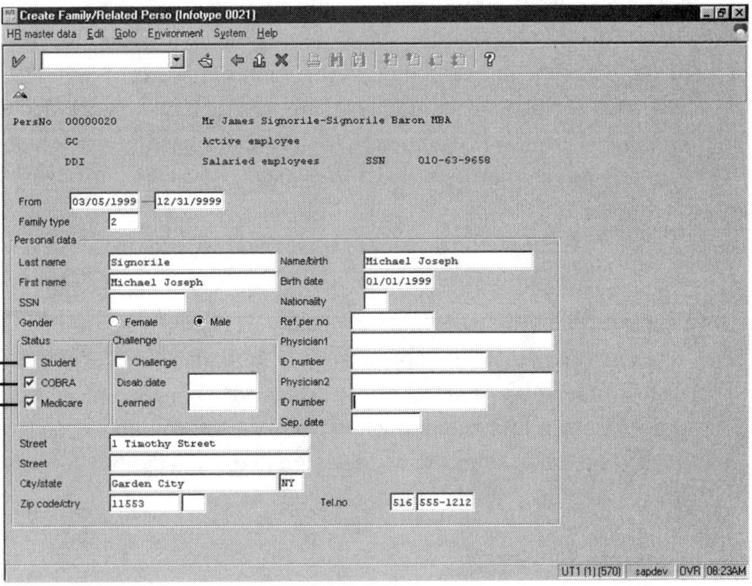

FIGURE 6.10

Check boxes are used for a yes or no selection.

Multiple check boxes in a group can be selected

Check boxes are used when a person has the option of selecting more than one option. On a single screen, a person can select multiple check boxes.

Radio Buttons

When you are permitted only one option among a selection, you will see a group of radio buttons. A group of radio buttons will only accept one selection for the group. You cannot mark more than one radio button in a group.

A mark placed in the circle indicates that the radio button is selected, and an empty circle indicates that the radio button is not selected (see Figure 6.11). An example of a radio button would be the designation of an employee in the Human Resources module as male or female.

FIGURE 6.11

Radio buttons are always shown in a group of at least two or more.

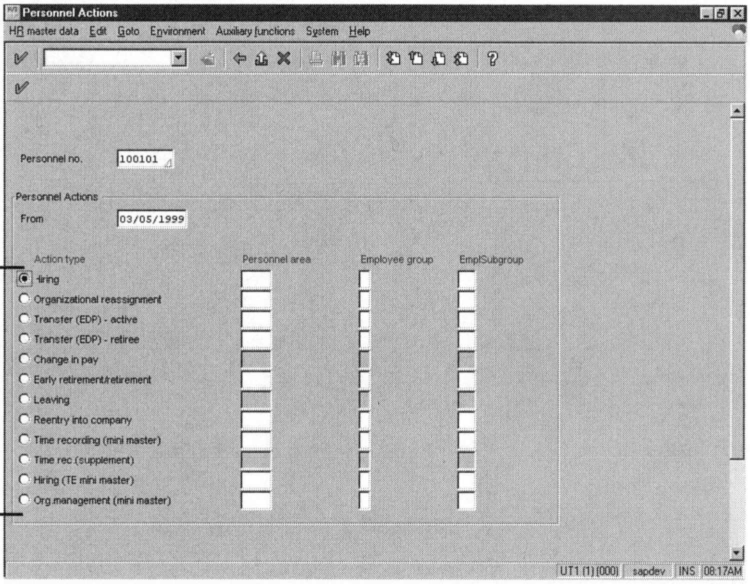

You can select only one radio button in a group

Dialog Boxes

A dialog box is a fancy term for a window that pops up to give you information (see Figure 6.12). Two situations in which a dialog box will appear on your screen are described as follows:

- The system needs more information from you before it can proceed.
- The system needs to give you feedback, such as messages or specific information about your current task.

FIGURE 6.12

*In Hour 4,
"Customizing Your
R/3 Display," you
learn how to set dia-
log boxes to appear
for warning and
error messages in
your R/3 system.*

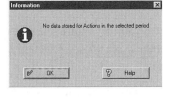

For example, you might receive a dialog box on your screen when you are logging off
the SAP R/3 system. If you select the SAP icon in the top left side of your screen and
then select the Close button, you will be prompted with a dialog box confirming that you
want to log off the system.

Table Controls

Another object you will see on SAP R/3 screens is Table Controls, as shown in Figure
6.13. Table controls display data in a tabular format similar to a Microsoft Excel spreadsheet. Table controls are popular for displaying or entering single structured lines of data.
The term *table control* comes from the R/3 Screen Painter, covered in Hour 17. Just as
you can use a check box object for selection for some data, you can use a table control
object to display data in a tabular format.

FIGURE 6.13

*Table Controls are
very popular in SAP
for presenting data in
a simple structured
format.*

SAP Table Control ——

Summary

At this juncture, you should feel very comfortable working in the SAP system. Many of the obscure objects and functions should be familiar. You are now well equipped to enter data into the SAP system, and you are quite familiar with the SAP objets that you will encounter on the different screens, including dialog boxes and radio buttons. You also should feel more comfortable with the SAP terminology.

Q&A

Q How is case used in SAP?

A This is a popular question during implementations of SAP. As technology moves away from the old mainframe systems, uppercase entries are moved toward a mixture of upper- and lowercase entry of data for better presentation. Data that comes delivered with SAP is presented in title case, and all data converted into SAP from your existing systems should first be translated to title case as well for consistency.

Q Is there a standard setting that companies should be using with regards to the insert and overwrite modes of SAP?

A Generally this setting is usually unique to an individual and should be permitted to be maintained by the individual on their own workstation.

Q Can you set your own required fields?

A In SAP, you can configure your own required fields. Keep in mind that any fields you configure as required will prevent the user from proceeding if the data is not readily available to them. Be cautious when setting required fields.

Workshop

The workshop is designed to help you anticipate possible questions, review what you've learned, and begin thinking ahead to putting your knowledge into practice. The answers to the quiz that follows can be found in Appendix A, "Answers."

Quiz

1. How do you check your entries on a screen?

2. Is it the Hold Data or Set Data option that allows you to overwrite the default entry in an input field?

3. What item on an SAP screen that contains a SAP tree do you need to select in order to expand the tree?

6

4. What is the name of a window that pops up to give you more information or supplies you with feedback on your current task?

5. When looking at a screen, what determines how many characters you can enter in an input field?

6. How do change your system setting to toggle between Insert and Overwrite mode?

7. What do you need to do to display a list of available entries for an input field that is linked to a database table?

8. What type of fields contain a question mark?

Exercises

1. Navigate to transaction code /nFB02 and determine which of the three fields on the Change Document: Initial Screen contains Possible Entries Help.

2. Find two screens in SAP that contain required fields.

3. Use the Hold Data tool to hold the data in an SAP field.

4. Use the Set Data tool to set data in an SAP field.

PART II
Implementing SAP R/3

Hour

HOUR 7

Implementing SAP

Implementing SAP is a very large undertaking that usually comes at the culmination of a long "needs analysis" and vendor comparison process. Equally as important as the SAP product is the SAP team that you comprise to implement and manage your SAP system. This hour is designed to give you an idea of what an SAP implementation entails and provides some suggestions for accomplishing a successful implementation of SAP into your organization. Highlights of this hour include

- Compiling successful Project Teams
- SAP training
- SAP training class levels
- The importance of a committed Project Team

Assembling the Project Team

Your SAP Project Team is very critical to the success of your implementation. The design and structure of this team needs to encompass all areas of your company's business as well as management support from a higher level. Areas of consideration in determining the structure of your team should include the following:

- Assessment of the business areas that will be effected by the SAP R/3 installation (Finance Dept, Accounting Dept, Receiving Dept. and so on).
- Assessment of the necessary skills that your company feels are required of your team member, both professional and technical.

When you determine what areas will be effected and what skill sets you want your Project Team members to possess, you also need to look for individuals who possess the necessary vision that your SAP R/3 implementation requires. More specifically, the vision of change and the reengineering of your current processes is essential to the implementation.

Your company's Project Team needs to be comprised of individuals from all level of the business who will be impacted by the SAP implementation. Even more importantly, upper-management support is required for efficient decision making and project direction. An ideal Project Team skeletal structure is shown in Figure 7.1.

FIGURE 7.1

Project Team structure.

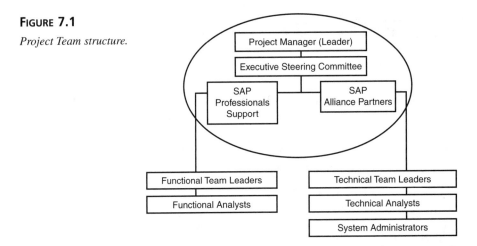

Five key characteristics that your ideally structured Project Team should possess are as follows:

- Ability to assess how the new system will enable or affect individual and collective business processes company wide.
- Ability to identify the impact on current business processes.
- Ability to comprehend the requirements for reengineering identified business processes with the R/3 system.

- Individuals who collectively have the knowledge to design the integration of the SAP R/3 structure, hierarchies and configuration across your enterprise.
- Individuals who will provide an efficient transfer of knowledge throughout the duration and maintenance of your SAP implementation.

Project Manager (Lead)

The *project manager* (or *project lead*) is responsible for the overall management of your SAP implementation. This individual will be responsible for coordinating a cooperative productive environment between all your different team members and ensures that your SAP implementation is ultimately a success. This position is often held by a consultant.

Executive Steering Committee

The highest level within your Project Team structure should consist of your high-level managers and decision makers. It is their ability to steer the project in the right direction with their management experience and decision making power that makes them the vital foundation of a successful Project Team. Tasks crucial to the Executive Steering Committee include

- Approving scope of project
- Setting priorities
- Settling queries and disputes
- Committing the resources to the project
- Monitoring the progress and impact of the implementation
- Empowers the team to make decisions

The importance of upper management's buy-in, support and facilitation of end-user training will have a direct impact on the success of the implementation. The projects that have the most problems are the ones where support in these areas is not provided.

Project Management Support

The second highest level in an ideal Project Team structure would include your Project management support. The project management team is usually comprised of SAP support professionals and your SAP alliance partners. It is their job to work in conjunction to assure that your SAP implementation is a success.

7

SAP Professionals Support

The support you receive from SAP should ensure that you take better control and ownership of your SAP project. Your SAP support professionals are also crucial in accelerating your teams' learning process through education and instruction by using their SAP knowledge and experience. The SAP Support professionals should also assist your team with the project organization throughout the duration of the project.

SAP Alliance Partners

SAP Alliance partners would consist of any SAP approved partnering company that offers an additional level of support for your SAP system. This includes additional general SAP support as well as support for SAP partnered third-party products.

 SAP has a Web site that details its partners and products, which can be found at `http://www.SAP-ag.de/partner/`.

Team Leaders

It is the responsibility of your team leaders to work with the project manager to plan and manage your project's scope, schedule, and resources. They identify the impact on and the requirements for business processes to support the organizations re-engineered vision through the use of the SAP system.

The Team Leaders hold the responsibility for designing the integration of the R/3 system across your company's functional business processes. They also need to serve as a leader and role model for their teams and are an integral part of the knowledge transfer mechanism between team members, consultants, and teams.

Functional Analysts

Functional Analysts design your SAP solution for your company based on your individual and unique requirements. These are usually non-technical managers who, on a day to day basis, manage some functional area of your business. Examples of Functional Analysts include

- Financial Accounting Manager
- Supervisor of Human Resources
- Shipping and Receiving Manager

It is their job to foresee the impact that the implementation will have on your employees and your company's business processes. They also need to evaluate the output that is currently generated and determine the functions and processes that will produce the output in the future. A very important function for a Functional Analyst is to determine the teams' training requirements and performance support.

Technical Analysts

As opposed to the Functional Analysts, the Technical Analysts are your skilled Information Technology professionals. These individuals have the computer skills and savvy and will serve as the technical leaders and support for your team. It will be the responsibility of the Technical Analysts to configure your SAP system to successfully manage your company's unique processes.

They are also responsible for designing any interfaces or customizations that your SAP R/3 system might require. These technically inclined associates also hold the task of designing your conversion plan and the actual movement of data from your old system to the new.

System Administrators

System Administrators are responsible for the maintenance of your actual hardware and your SAP installation. It is their duty to administer and maintain your SAP data. This includes preparing scheduled backups, maintaining spools, installing upgrades, hot packages, and legal change packages (LCPs).

NEW TERM *Hot packages* are fixes that you will receive from SAP on a periodic basis. They are designed to correct or enhance your current SAP version. Hot packages include any tweaking done to the SAP system that can be installed as a fix before the next release of the product.

NEW TERM *Legal change packages* are enhancements that are issued occasionally to accommodate legislative and governmental regulation changes that are required before the next official release of the software.

Training the Project Team

It is the role of the Project Team Manager to develop a training strategy for all the different levels of the Project Team. SAP has identified three levels of training, as illustrated in Figure 7.1, summarized in Table 7.1, and described in the following sections.

7

TABLE 7.1 TRAINING LEVEL CLASS DESCRIPTIONS

Level	Prerequisites	Description
1	None	Level 1 courses identify entry-level or high-level overview classes designed to introduce a general theme to the student for the first time. (that is, SAP R/3 Overview)
2	Level 1	Level 2 courses are usually an introduction to a specific subject matter. (that is, ABAP Workbench Basics)
3	Level 1 and level 2	Level 3 courses delve deeper into subject content introduced in Level 2 courses.

The SAP training methodology is based on three principles: Awareness, Readiness, and Proficiency.

Level 1 Training

Level 1 focuses on *customer awareness*. Level 1 courses generally focus on introductory features and functions to familiarize you with the SAP environment and terminology. Level 1 classes include

- SAP R/3 Overview
- SAP R/3 Basis Overview

Level 2 Training

Level 2 training is also known as the *readiness phase*. At this level, you begin to focus on the core business process courses that will empower you with the skills to apply SAP to your company's way of doing business. Level 2 classes include

- Introduction to Human Resources
- Introduction to Financial Accounting

Level 3 Training

When embarking on the Level 3 training, you generally want to master or become proficient in a particular area. Level 3 classes are more advanced courses that help you to acquire specific expertise in a particular SAP area. Level 3 classes include

- Advanced Customizing and Configuration
- Joint Venture Accounting: Processing and Configuration
- Advanced Payroll

FIGURE 7.2

SAP training courses are broken down into three levels based on complexity.

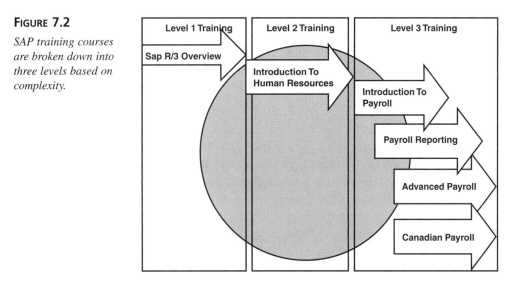

SAP Training Catalogs

SAP publishes training catalogs approximately every six months. You can obtain hard copies of these catalogs from your SAP sales contact or you can download them from SAP's Web site at `http://wwwext03.SAP.com/usa/trainsupp`.

Summary

The careful preparation and groundwork dedicated to your SAP R/3 implementation is essential in assuring a smooth transition to the SAP environment. One of the most important aspects that will contribute to the success of your R/3 implementation is a skilled and diversified Project Team. The level of expertise and project commitment of the team will have a direct relationship to the success of your SAP R/3 project.

Workshop

The workshop is designed to help you anticipate possible questions, review what you've learned, and begin thinking ahead to putting your knowledge into practice. The answers to the quiz that follows can be found in Appendix A, "Answers."

7

Q&A

Q At what point should training begin?

A After SAP is selected as your vendor of choice, Level 1 training, to familiarize user with the basic SAP environment, should begin almost immediately.

Q Should your project manager (project lead) be an employee or a consultant?

A If you have an employee with SAP and project management experience for SAP implementations, by all means an employee should hold this role. In most cases, however, a consultant usually fits the skill-set better than any employee. It is a good idea to have an employee shadow the project lead so that when it is time for the consultant to move on, there will have been a transfer of knowledge to the employee.

Q How much do these SAP courses cost?

A The easy answer is that the price varies depending on the course, length of the course, location, and so on. Courses generally cost a couple of thousand dollars each.

Q Where can you get more information on different options available for SAP Training and Support?

A For more information on different options available for SAP Training and Support, visit their Web site at http://wwwext03.SAP.com/usa/trainsupp/flexible.asp.

Q How can I find out when new courses become available for SAP training?

A For more information on new courses available for SAP training, visit their Web site at http://wwwext03.SAP.com/usa/trainsupp/course/index.asp.

Quiz

1. How many levels of SAP training are available?

2. What level of SAP R/3 training does not require any perquisites?

3. What is the difference between a functional and a technical analyst on your Project Team?

4. What is one of the most important factors contributing to the success of your SAP R/3 implementation?

5. What is the highest level of structure in your Project Team hierarchy?

Hour **8**

R/3 Implementation Tools

Implementing SAP is no easy task. SAP is aware of this, and accordingly has developed options for enhancing and perfecting an efficient SAP implementation. This hour I will discuss two rapid SAP implementation tools: ASAP AcceleratedSAP and Ready To Run R/3. Highlights of this hour include

- Reviewing your implementation options
- Learning about the R/3 Roadmap
- Concepts of The Phase approach
- Finding more information on SAP's Partners

ASAP AcceleratedSAP

Everyone knows that the integration of the SAP R/3 system into your organization can be challenging. It's not quite like installing a new product like Microsoft Office. It entails a re-engineering of your current environment, structure, system, and processes. AcceleratedSAP (ASAP) is a tool to help make this transformation easier by assisting in the implementation of R/3 solutions.

Its purpose is to help design your SAP R/3 implementation in the most efficient manner possible. Its goal is to effectively optimize time, quality, and the efficient use of resources. ASAP focuses on tools and training, wrapped up in a five-phase roadmap for guiding implementation.

The AcceleratedSAP Roadmap delivers a process-oriented strategy to provide step-by-step direction throughout your implementation of R/3. The roadmap is comprised of five consecutive phases that will ultimately lead you to a successful implementation:

Phase 1: Project Preparation

Phase 2: Business Blueprint

Phase 3: Realization

Phase 4: Final Preparation

Phase 5: Go Live and Support

The roadmap is illustrated in Figure 8.1, and the five phases are described in the following sections.

FIGURE 8.1

ASAP Roadmap.

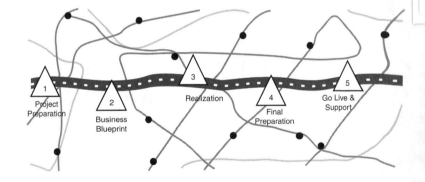

Phase 1: Project Preparation

Phase 1 initiates with a retrieval of information and resources. It is an important time to assemble the necessary components for the implementation. Some important milestones that need to be accomplished for Phase 1 include

- Senior Level Management Support
- Clear Project Objectives
- An Efficient Decision Making Process

- Environment Suitable For Change and Re-engineering
- Representative and Qualified Team

Senior Level Management Support

One of the most important milestones with Phase 1 of ASAP is the full agreement and cooperation of the important company decision makers. It is their backing and support that is crucial for a successful implementation.

Clear Project Objectives

Be concise in defining what your objectives and expectations are for this venture. Vague or unclear notions of what you hope to obtain with SAP will handicap the implementation process. Also make sure that your expectations are reasonable considering your company's resources. It is essential to have clearly defined ideas, goals, and project plans devised before embarking on Phase 2 of ASAP.

An Efficient Decision Making Process

One obstacle that often stalls implementations is a poorly constructed decision making process. Before embarking on this venture, individuals need to be clearly identified, who will be responsible for different decisions along the way. From day one, the implementation decision makers from each area must be clearly defined, and they must be aware of the onus placed on them to return good and fast decisions. Through the course of the implementation, many important decisions will need to be made that will tap into a multitude of areas within your organization.

Environment Suitable for Change and Re-engineering

Your team must be willing to accept that, along with the new SAP R/3 software, things are going to change. SAP is not going to be configured to exactly fit the mold of your current business practices. You are implementing SAP to help you redesign your current practices to model more efficient or predefined best business practices. Resistance to this change will impede the progress of your implementation.

Representative and Qualified Team

Probably the most important milestone in Phase 1 is assembling a Project Team for the implementation. Your Project Team has to be a representative sample of the population of your company. If you are implementing the Materials Management and Plant Maintenance modules, you will need to include people from both of these departments, as well as from your Information Technology department, on your team. The team should also represent management level as well as non-management personnel because sometimes the management level is not always aware of the day-to-day functions that will be influenced by the SAP R/3 system. (In Hour 7, "Implementing SAP," you learned how a Project Team should be constructed.)

TeamSAP Support

Right from the beginning of Phase 1, your TeamSAP consultants work with you to assess your needs and expectations for the SAP implementation. The ASAP implementation method provides you with an AcceleratedSAP's Project Estimator. This tool guides your team through a series of predefined questions, and conducts interviews with your company's senior executives and decision making managers to derive the necessary information for the course of the implementation. Your representative's response to the estimator's queries will be evaluated to provide a project scope and resource requirements basis for you to begin the implementation in terms of identifying project time, cost, and resources.

When your implementation Project Team has been identified (and your SAP contract has been signed), introductory training (Level 1) should begin. A table defining the different levels of SAP training can be found in the section "Training the Project Team" in Hour 7.

This introductory training will acquaint team members with the SAP structure, terminology, and environment. The sooner key members are familiar with these concepts, the better prepared they will be in the implementation process.

Phase 2: Business Blueprint

SAP has defined Business Blueprints to help extract pertinent information about your company that is necessary for the implementation. These blueprints are in the form of questionnaires that are designed to probe for information on how your company does business. These blueprints are also a very useful documentation tool that serves as the global source for implementation information for your company.

This business blueprint document will house your future business processes and business requirements. Two sample questions from the business blueprint document are

- What information do you capture on a purchase order?
- What information is required to complete a purchase order?

AcceleratedSAP Question and Answer Database

The Question and Answer database is a tool to facilitate the creation of your business blueprint. This database stores the questions and the answers and serves as the heart of your blueprint. Customers are provided with a Customer Input Template for each application that collects the data. The question and answer format is standard across applications to facilitate easier use for your Project Team.

Issues Database

Another tool used in the blueprinting phase is the Issues Database. This stores any open concerns and pending issues that relate to the SAP R/3 implementation. The central storage of this information assists in the gathering of the issues as well as helps so that important issues are not forgotten in the process. Issues in the database can be tracked, assigned to team members and updated accordingly.

R/3 Reference Model

The R/3 Reference Model is a visual tool that helps your implementation team with seeing the "big picture" in terms of your implementation plans. The reference model can be accessed through your SAP system using the Business Navigator Tool. The Business Navigator Tool in the R/3 system links the process models to actual transactions in the R/3 system in an effort to ensure consistency and support for your SAP projects.

Because your data is being collected and organized into a source, it is important for your Project Team to begin Level 2 training. (See the section "Training the Project Team" in Hour 7.) Level 2 training will provide your Project Team with a deeper understanding of the SAP system and the application components that they are installing and configuring. With Level 2 training complete, your team will be ready to press on and enter Phase 3.

Phase 3: Realization

With the completion of the business blueprint in Phase 2, you are now ready to begin to configure your SAP R/3 system. The Realization phase is broken into two parts:

1. Your TeamSAP consultant will help you configure your baseline system, which I will call the Baseline Configuration.

2. Your implementation Project Team will fine-tune that system to meet all your business and process requirements as part of the Fine Tuning Configuration.

The initial configuration completed during the baseline configuration will be based on the information that you provided in your blueprint document. The remaining approximately twenty percent of your configuration that was not tackled during the Baseline Configuration will be completed during the Fine Tuning configuration. Fine Tuning usually deals with the exceptions that are not covered in Baseline configuration. This is the actual tweaking of the SAP system to fit your special needs.

Configuration Testing

With the help of your TeamSAP consultant, you will segregate your business processes into cycles of related business flows. The cycles will serve independent units that will allow you to test specific parts of the business process. You will also work through configuring the SAP Implementation Guide (IMG), a tool used to assist you in configuring your SAP system in a step-by-step manner. (The Implementation Guide is covered in detail in Hour 9, "The SAP Implementation Guide (IMG).")

During this configuration and testing process, it will be necessary to send your Project Team for Level 3 SAP training. (See the section "Training the Project Team" in Hour 7.) This in-depth instruction will provide your team members with expertise specific to your business' requirements.

Knowledge Transfer

As the configuration phase comes to a close, it will be necessary for the Project Team to be self sufficient in their knowledge of the configuration of your SAP system. A transfer of knowledge from the TeamSAP consultants to the configuration team needs to be completed at this time.

In addition, although the SAP Implementation Project Team is SAP savvy, it is now time to train the end users. End users are people—not members of your Project Team—but people who will be using the SAP system. Level 1 and Level 2 training should now begin for the people who will be using the SAP system on a daily basis. This is also a good opportunity to send the implementation Project Team for additional functional Level 2 and Level 3 training in the areas they want to focus on in the live system.

Phase 4: Final Preparation

As Phase 3 merges into Phase 4, your implementation Project Team and your end users will be attending SAP training. There will also be rigorous testing being conducted on your SAP system. Phase 4 concentrates on the fine tuning of your configuration before you Go Live and more importantly, the migration of data from your old to your new system.

Volume, stress, and integration tests will be conducted to ensure the accuracy of your data and the stability of your SAP system. Because you began testing in Phase 2, you do not have too far to go until the Go Live. Now is an important time to perform preventative maintenance checks to ensure optimal performance of your R/3 system.

At the conclusion of Phase 4, you are planning your Go Live strategy. Preparing to Go Live means preparing for your end-users' questions as they start actively working on the new SAP R/3 system.

Phase 5: Go Live and Support

The Go Live is the easy part. You have been preparing for it for some time. The focus on supporting your Sap R/3 system is more important and you are not alone. In addition to your internal SAP resources who you have trained and the TeamSAP consultants who are assisting you, there is also a wealth of information available to you. Some of these additional resources are discussed in Hour 24, "Additional SAP Resources."

Ready-to-Run R/3

8

Ready-to-Run R/3 (RRR) is a program that continues SAP's effort to make the implementation of the R/3 system faster and more efficient. Ready-to-Run R/3 (RRR) became an option for the United States in August of 1996 and in Europe in June of 1997. The Ready-to-Run R/3 is ideally suited for small to medium-sized companies.

RRR can serve to complement the AcceleratedSAP program by combining bundled server and network hardware systems with a pre-installed, pre-configured base R/3 System, operating system, and database. Putting aside the technical jargon, this means that you will receive a SAP system, which already contains the SAP software and configuration that is required for your company right out of the box.

Two distinctive advantages to using the RRR method is the cost and time savings. SAP estimates that implementing with the RRR solution can knock off 15–30 days of your implementation schedule.

Ready-To-Run System Administration Assistant

This implementation methodology includes a specially-developed online tool for system administration called the System Administration Assistant. The Assistant is designed to assist your system administrator in their tasks on a daily, weekly, and monthly basis. The system administrator can perform the required R/3 functions, transactions, and programs directly from the System Administration Assistant with tips and instructions provided along the way. This not only saves time and resources, but it also allows you to have a minimally trained system administrator effectively managing your system.

Participating Partners

A SAP Ready-To-Run R/3 solution can be purchased through any of the SAP hardware vendor partners listed in Table 8.1.

TABLE 8.1 SAP HARDWARE VENDOR PARTNERS

Partner	Web site
Bull Corp.	www.bull.com
Compaq	www.compaq.com
Digital	www.digital.com
Hewlett-Packard Co.	www.hp.com
IBM Corp. (NT and AS/400)	www.ibm.com
NCR Corp.	www.ncr.com
Siemens Corp.	www.siemens.de
Sun Microsystems, inc.	www.sun.com

Operating Systems

An SAP Ready-To-Run R/3 solution can be supported using any of the operating systems listed in Table 8.2.

TABLE 8.2 SAP OPERATING SYSTEMS

Partner	Web site
Microsoft Windows NT	www.microsoft.com
IBM AS/400	www.ibm.com
UNIX (Sun Microsystems Only)	www.sun.com

Supported Databases

An SAP Ready-To-Run R/3 solution can be supported using any of the databases listed in Table 8.3.

TABLE 8.3 SAP SUPPORTED DATABASES

Partner	Web site
Microsoft SQL Server	www.microsoft.com
DB2/CS	www.ibm.com
DB2/400	www.ibm.com
Informix	www.informix.com
Oracle	www.oracle.com
Dynamic Server	www.informix.com
DB2/UDB	www.ibm.com

Summary

The decision on the implementation strategy will affect the time, cost, and path you follow in your SAP implementation. SAP rapid Ready-To-Run R/3 and AcceleratedSAP implementation options are both effective, efficient solutions that may or may not be the best fit for your company. Because no two companies are alike, you should discuss your company's individual needs with your SAP representative and take it from there.

Q&A

Q Why use an accelerated solution in your implementation?

A The use of an accelerated solution can incorporate best business practices using a bundled hardware/software solution, which includes a dedicated team of experts assembled to get your system up and running; a range of tools, including AcceleratedSAP, to streamline your implementation; and training to bring you and your user community up to speed quickly.

Q Where can you get more information on Ready-to-run solutions?

A You get more information on Ready-to-run solutions on SAP's Web site at `http://wwwext03.SAP.com/usa/solutions/midsize/run/index.asp`.

Q What does the Ready-to-run solution come with?

A The Ready-to-run solution contains configured hardware with a complete operations concept, including an online administration assistant with years of experience in Basis consulting. It also provides access to the Internet and to all SAP services, such as the Online Service System (OSS), and a preconfigured Workbench Organizer specifically optimized for mid-size businesses.

8

HOUR 9

The SAP Implementation Guide (IMG)

The Implementation Guide is a tool to assist you in the configuration of your SAP system. It is a large tree structure diagram that lists all actions required for implementing the SAP System, and guides you through each of the steps in all the different SAP areas that require configuration. Highlights of this hour include

- Learning about the different IMG views
- Viewing the R/3 Procedure Model
- Tracking Tasks in the IMG
- Getting help in the IMG

The guide begins with very basic settings including "what country are you in?" to very specific settings like "what number do you want your purchase orders to begin with?". All in all, you basically cannot get started on SAP without being familiar with the SAP Implementation Guide. To begin your look at the SAP Implementation Guide, go to transaction code /nSPRO or follow the menu path Tools, Business Engineer, Customizing. The main screen appears similar to the one in Figure 9.1.

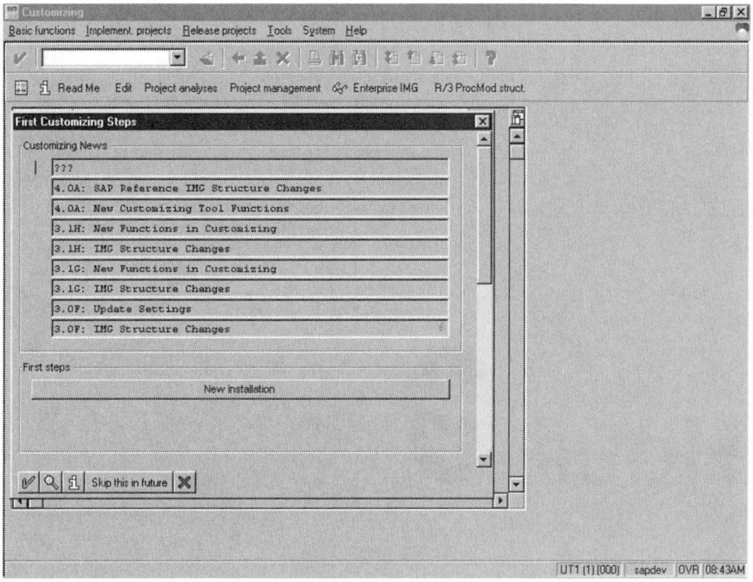

FIGURE 9.1

The Implementation Guide main screen will vary depending upon your installation and the amount of configuration that has been done.

It is important to note that the screens depicted in this hour might not appear exactly as the screens appear on your system. With the modules being implemented, your SAP R/3 version number, progress in the implementation, and authorization access will all affect the way the screens appear on your system.

For each business application, the SAP Implementation Guide (IMG)

- Explains all the steps in the implementation process
- Tells you the SAP standard (default) settings
- Describes system configuration work (tasks or activities)

There are four levels of the SAP Implementation Guide (IMG):

- The SAP Reference IMG
- SAP Enterprise IMGs
- SAP Project IMGs
- SAP Upgrade Customizing IMGs

Different Views of the IMG

There are different ways that you can look at your Implementation Guide (IMG) within SAP. Each of the different ways is called a view. Depending on the type of information that you wish to see and the order in which you want it presented on the screen, you will select a different view of the IMG. You can also create your own custom views of the IMG.

The SAP Reference IMG

The SAP Reference IMG contains documentation on all the SAP business application components supplied by SAP and serves as a single source for all configuration (see Figure 9.2).

FIGURE 9.2

Using the SAP Reference IMG, you can customize your entire SAP implementation in a single place.

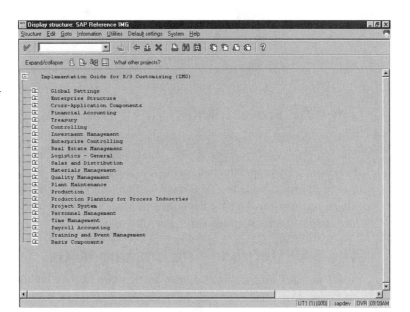

The SAP Enterprise IMG

This SAP Enterprise IMG is a subset of the SAP Reference IMG containing documentation only for the components you are implementing. It appears the same as the reference IMG, but only lists the configuration steps necessary for your company's implementation. For example, if you are implementing only the Logistics module, your IMG would not contain any information on configuring payroll from the Human Resources module (see Figure 9.3).

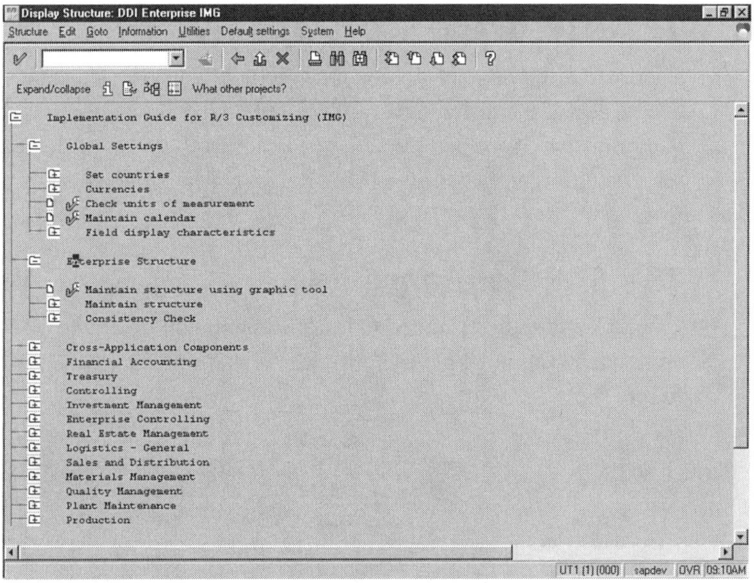

FIGURE 9.3

This example step in the Enterprise IMG is the configuration of your Country Global Parameters.

The SAP Project IMGs

SAP Project IMGs are Enterprise IMG subsets containing only the documentation for Enterprise IMG components you are implementing in particular Customizing projects. For example, if you are implementing the Logistics module only, but you have divided it into two projects—one for Sales and Distribution and a second for Materials Management—you can have them set up as two different projects here. Figure 9.4 gives an example of a Human Resources Payroll Project IMG.

The SAP Upgrade Customizing IMGs

SAP Upgrade Customizing IMGs are based either on the Enterprise IMG or on a particular Project IMG. They show all the documents linked to a Release Note for a given release upgrade (see Figure 9.5).

The R/3 Procedure Model

The R/3 Procedure Model shows the structure of your R/3 implementation projects and serves as the methodological framework for your implementation. It divides the implementation into four phases, each phase consisting of several work packages (see Figure 9.6):

FIGURE 9.4

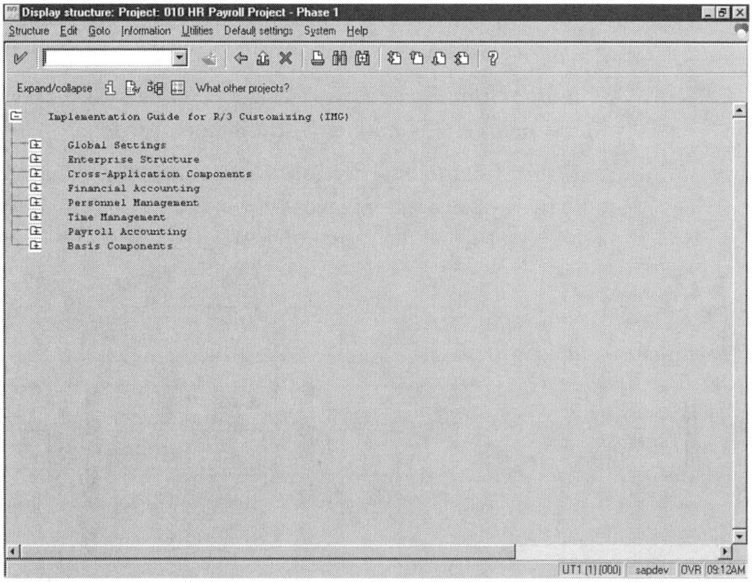

*The SAP Project
IMG for the Human
Resources Payroll
Project only includes
configuration steps
necessary for the
configuration of
Payroll.*

FIGURE 9.5

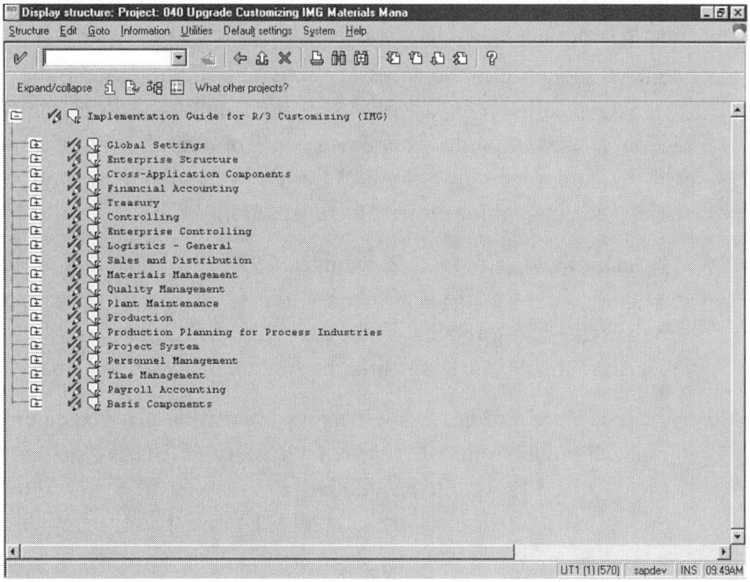

*The SAP Upgrade
Customizing IMG
allows you to specify
configuration based
on specific SAP
releases.*

1. *Organization and Conceptual Design*: The basic concepts are mapped out and a strategy is outlined for the path the project is going to take.

2. *Detailed Design and System Setup*: This phase is the detailed configuration of the system for your needs.

3. *Preparations for Going Live*: Stringent unit and parallel testing is performed to see if the systems configuration is working up to speed.

4. *Productive Operation*: This final phase entails the actual maintenance and support of the live system, and involves carrying out a quality check on the status of the items and releasing the results.

FIGURE 9.6

Each phase of the R/3 Procedure Model delineates specific goals and tasks.

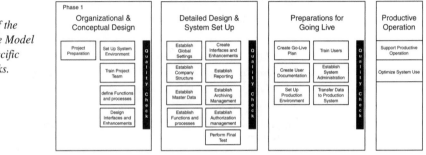

The R/3 Procedure Model provides a hierarchically structured plan of the activities, a detailed sequence of the necessary activities, and the link to the system setting activities that you need in order for your implementation to be successful. The R/3 Procedure Model is used in your Customizing configuration. It is helpful for navigation through the Customizing functions of the R/3 System, general administration of your R/3 implementation project, and for project documentation.

The main focus of the R/3 Procedure Model is to provide a structure for your R/3 implementation. To take a look at the procedure Model, follow the menu path Tools, Business Engineering, Customizing, Basic functions, R/3 Procedure Model, Display structure. The Procedure model appears similar to the screen shown in Figure 9.7.

The procedure also has a graphical representation that you can use. To take a look at the graphical model, follow the menu path Tools, Business Engineering, Customizing, Basic functions, R/3 Procedure Model, Display graphic. The Procedure model appears in a new window (using SAP Network Graphics) similar to the screen in Figure 9.8.

The boxes displayed in the structural graphic are linked to the same objects that appear in the structure display.

FIGURE 9.7

The R/3 Procedure Model is the basic element of Customizing.

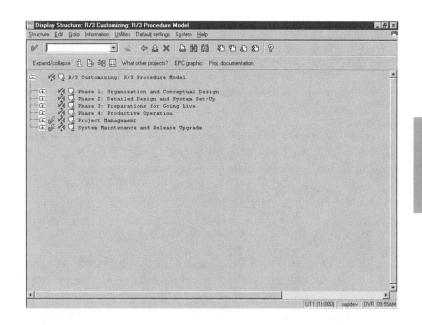

FIGURE 9.8

The SAP Procedure Model graphical structure.

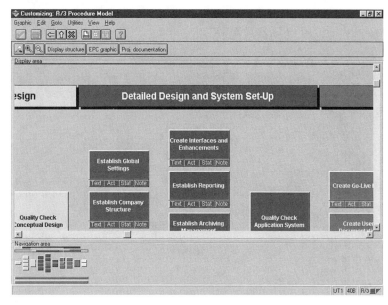

IMG Basics

You can start by taking a look at a basic IMG structure. Start by using transaction code /nSPRO or the menu path Tools, Business Engineering, Customizing. You will take a look at the Procedure Model structure view by selecting the menu path Basic functions, R/3 Procedure Model, Display structure.

Your initial view of an IMG structure will always be a tree diagram with symbols shown to the left, like the example shown in Figure 9.2. The plus signs to the left of each item in the tree structure can be used to expand that branch of the tree to view its sub structure. You can also expand branches by placing your cursor on a line item and then following the menu path Edit, Expand/Collapse or by placing your cursor on a line item and pressing F5. To expand all possible branches, place your cursor on the highest level and select Edit, All subnodes.

Looking at the IMG with the subnodes expanded gives you a good idea of what the IMG is used for. Taking a look at each of the different line items, you can see how this tool can assist you in the implementation. The IMG that you are currently viewing is for the Procedure model, and it has your implementation activities segregated by phases.

Icons in the IMG

The Implementation Guide contains different symbols (or pictures) next to each line item. These symbols and their functionality are explained in Table 9.1.

TABLE 9.1 TABLE OF IMG ITEMS

Symbol	Name	Description
	Expand Node	Plus sign expands the tree to view any available subnodes
	Collapse Node	Minus sign (-) collapses any expanded subnodes
	Empty Node	Indicates a node without subnodes
	Create Note	Opens note maintenance for this particular activity
	Read Note	Opens the attached note for this particular activity
	Execute	Indicates an executable function and launches the executable function.
	Activity	Used to enter the status maintenance for the selected activity
	Release Note	Used to retrieve Release Notes specific to the selected node.

Help in the IMG

The first thing you should learn about the IMG window is how to retrieve help for any individual line item. Just by looking at the description of each line item, it is not always clear exactly what the configuration of that item entails. Selection-specific Help can be launched by double-clicking any activity (line item) in the IMG. This will bring you detailed help on the configuration activity that you have selected. In some cases, it will launch a small window describing the reasons for the activity and what it entails, including describing actual examples of what the activity is used to configure. In other instances it will launch your SAP Help application, allowing you to navigate your SAP Help application for more information. Help is also available after you execute a line item in the IMG. Most activities in the IMG will bring you to a screen where you will need to add or modify values in a table in order for you to configure your SAP system. The field descriptions and selection-specific Help may not have provided all of the information necessary for you to understand what to do. Placing you cursor in any field and then pressing F1 from any IMG activity screen will launch field-level selection-specific Help. The Help file will be presented as a small window describing the possible values for entry in that field. Using the Help in the IMG is essential to obtain additional information on the activities required for configuring your SAP system.

Documentation in the IMG

The Implementation Guide is usually your main source for configuration. That is essentially why it is the ideal location for documenting your configuration. As you have learned, the IMG gets very specific about different steps that you need to configure in your system. Place your cursor on the top line that reads R/3 Customizing: R/3 Procedure Model. Next select the Create Note symbol to the left of the line (see Table 9.1).

Using this symbol, you can write comments, notes, or configuration information pertaining to this particular line in the IMG. Use your cursor to select the documentation symbol, and your screen launches into a documentation editor like the one shown Figure 9.9.

The SAP documentation editor is used to record configuration specific notes for each line item in the IMG. This is a very helpful tool and a great reference to be used after your implementation is complete and as a reference for SAP upgrades and changes. Configuration notes can be typed into the editor and saved with that line item in the IMG. The Read Note symbol is used to read any documentation notes added for the line item.

FIGURE 9.9

*The IMG documenta-
tion editor is an ideal
resource for writing
configuration notes
for particular activi-
ties.*

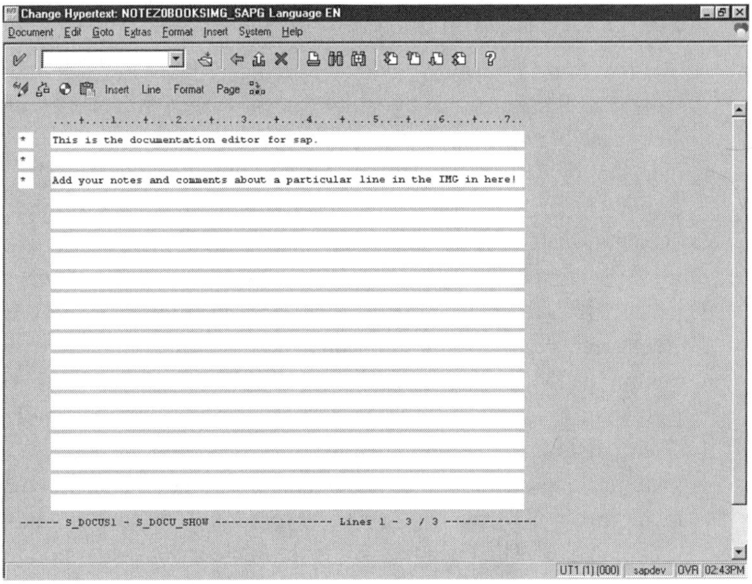

Activity Data

Selecting the Activity symbol, like the one shown in Table 9.1, will bring you to the
Change Activity data screen, as shown in Figure 9.10. The Change Activity data screen is
the place where you record the status and progress of your configuration for a particular
line item.

Status

The purpose of the Change Activity Data Screen is to keep a record of your configuration to date and to track your implementation progress. It is also a good place to see who
is working on what. One of first things that you need to assign on this screen is the
Status field. Example Status types include

- In Process
- In Q/A Testing
- Completed

The different status levels are set up by you to your company's specifications. This Status
designation will segregate your configuration tasks into different completion categories.

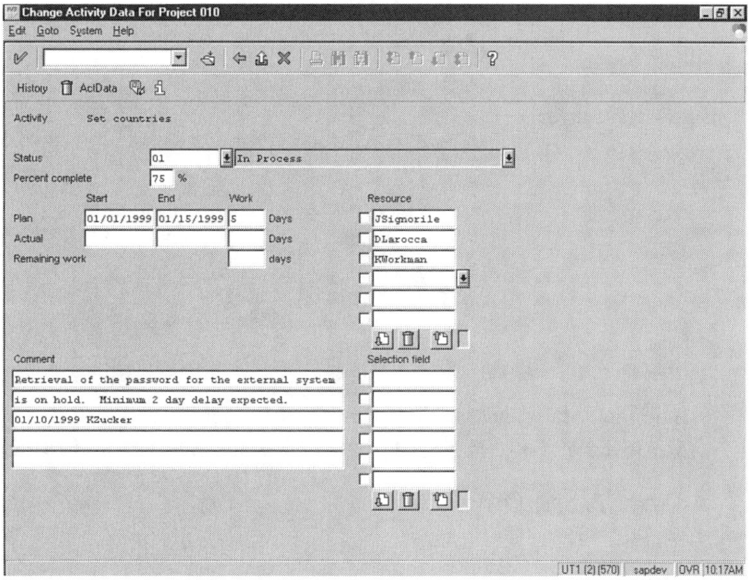

FIGURE 9.10

The Change Activity Data screen records the status of the item, the individuals assigned as well as the percentage complete.

Percent Complete

The Percent Complete field is used to display a processing status for an activity expressed as a percentage. Example percent completed values include

25%

50%

75%

100%

Again, these values are up to you. Your company will decide which values are appropriate for your organization.

Plan Start Date

The Plan Start Date is where you record the initial projected date that this particular activity should commence. Select the Possible Entries Help button on this field to display a calendar that allows you to select the date rather than entering it. The SAP Calendar Control appears similar to the one shown in Figure 9.11.

The date is selected using the calendar control by selecting the month, date, and year, and then double-clicking or by selecting the green check mark.

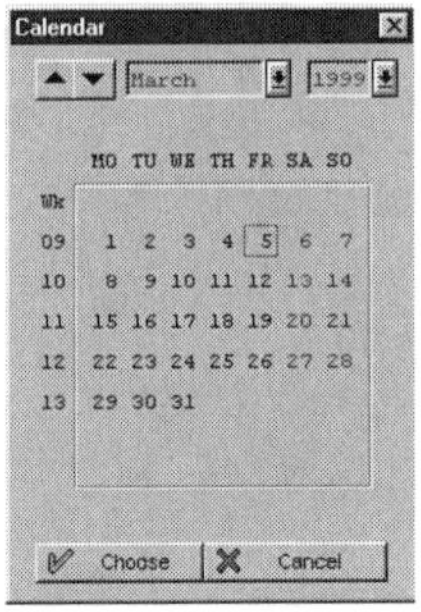

FIGURE 9.11

*SAP Calendar
Controls appear on
most SAP date fields
to assist in the entry
of dates.*

Plan End Date

The Plan Start Date is where you record the projected activity completion date for this particular activity. The SAP calendar is also available on this field.

Plan Work Days

The Plan Work Days field records the planned duration of an activity in days. The planned expenditure can be maintained manually. If neither actual expenditure nor processing status are maintained, the remaining expenditure is calculated.

Actual Start Date

In the real world, sometimes things do not always go as planned. The Actual Start Date field records the actual date that the activity was commenced on. This field is usually maintained only when the Planned Start Date and the Actual Start Date differ.

Actual End Date

The Actual End Date field records the actual date that the activity was completed. This field is usually maintained only when the Planned End Date and the Actual End Date differ.

Actual Work Days

The Actual Work days field records the actual duration in days of an activity. This field is usually maintained only when the Planned Start and End Date conflict with the Actual Start and End Date.

Remaining Work Days

The Remaining Work Days field records the remaining expenditure for an activity in days. The remaining expenditure is calculated from the actual expenditure and the processing status, or from the planned expenditure, if these fields are not maintained. You can also set the remaining expenditure manually.

Resource Assignment

For each particular task in the IMG, you can assign resources (or people) who are responsible for that task. The Resource boxes on the right side of the screen are where you denote this assignment. By using the Possible Entries Help button in the resource field, you can select the resources responsible for performing an activity. As the multiple resources boxes depict, you can assign multiple resources to a single task.

The check boxes listed next to each resource are used if you want to remove that resource from the activity. Place a check mark in a box next to a resource name and then select Edit, Delete Resource from the menu bar to remove the marked resource from the assignment.

Selection Fields

The Selection fields are used to define organizational criteria for project control using the selection fields.

The check boxes listed next to each selection field are used if you want to remove that selection field from the activity. Place a check mark in a box next to a selection field and then select Edit, Delete SelectField from the menu bar to remove that selection field from the assignment.

Comments

The comments section is where you would add any relevant notes that pertain to the status of the activity. Helpful notes would include reasons for delay or problems encountered. For example, there is a setting in the IMG where you set up the number of decimals places that you want stored for your currency amounts. This setting may be different for each of the different currencies. If you contacted your remote office in Turkey to determine how many decimal places they use for their Turkish Lira and you were unable to find a translator to translate the answer, you can note that delay in the comments section.

Viewing Activity Status on the IMG Main Screen

You can change an IMG setting so that the status of all your IMG tasks is displayed in the IMG tree structure. From the main IMG tree structure screen, follow the menu path Information, Title and status. Your tree structure will now include the status of each item in your IMG listed to the right of each line item (see Figure 9.12).

FIGURE 9.12

You can modify your IMG setting to display each line item with its status.

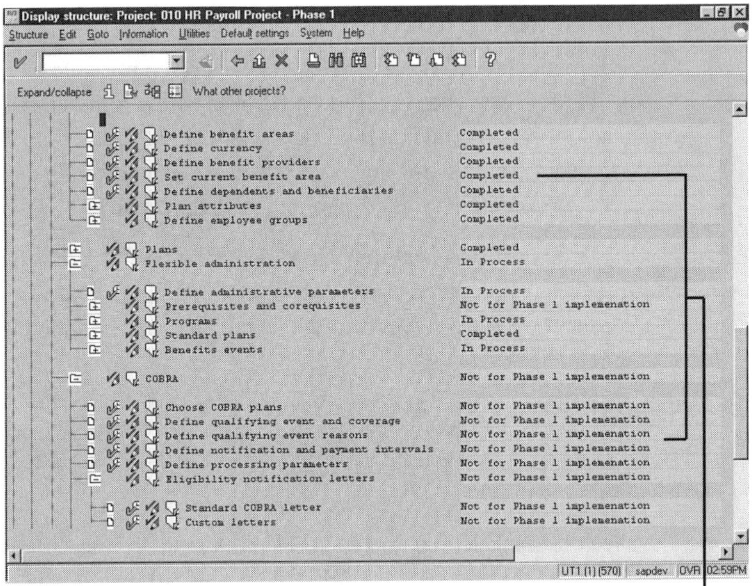

Completion status now listed next to each item in the IMG

Release Notes

Release Notes contain specific relevant information on changes to the SAP system since the last release. They contain functionality and screen changes, as well as menu path and table structure changes. Release Notes are helpful when you are migrating from one SAP version to another. They are also a good tool for retrieving additional information about how something works in the SAP system.

There is an indicator, which you can turn on in your IMG, that displays a marker next to each activity revealing whether the Release Notes are available for that particular activity (see Figure 9.13).

Activate this feature by following the menu path from the main IMG tree structure: Information, Title and IMG Info, Release Notes. Your Tree structure will now include the hand graphic next to each line item in your IMG that has relevant Release Notes. The Release Notes screen will display as text with hypertext links that you can use to navigate to other relevant topics. Hypertext links appear in highlighted text (see Figure 9.14). Another way to tell which words in the text are hypertext links is when placing your cursor over the word, your pointer changes to a hand.

Sometimes these hypertext links will lead you to additional text descriptions, and sometimes they will take you to actual SAP screens. To return to the IMG from these additional screens, use the green back arrow on the SAP standard toolbar.

FIGURE 9.13

Selecting the Release Notes symbol brings you to a screen containing documentation about the line item and how it has been changed since an earlier release (see Table 9.1).

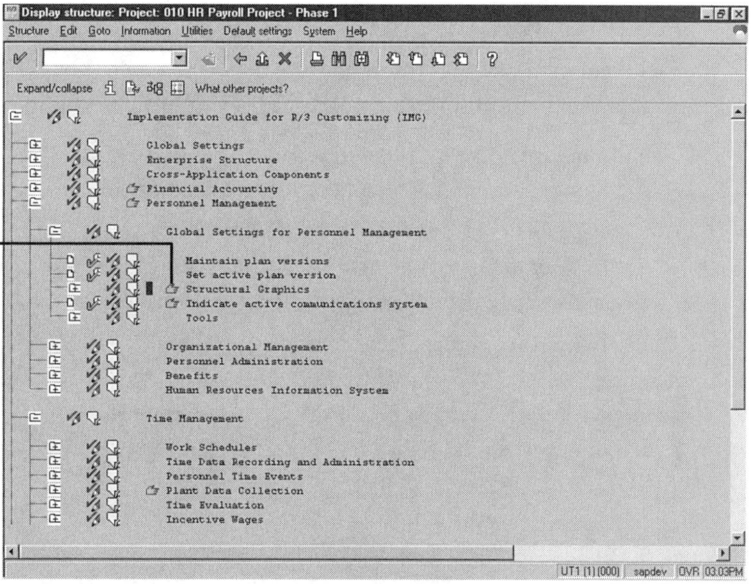

Highlighted items in text indicate hypertext links that will lead you to additional information about the subject

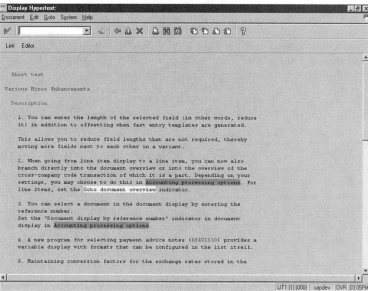

FIGURE 9.14

In some cases, when you display Release Notes, they will appear with hypertext links.

9

Activity Requirement Level

Each item in the IMG contains an Activity Requirement Level. This level determines the level of requirement for that activity. The possible values for this setting are as follows:

- *Mandatory activity*: Activities for which SAP cannot deliver standard defaults settings. In these fields, you must store your own company-specific requirements for activities that are categorized as mandatory.

- *Optional activity*: SAP delivers default settings for these activities in the IMG. You can use these default settings or change them to meet your company-specific needs.

The Activity Requirement level setting is configured by SAP. To view the Activity Requirement level for your IMG from the main IMG tree structure screen, follow the menu path Information, Title and IMG Info, Activity Requirement level. The requirement level will appear in the right side of your screen for each activity in the IMG (see Figure 9.15).

FIGURE 9.15

Viewing Activity Requirement Levels in the IMG provides you with an instant view of the status of the different line items.

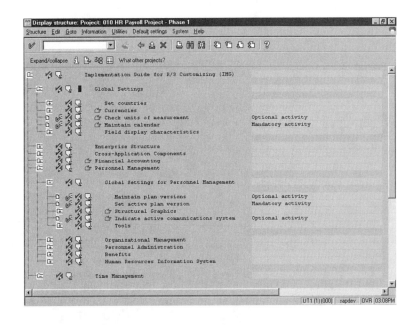

Critical Activity Setting

Each item in the IMG contains a Critical Activity setting. This setting determines the critical nature of the activity. The possible values for this setting are

- *Critical activities*: The activities performed for this item are critical and might have far reaching implications in your SAP implementation. You need to proceed with caution in carrying out these activities.

- *Non-Critical Activities*: You should also proceed with caution when completing these activities, but the implications of these configurations are not as far reaching and or damaging if not configured correctly.

The Critical Activity setting is configured by SAP. To view the Critical Activity setting for your IMG, from the main IMG tree structure screen follow the menu path Information, Title and IMG Info, Critical Activity. The Critical Activity setting will appear in the right side of your screen for each activity in the IMG (see Figure 9.16).

FIGURE 9.16

Viewing Critical Activities in the IMG provides you with an instant view of the critical nature of the different line items.

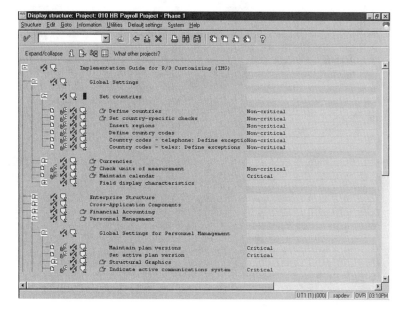

Information Settings

There are a couple of different viewing selections that you can use to view the main tree structure of the IMG. The Information item on the SAP menu bar expands to offer different viewing options:

- Title Only
- Title and Key
- Title and Status

Title Only

The default setting shows the basic tree structure on the left-hand side of the screen with no information displayed on the right-hand side of the screen. This view is called Title Only and can be reset by following the menu path Information, Title Only.

Title and Key

The Title and Key setting will display the name of the customizing transaction that the particular line item is attached to, as shown in Figure 9.17, and can be set by following the menu path Information, Title and Key.

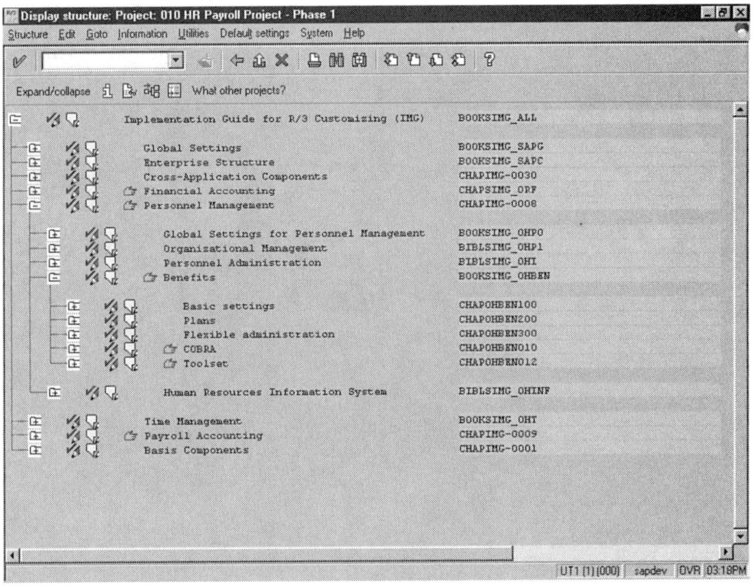

FIGURE 9.17

Title and Key settings are generally used by advanced configuration specialists who want to know the name of the program that the line item is attached to.

Title and Status

The Title and Status setting displays completion status of the current activity on the right-hand side of the screen and can be set by following the menu path Information, Title and Status, which appears similar to the picture in Figure 9.11.

Summary

The Implementation Guide is a tool to assist you in the customizing and implementation of your SAP system. The Implementation Guide is designed to pinpoint all the configuration activities that you will be required to perform in order for your SAP implementation to be a success. It also allows you to tweak your SAP system to ideally suit your company's individual needs through custom configuration.

Q&A

Q Is there a general method to working through the IMG?

A The IMG is designed so that steps that need to be completed first are contained at the top so that you work your way down through the IMG.

Q How many different project IMGs should you create?

A You generally only need to create a single project IMG for each module. In some cases module's like Human Resources two project IMGs can be created.

Workshop

The workshop is designed to help you anticipate possible questions, review what you've learned, and begin thinking ahead to putting your knowledge into practice. The answers to the quiz that follows can be found in Appendix A, "Answers."

Quiz

1. What is the difference between an Optional and a Mandatory activity in the IMG?

2. What is the difference between Critical and Non-Critical activities in the IMG?

3. Which view of the IMG contains only the relevant documentation for the SAP components that your company is implementing?

4. What does the icon symbol of the hand indicate?

5. What are three different project views of the IMG?

6. What model displays the structure of your R/3 implementation projects?

7. What is the transaction code to launch the IMG?

Exercises

1. Navigate to the Reference IMG and display all activity requirement levels.

2. Navigate to the Enterprise IMG and display the names of the customizing transactions.

3. Navigate to the Reference IMG and turn on the setting that displays the Release Notes icon. Select a Release Notes icon and access the release note text. From within the text, look for any hypertext links and use them to navigate deeper into the release note. When done, navigate back to main SAP screen.

4. Navigate to a Project IMG and review the Activity status for any line item in the IMG.

PART III
R/3 Function Modules

Hour

SAP Financials

Many people believe that SAP's Financials is its most popular product. Because the Financials module is such a large module encompassing many different components, I will only scratch the surface of its structure and design, yielding a basic overview of its capabilities. In the next hour, I will take a high level overview of SAP's Financials. Highlights of this hour include

- A look at a sample of SAP's Financials screens
- A survey General Ledger Management in SAP
- An introduction to SAP'S Real Estate component

The Financials module of the SAP system is an integrated suite of financial applications designed to effectively manage your company's bottom line. The SAP R/3 Financials application resides at the core of your enterprise and contains the following submodules :

- Financial Accounting
- Controlling
- Investment Management

- Treasury Cash Management
- Enterprise Controlling
- Real Estate

Each of the submodules listed previously represent a different area of your company's financial business and is designed to uniquely satisfy the needs that the different areas of your business require. The main menu options for SAP's Financials from the main R/3 window is shown in Figure 10.1.

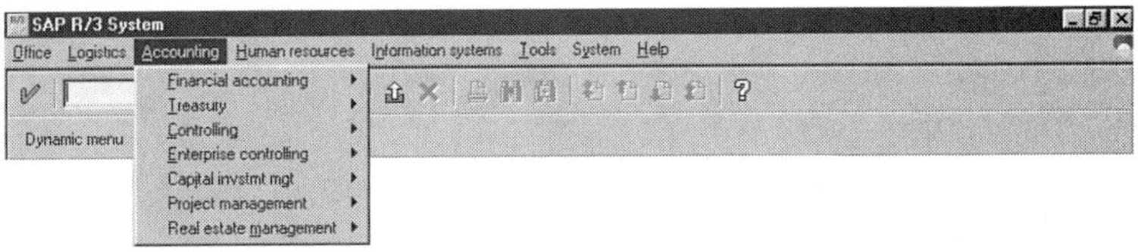

FIGURE 10.1

The initial SAP Financials screen.

Financial Accounting

The R/3 Financial Accounting sub module gives you the ability to enhance the strategic decision making processes for your company's financial needs. It allows companies to centrally track financial accounting data within an international framework of multiple companies, languages, currencies, and charts of accounts. SAP reports that the Financial Accounting sub module complies with international accounting standards, such as GAAP and IAS, and fulfills the local legal requirements of many countries, reflecting fully the legal and accounting changes resulting from European market and currency unification.

The Financial Accounting sub module contains the following components:

- General Ledger Accounting
- Accounts Payable
- Accounts Receivable
- Asset Accounting
- Funds Management
- Special Purpose Ledger
- Travel Management

General Ledger Accounting

Essentially, the General Ledger serves as a complete record of all your company business transactions. The central function of G/L Accounting is to provide an inclusive, integrated illustration of how your company's accounts are managed. This integral part of the Financials module is integrated with all your company's relevant financial operations.

The ledger provides a place to record business transactions throughout all facets of your company's business to ensure that the accounting data being processed in your R/3 system is factual in its entirety.

The SAP Financials General Ledger contains the following features:

- Free choice of level: corporate group or company
- Automatic and simultaneous posting of all subledger items in the appropriate General Ledger accounts
- Simultaneous updating of General Ledger and cost accounting areas
- Real-time access to, evaluation of, and reporting on current accounting data stored in SAP

A sample screen from the Financials, General Ledger application is shown in Figure 10.2.

10

FIGURE 10.2

G/L account postings are entered on the Enter G/L Account Posting: Header Data screen.

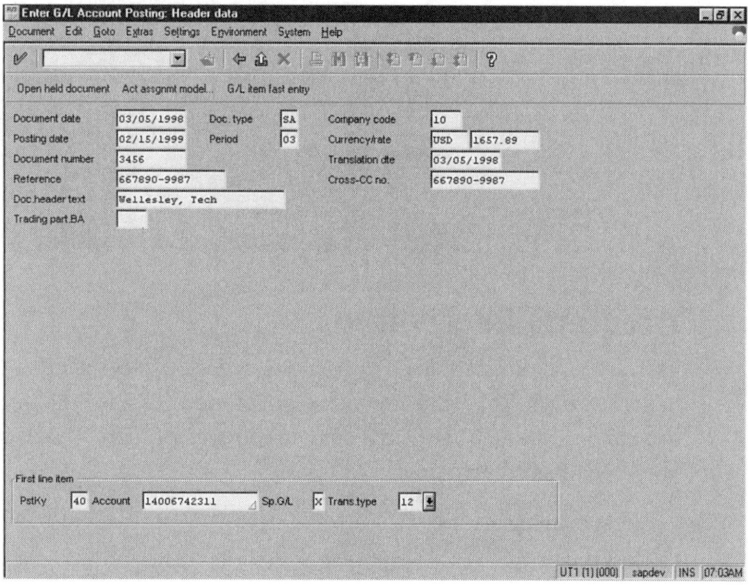

Accounts Payable

The Accounts Payable application records and administers accounting data for all vendors in your SAP R/3 system. The following are the accounts payable functions:

- Internet integration
- Document management
- Electronic Data Interchange (EDI)

- Integration with cash management
- Comprehensive, flexible reporting

A sample screen from the Financials, Accounts Payable application is shown in Figure 10.3.

FIGURE 10.3

Outgoing payments are posted on the Post Outgoing Payments: Header Data screen.

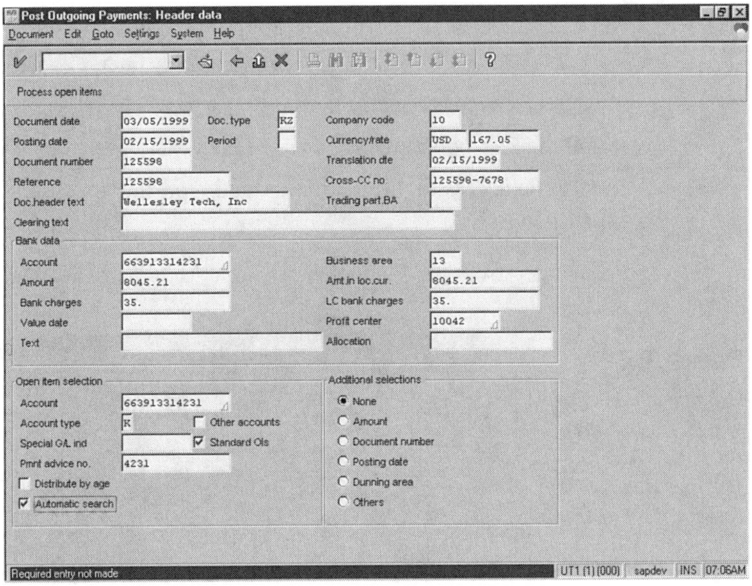

Accounts Receivable

The Accounts Receivable component manages the most integral parts of your company's Sales activities. This application component records and administers the accounting data of your customers. The system contains a range of tools, which can be used to monitor your open items, including:

- Account analyses
- Alarm
- Reports
- Due date lists
- Flexible dunning programs

A sample screen from the Financials, Accounts Receivable application is shown in Figure 10.4.

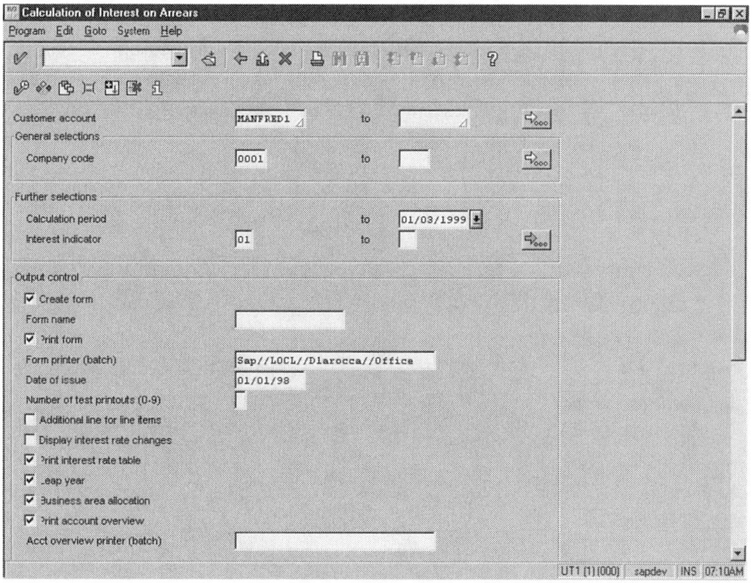

FIGURE 10.4

Interest can be determined on the Accounts Receivable, Calculation of Interest on Arrears screen.

```
Calculation of Interest on Arrears                                    _ 8 X
Program  Edit  Goto  System  Help

Customer account          MANFRED1        to                     [icon]
General selections
   Company code           0001            to                     [icon]

Further selections
   Calculation period                     to    01/03/1999
   Interest indicator     01              to                     [icon]

Output control
   ☑ Create form
   Form name
   ☑ Print form
   Form printer (batch)          Sap//LOCL//Dlarocca//Office
   Date of issue                 01/01/98
   Number of test printouts (0-9)
   ☐ Additional line for line items
   ☐ Display interest rate changes
   ☑ Print interest rate table
   ☑ Leap year
   ☑ Business area allocation
   ☑ Print account overview
   Acct overview printer (batch)

                                      UT1 (1)(000)  sapdev  INS  07:10AM
```

The accounts receivable functions are the same as those listed for accounts payable in the preceding section:

- Internet integration
- Document management
- Electronic Data Interchange (EDI)
- Integration with cash management
- Comprehensive, flexible reporting

> Accounts Payable and Accounts Receivable sub-ledgers are integrated both with the General Ledger and with different components in the Sales and Distribution module. Accounts Payable and Accounts Receivable transactions are performed automatically when related processes are performed in other R/3 modules.

Asset Accounting

This component manages your company's fixed assets. Asset Accounting is designed to manage and supervise your fixed assets within the SAP R/3 System. It also serves as a subsidiary ledger to the R/3 Financials General Ledger, providing detailed information on transactions involving fixed assets.

The R/3 Financials, Asset Accounting component is intended for international use in many countries, irrespective of the nature of the industry. In simpler terms, no country-specific valuation rules are hard-coded in the system. Any country-specific settings that you require need to be configured as part of your system configuration.

A sample screen from the Financials, Asset Accounting application is shown in Figure 10.5.

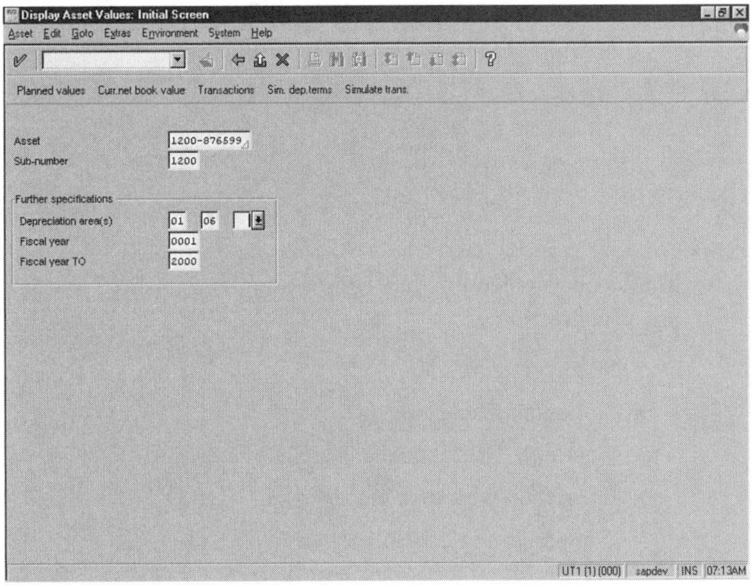

FIGURE 10.5

Asset values can be enetered and then displayed on the Asset Accounting, Display Asset Values: Initial screen.

Funds Management

The Funds Management component is designed to support you in creating budgets. It also provides you with a tool set for replicating your company's budget structure for the purpose of planning, monitoring, and managing your company's funds. Funds Management provides the following three essential tasks:

- Budget all revenues and expenditures for individual responsibility areas.
- Monitor future funds movements in light of the budget available.
- Prevent budget overruns.

A basic requirement for the use of SAP Funds Management is integration with the General Ledger Accounting component.

A sample screen from the Financials, Funds Management application is shown in Figure 10.6.

FIGURE 10.6

Budget's can be manipulated on the Funds Management, Roll-up Original Budget: Initial Screen.

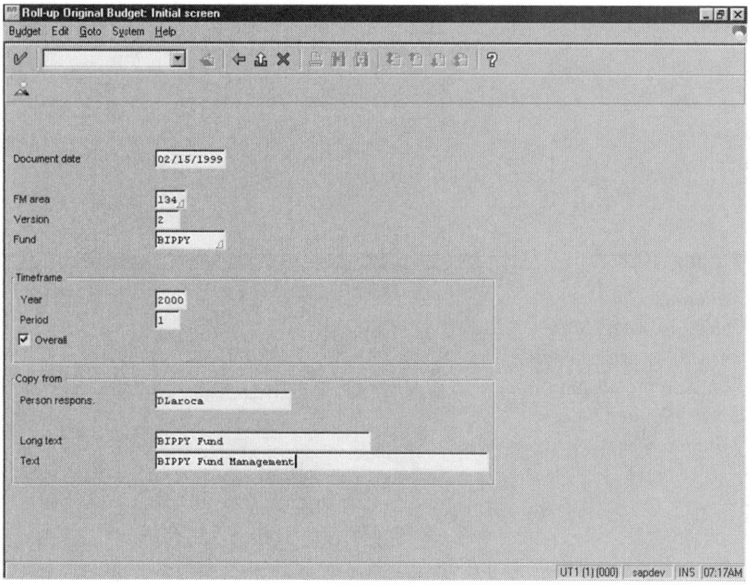

```
Roll-up Original Budget: Initial screen                                    _ 8 X
Budget  Edit  Goto  System  Help

              ▼  ◄  ← ⌂ X  ▤ ⊞ ⍓  ⬆ ⬇ ⬅ ➡  ?
  ▲

  Document date        02/15/1999

  FM area              134
  Version              2
  Fund                 BIPPY

  Timeframe
  Year                 2000
  Period               1
  ☑ Overall

  Copy from
  Person respons.      DLaroca

  Long text            BIPPY Fund
  Text                 BIPPY Fund Management

                                           UT1 (1) (000)  sapdev  INS  07:17AM
```

Special Purpose Ledger

The Special Purpose Ledger is designed to provide summary information from multiple applications at a level of detail that you specify according to your business's needs. This function allows you to collect, combine, summarize, modify, and allocate actual and planned data that originates from SAP or other external systems. In the Financials, Special Purpose Ledger, the operating functions of the individual applications remain unchanged, as shown in Figure 10.7.

A sample screen from the Financials, Special Purposes Ledger application is shown in Figure 10.8.

10

FIGURE 10.7

*The Financials,
Special Purpose
Ledger overview.*

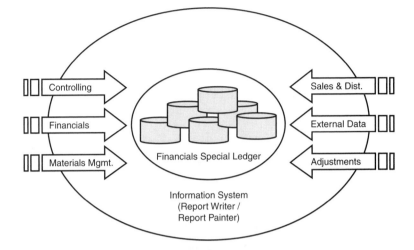

FIGURE 10.8

*Within the Special
Purpose Ledger, differ-
ent Values can be eval-
uated on the Display
Local Planned Values:
Initial Screen.*

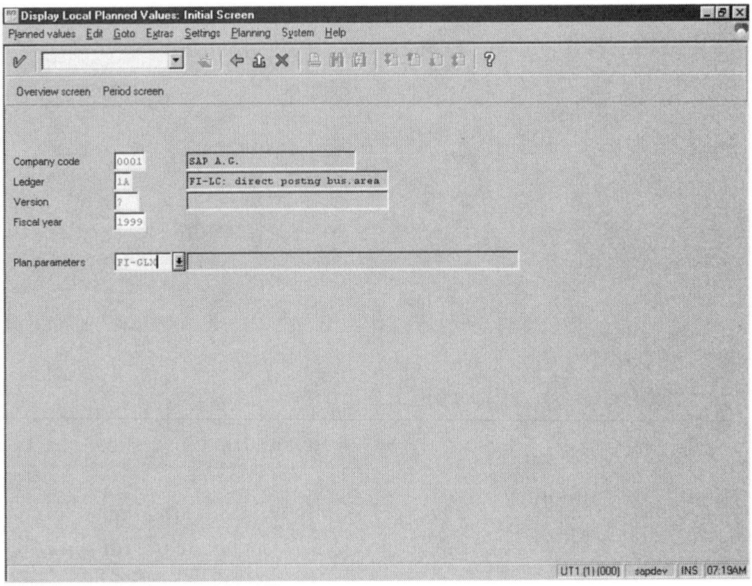

Travel Management

SAP's Financials, Travel Management component offers an integrated spectrum of procedures used for processing your company's business trip data. This management includes
entering receipts, approving reimbursement requests, and posting actual trip costs.

The Travel Management component is completely integrated with your Financial
Accounting, Controlling, and Payroll Accounting applications to ensure accurate posting,
taxation, and trip reimbursement. The Travel Management accounting can be forwarded to

your Financial Accounting module, HR Payroll module, or your non-SAP systems. A sample screen from the Financials, Travel Management application is shown in Figure 10.9.

FIGURE 10.9

Trip record receipts can be reviewed in the Travel Management, Overview of Trip Data in Receipt Entry screen.

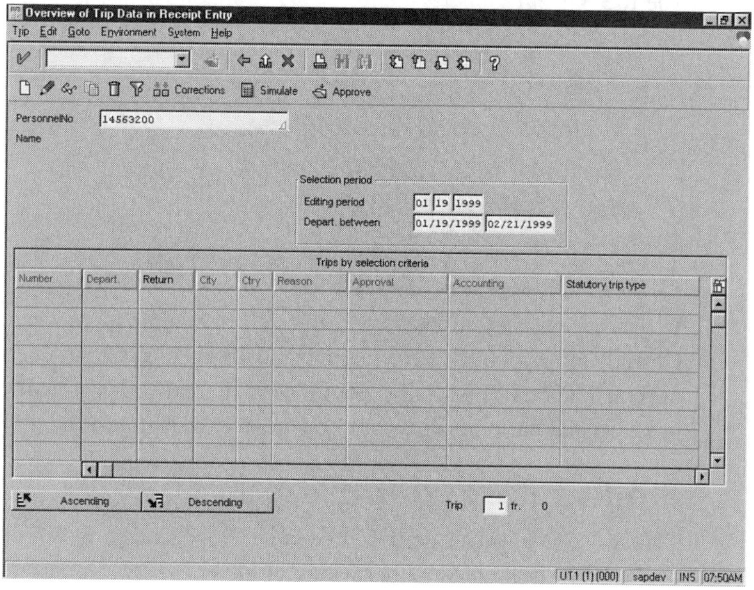

Controlling

The R/3 Controlling sub module provides the functions necessary for effective and accurate internal cost accounting management. Its complete integration allows for value and quantity real-time data flows between Financial Accounting and Sap R/3 Logistics.

The Controlling sub module contains the following components:

- Overhead Cost Controlling
- Activity Based Coding
- Product Cost Controlling
- Profitability Analysis

Overhead Cost Controlling

The Overhead Cost Controlling component focuses on the monitoring and allocation of your company's overhead costs and provides all the functions that your company requires for planning and allocation. The functionality contained within the Controlling sub module supports multiple cost controlling methods, which give you the freedom of deciding which functions and methods are applied to your individual areas.

NEW TERM In SAP, any costs that cannot be assigned directly to cost objects in SAP are designated as *overhead costs*.

The R/3 System supports the following common cost controlling methods in the Overhead Cost Controlling component:

- Assessment
- Overhead Percentages
- Standard Costing
- Marginal Costing

Activity Based Costing

In contrast with traditional overhead cost accounting approaches, Sap R/3 Activity-Based Costing allows you to charge organizational overhead to products, customers, sales channels, and other segments, and permits a more realistic profitability analysis of different products and customers because you are able to factor in the resources of overhead.

Product Cost Controlling

This R/3 component is used to determine the costs arising from manufacturing a product or providing a service by evoking a real-time cost control mechanism. The Sap R/3 Product Cost Controlling application component contains three subcomponents:

- Product Cost Planning
- Cost Object Controlling
- Actual Costing

Profitability Analysis

This component provides your company with an effective tool for analyzing profitability in your organization. Profitability Analysis gives you the ability to analyze the profitability of segments of your market structured according to:

- Products
- Customers
- Orders
- Combined summaries of products, customers, and orders

The goal is to provide your sales, marketing, planning, and management organizations with decision support from a market-oriented point of view. A sample screen from the Controlling, Profitability Analysis application is shown in Figure 10.10.

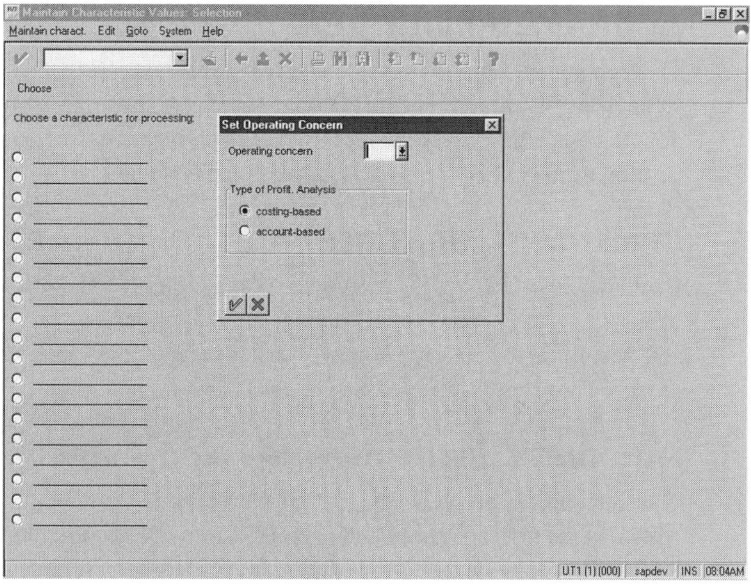

FIGURE 10.10

*Profitability analysis
characteristic values
can be displayed for
activity-based or
account-based values.*

FIGURE 10.10

*Profitability analysis
characteristic values
can be displayed for
activity-based or
account-based values.*

Investment Management

The R/3 Investment Management component provides functions to support the planning,
investment, and finance processes for capital investment measures for your company. The
Investment Management component provides you with tools to assist your company with
the following:

- Corporation wide budgeting
- Appropriation requests
- Investment measures
- Automatic settlement of fixed assets
- Depreciation forecast

NEW TERM A *capital investment* is any measure that initially causes costs and might only generates revenue or provides other benefits after a certain time period has lapsed.

Corporationwide Budgeting

Corporationwide budgeting promotes Wide Budgeting Management, strategizing, and
budgeting at a higher level than specific orders or projects. Using the corporationwide
budgeting functions of the Investment management component allows your company the
capability to monitor and avoid budget overruns.

Appropriation Requests

This component supports your company's investment process in terms of planning and strategizing about investments to be implemented. In the investment process, appropriation requests allow you to represent investment inclinations, including research and development strategies, prior to an actual implementation.

Investment Measures

Using the Investment Measures component, investment measures that require individual monitoring can be represented either as internal projects or orders promoting automatic and flexible settlement. Investment measures are slightly different from other internal orders or projects because of special asset accounting features.

Automatic Settlement of Fixed Assets

This component automatically distinguishes between costs requiring capitalization from costs that are not capitalized and debits the correct costs to the asset under construction. SAP can accommodate for your different accounting requirements using different capitalization rules. For each of your transactions that affect acquisition and production costs, the automatic settlement of fixed assets provides an accurate proof of inception.

Depreciation Forecast

Using the Depreciation Forecast component, automatic transference of planned depreciation values for appropriation requests and investment measures can be made directly to ongoing overhead cost planning. Current values are maintained on budget balance sheets, and cost planning and expected depreciation amounts are recalculated.

Treasury

New to Release 4.0 is the introduction of Treasury Management. SAP's Financials, Treasury sub module contributes the functionality that your company needs to control liquidity management, risk management and assessment, and position management. Treasury Management is a separate sub module including components for the following:

- Cash Management
- Treasury Management
- Market Risk Management
- Funds Management

Cash Management

The Cash Management component is designed to facilitate an optimum amount of liquidity to satisfy required payments as they become timely and to supervise cash inflows and outflows. The three main benefits of this application are

- A check deposit register is automatically generated.
- The data is updated in the cash management system.
- The suitable clearing entries for Financial Accounting are generated.

A sample screen from the Treasury, Cash Management component is shown in Figure 10.11.

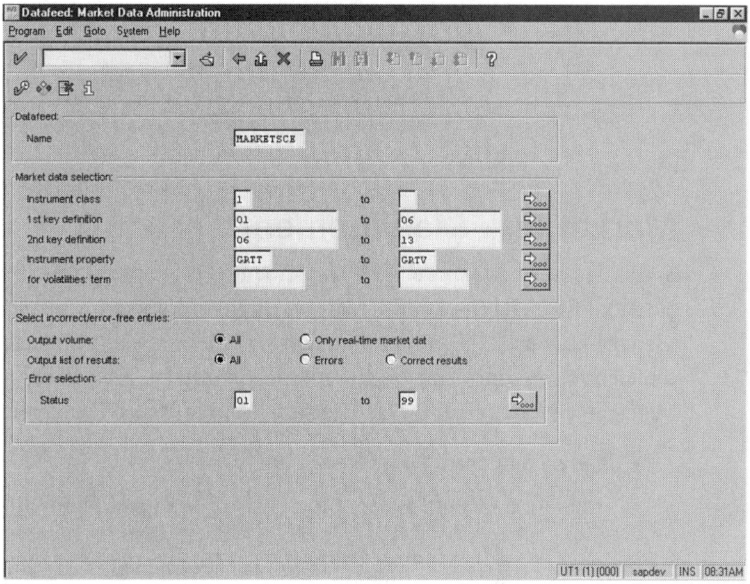

FIGURE 10.11

Value dates can be compared on the Cash Management, Compare Value Dates with Bank Postings screen.

Treasury Management

Your company's financial transactions are entered into SAP's Treasury Management component. The focus of SAP's Treasury Management is to support the management of your company's financial transactions and positions through back office processing to the Financial Accounting sub module. It also provides a versatile reporting platform that your company can use to examine its financial positions and transactions. A sample screen from the Treasury, Treasury Management application is shown in Figure 10.12.

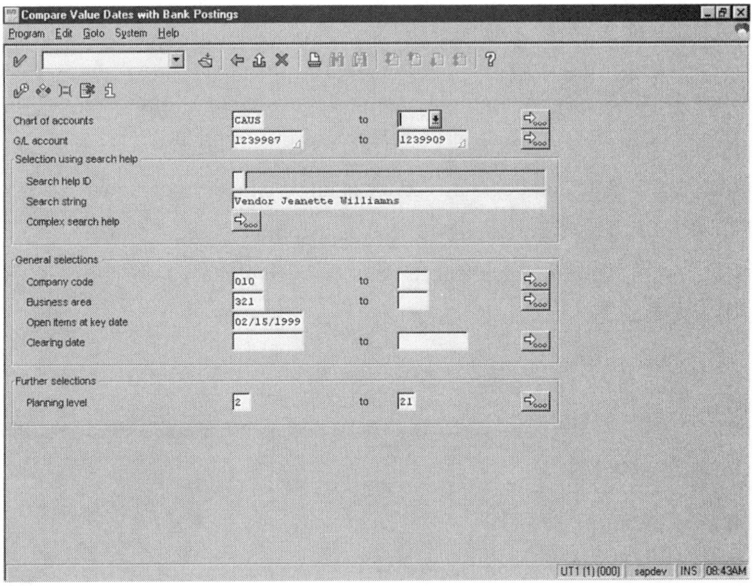

FIGURE 10.12

Bank reconcilliations can be performed on the Treasury Management, Compare Value Dates with Bank Postings screen.

Market Risk Management

SAP's Treasury, Market Risk Management is effective in quantifying the impact of potential financial market fluctuations on your company's financial assets. The Cash Management package, in combination with the Treasury Management package, sets the foundation for your database for controlling market risks using the Market Risk Management component. The Treasury, Market Risk Management component includes:

- Interest and currency exposure analysis
- Simulation of portfolios on the basis of both real and fictitious financial transactions
- Market-to-market valuation

Funds Management

The Treasury, Funds Management component is a self-sufficient tool designed to sustain your company's funds management processing from the planning stage clear through to the payments. Using this component, your company can create different budget versions, making it possible to work with rolling budget planning.

Another advantage of the Treasury, Funds Management component is that it provides you with a real-time status of fund commitments resulting from purchase orders and release orders in your R/3 Materials Management component.

Enterprise Controlling

SAP's Financials, Enterprise Controlling sub module is divided into the following four components:

- Executive Information System
- Business Planning and Budgeting
- Consolidation
- Profit Center Accounting

Executive Information System

In SAP, the Enterprise Controlling, Executive Information System provides an up to the minute overview of the critical information required in order for your company to effectively manage its resources.

NEW TERM In SAP, an *Executive Information System (EIS)* provides information about all the factors that influence the business activities of a company.

SAP's Enterprise Controlling, Executive Information System collects and appraises information from various areas of your business, including financial information and information contained within your Human Resources Information System and the Logistics Information System. A sample screen from the Enterprise Controlling, Executive Information System application is shown in Figure 10.13.

FIGURE 10.13

Different characteristics can be processed on the Executive Information System, Maintain Master Data: Characteristics screen.

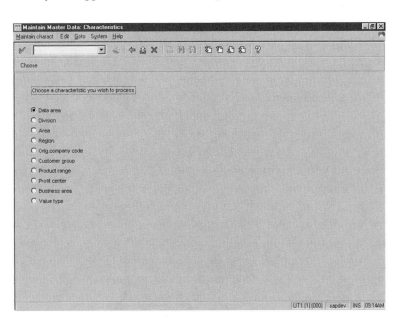

Business Planning and Budgeting

This component is designed to assist in creating high-level enterprise plans that allow for the adaptable representation of customer-specific plans and their inter-relationships. This also takes in to consideration the connections between profit and loss, balance sheet, and cash flow strategies.

Using the Enterprise Controlling, Business Planning and Budgeting applications, you can create simulations based on user-defined planning models.

Consolidation

The Consolidation component enables you to enter reported financial data online using data entry formats and provides consolidated reports for your company's legal and management reporting. Some methods for data collection in the Consolidation application include online data entry, automatic data transfer from R/3 or R/2 Systems, data transfer from non-SAP systems (using the flexible upload program), and data transfer using the offline data entry program on the basis of Microsoft Access. The Consolidation component supports:

- Internal accounting
- External accounting
- Parallel reporting (complying with U.S. GAAP IAS standards)

A sample screen from the Enterprise Controlling, Consolidation component is shown in Figure 10.14.

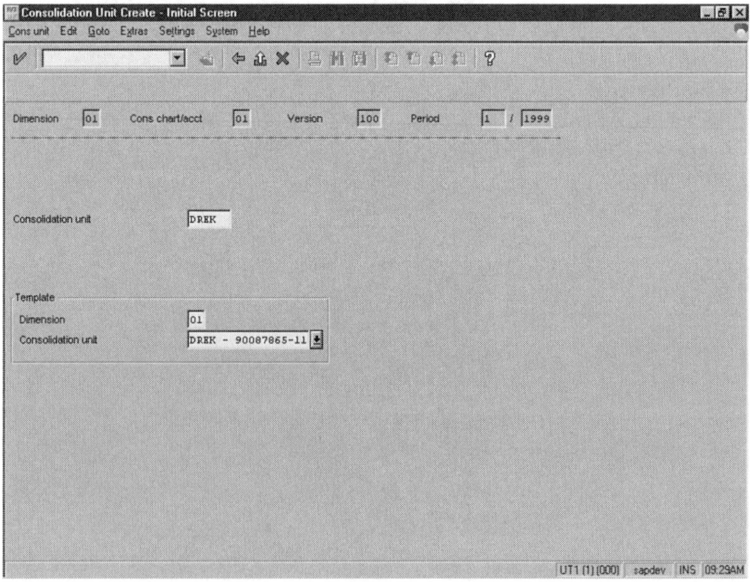

FIGURE 10.14

Consolidation units can be created on the Consolidation Unit Create: Initial Screen.

Profit Center Accounting

The function of Enterprise Controlling, Profit Center Accounting is to analyze the profitability of internal responsibility centers.

NEW TERM In SAP, a *profit center* is a management-oriented organizational unit used for internal controlling purposes.

Using either period accounting or the cost-of-sales approach, Profit Center Accounting allows you to effectively determine profits and losses, by profit center, and allows you to investigate fixed capital and statistical key figures including return on investment, cash flow, and so on. A sample screen from the Enterprise Controlling, Profit Center Accounting component is shown in Figure 10.15.

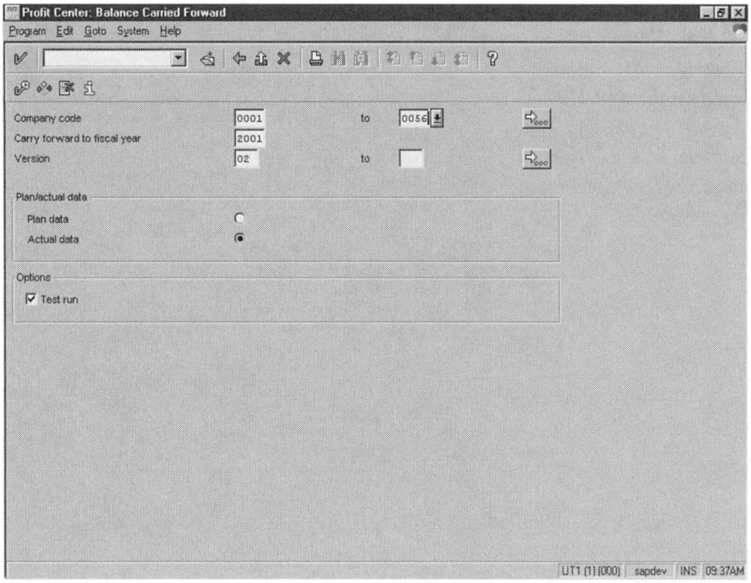

FIGURE 10.15

Balance adjustments can be managed on the Profit Center Accounting, Profit Center: Balance Carried Forward Screen.

Real Estate

SAP's Financials, Real Estate sub module integrates Real Estate processes into your company's overall organizational structure. The Corporate Real Estate Management model is divided into the following two components:

- Rental Administration and Settlement
- Controlling, Position Valuation, and Information Management

In order for your company to successfully use the Real Estate components, necessary configurations are required in your Plant Maintenance, Materials Management, Project System and Asset Accounting components. As a new component, not much information is available on its functionality.

Rental Administration and Settlement

Functions contained in this component focus on the entry, administration, and controlling of costs and revenues, in addition to rental and settlement processing. A sample screen from the Real Estate, Rental Administration and Settlement component is shown in Figure 10.16.

FIGURE 10.16

Postings can be managed on the Rental Administration and Settlement, One-time Postings Rntl agreements screen.

Controlling, Position Valuation, and Information Management

Controlling, Position Valuation, and Information Management focuses on the real-time supervision, monitoring, updating, and settling of costs and revenues arising in the Real Estate Management sub module. A sample screen from the Real Estate, Controlling, Position Valuation, and Information Management component is shown in Figure 10.17.

FIGURE 10.17

Settlement management can be performed on the Position Valuation, and Information Management, Actual settlement: Real estate objects screen.

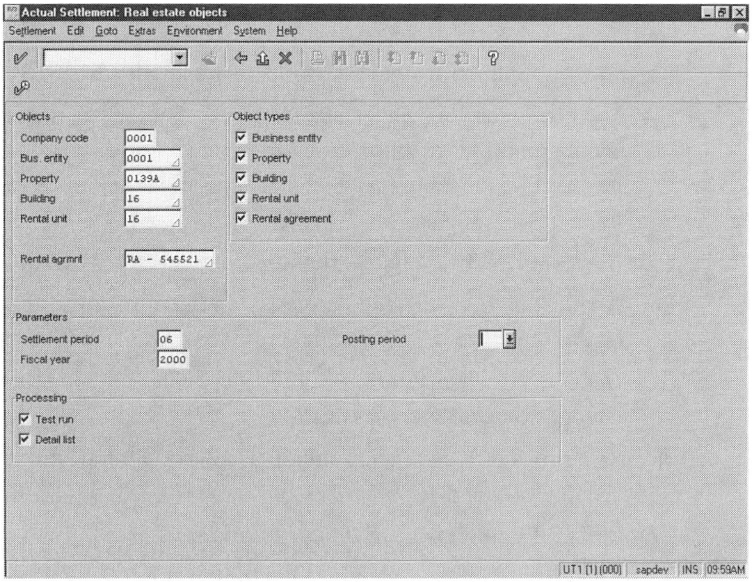

10

Summary

This hour gives you a very high-level overview of the components of the SAP Financials module. As I am sure that you have discovered over the course of this hour, the Financials component contains some very comprehensive submodules, each of which could probably satisfy an hour of its own. This introduction to the Financials module should have made you familiar with what the application has to offer and possibly give you some ideas on different areas that require focus if your company will be working with the SAP Financials module.

There are many helpful books available on the market that cover the SAP R/3 Financials module. Some good titles to check out are

ASAP World Consultancy, et al., *Administering SAP R/3: The Fi-Financial Accounting and Co-Controlling Modules* (ISBN: 0789715481). Indianapolis: Que, 1998.

ASAP World Consultancy et al., *Special Edition Using Sap R/3 Third Edition* (ISBN: 0789718219). Indianapolis: Que, 1998.

ASAP World Consultancy, et al., *Administering SAP R/3: Sd-Sales and Distribution Module* (ISBN: 0789717557). Indianapolis: Que, 1998.

Ben W. Rockefeller, *Using SAP R/3 FI: Beyond Business Process Reengineering* (ISBN: 0471179965). New York: John Wiley & Sons, 1998.

Q&A

Q Can you add your own functions to work with the SAP Financials module?

A You can tailor your Financials module to suit the requirements of your company by adding non-SAP functions and developing your own solutions using R/3 components. Also there are many industry specific components that supplement the R/3 functions.

Q Does your R/3 Financials module have the ability to link to older R/2 systems?

A Application Link Enabling (ALE) technology permits the linking of your R/3 system to other R/3, R/2 (regardless of release level), and non-SAP systems.

Q Does SAP have a solution to the European and Monetary Union (EMU) changes that affect currency?

A SAP provides a complete solution and a smooth transition utilizing currency conversion tools and services.

Q Is SAP Financials year 2000–compliant?

A The answer is yes. From the beginning the R/3 SAP system was designed with a four digit year code.

Q What new country versions are available in 4.5?

A Country versions Columbia, Korea, Poland, the Slovak Republic and Venezuela have been added in version 4.5.

Q Is the Pre-Configured client available for the Financials module?

A The Pre-Configured client is available for the Financials module.

Workshop

The workshop is designed to help you anticipate possible questions, review what you've learned, and begin thinking ahead to putting your knowledge into practice. The answers to the quiz that follows can be found in Appendix A, "Answers."

Quiz

1. Which Financials submodule is designed to support your company in creating budgets?

2. Which Financials submodule provides the functions necessary for effective and accurate internal cost accounting management?

3. What are the four components of the Treasury sub module?

4. What are the six components of the Financials module?

5. In the Financials module, what subcomponent serves as a complete record of all your company's business transactions?

6. In which component can automatic transference of depreciation values for appropriation requests and investment measures be made?

7. How does SAP define the term *profit center*?

10

146

SAP Human Resources

The Human Resources module offers a global human resources management solution including standard language, currency, and regulatory requirements for more than 30 countries. The Human Resources module also serves as a standalone product. The innovative conceptual design of SAP Human Resources takes into consideration all the different aspects of managing your company's Human Resource functions, including Recruitment, Training, and Organizational structure management. Highlights of this hour include

- SAP's distinction between Personnel Administration and Personnel Development
- An introduction to infotypes
- SAP's Payroll system overview

SAP's Integrated Human Resources

The Human Resources module is divided into two different submodules, which follow, that are fully integrated with SAP's suite of products:

- Personnel Administration (PA)
- Personnel Planning and Development (PD)

Each of these submodules contains different aspects of your company's Human Resource functions; and the integration between the two produces a well-oiled Human Resources machine that also attaches itself to other areas of your company's business through integration. Both of these areas are supported by the Human Resources Information System (HRIS), which is discussed later in the hour.

NEW TERM Functions performed in the Personnel Administration submodule are directly linked and connected to functions performed in the Personnel Planning and Development submodule, as well as to the SAP R/3 Financials and R/3 Logistics modules. This is referred to as *integration*.

R/3 Concepts Unique to Human Resources

Some concepts are unique to SAP's Human Resources and make it stand apart from SAP's other applications. The most remarkable concept in the Human Resources component is its use of infotypes.

Introduction to Infotypes

In simple terms, an infotype is a screen in your Human Resources application that stores particular information about an employee, like payroll data or personnel data. There are hundreds of infotypes in the R/3 Human Resources application. Table 11.1 lists a sample of some SAP infotypes.

NEW TERM SAP defines an *infotype* as a carrier of system-controlling characteristics such as attributes, time constraints, and so on.

TABLE 11.1 A SAMPLE OF SAP HUMAN RESOURCES INFOTYPES

Infotype Number	Description	PA/PD
1000	Object	PD
1001	Relationship	PD
1002	Description	PD
1003	Department/Staff	PD
1005	Planned Compensation	PD
1007	Vacancy	PD
1008	Acct. Assignment Features	PD

Infotype Number	Description	PA/PD
1010	Authorization/Resources	PD
1011	Work Schedule (Working Time)	PD
1013	Employee Group/Subgroup	PD
1014	Obsolete	PD
1015	Cost Planning	PD
1016	Standard Profiles	PD
1017	PD Profiles	PD
1027	Site-Dependent Info	PD
1028	Address	PD
1032	Mail Address	PD
1037	Billing/Allocation Info	PD
1039	Shift Group	PD
1050	Job Evaluation	PD
1051	Survey Results	PD
1208	SAP Organizational Object	PD
1610	EEO/AAP Category	PD
1613	WC State, Code, Attribute	PD
0000	Actions	PA
0001	Organizational Assignment	PA
0002	Personal Data	PA
0003	Payroll Status	PA
0006	Address	PA
0007	Planned Working Time	PA
0008	Basic Pay	PA
0009	Bank Details	PA
0027	Absence Quotas	PA
0207	Residence Tax Area	PA
0208	Work Tax Area	PA
0209	Unemployment State	PA
0210	Withholding Information	PA
0169	Savings Plan	PA

11

All infotypes are assigned a four-digit number. SAP makes it easy to distinguish which infotypes are relevant to the different R/3 components based on their infotype number, as shown in Table 11.2.

TABLE 11.2   HUMAN RESOURCES INFOTYPE DISTINCTIONS

Range	Description
0000-0999	Personnel Administration (PA) Data
1000-1999	Personnel Planning and Development (PD) Data
2001-2999	Time Data
4000-4999	Recruitment Data

Each infotype stores a group of relevant data. In the example shown in Figure 11.1, infotype 0002 from Personnel Administration is displayed. It stores employee basic personal data, including name, marital status, social security number, birth date, and so on.

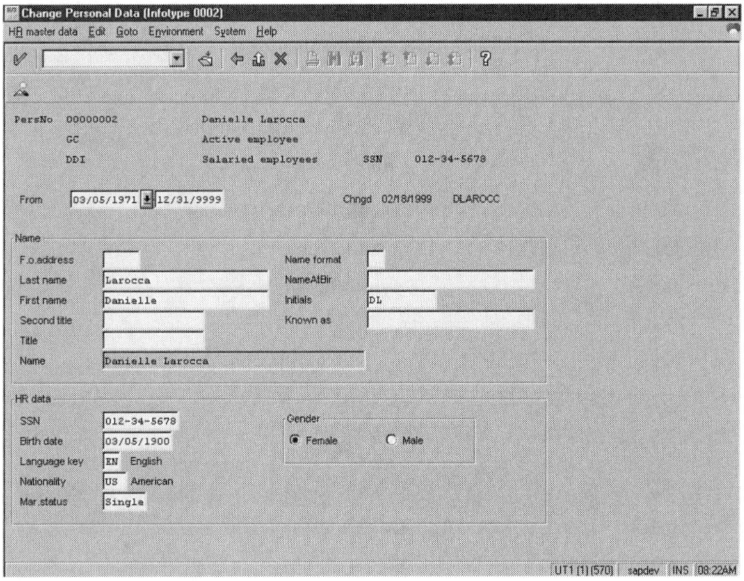

FIGURE **11.1**

Change Personal Data (Infotype 0002) is a Personnel Administration infotype used to store employee personal data.

Introduction to Actions

When a series of infotypes are bundled together, it is considered an action. For example, combining infotypes 0001 Organizational Assignment, 0007 Planned Working Time, 0008 Basic Pay, 0041 Date Specifications, and 0019 Date Monitoring will yield all the necessary infotypes (or screens) that you will need to go through in order to perform the Pay Change action.

NEW TERM A series of infotypes combined to complete a logical unit of work is a called an *Action*. (In earlier versions of SAP, Human Resource Actions were called *Events*.)

During your configuration, your company will decide which infotypes must be bundled together to create the actions necessary for your company. The Actions infotype (0000) is used to control the entry of HR master data and is automatically included as the first infotype for all actions. Sample actions and infotypes are shown in Table 11.3.

TABLE 11.3 HUMAN RESOURCES SAMPLE ACTIONS

Sample Action	Sample Infotypes Included in the Action
New Employee Hiring Action	0000, 0001, 0002, 0006, 0007, 0008, 0009, 0207, 0208, 0209, 0210, 0014, 0040, 0041, 0019
Employee Termination Action	0000, 0001, 0014, 0015, 0019, 0040, 0041, 0171
Benefit Enrollment Action	0000, 0019, 0021, 0041, 0167, 0168, 0170, 0171, 0219, 0236
Compensation Action	0000, 1050, 1051, 1005, 0041, 0019
Enter Payroll Details Action	0000, 0003, 0007, 0008, 0009, 0010, 0014, 0015,

Your SAP actions are configured using your Implementation Guide during the initial configuration of your SAP system. (The Implementation Guide IMG is covered in Chapter 9.) Depending on the users' security access in the system, different actions are available for execution.

R/3 Personnel Administration Components

The Personnel Administration module is used to manage company procedures including payroll, employee benefits enrollment, and compensation. This module's focus serves all the required Human Resource functions that most companies use. SAP's Human Resources Personnel Administration submodule contains the following components:

- Benefits Administration
- Compensation Management
- Recruitment

- Time Management
- Travel Management
- Payroll

Benefits Administration

The Human Resources, Benefits Administration component provides all the functionality required to offer and enroll your employees into benefit plans. This includes the functionality to manage eligibility requirements, evidence of insurability, cost tracking and management, Flexible Spending Account (FSA) claims processing, benefit terminations, and COBRA. The relevant infotypes for Benefits Administration are listed in Table 11.4.

TABLE 11.4 SAMPLE BENEFITS ADMINISTRATION INFOTYPES

Infotype	Description
Infotypes Used For Enrollment	
0171	General Benefits Data
0378	Event Permissions
0376	Medical Service Data
Infotypes Created By Enrollment	
0167	Health Plan
0168	Insurance Plan
0169	Savings Plan
0236	Credit Plan
0377	Miscellaneous Plan
0170	Spending Account (United States only)
Additional Benefits Infotypes	
0021	Family Related person
0219	Organizations
0019	Monitoring of Dates
0041	Date Specifications
0375	HCE Information (United States only)
0211	COBRA Qualified Beneficiary

Samples of Human Resources, Benefits Administration screens are shown in Figures
11.2 and 11.3.

Compensation Management

The Human Resources, Compensation Management component administers your company's remuneration policies. Functions managed by the Compensation Management component include salary administration, job evaluations, salary reviews, salary survey results, compensation budget planning and administration, and compensation policy administration.

In addition, Compensation Management gives you the ability to create pay grades and salary structures to identify the internal value of the jobs and positions within your organization. A sample of Compensation Management infotypes is listed in Table 11.5.

TABLE 11.5 SAMPLE COMPENSATION MANAGEMENT INFOTYPES

Infotype	Description
0050	Job Evaluation
1051	Salary Results
1005	Planned Compensation

Samples of the Human Resources, Compensation Management screens are shown in Figures 11.4 and 11.5.

FIGURE 11.4

The Human Resources, Compensation Management sample screen, Planned Labor Costs screen.

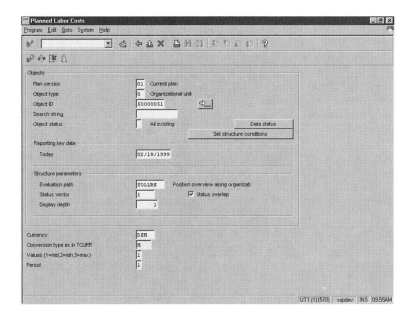

FIGURE 11.5

The Human Resources, Compensation Management sample screen, Budgeting: Compensation management Salary Increase: Change, Revalue Budget Amount screen.

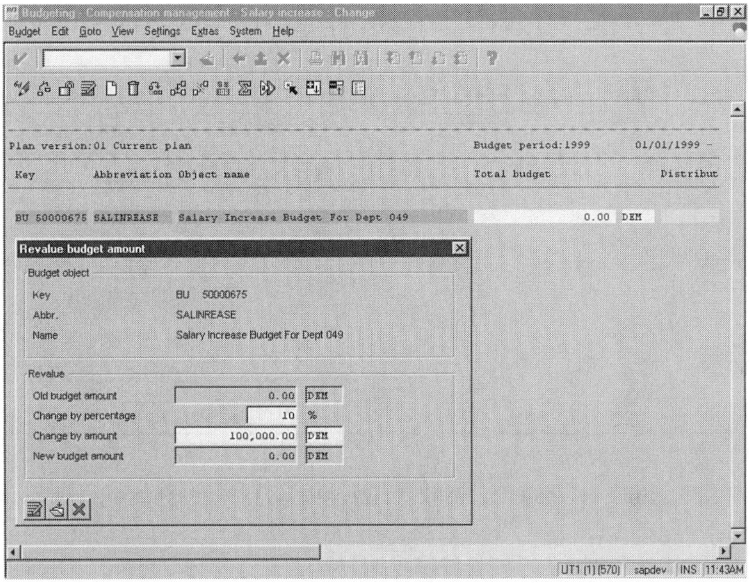

Recruitment

The R/3 Human Resources Recruitment component gives the flexibility to manage all areas of employee recruitment. Recruitment initiates from the creation of a position vacancy through the advertisement and applicant-tracking of potentials, concluding with the notification of successful and unsuccessful applicants and the hiring of the best candidate.

The main benefit from the Recruitment component is its automation. The Recruitment component contains the following:

- Workforce Requirements and Advertising
- Applicant Administration
- Selection of Applicants

In order to use all of the functions in the recruitment component, it is recommended that you implement Personnel Administration, Organizational Management, and Personnel Development.

A sample of Human Resources, Recruitment infotypes is listed in Table 11.6.

TABLE **11.6** SAMPLE RECRUITMENT INFOTYPES

Infotype	Description
4000	Applicant Actions
4001	Applications
4002	Vacancy Assignment
4003	Applicant Activities
4005	Applicant's Personnel Number
0139	Employee's Applicant Number
4004	Status of Actions

Samples of the Human Resources, Recruitment screens are shown in Figures 11.6 and 11.7.

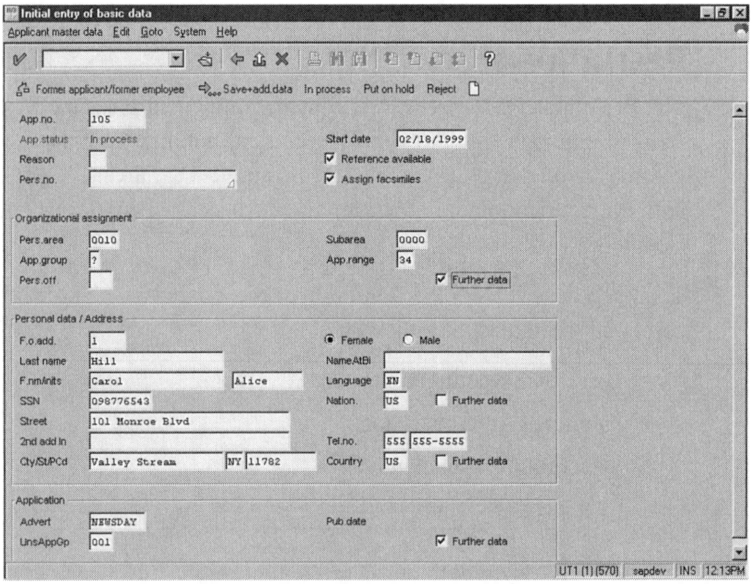

FIGURE **11.6**

The Human Resources, Recruitment sample screen, Applicant Initial entry of basic data screen.

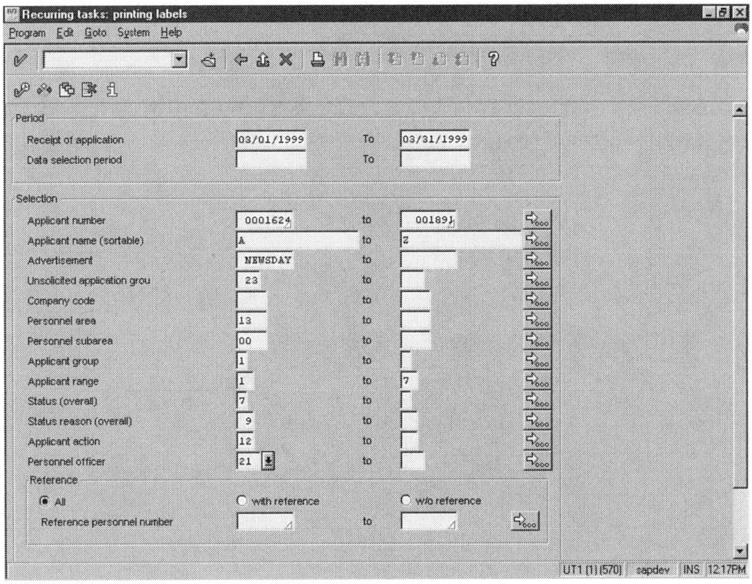

FIGURE 11.7

The Human Resources, Recruitment sample screen, Recurring tasks: printing labels screen.

Time Management

SAP's Human Resources, Time Management component provides a flexible methodology for recording and evaluating employee work time and absence management. Time Management is also integrated to other R/3 components that can make use of this data.

A key benefit of the Time Management component is that it enables you to represent the time structures in your company in accordance with your actual conditions, using the calendar as a basis. These include

- Actual working time models such as flextime, normal working time, and shift operation
- Planned working times, break schedules, and compensation times
- Exceptions such as substitutions, availability, and business trips
- Regulations for the payment of attendance and absences, breaks, and work or non-work days (weekends and public holidays)

A sample of Human Resources, Time Management infotypes is listed in Table 11.7.

TABLE 11.7 SAMPLE TIME MANAGEMENT INFOTYPES

Infotype	Description
Data Recording Infotypes	
2001	Absences
2002	Attendance
2003	Substitutions
2004	Availability
2005	Overtime
2010	Employee Remuneration
2011	Time Events
2012	Time Balance Revisions
Quotas Infotypes	
2006	Absence Quotas
2007	Attendance Quotas
2013	Quota Corrections
0005	Leave Entitlement
0083	Leave Compensation
Time Management Master Infotypes	
0001	Organizational Assignment
0002	Personal Data
0003	Payroll Status
0007	Planned Working Time
0050	Time Recording Information
Special Absences Infotypes	
0080	Maternity Protection
0081	Military Service

Samples of the R/3 Human Resources, Time Management screens are shown in Figures 11.8 and 11.9.

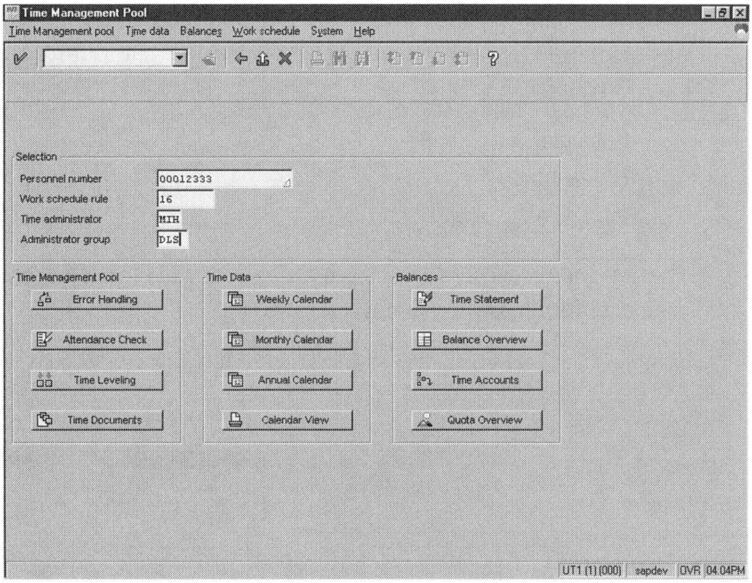

FIGURE **11.8**

The Human Resources, Time Management sample screen, Time Management Pool screen.

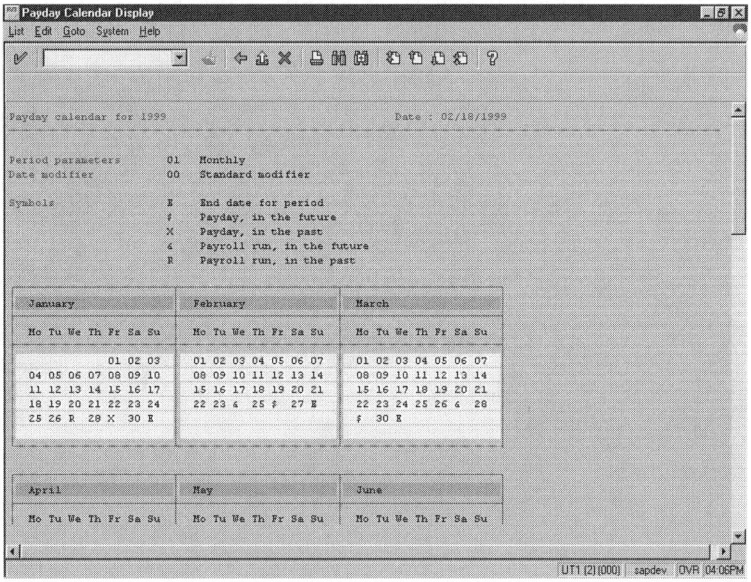

FIGURE **11.9**

The Human Resources, Time Management sample screen, Payday Calendar Display screen.

Travel Management

R/3's Human Resources, Travel Management component offers a wide range of functionality encompassing all areas of Travel management, which includes entering, approving, and processing trip data, travel requests, and trip cost management. Travel Management was first introduced in Hour 10, "SAP Financials," and is also integrated with the following R/3 systems:

- Financial Accounting
- Controlling
- Payroll Accounting

This integration ensures the integrity of the data and the efficient posting, taxation, and payment of trip costs to employees.

Samples of R/3 Human Resources, Travel Management screens are shown in Figures 11.10 and 11.11.

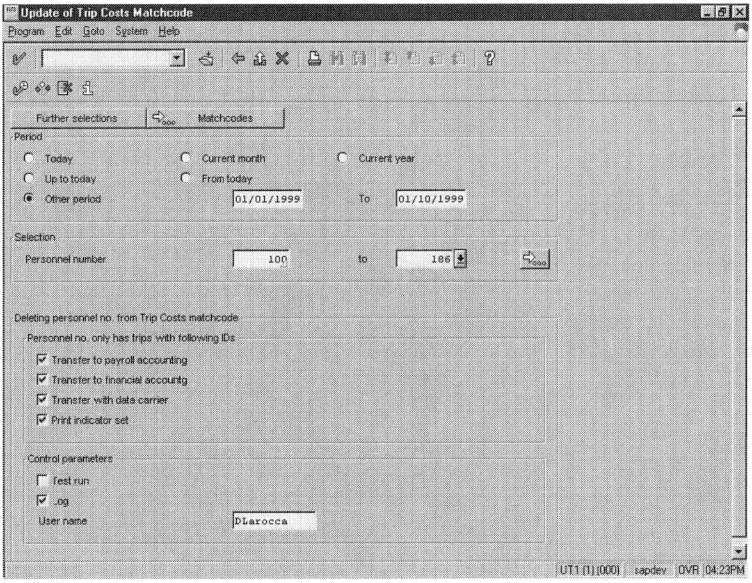

FIGURE 11.10

The Human Resources, Travel Management sample screen, Update of Trip Costs Matchcode screen.

FIGURE 11.11

The Human Resources, Travel Management sample screen, Create Travel Privileges (Infotype 0017) screen.

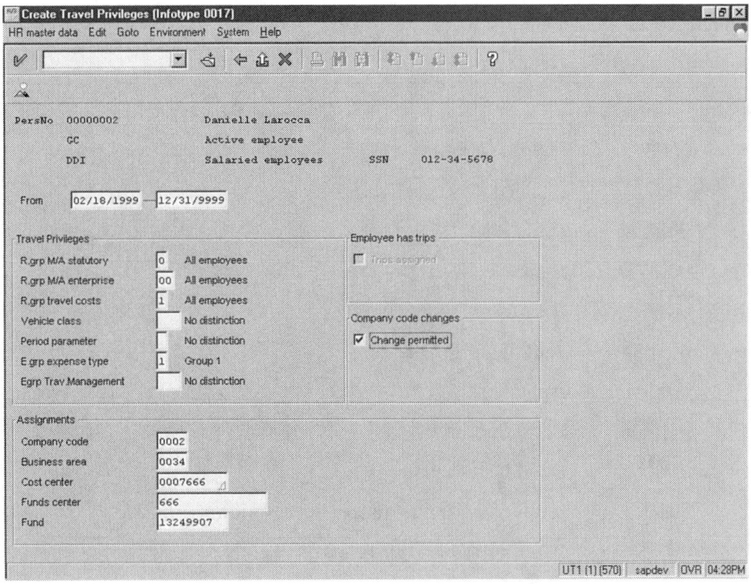

Payroll

The Human Resources Payroll component is designed to efficiently and accurately calculate remuneration for work performed by your employees, regardless of their working schedule, working calendar, language, or currency. This includes your fluctuating reporting needs as well as the constantly changing compliance requirements with federal, state, and local agencies.

Because of the complexity of the component, including the calculation of gross-to-net, net-gross, regular, and off-cycle payroll processing, the Payroll component of SAP requires the most training compared to the other Human Resource components available. A sample of Human Resources, Payroll infotypes is listed in Table 11.8.

R/3 Payroll Accounting is based on an international payroll driver modified for each country. These country-specific payroll drivers consider the statutory and administrative regulations of each country. When you are processing in payroll accounting, the payroll driver calls a sequence of functions.

TABLE 11.8 SAMPLE PAYROLL INFOTYPES

Infotype	Description
General Payroll Data	
0003	Payroll Status
0007	Planned Working Time
0008	Basic Pay
0009	Bank Details
0014	Recurring Payments
0015	Additional Payments
0025	Appraisals
0103	Bond Purchases
0104	Bond Denominations
2010	Employee Remuneration Information
0011	External Bank Transfers
0083	Leave Compensation
0165	Limits Deductions
0057	Membership Fees
0128	Notifications
0052	Wage Maintenance
0076	Workers' Compensation
Garnishment	
0194	Garnishment Document
0195	Garnishment Order
0216	Garnishment Adjustment
Tax and Insurance	
0207	Residence Tax Area and Deductions
0208	Work Tax Area
0209	Unemployment State
0210	Withholding Information
0234	Additional Withholding Information
0235	Other Taxes
0161	IRS Limits
0037	Insurance

Samples of the R/3 Human Resources, Payroll screens are shown in 11.12 and 11.13.

FIGURE 11.12

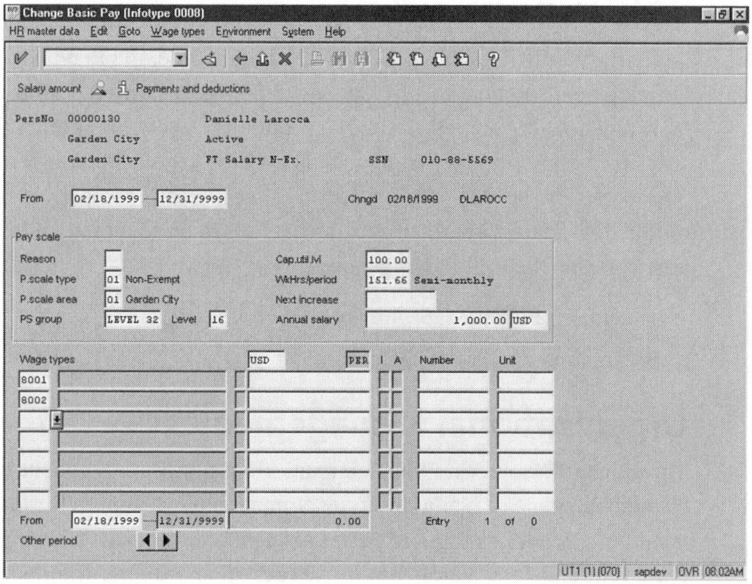

The Human Resources, Payroll sample screen, Change Basic Pay (Infotype 0008) screen.

FIGURE 11.13

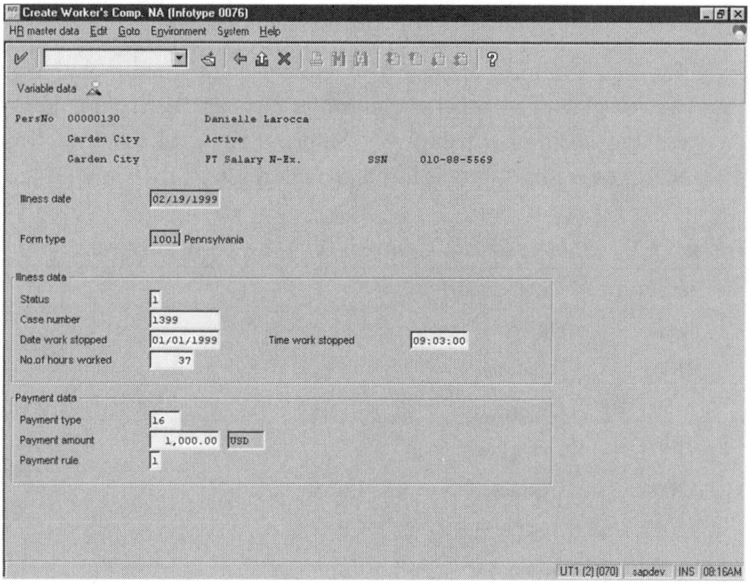

The Human Resources, Payroll sample screen, Create Workers' Comp. NA (Infotype 0076) screen.

R/3 Personnel Planning and Development (PD)

In contrast to the Personnel Administration module, the Personnel Planning and Development submodule's functions are not necessarily required by your company but their functionality serves as a tool to better manage your Human Resource functions. Advanced organizational management and workforce planning are well valued tools for your company, but are not required in order for your company's Human Resource tasks to function. The R/3 Human Resources, Personnel Planning and Development component contains the following components:

- Organizational Management
- Training and Events Management

Organizational Management

The Human Resources, Organizational Management component is designed to assist in the strategizing and planning of the comprehensive Human Resource structure. Through the development of proposed scenarios using the flexible tools provided, you can manipulate your company's structure in the present and future. Using the basic organization objects in SAP, units, jobs, positions, tasks, and work centers are all structured as the basic building blocks of your organization.

The Organizational Management component also comes with a graphical tool that you can use to manipulate your companies company's structure graphically, with an easy-to-use drag and drop capability. A sample of Human Resources, Organizational Management infotypes is listed in Table 11.9.

TABLE 11.9   SAMPLE ORGANIZATIONAL MANAGEMENT INFOTYPES

Infotype	Description
1000	Object
1001	Relationships
1002	Descriptions
1003	Department/Staff
1004	Character
1006	Restrictions
1007	Vacancy
1008	Account Assignment Features

Infotype	Description
1009	Health Examinations
1010	Authorities and Resources
1011	Work Schedule
1013	Employee Group/Sub Group
1014	Obsolete
1015	Cost Planning
1016	Standard Profiles
1027	Site Dependant Info
1028	Address
1032	Mail Address
1037	Sales Area
1039	Shift Group
1040	Override Requirement
1208	SAP Organizational Object

Samples of the R/3 Human Resources, Organizational Management screens are shown in Figures 11.14 and 11.15.

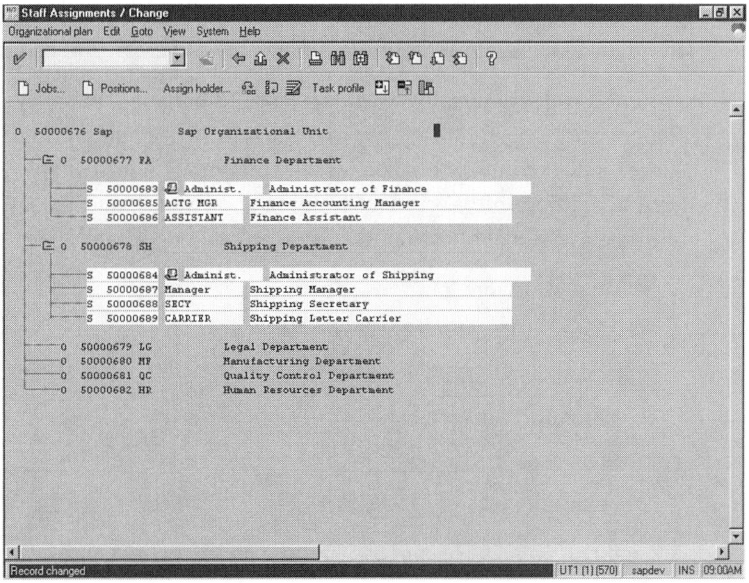

FIGURE 11.14

The Human Resources, Payroll sample screen, Staff Assignments/Change screen.

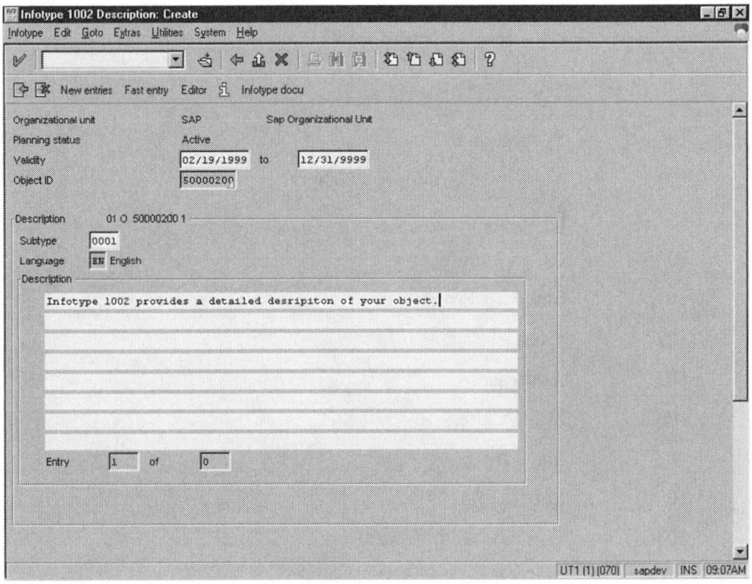

FIGURE 11.15

The Human Resources, Payroll sample screen, Infotype 1002 Description: Create screen.

Training and Events Management

The R/3 Human Resources, Training and Events Management component assists your company in coordinating and administering its business events, including conventions, seminars, and training. It contains functionality to plan, execute, confirm, and manage cost allocations and billing for your company's events.

The enhanced functionality of the Human Resources, Training and Events Management component gives you the ability to create business event procedures, maintain attendance, and control the output of notifications and confirmations, including a direct connection to Microsoft Word. The Training and Event Management component is integrated with the following R/3 application components:

- Time Management
- Personnel Development
- Organizational Management
- Materials Management
- Sales and Distribution
- Controlling

A sample of Human Resources, Training and Events Management infotypes is listed in Table 11.10.

TABLE 11.10   SAMPLE TRAINING AND EVENTS MANAGEMENT INFOTYPES

Infotype	Description
1021	Prices
1024	Capacity
1027	Site-Dependent Info
1029	Business Event Type Info
1032	Mail Address
1035	Schedule
1037	Billing/Allocation Info
1042	Schedule Model
1023	Availability Indicators
1026	Business Event Info
1028	Address
1030	Procedure
1034	Name Format
1036	Costs
1041	Business Event Blocks
1060	Demand

A sample of R/3 Human Resources, Training and Events Management screens is shown in Figures 11.16 and 11.17.

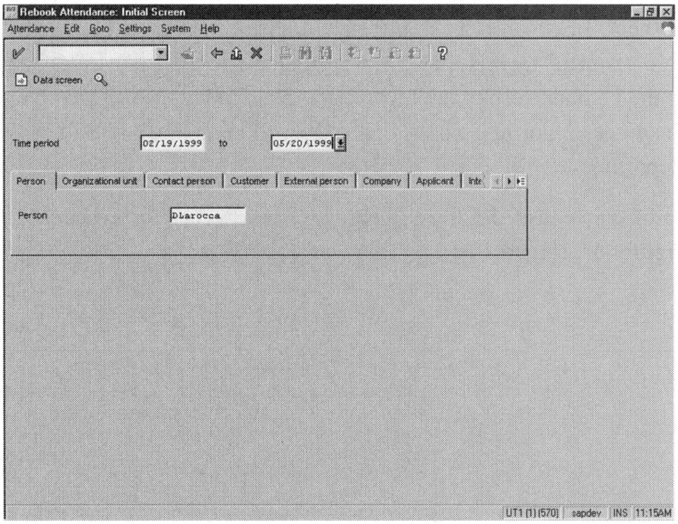

FIGURE 11.16

The Human Resources, Organizational Management sample screen, Rebook Attendance: Initial Screen.

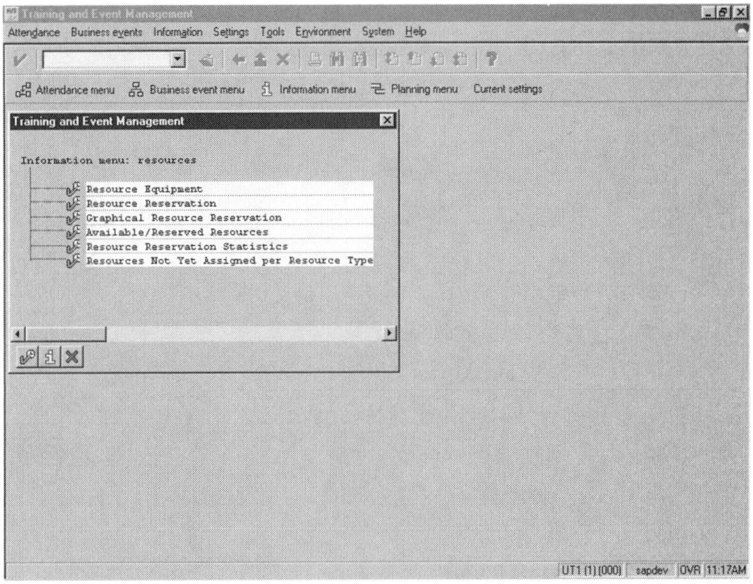

FIGURE 11.17

The Human Resources, Training and Event Management sample screen.

Human Resources Information System (HRIS)

The Human Resources Information System (HRIS) is a tool to help you extract output from your Human Resources module.

The Human Resources Information System (HRIS) component also allows you to request reports from inside R/3's Structural Graphics. The HRIS offers reports that come from both the Personnel Administration and Personnel Planning and Development components of the R/3 Human Resources module. From the report tree in HRIS, you can view delivered (canned) reports that come pre-installed with your R/3 system. Another tool found in the Human Resources Information System is the Ad Hoc Query used for Human Resources reporting. The Ad Hoc Query tool is discussed in Hour 20, "Ad Hoc Query Reporting (HR Module)."

Sample screens from the R/3 Human Resources Information System are shown in Figures 11.18 and 11.19.

FIGURE **11.18**

*The Human
Resources
Information System
sample screen, HRIS
Display Report Tree
screen.*

FIGURE **11.19**

*The Human
Resources
Information System
sample screen,
Structural Graphics.*

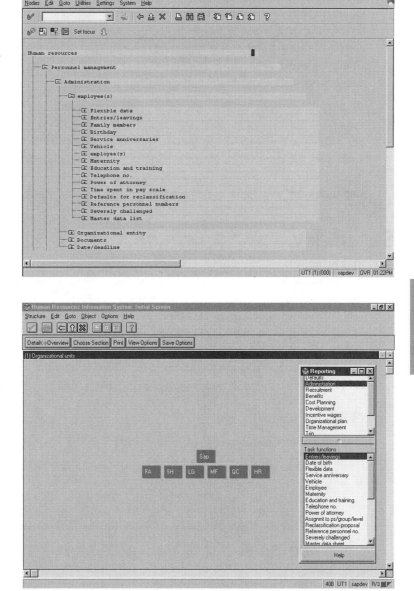

Employee Self-Service

The number one complaint from Human Resources professionals is that they spend a
large percentage of their time responding to employee inquires. Questions like "How

many dependants am I claiming?" or "Who is named as the beneficiary of my life insurance policy?" seem to take up a large portion of the their time. SAP has developed a product that empowers employees to retrieve, and in some cases, modify their own employee data via Web-based technology and interactive voice-response functionality. Employee Self Service (ESS) is an effective means for providing real-time access and data upkeep capabilities to the employees.

With SAP Employee Self Service, employees can be responsible for the preservation of their own data and can get access to their information, on their own time, without requiring a PC connected to SAP and without any SAP training. This saves time for the employees because they no longer need to stop work and visit the Human Resources department, and it saves time for the Human Resources professionals who would need to stop their work to help the employee.

Summary

This hour gives you a very high-level overview of the components of the SAP Human Resources module and its components. It is easy to see why people say that nothing is easy in SAP, just by looking at any particular module. Each module seems to have submodules, which in turn have components which in some cases have sub-components, and so on, and so on. Because R/3 Human Resources is a relatively newer module, there are not a lot of resources available to the user as with the other R/3 modules. Over the course of this hour, you should, however, have become familiar with the basics of the Human Resources module and the functionality it contains.

Q&A

Q What does a standalone product mean?

A The component structure means that you can establish an implementation and maintenance schedule for your SAP HR system that is separate from the rest of the enterprise.

Q Is the Pre-Configured Client available for the Human Resources module?

A A Pre-Configured Client solution for Human Resources is available to SAP customers as part of the Accelerated Human Resources solution. Accelerated HR is available for R/3 release 4.0B, and is compatible with the Pre-Configured Client 40B.

Q Is there a tool to assist in the transference of data from a non-SAP system into SAP R/3 Human Resources?

A As of Release 4.0A, the Data Transfer Workbench tool can be used to assist in the transference of data from a non-SAP system into SAP R/3 Human Resources.

Q If you are using SAP R/3 Human Resources, is configuration required in any of the other modules?

A Configuration of a couple of items in the Financials module, for example cost centers, would need to be performed in order for successful implementation of the SAP R/3 Human Resources as a standalone product to occur.

Q Can R/3 Workflow be used to increase efficiency of the Human Resources functions and procedures?

A R/3 Business Workflow can be used to automate many of the tasks, functions, and procedures of the Human Resources department. R/3 Business Workflow for your company's Human Resources can be based on best practices established for your industry.

Q What are some of the initial configuration decisions required when implementing R/3 Human Resources?

A Some of the initial configuration decisions required when implementing R/3 Human Resources are determining an Enterprise, Personnel, and Organizational structure for your company. These original structures will help dictate how your Human Resources module will ideally perform for your company.

Q Can you use R/3 Human Resources with an external payroll system?

A R/3 Human Resources can be used to manage your company's Human Resources and organizational functions and still be connected to an external payroll system. Your R/3 Payroll component can also record the time and wages and feed this data to an external source for check generation.

Q Can your R/3 Human Resources module be linked to a time- and attendance-recording system?

A The R/3 Human Resources can be interfaced with external time and recording systems. SAP has many partners that have SAP certified interfaces that can be used to work with external systems.

11

Q **Can security in the R/3 system prevent users from seeing sensitive payroll information?**

A Yes. Many different methods can be used to restrict users' ability to see different types of sensitive data in your R/3 system.

Workshop

The workshop is designed to help you anticipate possible questions, review what you've learned, and begin thinking ahead to putting your knowledge into practice. The answers to the quiz that follows can be found in Appendix A, "Answers."

Quiz

1. Define the SAP term *Actions*.
2. Knowing that SAP infotypes are named according to number range specifications, what category would infotype 0001 Organizational Assignment fall under?
3. What is the main benefit from the Human Resources, Recruitment component?
4. The Human Resources module is divided into what two submodules?
5. Define the SAP term *infotype*.
6. What are two methods that can be used for R/3 Employee Self-Service?
7. What is the name of the graphical tool that can be used when generating reports in R/3 Human Resources?

HOUR 12

SAP Logistics

In this hour, you will take a look at SAP's R/3 Logistics module. Not unlike the Financials module, the Logistics module encompasses a large area of your company's business. R/3 logistics encompasses all processes related to your company's purchasing, plant maintenance management, sales and distribution, manufacturing, materials management, warehousing, engineering, and construction. This hour covers a high-level overview of how the Logistics module and the applications contained in the module are structured. Highlights of this hour include

- Overview of R/3 Logistics module
- Review of sample screens from the different submodules in the Logistics module
- An introduction to the Logistics Information System

The Logistics module of the R/3 system allows you to arrange your business functions in a manner that encourages the creativity, competency, and flexibility that your company desires. The Logistics applications are linked to, and coordinated with, all the R/3 modules and contain the following submodules:

- Sales and Distribution
- Production Planning

- Materials Management
- Quality Management
- Plant Maintenance
- Logistics Information System
- Project System
- Product Data Management

Sales and Distribution

The R/3 Logistics, Sales and Distribution submodule provides you with the necessary instruments to use a wealth of information relating to your company's sales and marketing. Data on products, marketing strategies, sales calls, pricing, and sales leads can be accessed at any time to facilitate sales and marketing activity. The information is online, up-to-the-minute support to be used to service existing customers as well as potential customers and leads.

Also included within the Sales and Distribution submodule is a diverse supply of contracts to meet every type of business need. Agreements concerning pricing, delivery dates, and delivery quantity are all supported within this submodule. The components of the R/3 Logistics, Sales and Distribution module include

- Master Data
- Basic Functions
- Sales
- Shipping
- Billing
- Sales Support
- Transportation
- Foreign Trade
- Sales Information System
- Electronic Data Interchange

Some of the benefits of the Sales and Distribution application include

- Automatic order entry via a simple user interface
- Automatic pricing in the sales order using price lists, customer agreements or pricing according to products, and product group or product cost
- Performs a credit limit verification against credit, financial, and sales data to substantiate customers' credit limits

- Automatic product availability checks verify sufficient quantities

A few sample screens from the Logistics, Sales and Distribution submodule can be found in Figures 12.1–12.6.

FIGURE 12.1

The Sales and Distribution, Master Data sample screen, Customer Create: Initial Screen Sales area screen.

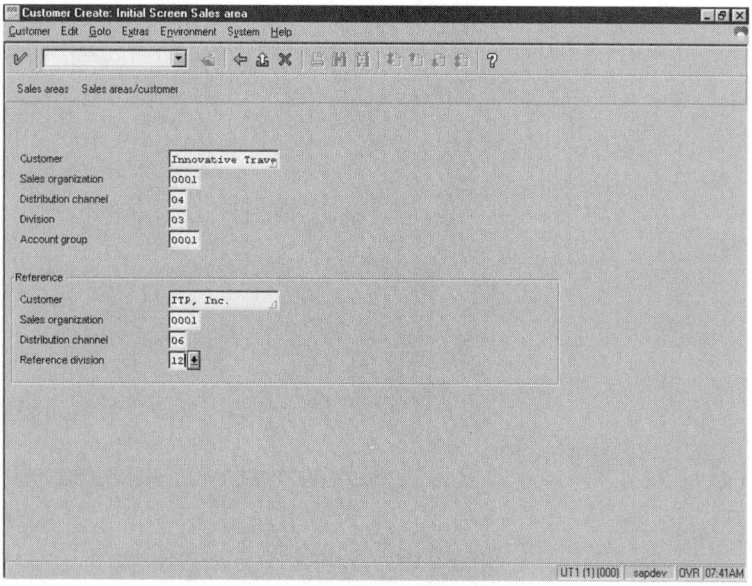

FIGURE 12.2

The Sales and Distribution, Sales sample screen, Incomplete SD Documents screen.

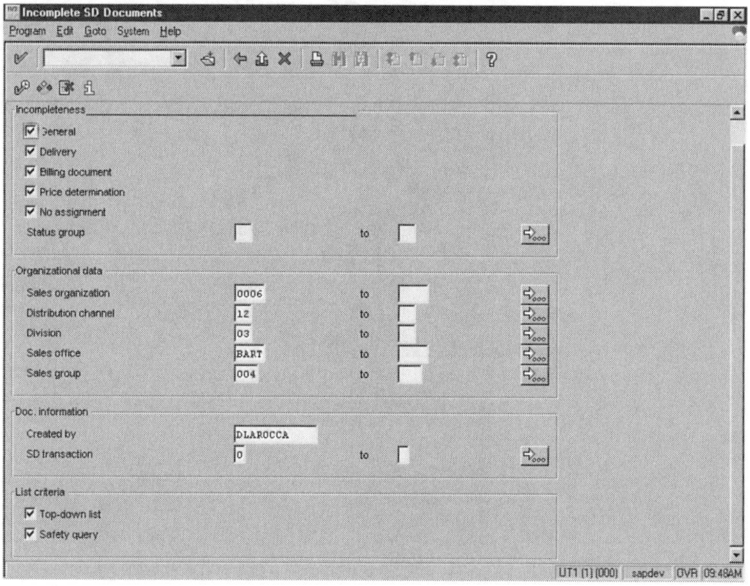

12

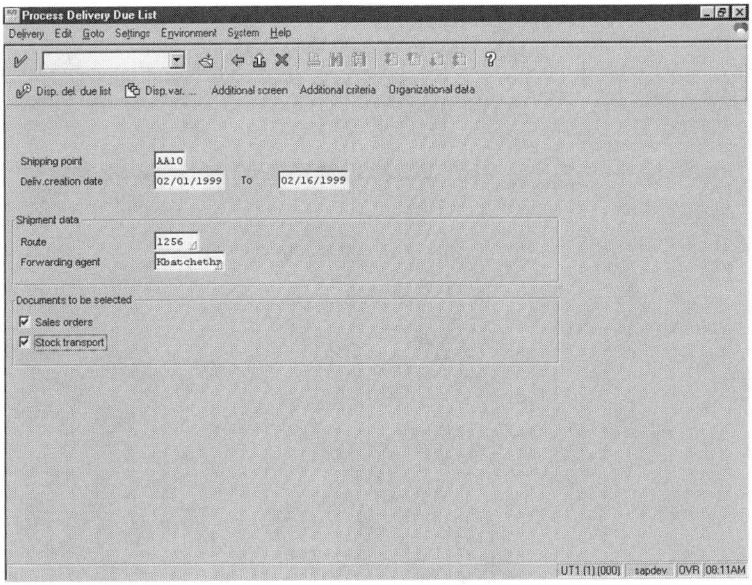

FIGURE 12.3

*The Sales and
Distribution, Shipping
sample screen, Process
Delivery Due List
screen.*

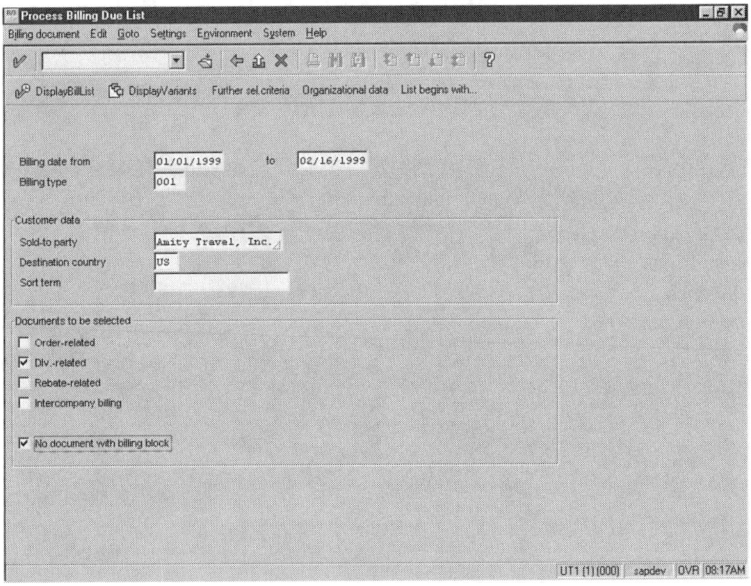

FIGURE 12.4

*The Sales and
Distribution, Billing
sample screen, Process
Billing Due List
screen.*

FIGURE 12.5

The Sales and Distribution, Sales Support sample screen, Create Mailing w.Fol.Act.:Overview Screen.

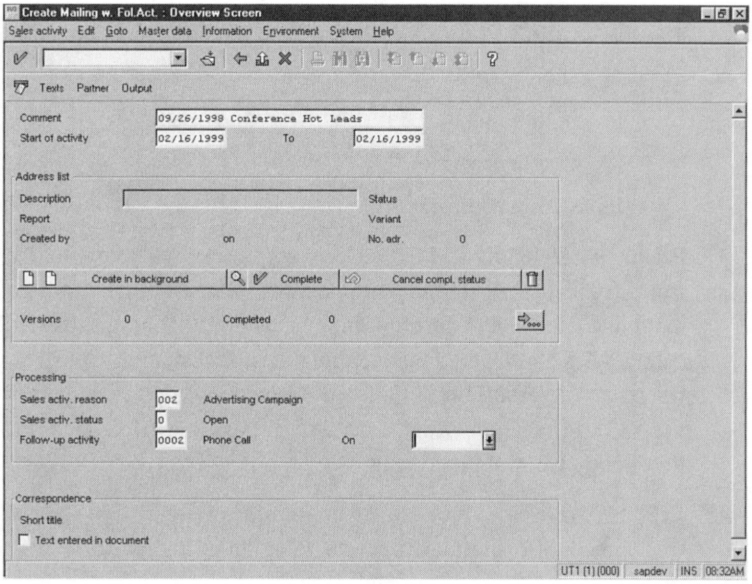

FIGURE 12.6

The Sales and Distribution, Sales information System sample screen, Customer Analysis: Selection screen.

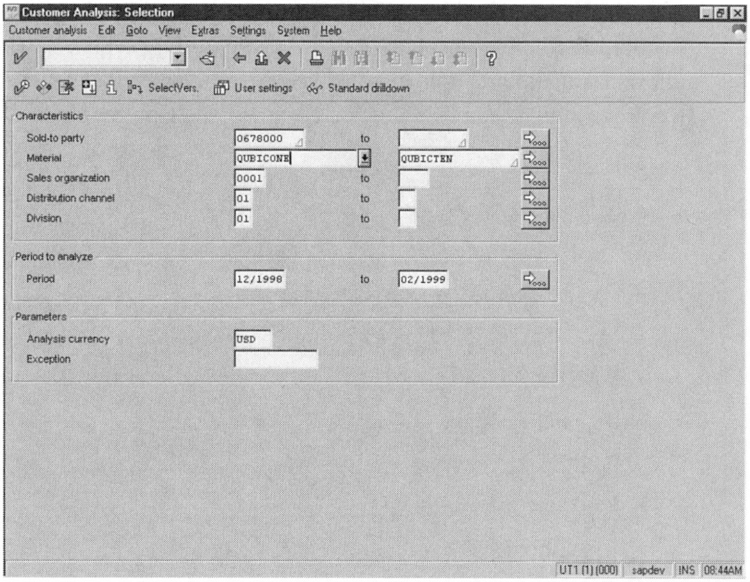

12

Production Planning and Control

The focus of R/3's Logistics, Production Planning and Control submodule is to contribute complete solutions for

- Production planning
- Production execution
- Production control

Production Planning and Control encompasses the comprehensive production process from its inception with the initial creation of master data through the production process, including control and costing. The Production Planning submodule includes a component called Sales and Operations Planning used for creating realistic and consistent planning figures to forecast future sales, and depending on your method of production, you can use R/3's Production Order Processing, Repetitive Manufacturing or KANBAN Production Control processing.

NEW TERM *KANBAN* is a procedure for controlling production and material flow based on a chain of operations in production and procurement.

One important benefit from the implementation of the Production Planning and Control submodule would be its elimination of routine tasks for the persons responsible for production scheduling, resulting in the increase of time available. This reduction in time allows for additional time to be dedicated to more critical activities within your company. Several components of Production Planning and Control module include

- Basic Data
- Sales and Operations Planning
- Master Planning
- Capacity Requirements Planning
- Material requirements Planning
- KANBAN
- Repetitive Manufacturing
- Production Orders
- Product Cost Planning
- Assembly Orders
- Production Planning for process industries
- Plant Data Collection
- Production Planning and Control Information System

A few sample screens from the Logistics, Production Planning and Control module can be found in Figures 12.7–12.11.

FIGURE 12.7

The Production Planning and Control, Sales and Operations Planning sample screen, Calculate Proportions for Planning Hierarchy screen.

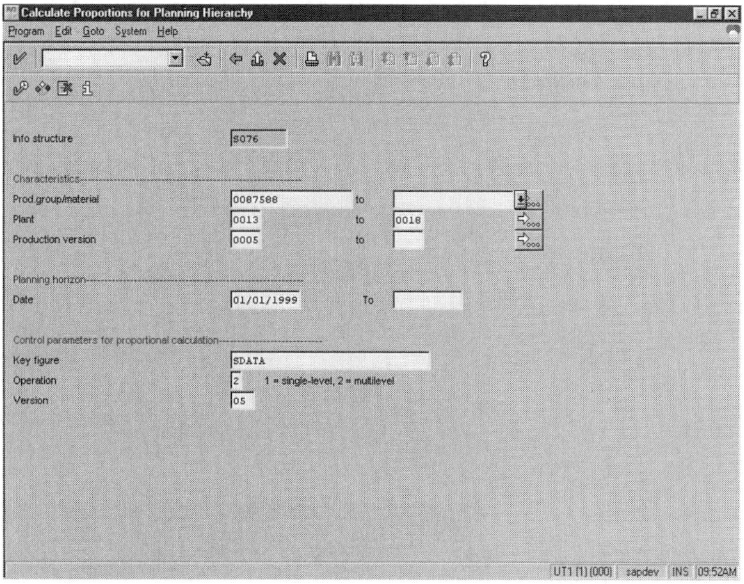

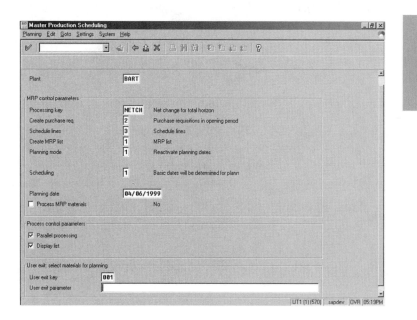

FIGURE 12.8

The Production Planning and Control, Master Planning sample screen, Master Production Scheduling screen.

12

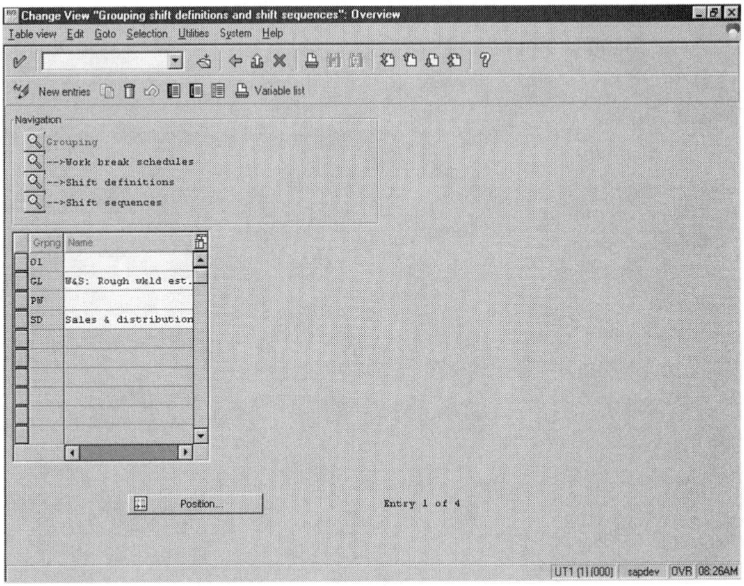

FIGURE 12.9

The Production Planning and Control, Capacity Requirements Planning sample screen, Change View "Grouping shift definitions and shift sequences": Overview screen.

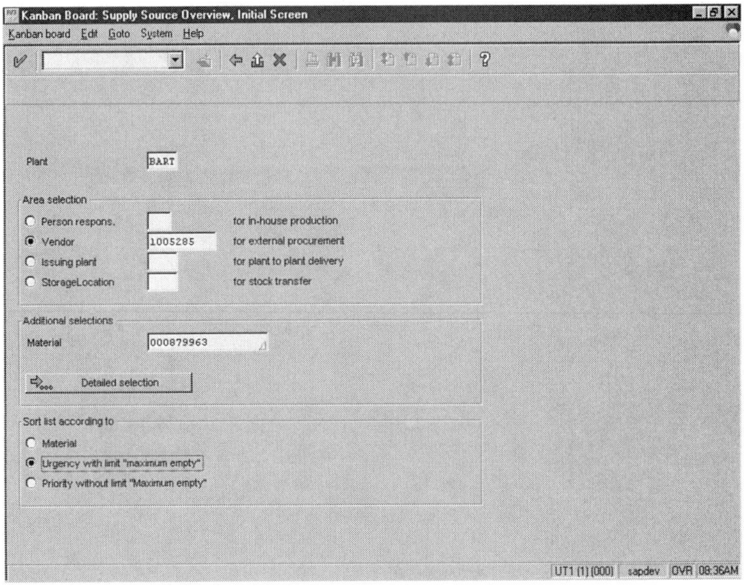

FIGURE 12.10

The Production Planning and Control, KANBAN sample screen, Kanban Board: Supply Source Overview, Initial Screen.

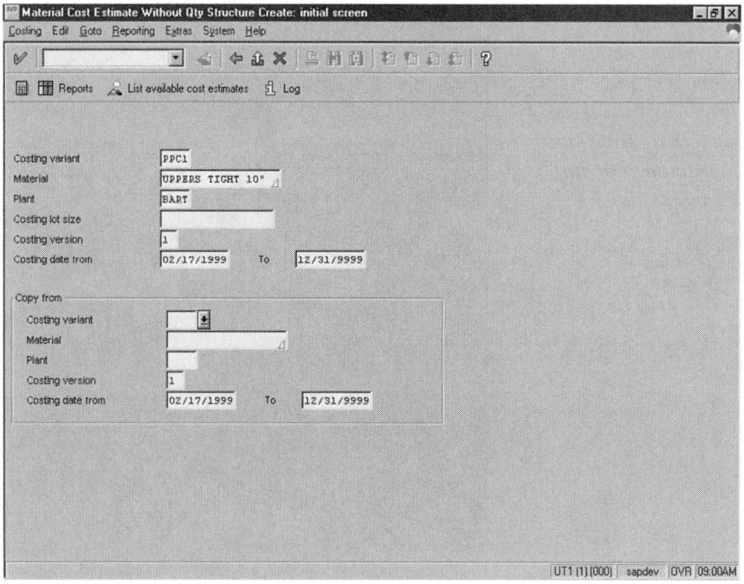

FIGURE 12.11

*The Production
Planning and Control,
Product Cost Planning
sample screen,
Material Cost Estimate
Without Qty Structure
Create: initial screen.*

Materials Management

Your company's business processes are essential to the success of your company. The
day-to-day management of your company's consumption of materials, including company purchasing, managing your warehouse and inventory, confirming your invoices, and
analyzing your processes, are all part of the R/3 Logistics, Materials Management submodule.

Savings of time, money, and resources are the three main benefits that you will derive
from your Materials Management submodule. The components of the R/3 Logistics,
Materials Management module include

- Inventory Management
- Warehouse Management
- Purchasing
- Invoice Verification
- Materials Planning
- Purchasing Information System

A few sample screens from the Logistics, Materials Management submodule can be
found in Figures 12.12–12.16.

12

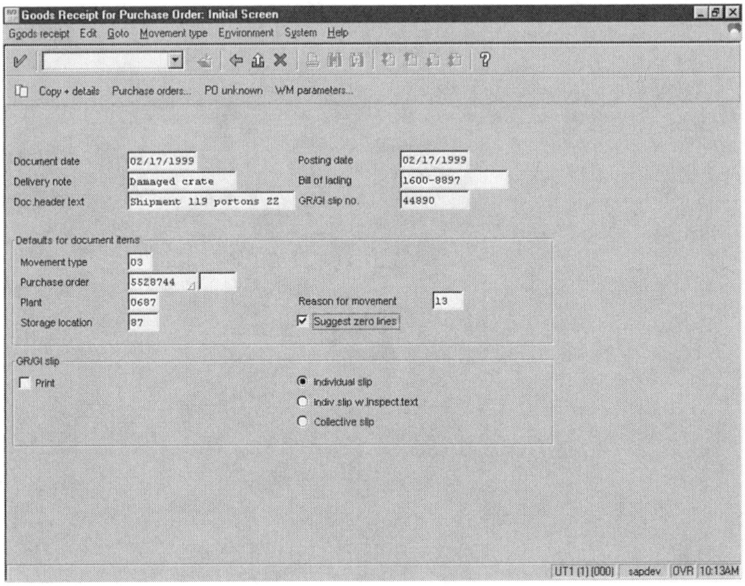

FIGURE 12.12

The Materials Management, Inventory Management sample screen, Goods Receipt for Purchase Order: Initial Screen.

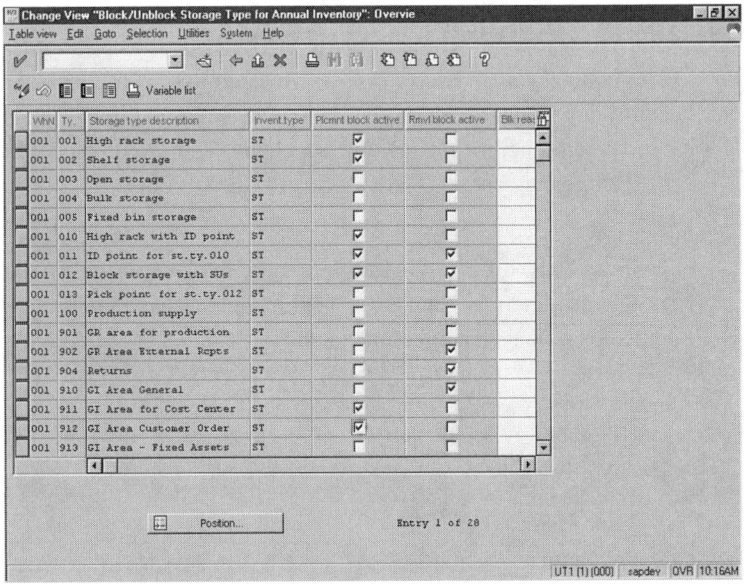

FIGURE 12.13

The Materials Management, Warehouse Management sample screen, Change View "Block/Unblock Storage Type for Annual Inventory": Overview.

FIGURE 12.14

The Materials Management, Purchasing sample Screeen, Create Purchase Order: Initial Screen.

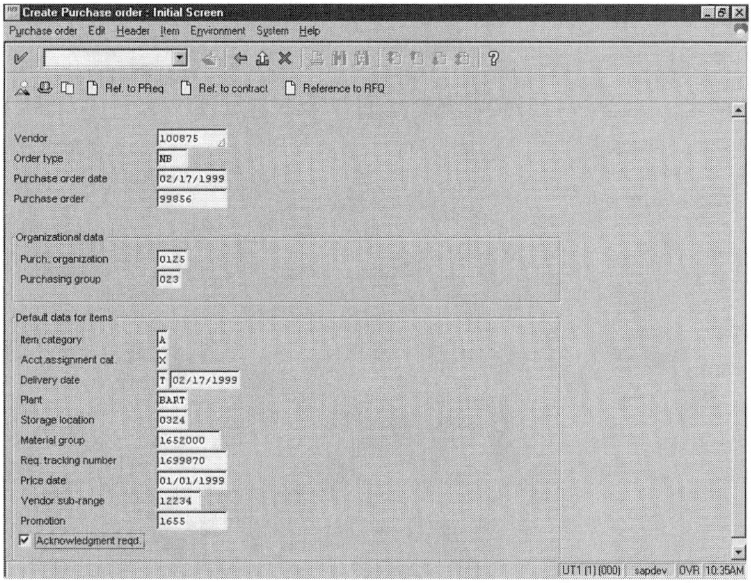

FIGURE 12.15

The Materials Management, Invoice Verification sample screen, Enter Invoice: Initial Screen.

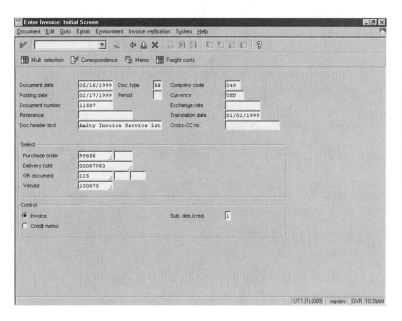

12

FIGURE 12.16

The Materials Management, Materials Planning sample screen, MRP— Single-Item, Single-Level screen.

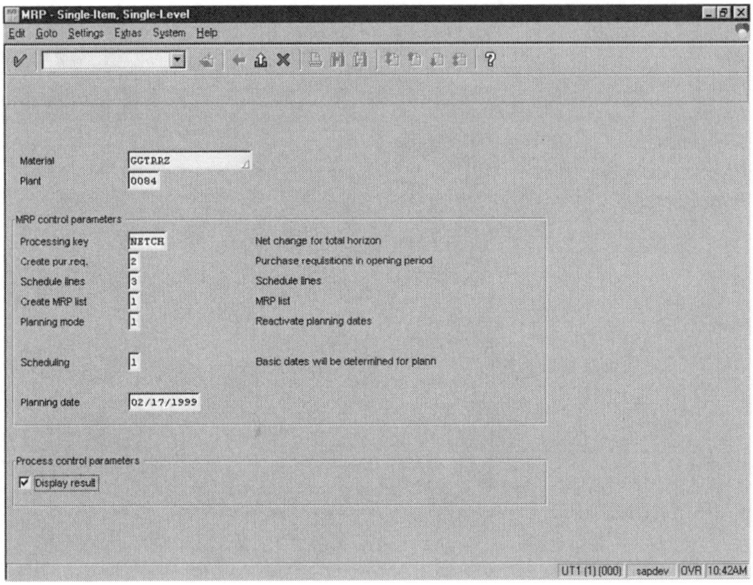

Quality Management

The Logistics, Quality Management submodule is directed at improving the Quality of your products. In order to produce high-quality products, a well-managed Quality Management system needs to be in place that assures the integrity of your products, which in turn helps foster good client relations and enhances a good reputation for your products and your company.

The Quality Management submodule gives you the ability to analyze, document, and improve upon the processes in your company. Applications contained in the Quality Management component include

- Quality Planning
- Quality Inspections
- Quality Control
- Quality Notifications
- Quality Certificates
- Test Equipment Management
- Quality Management Information System

A few sample screens from the Logistics, Quality Management submodule can be found in Figures 12.17–12.20.

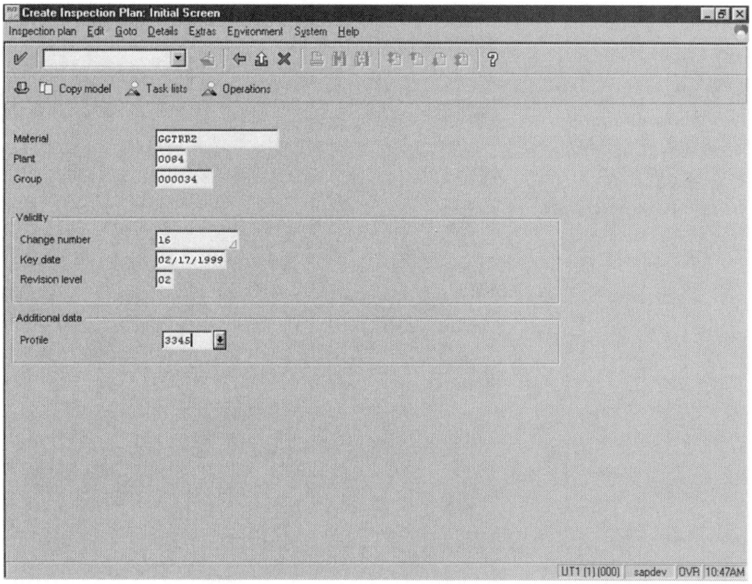

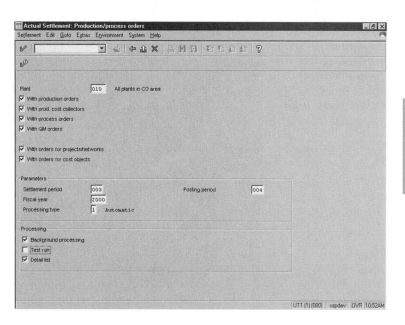

FIGURE 12.17

*The Quality
Management, Quality
Planning sample
screen, Create
Inspection Plan: Initial
Screen.*

FIGURE 12.18

*The Quality
Management, Quality
Inspections sample
screen, Actual
Settlement:
Production/process
orders screen.*

12

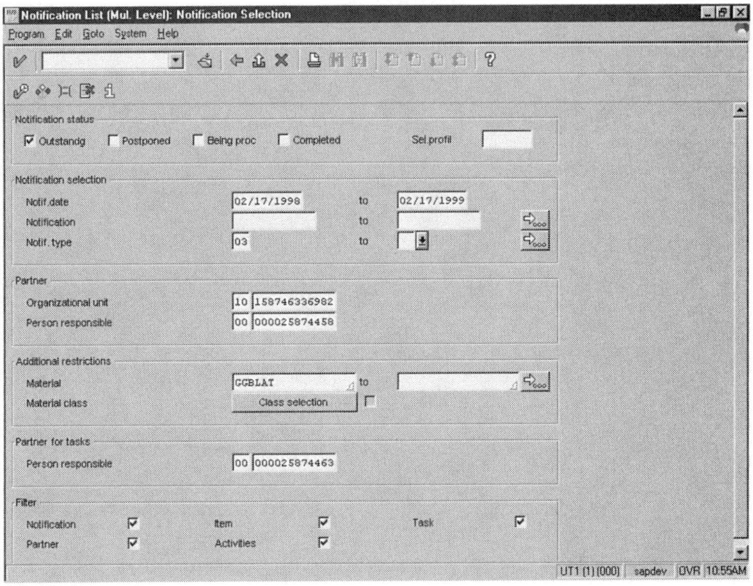

FIGURE **12.19**

The Quality Management, Quality Notifications sample screen, Notification List (Mul.Level): Notification Selection screen.

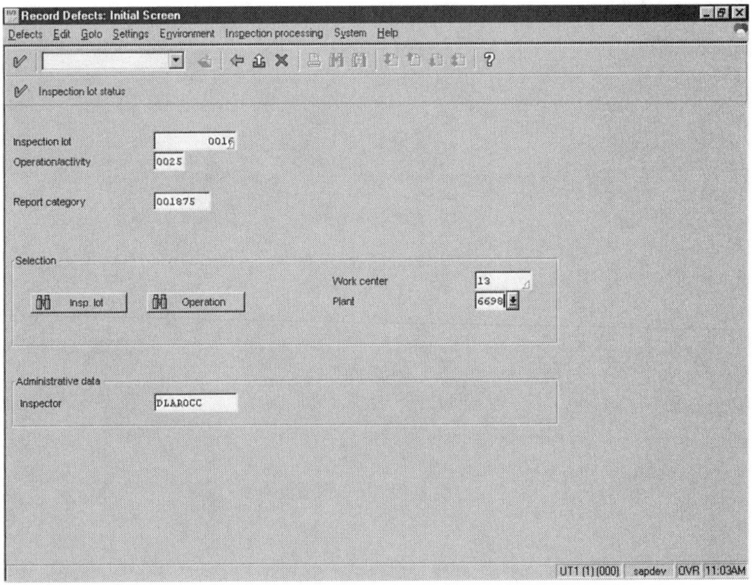

FIGURE **12.20**

The Quality Management, Test Equipment sample screen, Record Defects: Initial Screen.

Plant Maintenance

The main benefit to the R/3's Logistics, Plant Maintenance submodule is its flexibility to work with different types of companies to meet differing designs, requirements, and work forces. The Plant Maintenance submodule also contains a graphical interface, which makes it very user-friendly and enables it to cater to a larger population of your work force.

Different management strategies are supported within the application including Risk Based Maintenance and Total Productive Maintenance. Some benefits that your company will derive from the implementation of the Plant Maintenance submodule involve reduced down time and outages, optimization of labor and resources, and a reduction in the costs of inspections and repairs.

On the whole, the integration of the Plant Maintenance submodule will support your company in designing and executing your company's maintenance activities with regard to system resource availability, costs, materials, and personnel deployment. Components of Logistics, Plant Maintenance include

- Preventative Maintenance
- Service Management
- Maintenance Order Management
- Maintenance Projects
- Equipment and Technical Objects
- Plant Maintenance Information System

A few sample screens from the Logistics, Quality Management submodule can be found in Figures 12.21–12.23.

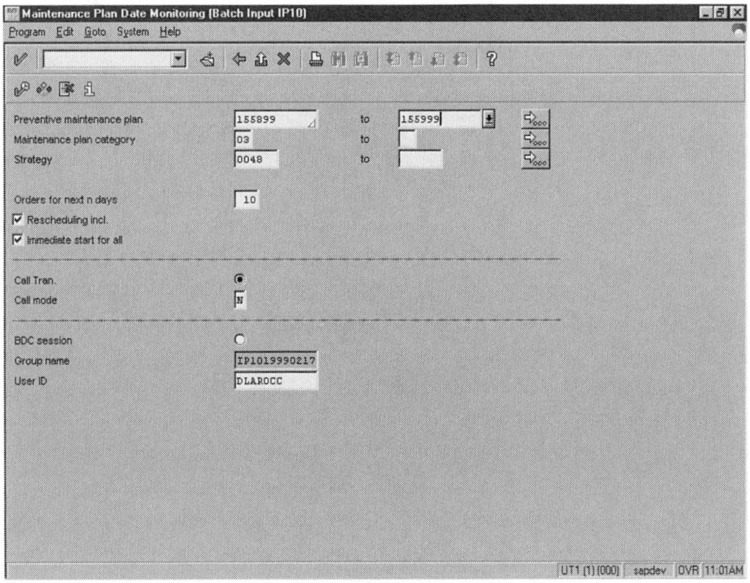

FIGURE 12.21

The Plant Maintenance, Preventative Maintenance sample screen, Maintenance Plan Date Monitoring (Batch Input IP10) screen.

12

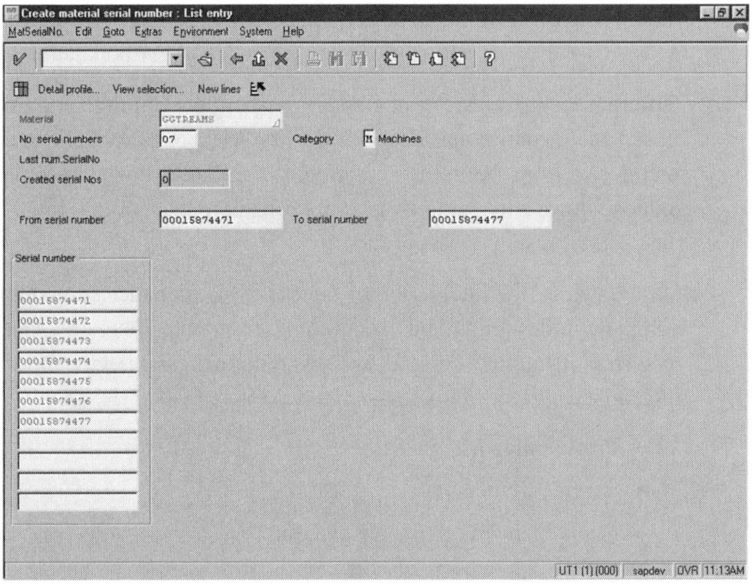

FIGURE 12.22

*The Plant
Maintenance,
Equipment and
Technical Objects
sample screen, Create
material serial
number: List Entry
screen.*

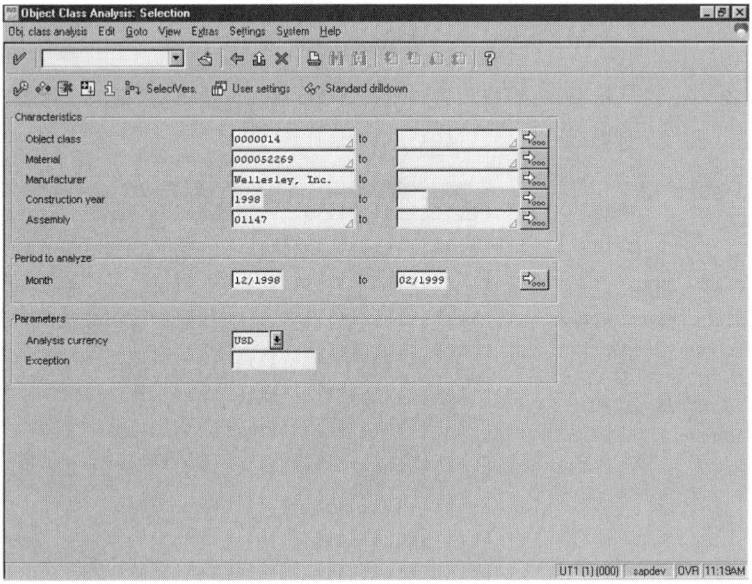

FIGURE 12.23

*The Plant
Maintenance, Plant
Maintenance
Information System
sample screen, Object
Class Analysis:
Selection screen.*

Logistics Information System

The Logistics Information System maintains real-time information derived from multiple R/3 components allowing you to evaluate actual data and forecast future data utilizing a technique called *Online Transaction Processing (OLTP)*. You can use the Logistics Data Warehouse to customize and design your company's Information System to meet your company's unique requirements and use the Early Warning System, which targets weak or bottlenecked areas in Logistics.

In addition to these two components, the Logistics Information System contains a Logistics Information Library which helps you to retrieve data via searches, enabling you to access key data when necessary. You use the Logistics Information Library (LIL) to record, classify, and retrieve key figures. The Logistics Information System is composed of the following information systems (see Figure 12.24):

- Sales Information System
- Purchasing Information System
- Inventory Controlling
- Production Planning and Control Information System
- Plant Maintenance Information System
- Quality Management Information System
- Project Information System
- Retail Information System (RIS)

FIGURE 12.24

Overview of the Logistics Information System.

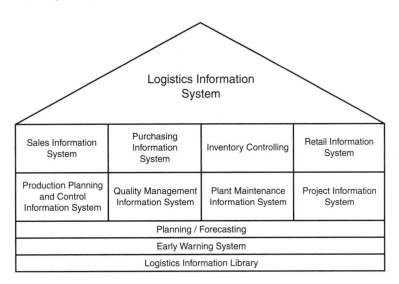

Project System

The Project System submodule is an instrument designed to assist your company in the management of its projects. The R/3 Project System is centered on the network of relationships within your integrated R/3 system, and it establishes links between project management and commercial information processing.

The Project System can be used in many different areas including investment management, marketing, software and consulting services, research and development, maintenance tasks, shutdown management, plant engineering and construction, and complex made-to-order production. The components of the Project System include

- Basic Data
- Operational Structures
- Project Planning
- Approval
- Project Execution and Integration
- Project System Information System

The Project System component is based on central structures called Work Breakdown Structures (WBS).

NEW TERM A structured model of work organized in a hierarchy format, to be performed in a project is called a *Work Breakdown Structure (WBS)*.

Three different views of the Project structure follow that are each based on different criteria:

- The Phases structure is logic oriented.
- The Function structure is function oriented.
- The Object structure is object oriented.

Work Breakdown Structures (WBS) are comprised of elements, which represent the individual tasks and activities in the project. Elements include tasks, breakdowns of tasks, and work packages. Within the Project System, they are referred to as *Work Breakdown Structure elements (WBS elements)*; see Figure 25 for an overview.

FIGURE 12.25

The Project Structure Overview.

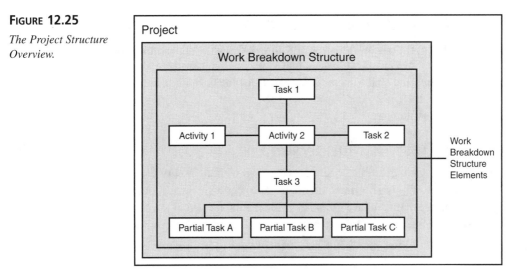

Product Data Management

By acknowledging the diversity and intricacies of today's products, R/3's Product Data Management component empowers you with the ability to access and control product data from every area of your company. The Product Data Management submodule also allows you to manage the following:

- Product data
- Product release and changes processes
- Product structures and configurations
- Product development projects

The entire spectrum of the Product Data Management functions is synthesized with the R/3 ERP system.

If your company decides to continue using your existing product data management system, it is possible to use an SAP R/3 interface to integrate that system into your SAP environment. Contact SAP to see if they have available a certified interface for your existing system.

Document Management System

The R/3 system also contains a Document Management System to assist you. The Document Management System helps you develop constant data arrangement for various documents and enables you to join those documents and their associated R/3 items. In addition, the Document Management System can also be linked to third-party optical archiving systems.

R/3 Classification System

The R/3 Classification System provides you with the ability to arrange your data within a structure of your specification. Items are categorized throughout the R/3 system based on the model that you have established and can be located at any time through a system search. For instance, a previously created document with specific characteristics can be retrieved through a search instead of creating a new document each time from scratch.

Summary

Over the past hour, you have taken a look at some of the very basics of the Logistics module. Many people say that the Logistics module is the largest of the applications offered by SAP and that in some cases it is the most complex. The high-level overview covered in this hour only introduces the different submodules and components of the Logistics system. This introduction to the Logistics module should have made you familiar with what the application has to offer and possibly gave you some ideas on different areas that might require focus if your company implements the Logistics module.

There are many helpful books available on the market that cover the SAP R/3 Logistics module or its submodules. Some good titles to check out are

Kasturi, Rajeev. *SAP R/3 Ale & Edi Technologies* (SAP Technical Expert Series) (ISBN: 0071347305). New York: McGraw-Hill, 1999

Hiquet, Bradley D., Kelley-Levey, et al. *SAP R/3 Implementation Guide : A Manager's Guide to Understanding SAP* (ISBN: 1578700639) Indianapolis: Macmillan Technical Publishing, 1998.

ASAP World Consultancy, et al. *Special Edition Using SAP R/3 Third Edition* (ISBN: 0789718219). Indianapolis: Que, 1998.

Q&A

Q **Does the Plant Maintenance submodule comply with the ISO 9000 and QS-9000 standards.**

A Yes, the Plant Maintenance submodule complies with the ISO 9000 and QS-9000 standards.

Q **Is the Quality Management submodule built on the ISO 9001 standard?**

A Yes, the Quality Management submodule is built on the ISO 9001 standard for quality management.

Q. **Is there a tool to assist in the transference of data from a non-SAP system into SAP R/3 Logistics?**

A As of version 4.0, the Data Transfer Workbench tool can be used to transfer your data from a non-SAP system into SAP R/3 Logistics.

Workshop

The workshop is designed to help you anticipate possible questions, review what you've learned, and begin thinking ahead to putting your knowledge into practice. The answers to the quiz that follows can be found in Appendix A, "Answers."

Quiz

1. Name the components available in the Materials Management submodule.

2. Name the components available in Quality Management submodule?

3. What are the eight components of the Logistics module?

4. The focus of the Production Planning and Control component is to contribute solutions for what three areas?

5. Describe the types of data available to facilitate sales and marketing activity in the Sales and Distribution submodule.

6. What component of the Production Planning submodule is used for creating realistic and consistent planning figures to forecast future sales?

7. What are the three main benefits that you will derive from your Materials Management submodule.

12

PART IV
SAP Technical Guide

Hour

HOUR 13

Basis Overview

In this hour, you will take a look at some of the basic components of the SAP R/3 Basis system. The introduction of the Basis system is your first look into the technical side of SAP. The Basis system is a behind-the-scenes layer that normal day-to-day users will not be required to become too familiar with. This hour will help you to understand some of SAP's basic concepts in terms of how your SAP system communicates. Highlights of this hour include

- Learning about the different types of R/3 Work Processes
- Understanding what Enqueue processing means
- Discovering Remote Function Calls (RFCs)

Application Architecture

In SAP R/3-speak, the Basis system is the *middleware* that allows the applications to run on different hardware and system platforms. The available platforms are shown in Figure 13.1.

Middleware is the software that functions as a conversion or translation layer between two different layers.

FIGURE **13.1**

SAP Basis available platforms.

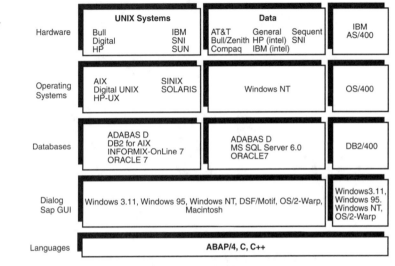

The Basis middleware manages all your application modules within your SAP R/3 system and assures that these modules are integrated and platform independent. Some important functions of the R/3 Basis System include

- Contributes the runtime environment for your R/3 system
- Is the heart of the administrative functions of your SAP system
- Manages the distribution of your SAP components and resources
- Permits optimal integration of the applications into the system environment
- Establishes a stable structural framework for system enhancements
- Offers the interfaces to your third-party vendors and products

Basis Tools

The R/3 Basis system provides for the integration of software and technology through the use of the tools outlined as follows (see Figure 13.2):

- Remote Function Calls (RFC)
- Common Program Interface Communications (CPI-C))
- Electronic Data Interchange (EDI))

- Object linking and embedding (OLE))
- Application Link Enabling (ALE))

Figure 13.2

Different SAP Basis integration tools are available in your R/3 system.

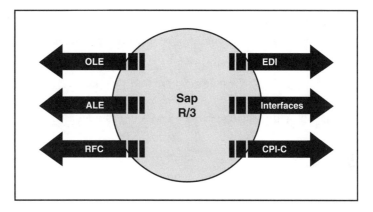

Remote Function Calls (RFC)

Remote Function Calls, or RFCs as they are referred to in SAP, are forms of interface communication.

NEW TERM *Remote Function Calls (RFCs)* allow for the simple programming of communication processes between systems.

In simpler terms, RFCs are used to pass communication throughout the SAP system and through interfaces into other systems. RFCs are also used for communication control, parameter passing, and error handling. RFCs are usually written in SAP's ABAP language and, without getting too technical, RFCs are used to call a program (see Figure 13.3).

Figure 13.3

Remote Function Calls (RFC) is code written in SAP's ABAP language for accessing function modules in other computers.

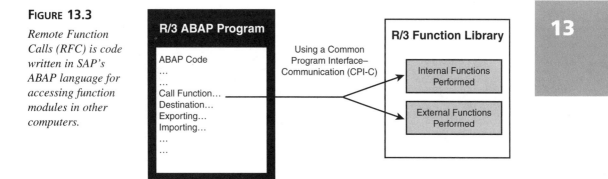

13

Common Program Interface Communications (CPI-C)

A SAP Common Program Interface Communications (CPI-C) is, just as its name implies, a type of program interface communication.

NEW TERM A *Common Program Interface Communication (CPI-C)* ensures a standard and consistent communication between two programs.

In non-technical terms, CPI-C facilitates the communication (talking back and forth) and the processing of applications and programs within the system. CPI-C is a communications protocol that consists of a series of rules governing communication between programs. These rules can be divided into four different areas:

1. Session setup
2. Session control
3. Communication
4. End of session

The difference between RFCs and CPI-Cs is that RFCs allow other systems to call R/3 functions and CPI-Cs allow program-to-program communications and exchange.

Electronic Data Interchange (EDI)

Electronic Data Interchange (EDI) is the communication of business transactions electronically. EDI permits two different systems to pass information back and forth in a standard format (see Figure 13.4). If you have ever purchased an item off of the Internet, you have used some form of EDI. The EDI architecture consists of the three elements listed in Table 13.1.

NEW TERM *Electronic Data Interchange (EDI)* is the electronic communication of business transactions. EDI permits two different systems to pass information back and forth in a standard format.

TABLE 13.1 EDI ELEMENTS

Element	Description
EDI capable applications	Applications that can effectively support the automatic processing of business transactions
EDI interface	Applications designed with an open interface and structure
EDI subsystem messages	Application that can convert the immediate structures into EDI

FIGURE 13.4

Electronic Data Interchange (EDI) uses a standardized scheme for exchanging business data between different systems.

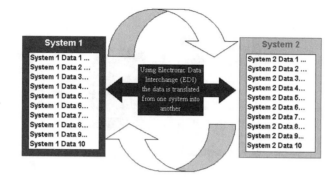

The standard format for EDI is ANSI X12 and was developed by the Data Interchange Standards Association.

Object Linking and Embedding (OLE)

Object linking and embedding (OLE) is used to integrate PC applications with the SAP R/3 system. OLE is the technology for transferring and sharing information among applications.

In Hour 22, "Communicating with Microsoft Office," you will see how to use OLE to create SAP R/3 reports with the Microsoft Office family of products.

OLE connects various PC applications to the R/3 system as RFCs to your SAPGUI presentation layer (see Figure 13.5).

Application Link Enabling (ALE)

13

Application Link Enabling (ALE) is the creation and operation of distributed applications. In other words, ALE, which is closely related to SAP Work Flow, is the technology used by your R/3 system to support distributed business processes.

Application integration is achieved not via a central database, but via synchronous and asynchronous communication. Synchronous transfer means that data is transmitted directly from program to program via a CPI-C interface. In asynchronous transfer, the sender and the receiver programs are independent of each other. This might sound a bit more technical than it actually is. An example of synchronous and asynchronous communication can be found in Figure 13.6.

FIGURE **13.5**

Object Linking and Embedding (OLE) enables the connection and incorporation of objects across platforms.

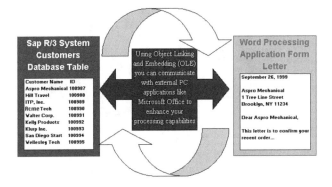

FIGURE **13.6**

Application integration is achieved via synchronous and asynchronous data transfer.

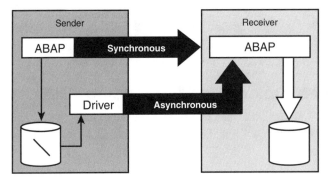

The following lists three different types of data that are transmitted through ALE:

- *Control and customizing data*: Any data that is entered into the system as part of your configuration process including user profiles, company codes, and business data.

- *Master data*: Any data that represents the organizational units of consolidation in the system, such as employee and vendor records.

- *Transaction data*: Records of transactions in the system: orders, shipments, purchases, payroll runs, and so on.

Work Processes

Several types of work processes go on behind-the-scenes in your SAP R/3 system, and they all perform different types of functions. Work processes perform the bulk of the processing carried out by your R/3 System, including performing dialog steps in user transactions, database updates, and record-lock management. If you are curious to see what work processes are happening at any given time in your SAP system, use the transaction code /nSM50. See the example in Figure 13.7.

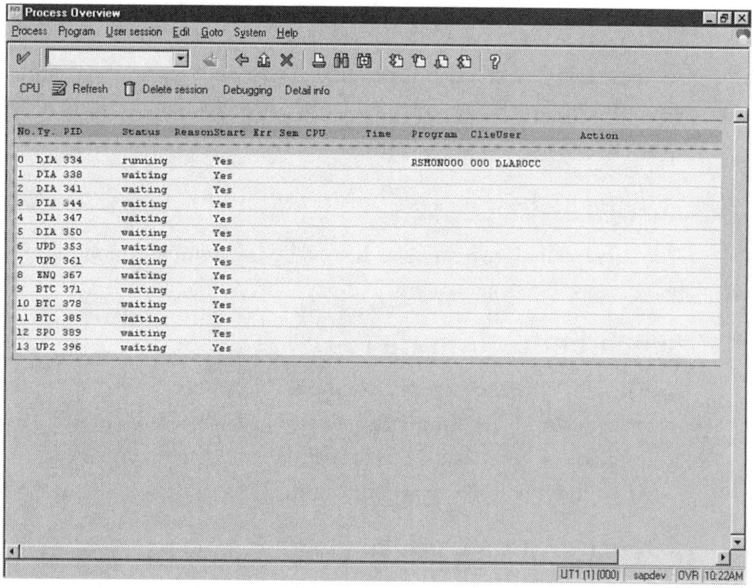

FIGURE 13.7

The SAP Process Overview screen will display a list of work processes.

Process Overview
Process Program User session Edit Goto System Help

CPU   Refresh   Delete session   Debugging   Detail info

No.Ty. PID	Status	ReasonStart Err Sem CPU	Time	Program ClieUser	Action
0 DIA 334	running	Yes		RSMON000 000 DLAROCC	
1 DIA 338	waiting	Yes			
2 DIA 341	waiting	Yes			
3 DIA 344	waiting	Yes			
4 DIA 347	waiting	Yes			
5 DIA 350	waiting	Yes			
6 UPD 353	waiting	Yes			
7 UPD 361	waiting	Yes			
8 ENQ 367	waiting	Yes			
9 BTC 371	waiting	Yes			
10 BTC 378	waiting	Yes			
11 BTC 385	waiting	Yes			
12 SPO 389	waiting	Yes			
13 UP2 396	waiting	Yes			

UT1 (1) (000)   sapdev   OVR 10:22AM

Types of work processes include

- Dialog
- Background
- Synchronous Update
- Asynchronous Update
- Enqueue
- Message
- Spool
- Gateway

Dialog Work Processes

Dialog work processes implement requests in your active work session and are based on synchronous communications.

Remember the Logical Units of Work (LUW) that we covered in Hour 1, "Introduction to SAP?" Well, a Dialog process is not complete until it completes a Logical Unit of Work.

13

Background Processing

As the name describes, Background processing tasks are usually executed in the background. This would include tasks run in batches and reports. Background processing is based on asynchronous communications.

Update Processes

Update processes are requests to update the database, and these are broken down into two categories: synchronous and asynchronous.

Synchronous Update (V1)

Synchronous updates are performed immediately. These are updates to the database that must be performed before you can proceed with the activity that you are processing in. Adding a new purchase order to the system is an example of a synchronous update because you would be required to immediately update the database with this information.

Asynchronous Update (V2)

Asynchronous updates are not performed immediately; rather, they are performed in batch and do not require an immediate update to the system.

Enqueue Processing

Enqueue is another word for lock. In this case, I further mean *lock management*. Lock management is meant to describe a sense of record management security in the system. In other words, if you have a record open (an employee record for instance) and are changing important data on that record (employee salary for instance), lock management prevents another user from opening the same record and making changes to it while you have it open.

Function modules to lock (enqueue) or release (dequeue) are generated from the lock objects that you define in your Data Dictionary. (The Data Dictionary is covered in Hour 15, "R/3 Data Dictionary.")

Message Processing

Message processing represents the communication between different application servers in your R/3 system.

Depending on your systems configuration, you might have only one application server. Not all companies have multiple application servers.

Spool Processing

Spool processing concerns output requests that are sent to a spool, which stores them temporarily until they are output. Spool processing usually encompasses reports and output in your R/3 system. See Figure 13.8 for an example.

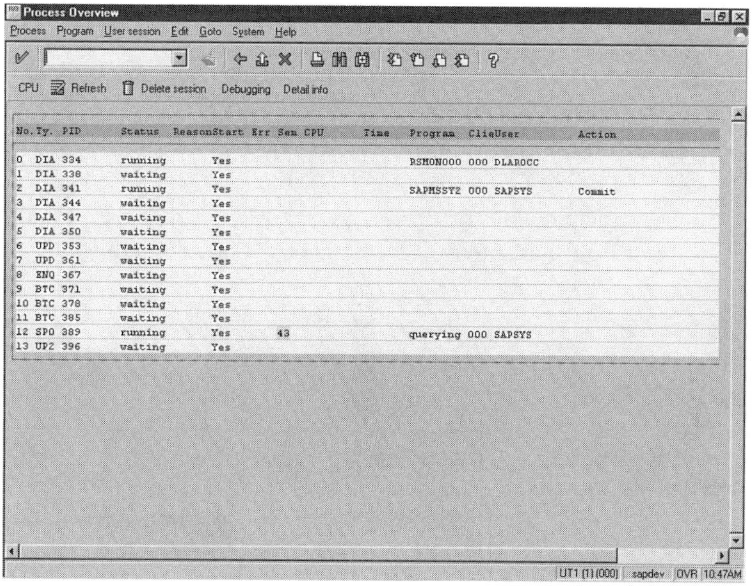

FIGURE 13.8

The SAP Process Overview screen displays your spool requests.

Gateway Process

Lastly, a Gateway process is a communication among other R/3 systems. An example of a Gateway process is between your SAP R/3 system and a mainframe computer system.

13

If you want to see what the work process is doing behind the scenes (in SQL*Net), navigate to the Process Overview screen (transaction code /nSM50) and select an item in the list by highlighting it with your cursor. Then follow the menu path Process, Trace, Display file.

Work Processes Review

The different types of work processes and the types of requests they manage are summarized in Table 13.2.

TABLE 13.2 SAP WORK PROCESSES

Work Process	Request Type
Dialog	Dialog requests
Update	Requests to update data in the database
Background	Background jobs
Spool	Print spool requests
Enqueue	Lock management
Message	Message management between application servers within an R/3 system
Gateway	Requests between multiple systems, including external non-SAP systems

The basic processes that go on, as we say, behind-the-scenes in SAP when tasks are performed are similar to the very basic depiction in Figure 13.9.

FIGURE 13.9

Work processes perform the bulk of the processing carried out by your R/3 System.

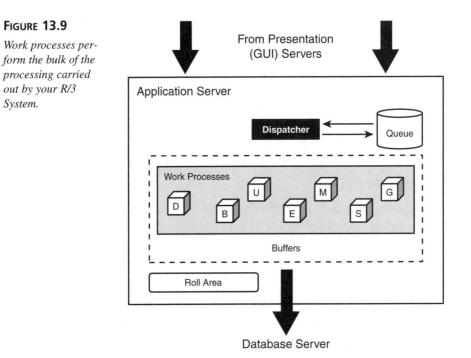

Summary

This hour provides you with a very elementary overview of some of the essentials of the Basis system and the functions that go on behind-the-scenes in your R/3 system. You will not need to "put into action," so to speak, many of the concepts you learned this hour because most of them concern things that are happening outside your view.

As an overview, there were many functions of the Basis system that were not covered in this hour. Some of these concepts are covered in Hour 14, "System Administration." This hour was designed to give you a very fundamental understanding of your Basis system. Unless you are planning a career in Basis or SAP system administration, the technical terms and R/3 functions that are discussed herein should suffice as a basic understanding of your SAP Basis system.

Q&A

Q Do all installations need to use the Basis system monitoring tools?

A Although not required, taking advantage of the system monitoring tools is an ideal way to ensure that the system maintains a good runtime environment, and is free of errors.

Q Are you required to have a systems professional specializing in Basis Administration in order to implement your R/3 system?

A You cannot have a successful installation and implementation without at least one knowledgeable Basis Systems Administrator. It is also useful to have an Administrator who is familiar with database management for your selected database (Oracle, UNIX, and so on.)

Workshop

The workshop is designed to help you anticipate possible questions, review what you've learned, and begin thinking ahead to putting your knowledge into practice. The answers to the quiz that follows can be found in Appendix A, "Answers."

Quiz

1. Which type of interface do Internet communications usually communicate with?
2. Which type of interface would be used to communicate with Microsoft Office?
3. What are the three different types of data transmitted through Application Link Enabling (ALE)?

13

4. What are two different types of update processes?

4. What does the term middleware represent?

6. What is a CPI-C?

7. What are the four different areas of rules that govern CPI-C communications protocol?

HOUR 14

System Administration

Administration and management of your SAP R/3 system is crucial.
Administration includes the monitoring, authorizations, and administrative
functions of your system. Highlights of this hour include

- System monitoring
- Introduction of the SAP System Log
- Authorization concepts

Monitoring the System

One of the tasks of your System Administrator is to perform general system
maintenance on your SAP R/3 system. System monitoring is one of the
basic maintenance functions. In system monitoring, your System
Administrator displays a list of the active instances and their services (see
Figure 14.1).

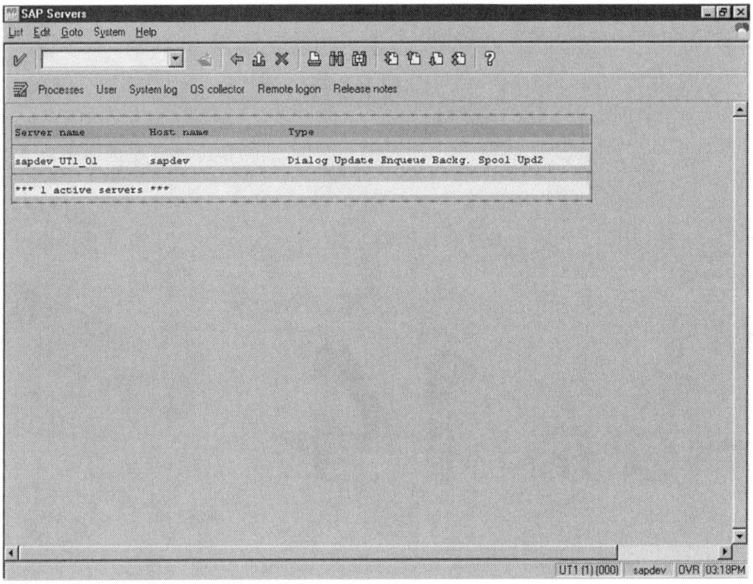

FIGURE **14.1**

The monitoring of your SAP Servers is a task performed by your Basis Administrator.

The SAP Servers System Monitoring screen can be reached by following the menu path Tools, Administration, Monitor, System Monitoring, Servers or by using the transaction code /nSM51. This screen will display all available instances in your R/3 system.

NEW TERM | An *instance* is an administrative unit, which groups together R/3 system components that provide one or more services.

SAP System Log

SAP contains a system log that records important events that occur in your R/3 system. The SAP System Log screen can be reached by following the menu path Tools, Administration, Monitor, System Log or by using the transaction code /nSM21. The selection screen that appears, which is similar to the one shown in Figure 14.2, allows the System Administrator to select certain criteria for which to display a system log.

After your System Administrator fills in this screen with dates, users, and so on, he selects the reread system log button to generate the log that will appear similar to the one shown in Figure 14.3.

FIGURE 14.2

You can specify certain system criteria to be displayed on your system log on the System Log: Local analysis screen.

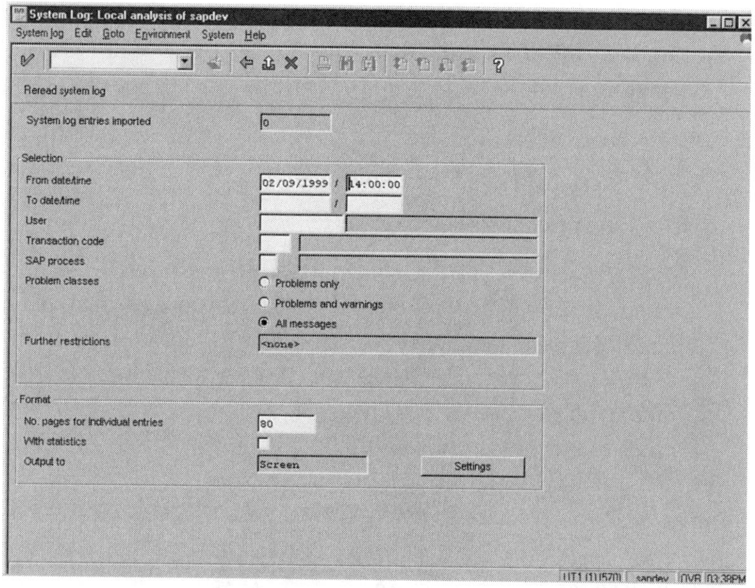

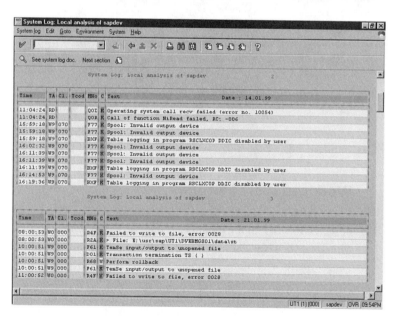

FIGURE 14.3

After specifying criteria you can display a log on The System Log Local analysis screen.

System Monitoring With CCMS

SAP's Computing Center Management System (CCMS) is a monitoring tool used for controlling, configuring, and managing your R/3 activities, database, operating systems,

14

and network functions. The CCMS main screen can be found by following the menu path Tools, CCMS or by using transaction code /nSRZL. CCMS covers the following functional areas:

- System management
- Load distribution and balancing
- Background processing

You can also use CCMS to monitor your R/3 installation. It collects and displays, in graphic form, detailed information on the response of your applications, software, operating system database, and network for your R/3 installation. It is an ideal tool to help identify problems and bottlenecks in your system and can help you project and identify future problems before they arise. An example of an SAP R/3 CCMS system monitoring screen can be found in Figure 14.4.

FIGURE 14.4

The CCMS support 24-hour unattended system management functions from within the R/3 System.

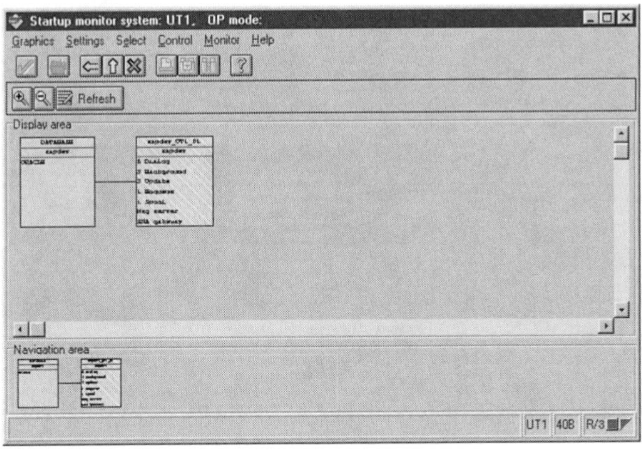

Workload Alert Monitor

With SAP R/3's release 4.0, CCMS has introduced a new alert monitor. This new tool is designed to assist in the monitoring of your R/3 system. The CCMS Workload Alert Monitor uses advanced object-oriented technology. Some highlights of the Workload Alert Monitor include:

- Comprehensive, detailed monitoring of the R/3 system, host systems, and database
- Easy-to-read status indicators (green, yellow, red) for all your R/3 components
- Alerts if a status indicator shows a problem
- Availability for analyzing reported alerts
- Alert tracking and management

To take a look at your CCMS Workload Alert Monitor, follow the menu path Tools, CCMS, Control/Monitoring, Alert Monitor (4.0), or use the transaction code /nRZ20. A Work Load Monitoring screen example appears in Figure 14.5.

FIGURE 14.5

The CCMS provides a series of graphical monitors and management utilities.

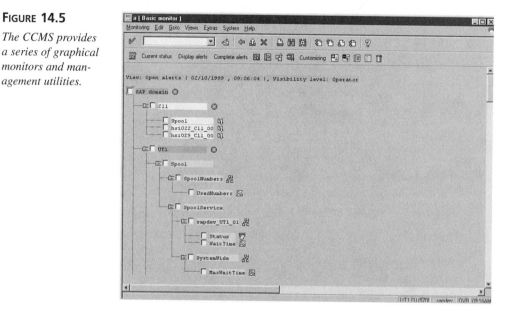

SAP Authorization Concepts

The data stored in your SAP system needs to be secure not only from outside intrusion, but also from within your organization as well. Assume that your company has the SAP Logistics and Human Resources components active on your R/3 system. You would not want individuals from your Materials Management department accessing Human Resources' confidential employee records and vice versa. SAP has designed an authorization concept based on the logical relationship between your user ID and available R/3 system authorizations with which it can be associated (see Figure 14.6).

User Authorizations

SAP user authorizations are stored in the master record of each user.

14

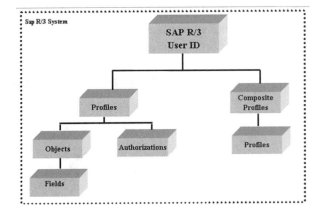

FIGURE **14.6**

The authorization structure is based on a relationship between the user ID and profiles created in R/3.

NEW TERM   The *Master Record* is a data record containing the principal employment and authorization data on a user that usually remains unchanged, including the user's system authorizations, standard printer and transaction settings.

The following are some of the fields that a user master record contains:

    User name
    Assigned client
    User password
    Company address
    User type
    Start menu
    Logon language
    Personal printer configuration
    Time zone
    Activity group
    Authorizations
    Expiration date
    Default parameter settings

Figure 14.7 shows the authorization users screen that your System Administrator would use to store your company's user master records.

FIGURE 14.7

FIGURE 14.7

The Maintain User screen stores the basic security data for your user profile.

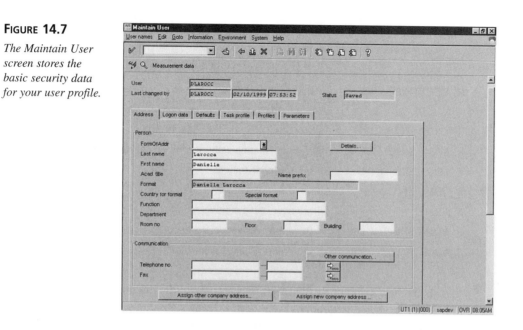

Authorization Profiles

You are assigned a user ID by your Systems Administrator. This concept was discussed in Hour 2, SAP basics. Your user ID is your user name in user master record. Your user ID refers exclusively to profiles when designating access privileges in your R/3 system. In turn, these profiles grant a certain level of system access authorities to the user. Examples of R/3 Authorization Profiles are listed in Table 14.1.

TABLE 14.1   SAP R/3 AUTHORIZATION PROFILES

R/3 Authorization Profile Name	Authorization Description
SAP_ALL	All authorizations
S-ABAP_ALL	All ABAP programming authorizations
S_ADMI_ALL	All system administration functions
SAP_NEW	All new authorization objects added during an R/3 upgrade for functions that already exist in your R/3 system
S_A.ADMIN	System operator authorization without configuration authorization
S_A.CUSTOMIZ	All customizing authorizations
S_A.DEVELOP	All development operations within the ABAP Workbench
S_A.DOKU	Authorizations for Technical Writers

14

R/3 Authorization Profile Name	Authorization Description
S_A.SHOW	Basis administration display authorization only
S_A.SYSTEM	(SAP Superuser) All authorizations for a system administrator
S_A.USER	Basis authorizations for a Basis user
S_ADDR_ALL	Authorizations for address administration
S_ADMI_SAP	Basic administration authorization except spool administration
S_ADMI_SPO_A	All spool administrations
S_ADMI_SPO_D	All spool device administration
S_ADMI_SPO_E	All extended spool administration
S_ADMI_SPO_J	All spool job administration
S_ADMI_SPO_T	All spool device type administration

You should develop your SAP user profiles specific to the job functions performed by individuals in your organization. For example, Human Resources Administrative Clerks will require access to the basic data entry screens to enter and maintain new employees' personal data; however, they might not need access to your company's organizational chart and reporting structure. Defining user profiles based on the roles individuals play in your organization is the key.

> Your SAP system contains some pre-installed standard authorization profiles. Although these might seem like a fast solution for security configuration, it is not a good idea to try to mold your organization into the standard. Creating specific profiles based on your organizations structure will serve you much better.

SAP R/3 Profile Generator

In SAP's release 3.0F, the R/3 Profile Generator was introduced. The Profile Generator was designed to assist in the implementation of your company's security and it was based on the concept of authorization objects, authorizations, and authorization profiles. Using the Profile Generator, the authorization profiles that you develop are no longer assigned to each user; rather, users are assigned to one or more activity groups.

New Term An *authorization object* is a logical entity used to group up to ten related fields that require authority checking within the system.

FIGURE 14.8

The Profile Generator automatically generates an authorization profile based on the activities contained in an activity group.

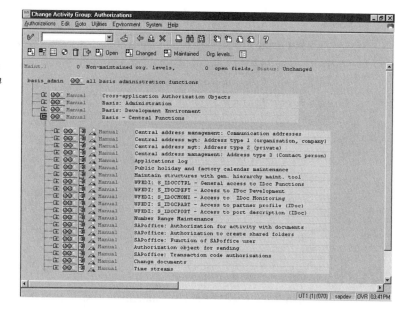

The SAP Simplification Internet homepage found at `http://207.105.30.51/simpweb/index.html` contains a document called "Authorizations Made Easy" that can assist you in the configuration of your company's security.

Summary

SAP R/3 system administration does not operate in a vacuum. It contains tools to assist you in the system administration and maintenance. Usually individuals are designated within your organization to perform the system monitoring tasks described in this hour. These individuals hold the responsibility for the day-to-day proper functioning of your R/3 system.

This hour is designed to give you an overview of some of the system administration tools used to manage your R/3 system. As a regular SAP user, you probably will not put any of the functions described here into practice at your company although it helps in your overall understanding of your SAP R/3 administration.

14

Q&A

Q **At what stage of the implementation should security issues be discussed?**

A Issues involving the security of your R/3 system should be considered throughout each stage of your implementation process. Identifying the structure of setup of your R/3 security is a serious task that should be addressed initially and throughout the project.

Q **Should you use the Profile Generator instead of manually creating user profiles?**

A There are many mixed reactions on this one. There is no clear-cut answer. Factors that should be considered when determining what tools you will utilize in implementing security should include, the size of your user population, the complexity of the data you wish to secure, and the level of security you feel your company requires.

Workshop

The workshop is designed to help you anticipate possible questions, review what you've learned, and begin thinking ahead to putting your knowledge into practice. The answers to the quiz that follows can be found in Appendix A, "Answers."

Quiz

1. Name three items that a user master record contains.

2. What is the name of the profile that gives you authorization access to everything in the SAP R/3 system?

3. What is the name of the SAP tool that helps administrators to create user profiles based on standards?

4. What does the acronym CCMS stand for?

5. What is the menu path to reach the SAP Servers System Monitoring Screen?

6. Define an SAP instance.

7. Where are user authorizations stored in your R/3 system.

Exercises

1. Take a look at your user profile by following the menu path Tools, Administration, User maintenance, Users and typing in your user name and selecting the Display (glasses) button from the application toolbar.

2. Navigate to the R/3 System Log to see what important events are happening in your R/3 system.

HOUR 15

R/3 Data Dictionary

In Hour 3, "Database Basics," you learned all about databases and how multiple tables store data that is related to data in other tables, creating a large relational database management system (RDBMS). In this hour, I take it one step further and show you the way in which SAP's database tables are arranged. You should take a quick look back first to review the database concepts in general, and then you will move forward to learn some of the more technical topics relating to the R/3 Data Dictionary.

In its simplest form, a database is composed of tables, which contain columns (called fields) and rows (called records or data), as illustrated in Figure 3.1 in Hour 3. The R/3 Dictionary describes the logical structure of the objects used in application development and shows how they are mapped to the underlying relational database in tables or views.

Highlights of this hour include

- Reviewing database structures
- Distinguishing between data elements and domains
- Taking a look at some of SAP's tables
- Learning some technical tricks with regard to the Data Dictionary

Database Tables

The SAP R/3 Dictionary contains four types of tables (or structures): cluster, transparent, pooled, and internal tables.

Pooled Tables

Pooled tables are a construct unique to SAP. Pooled tables appear to be separate distinguishable tables in SAP, but in fact, they are really all one colossal table in the R/3 system. Pooled tables contain a one-to-many relationship with other tables in the database. An example of a one-to-many relationship can be seen in Figure 15.1.

NEW TERM A *one-to-many* relationship between database tables means that a record in table A can have many matching records in table B, but a record in table B has only one matching record in table A.

FIGURE 15.1

In the R/3 Data Dictionary, pooled tables are comprised of a one-to-many database relationship.

Table A

☀ Vendor Table		
Vendor #	Vendor Name	Phone
B33124	Aspro Mechanical	555-555-9878
B33125	Innovative Travel Promotions	555-555-6321
B33126	Carol Hill Travel	555-555-7785
B33127	Wellesley Tech Supplies	555-555-1479
B33128	Acme Industries, Inc.	555-555-0036

One vendor in **Table A** can have multiple invoices in **Table B**.

Table B

☀ Invoice Table		
Invoice #	Vendor Name	Purchase Price
10002	Aspro Mechanical	$1,500.26
10003	Aspro Mechanical	$800.76
10004	Aspro Mechanical	$35.16
10005	Carol Hill Travel	$1,152.63
10006	Wellesley Tech Supplies	$100,085.21

The term one-to-many with regard to pooled tables, refers to the actual tables themselves. Just as shown in the preceding example in which the Vendor Name is the unique identifier, with pooled tables, the table name is the unique identifier. When you take a look at a pooled table in SAP, you will see a description of a table—but behind-the-scenes, as we say, it is really stored along with other pooled tables as part of a table pool.

NEW TERM A *table pool* is a database structure that contains multiple pooled tables.

Cluster Tables

R/3 cluster tables are becoming extinct in SAP. SAP is no longer creating any new cluster tables, but some remain from previous versions. Cluster tables are similar to pooled tables in that they are also based on a one-to-many relationship with other tables in the database. Like pooled tables, many cluster tables are stored together in a larger table called a table cluster.

> The specific distinction between cluster and pooled tables can get quite technical. One major distinction of note is that table pools hold a large number of tables, and table clusters hold only a handful of tables.

Internal Tables

Internal tables are a tricky concept in SAP. They are structures that have fields defined but do not store any data. They are tables used during programming that contain data only during the execution of a program. A simple way to define internal tables is to say that they are temporary storage holders of data during program execution and processing.

Transparent Tables

As explained previously, pooled tables and table clusters contain a one-to-many relationship to other tables in the database. A R/3 transparent table contains a one-to-one relationship with a table in the database. An example of a one-to-one relationship is shown in Figure 15.2.

NEW TERM A *one-to-one* relationship between database tables means that every record in table A must have only one matching record in table B.

The term one-to-one relationship with regard to transparent tables, like pooled tables, refers to the actual tables themselves. For R/3, transparent tables, the database table, and fields contain the same names as the R/3 table definition.

FIGURE 15.2

In the R/3 Data Dictionary, transparent tables are comprised of a one-to-one database relationship.

Table A

Vendor Table		
Vendor #	Vendor Name	Phone
B33124	Aspro Mechanical	555-555-9878
B33125	Innovative Travel Promotions	555-555-6321
B33126	Carol Hill Travel	555-555-7785
B33127	Wellesley Tech Supplies	555-555-1479
B33128	Acme Industries, Inc.	555-555-0036

Every vendor in **Table A** can have only one address in **Table B**.

Table B

Vendor AddressTable		
Vendor #	Vendor Address	Vendor City
B33124	111 Skillman Avenue	Brooklyn
B33125	30 Clearwater Ave	New Windsor
B33126	1400 Pearllink Drive Apt 5B	Friendly
B33127	2 Christopher Street	Maine
B33128	11793 Parkman Court	Wantagh

Table Components

The basic elements for defining data in the R/3 Data dictionary are

- Fields
- Data Elements
- Domains

The three table elements contained in the Data Dictionary are outlined in Figure 15.3.

Database Fields

Step back for one minute to review exactly what a database field is. The database field is the column that stored the data. If you had a table storing name and address information, the fields would be name, address, and phone number. Now, depending on the data that you store in each field (whether it is text or numbers, for example), the fields would require different formats. That's where data elements and domains come in.

Data Elements

R/3 data elements contain the descriptive field labels and online documentation for a database field. Fields contain data elements, and in turn, all data elements contain domains.

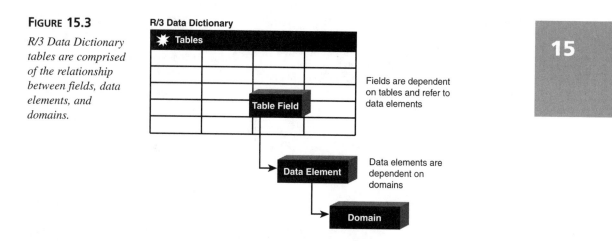

FIGURE 15.3

R/3 Data Dictionary tables are comprised of the relationship between fields, data elements, and domains.

15

R/3 Data Dictionary

Tables

Table Field

Fields are dependent on tables and refer to data elements

Data Element

Data elements are dependent on domains

Domain

NEW TERM   A data *element* provides the description for the field.

The data element description you provide for your field will be displayed on any screens that show your field. See the example in Figure 15.4.

Domains

A *domain* is an ABAP dictionary data object that describes the technical attributes of a table field, including the type, length, format, and values stored. For example, if you have a database field that contains employee salaries, the domain would specify that the field is of the type called currency and that it contains two decimal places.

Multiple fields can use the same domain. The domain I just described to store an employee's salary is also sufficient to store any currency value in your system that contains two decimal places. For example, this domain can also be used for Invoice and Purchase Order Amount fields.

FIGURE 15.4

The Data Element contains the field labels for the field.

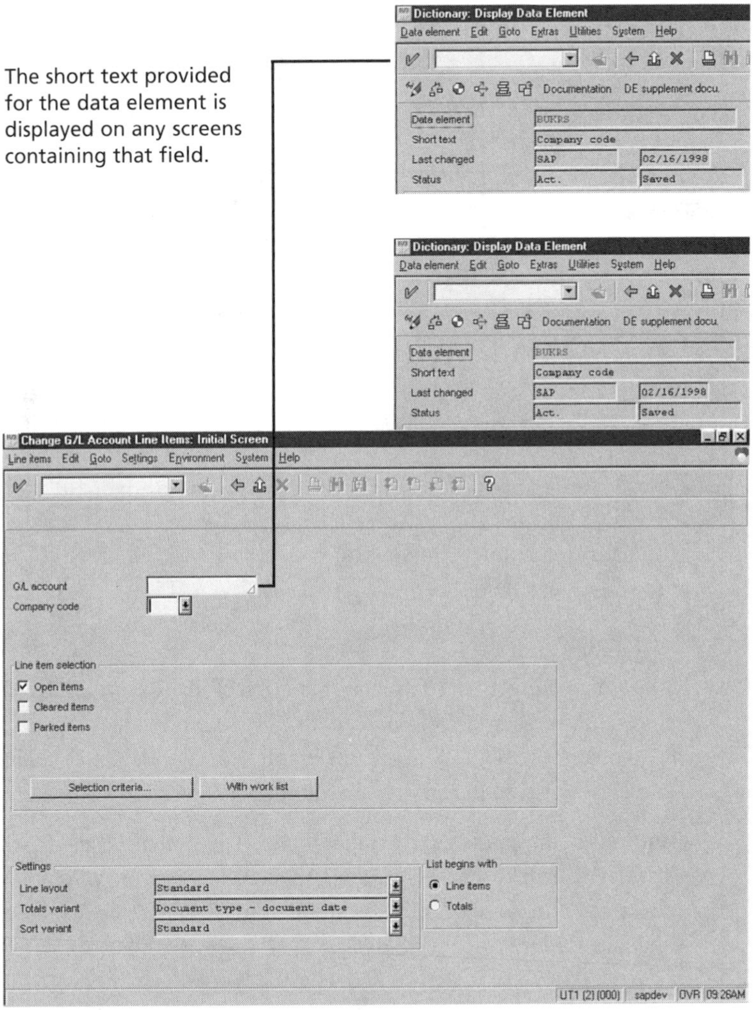

The short text provided for the data element is displayed on any screens containing that field.

Structures and Includes in the R/3 Data Dictionary

In addition to the different table types described earlier in the section "Database Tables," the R/3 Data Dictionary houses objects called *structures* and *includes*. Like tables, these objects globally define the structure of data used for the processing of programs or for transferring data between programs in the R/3 Dictionary.

Structures

A *structure* is a group of internal fields that logically belong together. Whereas data in tables is stored on the database, structures only contain data that is grouped together for a specific purpose temporarily during program runtime. A structure is like a table in the R/3 Dictionary and can be accessed from within ABAP programs. A structure does not have a corresponding object in the database.

Structures are commonly used in ABAP programming and follow the same naming conventions as transparent tables.

> You cannot have a table and a structure with the same name defined in your R/3 Data Dictionary.

Three main differences between R/3 Data Dictionary tables and structures are as follows:

1. Structures do not contain a primary key.
2. Structures do not contain any technical attributes.
3. A structure does not have an associated database table.

Includes

An R/3 structure can contain another structure, each nesting upon each other to build larger structures. Another component in the R/3 Data Dictionary is called an include, which is an example of this nesting.

This nesting of structures is used to eliminate redundancy and improve maintenance. If the same include is used in multiple structures, you only need to change it one time in order for that change to be effective in all structures that contain the include. Many of SAP's tables and structures contain includes because they are an ideal way to add fields—or a structure of fields—to a database table, so the fields would be included into the table or structure definitions, without having to manually add them.

Exploring the R/3 Data Dictionary

SAP's Data Dictionary main screen can be accessed by following the menu path Tools, ABAP Workbench and then selecting the Dictionary button from the application toolbar. The Data Dictionary can also be accessed by using the transaction code /nSE11. The main screen appears similar to the shown in Figure 15.5.

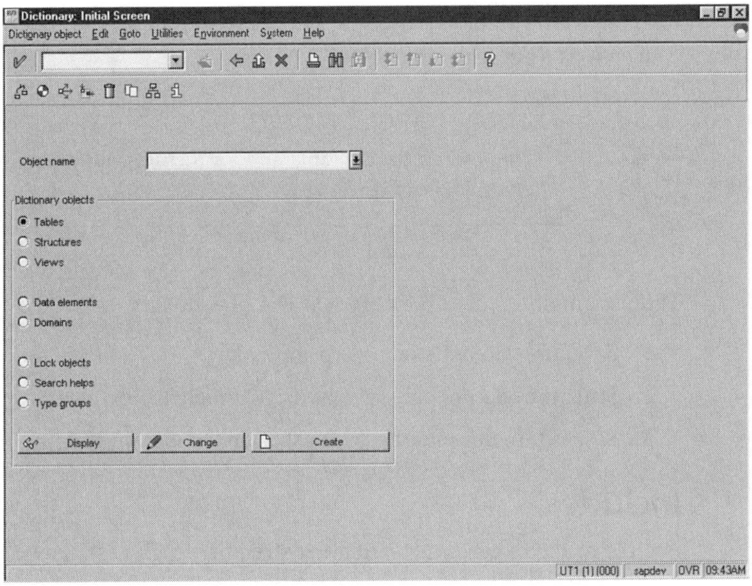

FIGURE 15.5

From the R/3 Data Dictionary Main Screen, you can display all the different tables and structures in the R/3 Data Dictionary.

The Data Dictionary is generally an area that only the technical folks dive into. I am just going to review the basics of the Data Dictionary here. To get started, look at an actual SAP table. Navigate to the SAP R/3 Data Dictionary main screen like the one shown in Figure 15.5. Type in the table name SFLIGHT and select the Display button. Your screen should appear similar to the one shown in Figure 15.6.

> The SFLIGHT table is a test table, delivered with your SAP system, that contains data for learning and testing purposes only and will not affect the performance of your SAP system.

You are viewing this table in Display Only mode. In this view, you are not permitted to make any changes. Remember from Hour 6, "Screen Basics," that fields shaded with a gray background are Display Only. If, on the R/3 Data Dictionary main screen, you typed in a table name (and modifications to the table were permitted) and selected the Change button, the screen would not appear gray and shaded, and you would be in Change mode.

15

FIGURE 15.6

You can view the attributes of an R/3 Data Dictionary Table by typing in the table name and selecting the Display button.

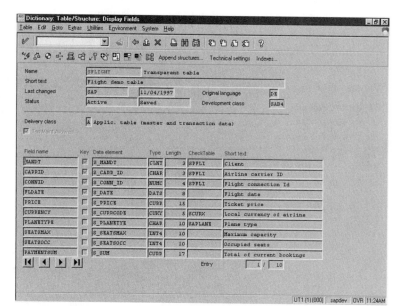

From this screen, you can see

- Table name and type
- Table description
- Modification information (Last changed by name and date)
- Table status
- Table language
- Development class
- Delivery class
- Field names
- Key
- Data element names
- Field types
- Field length
- Check tables (remember these from Hour 3?)
- Field descriptions

Data Dictionary Data Browser

The R/3 Data Dictionary contains a General Table Display function that allows you to
view the actual data in the tables. To access the General Table Display function, follow
the menu path Tools, ABAP Workbench, Overview, Data Browser or use the transaction
code /nSE16. The initial screen of the General Table Display appears similar to the one
shown in Figure 15.7.

FIGURE 15.7

*The Data Browser
allows you to view
the contents of your
R/3 Data Dictionary
tables.*

Display Table
Contents button

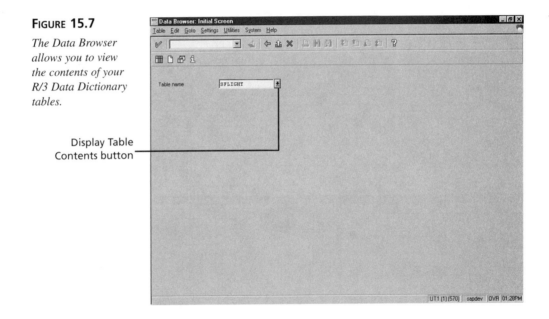

From this view, you can take a look at the data in your tables. Navigate to the general
Table Display screen, type in your SFLIGHT table name, and select the Display Table
Contents button (shown in Figure 15.7) from the application toolbar.

After selecting the Display Table Contents button, you will be presented with the Data
Browser: Table SFLIGHT Selection Screen like the one shown in Figure 15.8.

Selection Screens

The concept of selection screens is an important one. Whatever module you are processing in, you will be presented with SAP selection screens. Selection screens give you an
opportunity to specify certain criteria. For an example, take a look at the SFLIGHT table.
The selection screen gives you a chance to get more specific about what data you want to
see from the SFLIGHT table.

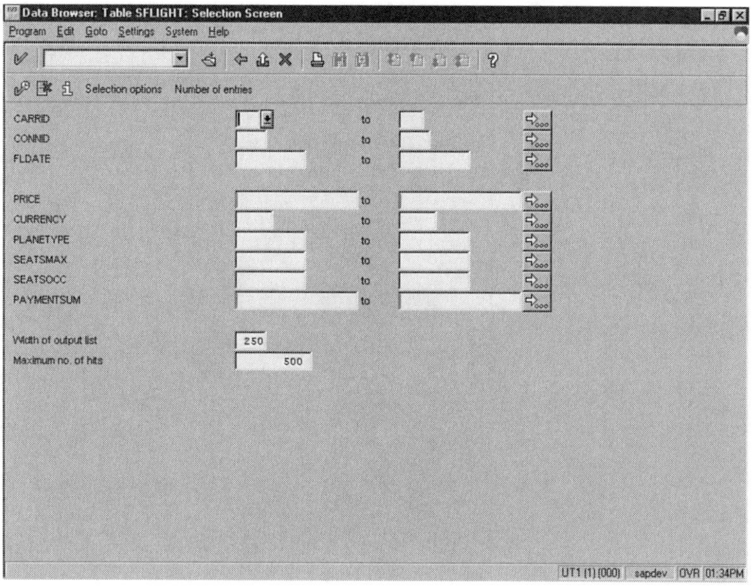

FIGURE 15.8

A Selection screen will appear after the execution of almost every program in SAP.

The first thing you will notice about the selection screen is that it contains all the fields that your table contains (with the exception of the MANDT field, which I cover in a few minutes). First, take a look at the table without any special criteria defined. Do not fill in any fields on your selection screen and select the execute button (green checkmark with the clock) from the application toolbar.

> If you are not sure if the button you want to select is the correct one, place your cursor just under the button and the description of its function will appear.

In this view, you can see all the records in the SFLIGHT table (see Figure 15.9).

In my example, the SFLIGHT table contains five records (yours might contain a different number of records). Take a look at the FLDATE (flight date) column. It should appear similar to the one in Figure 15.9. It lists the five records, two of which contain the date 2/28/1995.

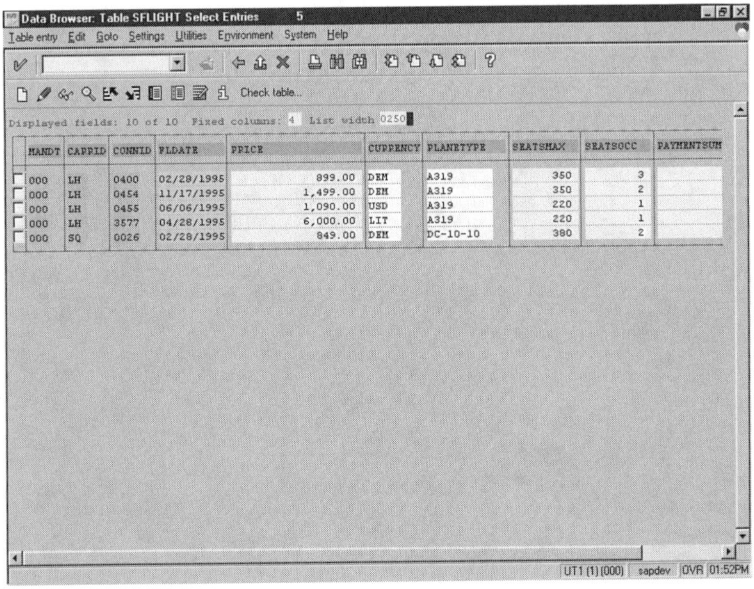

FIGURE **15.9**

*R/3 Table SFLIGHT
output will appear in
a colored list format.*

You learned that you can use the SFLIGHT selection screen to specify what database records you want to see, so give it a try. Use your green back arrow from the menu bar to return to the selection screen, which should appear like the one shown in Figure 15.8. This time, place your cursor inside the FLDATE field and enter the date 02/28/1995 (see Figure 15.10). Keep in mind you can also select the possible entries help button in the FLDATE field to access the calendar control, where you can use your mouse to select the date instead of typing it in.

After typing in your criteria (an FLDATE of 02/28/1995), select the Execute button from the application toolbar to yield only the records that you have specified on your selection screen (see Figure 15.11).

The selection screen is a great tool for helping you to pinpoint only the data that you are interested in. There is one other feature I want you to take a look at on your selection screen. Use the green back arrow to return to the selection screen.

On your selection screen, you can also specify a range of values to be included in your output. Say that you want to include all records that are within the dates of 02/28/1995 and 04/28/1995. You already have the starting point of your range filled in, as shown in Figure 15.11. Now you need to enter the ending value of the range. Place your cursor (or use the possible entries help calendar control) in the box next to the word To for the FLDATE field and type in the ending value date, 04/28/1995 (see Figure 15.12).

FIGURE 15.10

Selection screens are a useful way to specify output criteria in SAP.

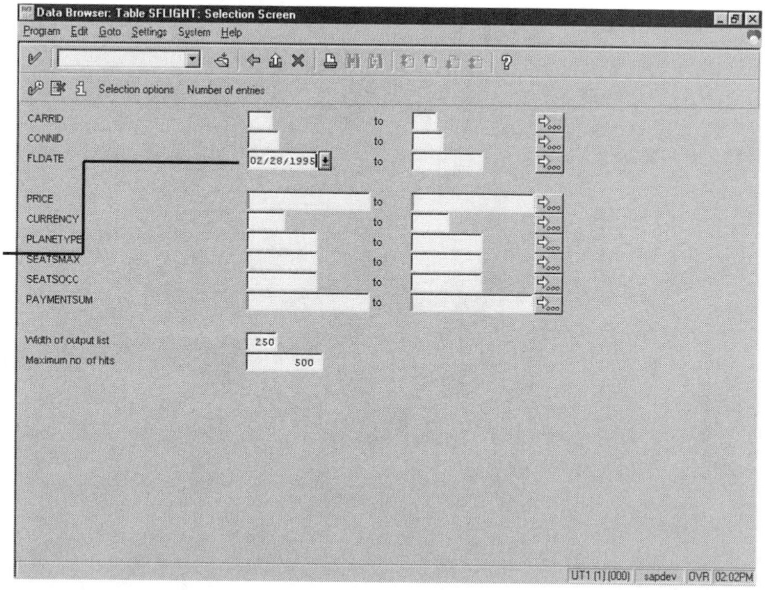

Fill in your selection criteria on the selection screen.

FIGURE 15.11

The Data browser will list your table contents based on the entries made in the selection screen.

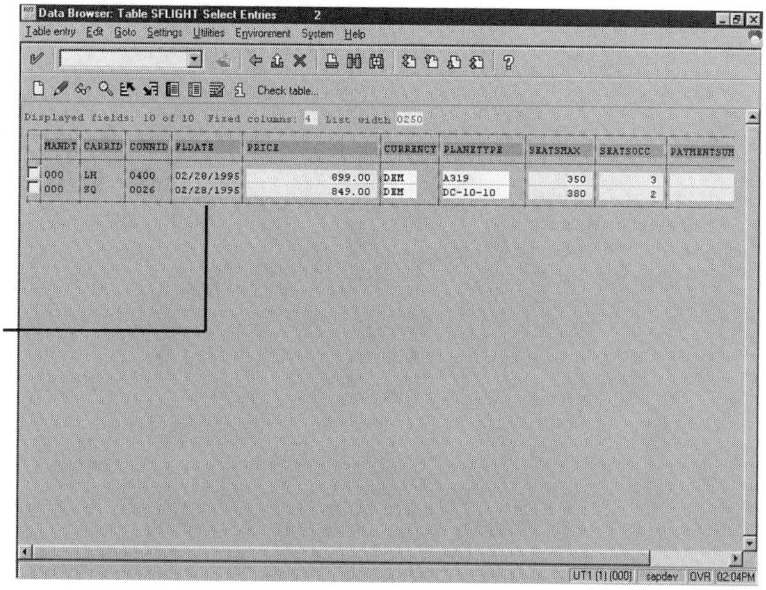

Using the selection screen, I have specified which data I want to see from my database table.

The output will now reflect the selection criteria (see Figure 15.13).

You can practice using selection screens on the SAP pre-delivered test tables: SFLIGHT, SBOOK, and SPFLI.

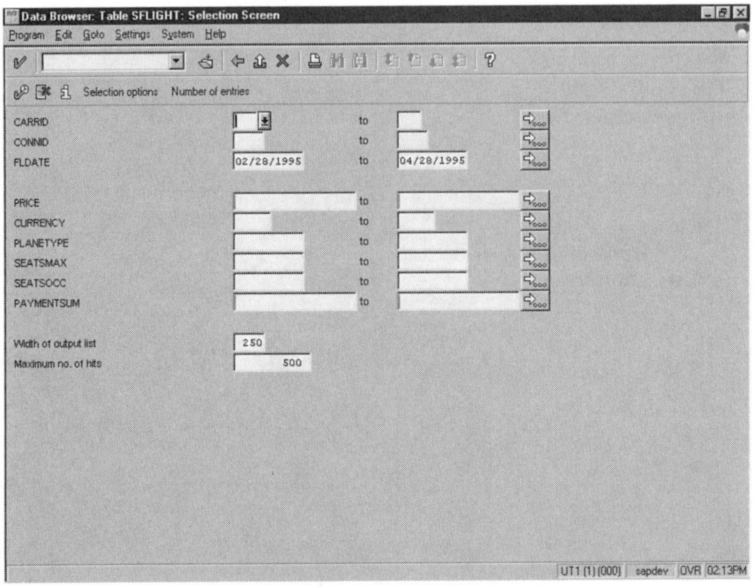

FIGURE 15.12

A range can also be entered to specify output criteria using a selection screen.

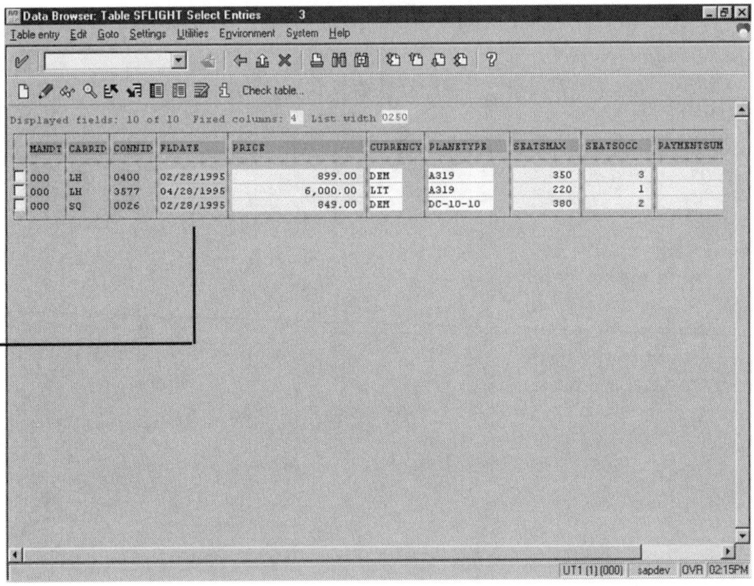

FIGURE 15.13

R/3 SFLIGHT output based on selection range.

Output contains only those records that you specified in your range on the selection screen.

> If for some reason your system does not contain the test tables, you can per-
> form these exercises on real tables (LFA1, for example). But always be care-
> ful when working with real SAP objects and obtain permission from your
> system administrator before making any changes or modifications.

Client Dependence and Independence

As you know, your SAP system can have multiple environments in which you can store
data called *clients*. Clients refer to separate logical entities within your SAP system.
These specifically self-contained units within R/3 contain separate master records and
their own set of tables. In your R/3 database, some tables are client specific, and some
tables can be seen in all clients.

Client-Independent Data

Some tables in your system—for example, tables that store SAP error codes and messages—are the same in all your SAP clients. The data in these types of tables are the
same no matter what client you are logged in to. These types of tables are called *client-
independent tables*.

Client-Dependent Data

Many of the tables that store your master data and your configuration data are unique to
each client. For example, your test client might contain fictional vendors and purchase
orders in your Vendor Master table (LFA1) wherein your real production client would
store your actual data. Data that is specific to a particular client is called *client-dependent
data*.

R/3 database tables that are client dependent always contain a MANDT field. The
MANDT field stores the client number that the data is specific to. When you took a look
at the SFLIGHT table through the Data Dictionary view back in Figure 15.6, the first
field was a MANDT field indicating that the SFLIGHT table stores client-dependent
data.

What Table and Field Is This Stored In?

In some situations, you might want to know where data that appears on your screen is
stored in the database. This is easy to do. For an example, navigate to the Logistics,
Batch Analysis Selection screen using the transaction code ⌐nMCBR. Place your cursor in
the Storage Plant field and select the F1 key on your keyboard. This launches the

selection sensitive help (covered in Hour 23, "Help Overview")and often provides a definition of the active field. On this dialog box, there is a button for Technical info (see Figure 15.14).

FIGURE **15.14**

R/3 Field Specific Help can be obtained on almost all SAP fields.

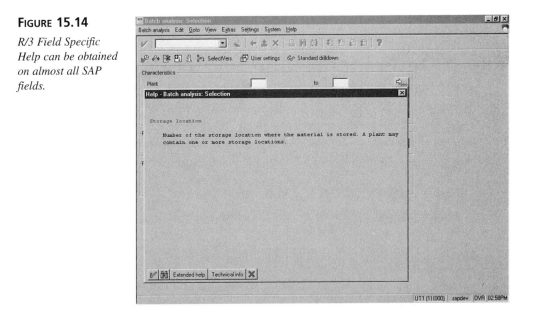

Select the technical info box to bring up a Technical Information window like the one shown in Figure 15.15. This Technical Information window contains the Table Name and Field Name of the selected field.

Summary

This hour gives you a behind-the-scenes look at the SAP R/3 Data Dictionary. You should now be quite familiar with the components of R/3 tables, including the different types of tables and structures, fields, data elements, and domains. Also, you should now be able to take a look at any database table's contents and select specific criteria that you want to see in these tables using selection screens. The basics that you have learned in this hour will be beneficial no matter which application module you are processing in.

FIGURE 15.15

R/3 Technical Information Window is available on most SAP fields.

The R/3 Data Dictionary information is contained on this screen.

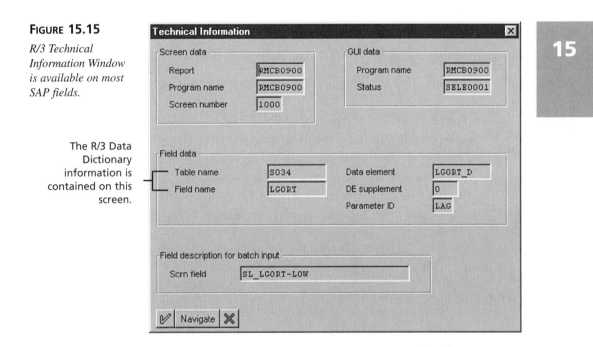

Q&A

Q What team members are generally involved with the maintenance of the R/3 Data Dictionary?

A The maintenance of the R/3 Data Dictionary is performed exclusively by skilled ABAP programmers and is generally not modified by regular system users?

Q Is there an SAP training course dedicated exclusively to the R/3 Data Dictionary?

A SAP offers a training class BC430 ABAP Workbench—R/3 Data Dictionary that is dedicated exclusively to concepts related to the R/3 Data Dictionary.

Q If you make a change to a client-independent database table while you are connected to one client, when will the effect appear in the other clients?

A Changes made to client-independent objects are reflected immediately in all clients.

Workshop

The workshop is designed to help you anticipate possible questions, review what you've learned, and begin thinking ahead to putting your knowledge into practice. The answers to the quiz that follows can be found in Appendix A, "Answers."

Quiz

1. What is the transaction code for the General Table Display function?

2. Define the term structure.

3. Name the three components for defining data in the R/3 Data Dictionary.

4. What are SAP selection screens used for?

5. Are pooled tables associated with a one-to-one relationship or a one-to many relationship?

6. What is a major distinction between cluster tables and pooled tables in the R/3 Data Dictionary?

7. What type of tables contain a one-to-one relationship with tables in the R/3 database.

Exercises

1. Use the Data Browser to view the contents of the SBOOK table.

2. Specify criteria on the selection screen for the SBOOK table to limit the number of records you retrieve.

3. Specify criteria on the selection screen using a range for the SBOOK table to limit the number of records you retrieve.

4. Use transaction code /nMB01 to navigate to the Goods receipt for Purchase Order: Initial Screen. Use the field specific help to find out the table and field name of the "storage location" field.

HOUR 16

Repository Information System

The Repository Information System is an R/3 tool designed to assist you in retrieving information on the objects in your R/3 ABAP/4 Dictionary. To continue focusing on some of the technical aspects of SAP this hour, I will discuss the features and functions of the Repository Information System, and you will learn why it is a useful tool in searching for information in your ABAP/4 Dictionary. Highlights of this hour include

- An overview of the basics of the Repository Information System
- Distinguishing the difference between Programming and Environment objects
- Learning how to search for objects in your R/3 system

R/3 Repository Information System

The R/3 Repository Information System is used as a tool to search for objects in your R/3 system. Objects that you can retrieve in the Repository

Information System include tables, views, fields, and domains (these elements are described in Hour 15, "R/3 Data Dictionary"). You can access the R/3 Repository Information System from the R/3 ABAP Workbench. The menu path to the Repository Information System is Tools, ABAP Workbench, Overview, Information system. You can also get there using transaction code /nSE84. The initial screen of the Repository Information System is shown in Figure 16.1.

FIGURE 16.1

You use the Repository Information System to search for objects in the R/3 System.

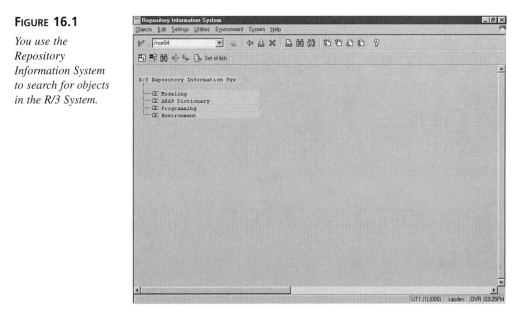

The main function of the R/3 Repository Information System is to serve as a comprehensive cross-reference tool that enables a system developer to research all R/3's development objects. In simpler terms, it serves as a technical encyclopedia for programmers developing in your R/3 system. This tool is primarily used by your technical team, and in this introduction, I will try not to get too technical.

I will start with the basics. Most developers use the R/3 Repository Information System to make requests similar to the following:

- *Search by an object's attributes*: For example, show me a list of objects that contain A but not B.

- *Research relationships between tables*: For example, show me the foreign key and check tables for table A.

- *Data Review*: For example, show me all the data records in Table A that have attribute B.

- *Modified Objects*: For example, show me all objects modified by user John Keller since last Thursday.
- *Where-used Lists*: For example, show me all objects of type A that use objects of type B, or show me all ABAP programs that use Table A.

Like many of SAP screens, the data presented appears in a tree structure. Use the menu path Edit, Expand node to get a view of what's available in the compressed tree structure. Your screen should appear similar to the one shown in Figure 16.2.

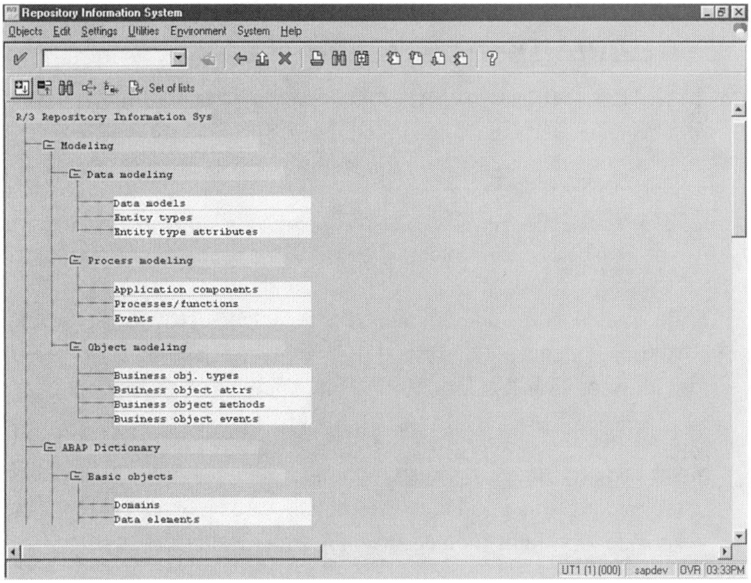

FIGURE 16.2

The Expanded Tree View of the Repository Information System screen shows each of the available nodes.

When expanded, the Repository Information System displays a hierarchical list of all the different types of objects in your R/3 system. This is divided into four categories, as follows:

- Modeling objects
- ABAP Dictionary objects
- Programming objects
- Environment objects

Modeling Objects

Modeling objects include the following three main subcategories:

- Data modeling
- Process modeling
- Object modeling

These subcategories can be further broken down. Data modeling includes data models, entity types, and entity type attributes. Process modeling can be divided into application components, processes/functions, and events. Object modeling encompasses business object types, business object attributes, business object methods, and business object events.

ABAP/4 Dictionary Objects

ABAP/4 Dictionary objects will be items that you are more familiar with from Hour 15, "R/3 Data Dictionary," and include:

- Basic objects
- Other objects
- Fields

Basic objects include domains, data elements, structures, tables, views, and type groups (these elements are described in Hour 15). These are concepts you should be familiar with from your look at the R/3 Data Dictionary.

You should also recognize some of the objects contained under the other objects subcategory including, search helps, matchcode objects, matchcode ID's, lock objects, table indexes and pooled/cluster tables (see Hour 15 for more information). The last subcategory fields include structure fields, table fields, view fields, matchcode fields, and lock object fields.

I am going to get a little technical in my description of what the programming and environment objects contain. I include their descriptions here only to be thorough(and in case a developer uses this book as a programming reference). Please do not be scared away by the technical lingo or worry about understanding most of it; it will be over shortly.

Programming Objects

Now I am starting to embark on some objects that might only be familiar to system developers and programmers. Object subcategories under the programming objects division include

- Function Builder
- Program Library
- Programming environment
- Program subobjects

The Function Builder subcategory contains your function groups and modules. The program library is a source for your programs, includes (you should recognize this term from Hour 13), dialog modules, and logical databases. I will cover logical databases in Hour 19, "ABAP Query Reporting."

The programming environment subcategory contains message classes and numbers, SET/GET parameters, transactions, and area menus. Lastly, program subobjects contain variants (which you will learn about in Hour 18, "R/3 Reporting Basics"), global data and types, subroutines, PBO and PAI modules, macros, screens, and GUI status, title and functions (which I will cover in Hour 17, "Designing Screens and Menus").

Environment Objects

The environment objects will contain the last of the technical jargon and contain the following three subcomponents:

- Development coordination
- Authorizations
- Automatic tests

The development coordination is composed of change requests and development classes, which are a group of logically related development objects. The authorizations group contains an item that you are familiar with from Hour 14, "SAP System Administration," called authorization objects, and lastly automatic tests contain Computer-Aided Testing Tool (CATT) procedures.

New Term A *change request* is an information source in the Workbench Organizer and Customizing Organizer that records and manages all changes made to Repository objects and customizing settings during a development project.

The Repository Information System Window

Now that you are familiar with what the Repository Information System is composed of, you must learn how to work with it. To follow along, begin at the main screen (transaction code /nse84) and expand all your sub nodes so that your screen appears similar to the one shown in Figure 16.2.

In Hour 2, "SAP Basics," you learned that each screen contains an application toolbar. On this screen, the application toolbar provides functionality to assist you in working with the Repository Information System (see Figure 16.3). The functions available on the application toolbar are as follows:

- *Expand Node Button*: This button serves the same function as following the menu path Edit, Expand node and expands all subnodes of the selected item.

- *Collapse Sub Tree Button*: This button serves the same function as following the menu path Edit, Collapse sub tree and collapses all subnodes of the selected item.

- *Find Button*: The Find button is probably the most useful button on your application toolbar as you will learn as the hour progresses. This button is used to search for objects in the R/3 Repository Information System. Selecting the find button serves the same function as following the menu path Objects, Find.

- *Where Used List Button*: This button serves the same function as following the menu path Objects, Where Used list and, like the Find button, is a search utility. The Where Used List function allows you to request and retrieve a hit list of locations where a specified object is used.

- *Environment Button*: You can use the environment analysis function to determine the external references of an object, in other words the referenced objects that do not belong to the object itself. This button serves the same function as following the menu path Objects, Environment.

- *Set of Lists Button*: Selecting this button brings you to the Repository Infosystem: Work list screen where you can detail selection criteria for the objects you are looking for. See Figure 16.3 for an example.

FIGURE 16.3

The Repository Information System application toolbar contains the necessary functionality for the Repository Information System.

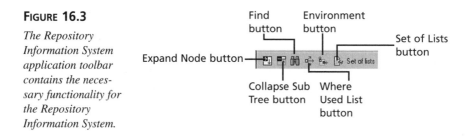

FIGURE 16.4

The Repository Infosystem: Work list screen.

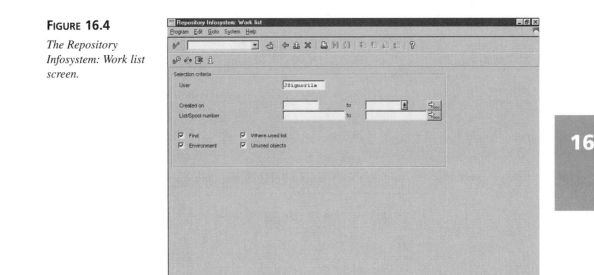

16

Searching in the R/3 Repository Information System

Now that you are familiar with the objects and features of the Repository Information System, you can put it to the test. You are going to work with something you are familiar with from Hour 15: tables and fields. If you would like to follow along, implement these steps:

1. Use Transaction code /oSE11 to create a new session (o for open) and navigate to the Dictionary initial screen.

2. On the Dictionary initial screen, type in the table name SBOOK and select the Display button.

You should now have two open SAP sessions. The first session should be on the Repository Information System main screen as shown in Figure 16.1 and the second should appear comparable to the one shown in Figure 16.5.

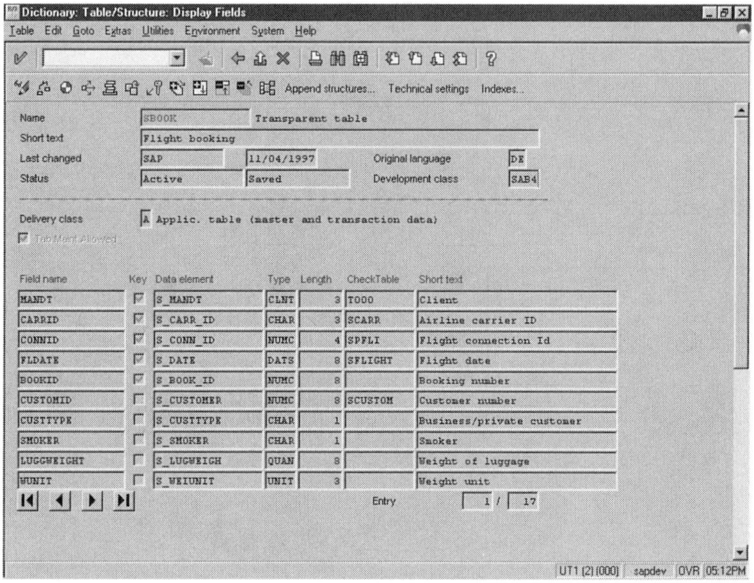

FIGURE **16.5**

Viewing table SBOOK in the R/3 Data Dictionary will give you a list of all the fields in the table.

Return to your first SAP session by selecting it from your Windows task bar or by using the keyboard combination Alt+Tab. You should now be looking at the Repository Information System main screen. We are going to try out the very basic searching capabilities. To follow along, implement these steps:

1. Place your cursor on the Table Fields subcomponent of the ABAP Dictionary node (see Figure 16.6).

2. Select the Find Button.mc

3. On this screen, enter the item that you are searching for. In the Field Name box, type in CARRID.

4. Select the Execute button.

Behind the scenes, the Repository Information System is searching through all its database tables for any fields named CARRID. Your results window should appear similar to the one shown in Figure 16.7.

FIGURE 16.6

*Selecting the Table
Fields Node in the
Repository
Information System.*

Select Table Fields

Select Find

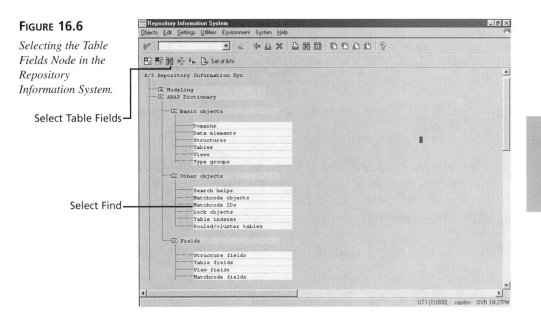

FIGURE 16.7

*The Table Fields'
results of search will
yield a list of all of
the items that
matched your search
criteria.*

The search yielded
a list of fields
matching your
search criteria.

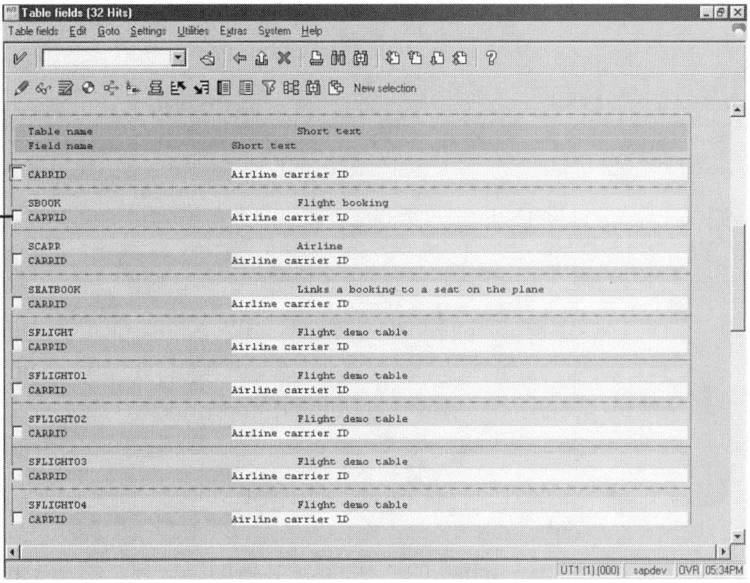

The Results screen lists all the database fields that contain the field CARRID. Remember
the second session that you created when you got started (at the beginning of this
section)? Navigate to the second SAP session by selecting it from your Windows task bar

or by using the keyboard combination Alt+Tab. This session contains the table view of the SBOOK table and should look similar to Figure 16.5. As you can see, this table contains a field CARRID. Return to your first session and see if you can find the listing for the table SBOOK field named CARRID.

Summary

Although I have only touched the surface of the capabilities of the R/3 Repository Information System, you can see that it can be a helpful tool for locating objects. Even though you might never have an occasion to require searching the R/3 system for objects, this is something that is done almost on a daily basis by programmers and developers of your R/3 system. Its introduction here is an attempt to give you a broad overview of what the R/3 Repository Information System is used for.

Q&A

QWould regular (non-technical) R/3 users use the Repository information System?

AThe Repository information System is primarily used by developers and system
     administrators as a tool for finding development objects within R/3.

Workshop

The workshop is designed to help you anticipate possible questions, review what you've learned, and begin thinking ahead to putting your knowledge into practice. The answers to the quiz that follows can be found in Appendix A, "Answers."

Quiz

1. ABAP Dictionary objects are broken down into what three components?
2. Environment objects are composed of what three subcomponents?
3. Which button on the Repository Information System application toolbar would you use to search or find?
4. What is the Find button on the menu bar used for?
5. Describe what the R/3 Repository Information System is used for.
6. Give an example of the types of queries you can request in the R/3 Repository Information System.
7. The Repository Information System displays a hierarchical list of the four different types of objects in the R/3 system: What are they?

Exercises

1. Search for field CONNID and see if you retrieve a listing for SPFLI-CONNID.
2. Search for the table SFLIGHT.

16

Hour **17**

Designing Screens and Menus

The R/3 Screen Painter is an ABAP Workbench tool designed for the purpose of creating and maintaining all elements of a screen. In simpler terms, you can create your own SAP screens using the R/3 Screen Painter. The R/3 Screen Painter is a part of the SAP R/3 Workbench and is generally used by your ABAP programmers. It is a programming tool because although the mechanics of creating a screen might be quite easy, the programming code or *flow logic* written to make the screen work is quite technical.

Creating SAP screens is a relatively simple task, but it does require the skills of an ABAP programmer. Over this hour, you will take a look at SAP's R/3 Screen Painter from a general overview perspective. Highlights in this hour include

- Introduction to the R/3 Screen Painter
- Introduction to the R/3 Menu Painter

R/3 Screen Painter

Screen Painter allows you to create user-friendly dialogs, with pushbuttons, graphical elements, and table controls. Creating screens using the R/3

Screen Painter uses *Transaction Processing*. In Transaction (or Dialog) Programming, screens are static objects not generated by ABAP code but designed graphically. The screens you design can be called from ABAP programs, and they in turn can call ABAP processing blocks from their *flow logic*. *The non-technical way to define transaction* programming is to define it as the code written to allow you to make your own transactions which are performed on SAP screens.

In German, SAP screens are sometimes referred to as *dynpros*. Dynpro is short for *dynamic program*, and means the combination of the screen and its accompanying flow logic. Creating or painting the screen is the easy part: it's the accompanying code, which makes the screen work, that requires ABAP programming skills. The creation of new screens in SAP is performed by an experienced ABAP programmer and is usually only done if you need to customize your SAP system. The four elements of a SAP screen include screen attributes, screen layouts, fields, and flow logic.

Screen Attributes

SAP screen attributes include the program the screen belongs to and the screen type. You will recall from earlier hours that you can obtain the screen attributes from any screen in the R/3 system by selecting the menu path System, Status (see Figure 17.1).

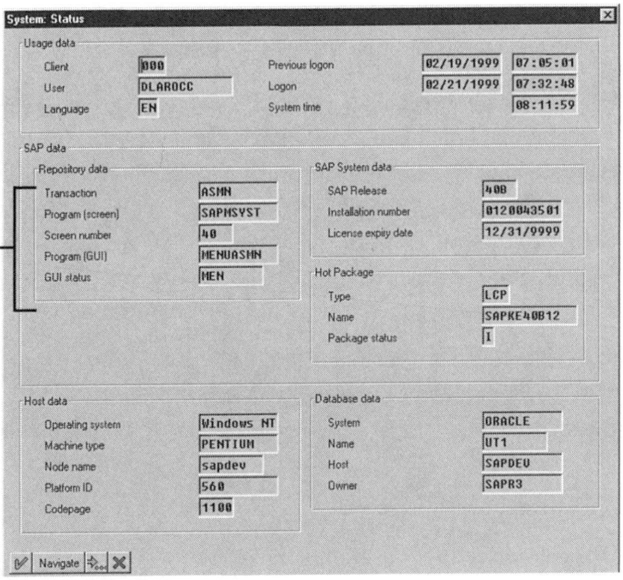

FIGURE 17.1

The System: Status screen gives you useful information about your system as well as the screen attributes for the selected screen.

Screen attributes ┘

Screen Layouts

Screen Layouts consist of the elements on your screen with which the user interacts, such as check boxes and radio buttons (see Figure 17.2). You took a look at the different types of screen elements in Hour 6, "SAP Screen Basics."

FIGURE 17.2

Screen Elements consist of the different items represented on your screen including check boxes, radio buttons, and pictures.

R/3 Screen Elements

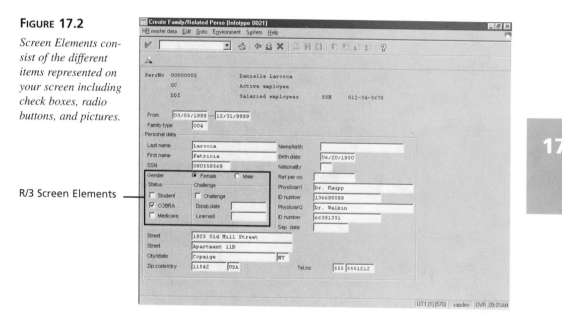

17

Fields

Fields are links to the ABAP Dictionary. Fields on your screen correspond to actual fields in your ABAP Dictionary. When painting a screen, you will use fields that are directly connected to your actual database (see Figure 17.3).

Field Validation

With Transaction Processing, screens allow you to both enter and display data. The fields on your screens can combine with the ABAP Data Dictionary to allow you to check the consistency of the data that a user has entered.

An example would be if you created a new screen for entering a new employee into your SAP Human Resources system. One of the required fields would be the employee's social security number. If you enter 123-45-123<u>B</u>, the system will check the validity of the entry and determine that the last value of B is not allowed as part of a social security number. The system would then halt and return the user to the social security input field, forcing the user to re-enter the correct value before proceeding. We took a look at this concept in Hour 3, "Database Basics."

FIGURE 17.3

Fields that you add on to your screen will be connected, via ABAP programming code, to fields in your ABAP Dictionary.

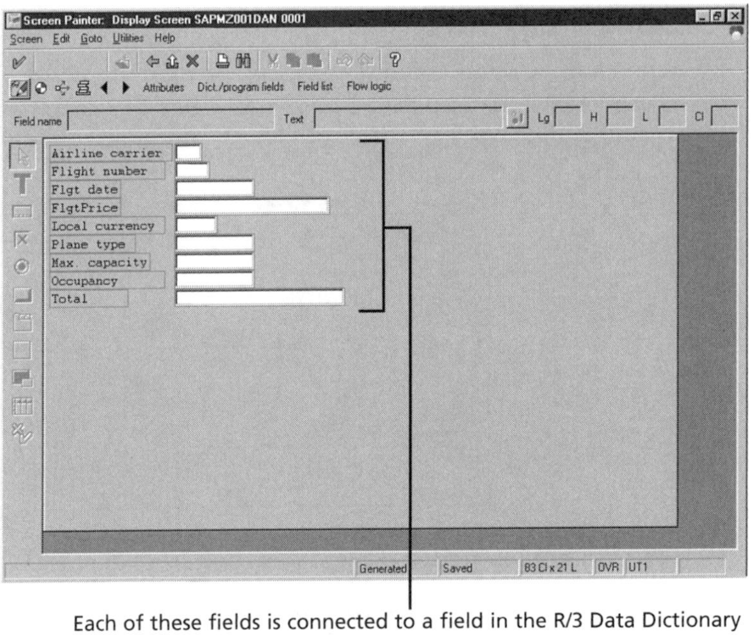

Each of these fields is connected to a field in the R/3 Data Dictionary

This behind-the-scenes integration to the ABAP Data Dictionary is already inherent in the Screen Painter and requires no special coding from you.

Flow Logic

Here is where things start getting technical. Flow logic controls the flow of your program and is the programming code that makes your screen work. Flow Logic is written in ABAP code in the Flow Logic Editor of the Screen Painter (see Figure 17.4).

These components combine to produce the architecture of the Screen Painter, as shown in Figure 17.5.

To start the Screen Painter, you can follow the menu path Tools, ABAP Workbench and then select the Screen Painter button from the application toolbar. The transaction code to get to this screen is SE51. The main screen of the R/3 Screen Painter is shown in Figure 17.6.

Selecting the different component views allows you to navigate to areas in the sequence of creating your screen. Your options consist of the Fullscreen Editor, Field list, Screen attributes, or flow logic as shown in Figure 17.6.

FIGURE 17.4

The Flow Logic Editor of the Screen Painter contains your actual screen code that makes the screen function in your SAP R/3 system.

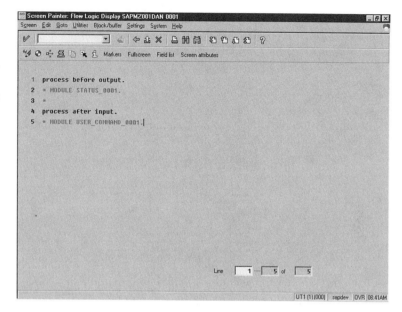

FIGURE 17.5

The screen attributes, layout, fields, and flow logic combine to produce the structure of the R/3 Screen Painter.

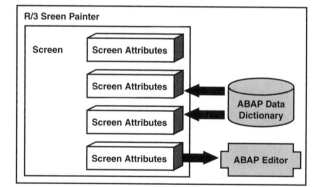

Fullscreen Editor

The Screen Painter contains the Fullscreen Editor, which you use to design your screen layout. The Fullscreen Editor works in two modes:

- Graphical Mode
- Alphanumeric Mode

FIGURE 17.6

*From the Screen
Painter: Initial
Screen, the Object
components text box
lists the different
screen component
views. Each view lets
you edit a different
aspect of a screen.*

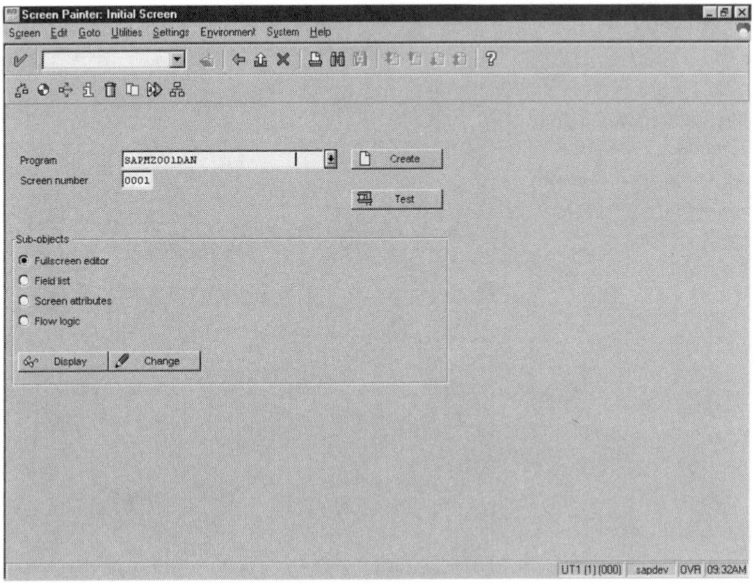

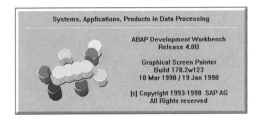

Both modes offer the same functions, but they use different interfaces. In graphical
mode, you use a drag-and-drop interface similar to a drawing tool. The graphical mode
of the R/3 Screen Painter is covered in this hour. In alphanumeric mode, you use your
keyboard and menus to design new SAP screens. Graphical mode is available only on
MS Windows 95, MS Windows NT, and UNIX/Motif platforms, and is not usually
installed with the default settings.

The graphical mode of the R/3 Screen Painter can be installed from your SAP GUI
installation disk. Ask your System Administrator for help.

Selecting the Fullscreen editor displays a splash screen similar to the one shown in
Figure 17.7 and launches the Graphical Screen Painter.

FIGURE 17.7

*Selecting the
Fullscreen Editor
component view
launches a new win-
dow before executing
the R/3 Graphical
Screen Painter.*

From Fullscreen Editor shown in Figure 17.3, you can maintain your screen's layout and graphical design.

The Field List Screen

The Field List component view of the R/3 Screen Painter is where you maintain the ABAP Dictionary or program fields for your screen (see Figure 17.8). You can access the Field List Screen by selecting it from the Screen Painter Initial Screen, as shown in Figure 17.6.

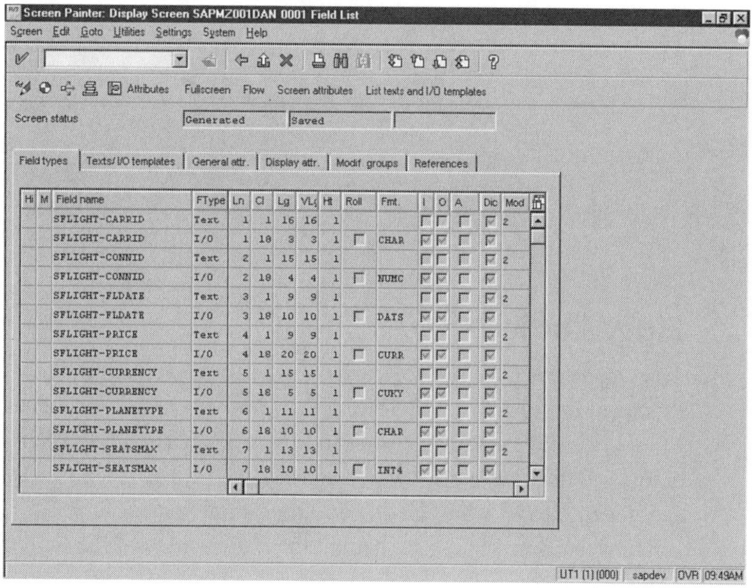

FIGURE 17.8

The Field List component view of the R/3 Screen Painter displays the field that you are using in your screen.

Screen Attributes

You can access the Screen attributes by selecting it from the Screen Painter Initial Screen, as shown in Figure 17.6. Selecting the Screen attributes is where you maintain a screen's attributes, including the name and short description of the program, as well as the screen type, status, and date of last modification (see Figure 17.9).

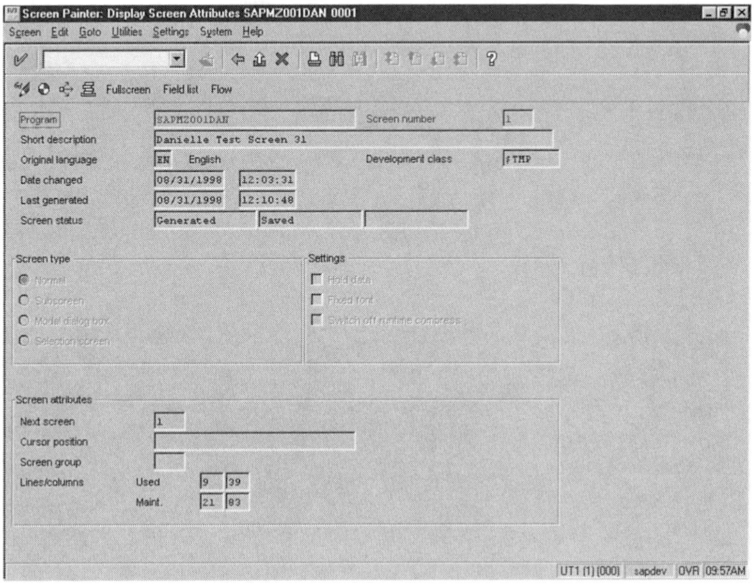

FIGURE 17.9

The Screen attributes component view of the R/3 Screen Painter displays the characteristics of your program.

Flow Logic

You can access the Flow logic view by selecting it from the Screen Painter Initial Screen, as shown in Figure 17.6. Selecting the Flow Logic view launches the R/3 Screen Painter Flow Logic Editor shown earlier in Figure 17.4. The Flow Logic Editor is where you define the flow logic of your screen. Flow logic is written in ABAP code. So that you can get an idea of what this screen programming code looks like, Figure 17.10 shows some of the flow logic code behind the main screen of the Screen Painter.

When writing the flow logic for your SAP screen, you need to establish a *static sequence of screens*—"what happens when" philosophy of how your new screen is going to function. SAP has two concepts used for this purpose:

- *PBO:* This refers to *processing before output*, and is the processing that occurs after a screen is called but before it is actually displayed on the screen.
- *PAI:* This term refers to *processing after output*, and is the processing that occurs after a screen has been displayed.

In combination, ABAP programmers use these two concepts when writing the code and sequence of their flow logic to determine how their newly created SAP screen will perform.

FIGURE 17.10

Flow logic code for every SAP R/3 screen is written in SAP's proprietary ABAP language.

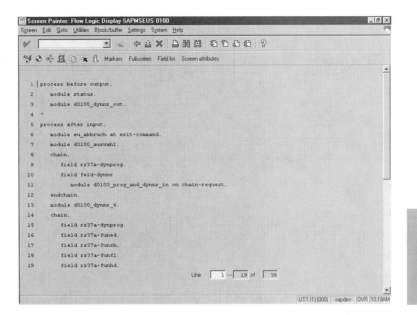

R/3 Menu Painter

The Menu Painter is another ABAP Workbench tool with which you design user interfaces for your ABAP programs. In other words, using the Menu Painter, you can create your own custom menus in SAP. Like the R/3 Screen Painter, creating your own menus requires the skills of an ABAP programmer. You will take a look at the basics here.

The Menu Painter can be accessed from the application toolbar in the ABAP Workbench or by following the menu path Tools, ABAP Workbench, Menu Painter or transaction code /nse41. The main screen of the Menu Painter is shown in Figure 17.11.

To use Menu Painter, it's crucial to understand GUI status: An instance of the *graphical user interface* (GUI), consisting of a menu bar, a standard toolbar, an application toolbar, and a function key setting, is called a GUI status.

The components of a User Interface are shown in Figure 17.12.

Two of the components of a GUI status, the Standard toolbar and the Application toolbar are covered in Hour 2, "SAP Basics." The Function Key Setting refers to the 12 functions listed atop your keyboard labeled F1–F12. The GUI status and GUI Title defines how the menu looks and performs in your R/3 program. Different GUI statuses can refer to common components, and a program can have multiple GUI statuses and titles.

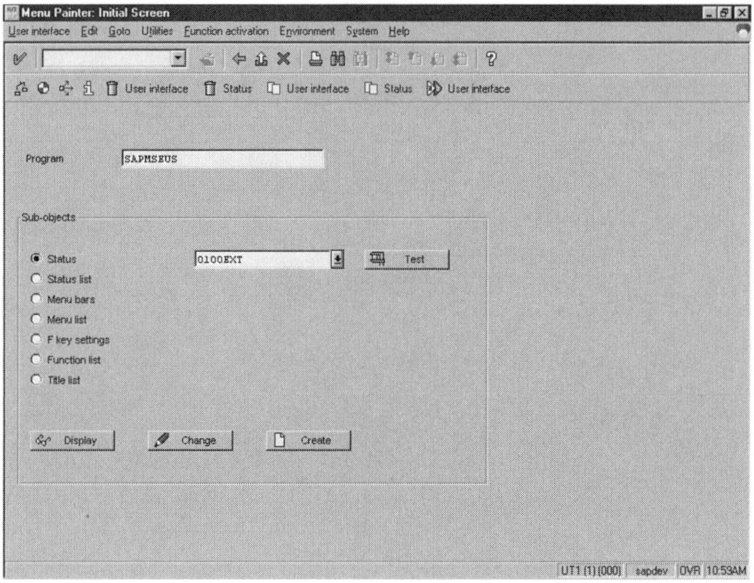

FIGURE **17.11**

The R/3 Menu Painter is used to design custom user menus and toolbars called the user interface.

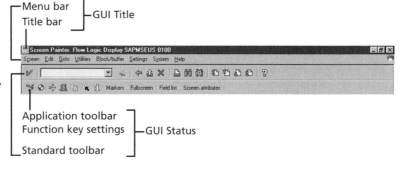

FIGURE **17.12**

The components of the GUI Title include the R/3 title bar and menu bar, and the components of the GUI status include the standard toolbar, application toolbar, and function key settings.

Menu Painter Object Components

From the main R/3 Menu painter screen, you can select the following options to modify:

- Status
- Status list
- Menu bars

- Menu list
- F key settings
- Function list
- Title list

Status

Selecting the Status sub-object from the main R/3 Menu Painter screen brings you to the Display Status screen. This tool is a little easier to work with than the Graphical Screen Painter, but it still requires ABAP programming skills. From the Display Status screen, you program the functions for the different items in the menu bar, Application toolbar, Standard toolbar, and function keys; see Figure 17.13 for an example.

FIGURE 17.13

The GUI status, menu bar, applica- tion toolbar, standard toolbar, and function keys can be modified by selecting the Status sub object from the main R/3 menu Painter window.

GUI Status

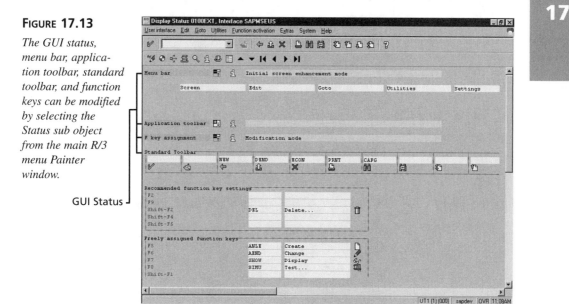

Status List

Selecting the Status list sub-object from the main R/3 Menu Painter screen brings you to the Display Status screen, listing all the screens contained in your program (see Figure 17.14).

FIGURE 17.14

The Status list screen displays a list of the statuses used in your program.

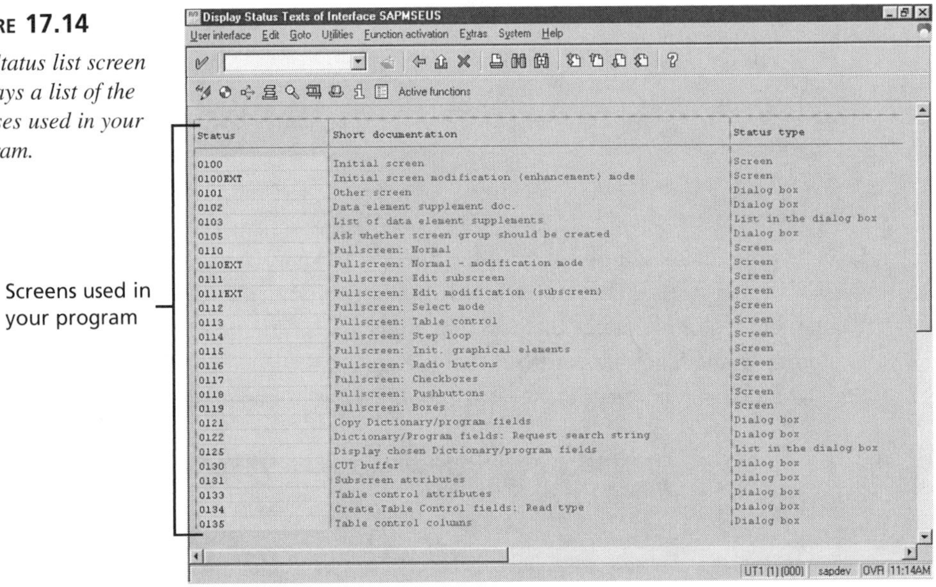

Screens used in your program

Menu Bars

Selecting the Menu bars sub-object from the main R/3 Menu Painter screen brings you to the Display Menu bars screen. This screen displays a list of menu bars sorted by status (see Figure 17.15).

FIGURE 17.15

The Display Menu bar's screen displays a list of menu bars.

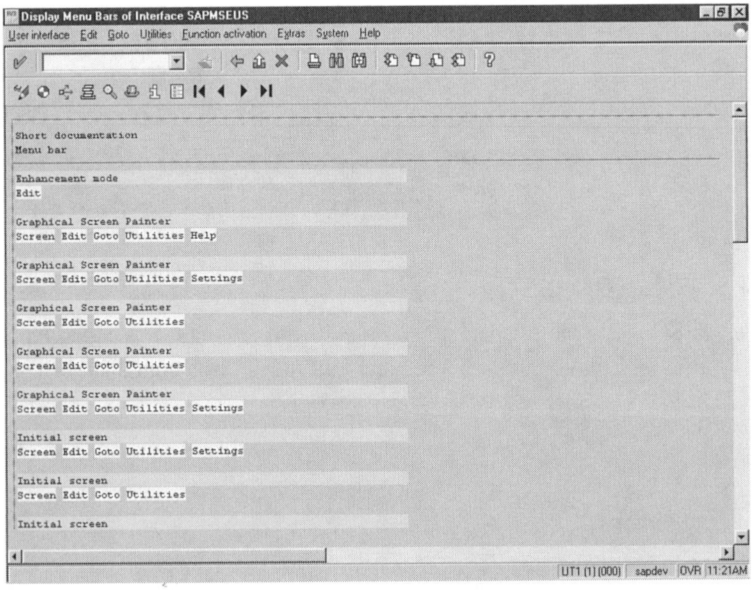

Menu List

Selecting the Menu list sub-object from the main R/3 Menu Painter screen brings you to the Display Menu lists screen. This screen displays a list of menus (see Figure 17.16).

FIGURE 17.16

*The Display Menu
list screen shows a
list of menus.*

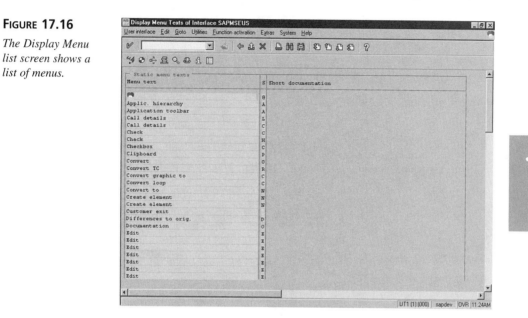

F Key Settings

Selecting the F key settings sub-object from the main R/3 Menu Painter screen brings you to the Display Function key settings screen. This screen displays a list of function key settings for your program (see Figure 17.17).

Function List

Selecting the Function list sub-object from the main R/3 Menu Painter screen brings you to the Display Function lists screen. This screen displays a list of program functions. See Figure 17.18.

Title List

The last sub-object from the main R/3 Menu Painter, Title list, brings you to the Display Title lists screen. This screen displays a list of the words that appear in the title bar for each of the screens in your program (see Figure 17.19).

FIGURE 17.17

The Display Function Key Settings screen displays a list of function key settings used for your program.

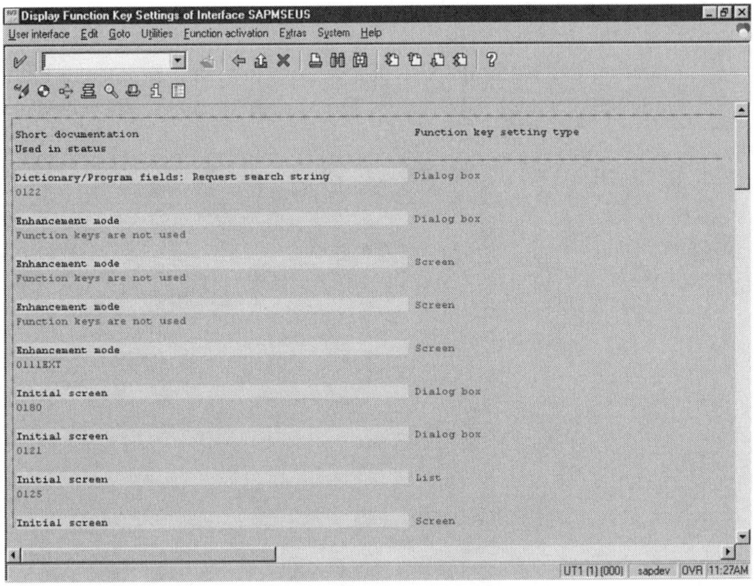

FIGURE 17.18

The Display Function list screen displays a list of program functions.

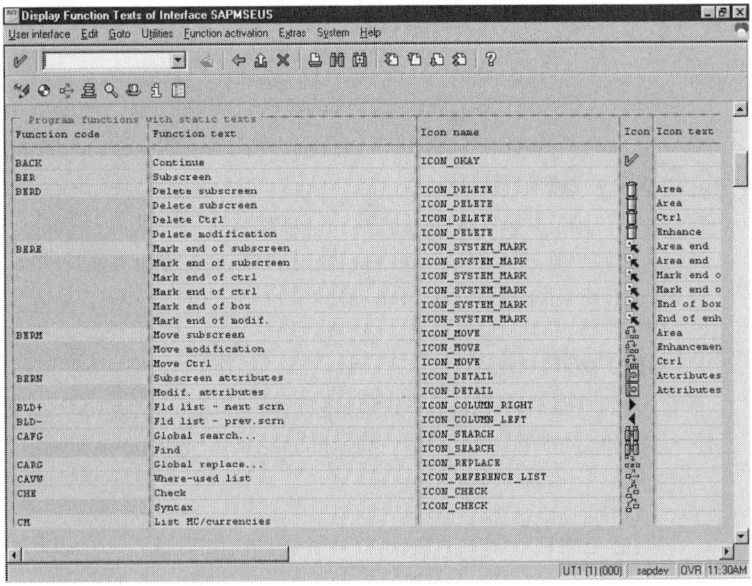

FIGURE 17.19

The Display Title list screen displays a list of your programs' titles.

Title number	Title
100	Screen Painter: Initial Screen
101	Get Other Screen
102	Data Element Supplement
103	Choose Data Element Supplement
105	Create Screen Group
110	Screen Painter: & Fullscreen & &
111	Screen Painter: & & &
112	Screen Painter: & Select Screen & &
113	Screen Painter: & Table Control &
114	Screen Painter: & Loop Definition
115	Screen Painter: & Graph. Elements, Screen & &
116	Screen Painter: & Radio Buttons, Screen & &
117	Screen Painter: & Checkboxes, Screen & &
118	Screen Painter: & Pushbuttons, Screen & &
119	Screen Painter: & Box, Screen & &
120	Screen Painter: & Dict. Fields, Screen & &
121	& Dictionary/Program Fields
122	Find Field Names
125	Display Selected Dictionary/Program Fields
130	Temporary Storage
131	Screen Element Attributes
133	Screen Element Attributes
134	Create Table Control Field
135	Table Control &: Column Fields
136	Tab Control &: Elements
138	Pushbuttons: Functions

Summary

This hour you have taken a look at the R/3 Screen Painter and Menu Painter. These ABAP tools are very useful in designing your own screens and menus. I have covered the basics here and you have a good understanding of how the different functions are designed. However, you will need to enlist the assistance of an ABAP programmer in order to create your own screens and menus.

Q&A

Q In what instances would you need to create your own SAP screens?

A Creating your own SAP screens is usually only done when you need to customize or enhance the functionality of your SAP system. Although SAP provides you with the tools to customize the system, they always recommend that you only customize the system when absolutely necessary.

Q Is the Alphanumeric mode of the Screen Painter still used?

A The Alphanumeric mode of the Screen Painter used to be the only tool available for customizing screens in earlier versions of R/3. Since the introduction of the easy drag-and-drop interface of the Graphical mode of the Screen Painter, its use has dropped significantly.

Workshop

The workshop is designed to help you anticipate possible questions, review what you've learned, and begin thinking ahead to putting your knowledge into practice. The answers to the quiz that follows can be found in Appendix A, "Answers."

Quiz

1. What are the two different modes of the R/3 Screen Painter?

2. What are dynpros?

3. Give two example of items considered as part of screen elements.

4. The programming code behind your screen that makes it work is called what?

5. On which screen do you maintain the ABAP Dictionary fields for your screen?

6. What are the four components of a GUI Status in the R/3 Menu Painter?

7. How could you view a list of all the title bars for each of the screens contained in your program?

Exercises

1. Locate the name of the program for the main SAP screen. (Hint: Refer to Figure 17.1).

2. Navigate to the R/3 Screen Painter Initial Screen and type in the program name for the main SAP screen. Take a look (display only) at each of the four R/3 components: Fullscreen editor, Fields list, Screen attributes, and Flow logic. (Refer to Figure 17.6 for help.)

PART V
Reporting in SAP

Hour

Hour **18**

R/3 Reporting Basics

As we have seen in earlier chapters, SAP has the ability to effectively manage all your company's data. Although this data is stored in the SAP system and can be presented to you on SAP screens, you might still want to produce output from the system in the form of SAP reports. You can use reports to extract and manipulate the data from your SAP database. This hour you will take a look at some basic reporting concepts in SAP R/3. Highlights in this hour include

- Overview of reporting options in SAP
- Introduction to variants
- Review of background processing

Reporting Tools

Several different methods that can be used to generate reports in SAP are as follows:

- ABAP List Processing (ABAP programming)
- ABAP Query Reporting

- Ad Hoc Query Reporting (HR Module)
- Structural Graphics Reporting (HR Module)
- Executive Information System
- SAP Information System (Report Trees)

> In newer versions of SAP, there is also a Web reporting tree that provides you with intranet access to canned R/3 reports.

This hour I will cover the basics of reporting concepts and introduce the SAP Information System, which contains the General Report Selection tree. The other reporting options are discussed briefly. The ABAP Query and the Ad Hoc Query are summarized in this hour, but are fully addressed in Hour 19, "ABAP Query Reporting," and Hour 20, "Ad Hoc Query Reporting (HR Module)," respectively.

ABAP List Processing (ABAP Programming)

Custom reports can be created in SAP by writing ABAP code to generate lists. This method is called *List Processing*. Using List Processing, ABAP programmers write statements in the ABAP Editor that generates reports. Writing reports using ABAP List Processing is reserved for your technical team.

This option might only be necessary if you require a report that the canned reports, or reports created through the ABAP Query, could not satisfy. This option is also used for creating interface files. For example, if you need your SAP R/3 system to be connected to other external systems like an outside third-party product, you would need to write a report using ABAP List Processing to create the output to be transmitted to that system.

ABAP Query

Custom reports can be created in SAP by creating queries using ABAP Query. ABAP queries are based on Logical Databases, Functional Areas, and User Groups. Creating reports using ABAP Query is covered in Hour 19.

Ad Hoc Query (HR Module)

The Ad Hoc Query is a reporting tool used in the Human Resources component. Like the ABAP Query tool, it is based on Logical databases, Functional Areas, and User Groups. Ad Hoc Queries are used as a one-time reference for posing queries to your SAP database to retrieve information. Creating reports using ABAP Query is covered in Hour 20.

Structural Graphics

Structural Graphics is an additional Human Resources tool used in the Organizational Management application component. Structural Graphics allows you to display and edit the structures and objects in your organizational plan and to select reports directly from the graphical structure for an object.

Executive Information System

The Executive Information System is just as its name sounds: a reporting tool for executives. The tool is designed for users who require quick access to information especially prepared for their use. Using the Executive Information System Report portfolio, you call up a hierarchy graphic defined for access to your own report portfolio. You can also use Report selection, in which you call up either the general report tree of drill-down reports or your own custom tree. Or you can use the Report portfolio report, in which you enter the name of an individual report portfolio report and then display it.

The Executive Information System provides you with information about all the factors that influence the business activities within your company. It combines relevant data from external and internal sources, providing you with the necessary current data that can then be analyzed quickly.

SAP Information System (Report Trees)

Most of the reports you need are available in the module in which you are processing. Each module contains its own Information System that contains the reports specific to that module. In earlier hours, you reviewed some of these module-specific Information Systems. An example would be the Human Resources Information System that was reviewed in Hour 11, "SAP Human Resources." However, all SAP canned reports can be found in the R/3 Information System.

R/3 General Report Selection

SAP has many tools in the R/3 system used to extract data in the form of reports. We are first going to take a look at the basics of SAP's reporting capabilities. From the main SAP screen, using the menu path Information Systems, General Report Selection, or transaction code /nSART, navigate to the SAP main reporting screen shown in Figure 18.1.

18

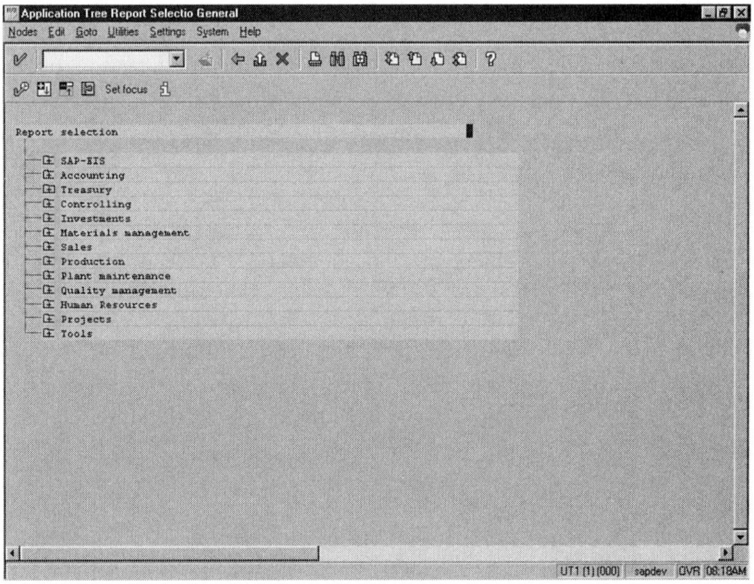

FIGURE **18.1**

*SAP's General
Report Selection
Screen allows users
to access business
information in R/3 by
starting reports and
displaying lists in
report trees.*

Application Tree Report Selectio General

Nodes Edit Goto Utilities Settings System Help

Report selection

- SAP-EIS
- Accounting
- Treasury
- Controlling
- Investments
- Materials management
- Sales
- Production
- Plant maintenance
- Quality management
- Human Resources
- Projects
- Tools

UT1 (1) (000)   sapdev   OVR 08:18AM

Take a good look at the title bar in Figure 18.1. Notice anything amiss? The word *Selection* is misspelled as *Selectio*. This is not rare: You will find many spelling mistakes in SAP, and a few of them are included in screen prints throughout this book.

SAP is written in German and then translated to each of the different languages. Throughout this process, many errors occur. Another interesting thing you will find is that some things appear on your screen in German regardless of the login language. This is especially prevalent in the SAP Help Online Documentation.

SAP refers to this main screen as the General Report Selection screen, which will display a series of report trees.

NEW TERM   *Report trees* are hierarchical structures that can contain standard SAP reports and your company's custom reports, as well as lists generated by starting reports.

General Report Selection is structured as a hierarchy containing the following four levels (see Figure 18.2):

- The top level contains the individual R/3 System applications.
- The second level contains the work areas of each application.
- The third level contains the objects of each work area.

- The fourth level generally contains the reports and saved lists available for each object.

FIGURE 18.2

SAP's General Report Selection is structured as a four-level hierarchy.

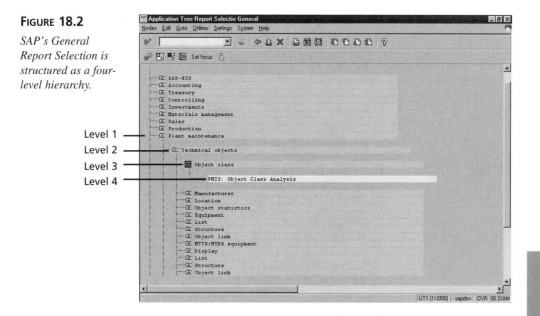

Your SAP R/3 system comes with predelivered (canned) reports for all its applications. You can modify the structure of the general reporting structure according to your company's specific needs. For example, if you are installing only the R/3 Financials component, you might want to remove the Logistics and Human Resources reports from your General Report Selection screen.

The customizing of the General Report Selection reporting tree is accomplished using the Implementation Guide (IMG). The Implementation Guide is discussed in Hour 9, "The SAP Implementation Guide (IMG)." Reports specific to a particular R/3 module can be located through the module's Information System. Module specific Information Systems were covered in Hour 10, "SAP Financials," Hour 11, "SAP Human Resources," and Hour 12, "SAP Logistics."

Executing Reports

Reports can be executed directly from this General Report Selection screen (see Figure 18.1). Depending on the modules currently installed on your system, different reports will be available to you. To execute a sample report, drill down in the report tree as follows:

1. Expand the Human Resources node

2. Expand the Payroll accounting node

3. Expand the Payroll accounting—USA node

4. Expand the Payday node

5. Expand the Payday calendar node

Your screen should appear similar to the one shown in Figure 18.3.

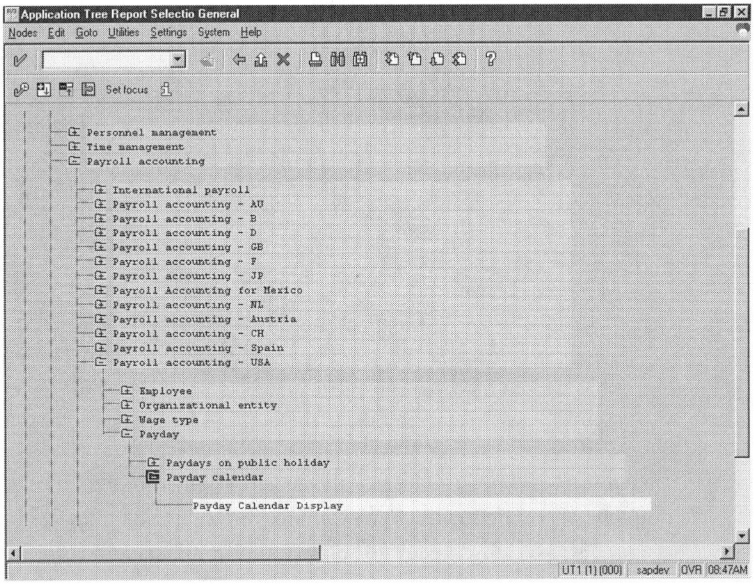

FIGURE **18.3**

SAP's General
Report Selection
screen drills down to
the Payday Calendar
report.

To execute the Payday Calendar Display report, select the report and then select the Execute button from the application toolbar, or double-click the report name. This launches the selection screen for the report.

Selection screens are used on almost all SAP reports to further clarify what output you are seeking. On the selection screen for the Payday Calendar Display report, shown in Figure 18.4, you are asked to create identifying markers for your payroll calendar.

For this example, you do not need to modify any of the data indicated on this selection screen. To execute the report, select the Execute button from the toolbar. The report will execute and should appear similar to the one shown in Figure 18.5.

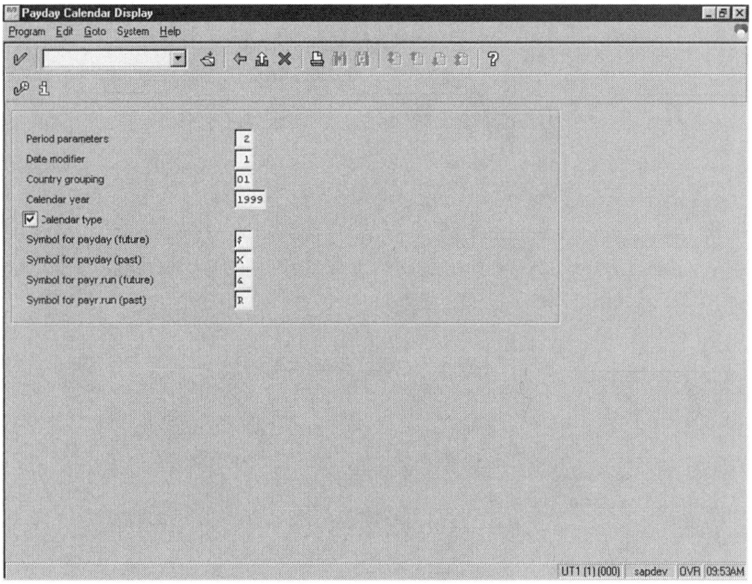

FIGURE 18.4

SAP's Payday Calendar Display selection screen allows you to specify identifying markers for different elements of the Payday Calendar.

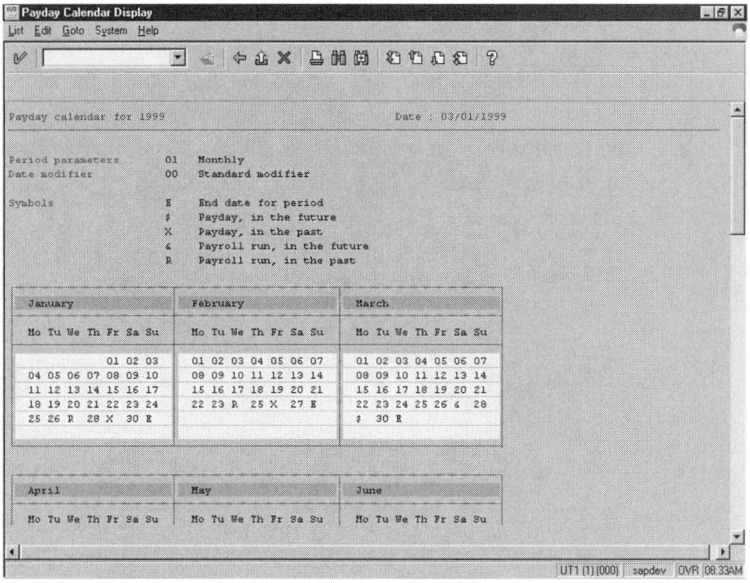

Payday Calendar Display
Program Edit Goto System Help

Period parameters	2
Date modifier	1
Country grouping	01
Calendar year	1999
☑ Calendar type	
Symbol for payday (future)	f
Symbol for payday (past)	x
Symbol for payr.run (future)	<
Symbol for payr.run (past)	R

FIGURE 18.5

SAP's Payday Calendar Display report is an example of a report executed from the General Report Selection Tree.

18

Payday Calendar Display
List Edit Goto System Help

Payday calendar for 1999   Date : 03/01/1999

Period parameters   01   Monthly
Date modifier   00   Standard modifier

Symbols   E   End date for period
                       $ Payday, in the future
                       X   Payday, in the past
                       <   Payroll run, in the future
                       R   Payroll run, in the past

January							February							March						
Mo Tu We Th Fr Sa Su							Mo Tu We Th Fr Sa Su							Mo Tu We Th Fr Sa Su						
01 02 03							01 02 03 04 05 06 07							01 02 03 04 05 06 07						
04 05 06 07 08 09 10							08 09 10 11 12 13 14							08 09 10 11 12 13 14						
11 12 13 14 15 16 17							15 16 17 18 19 20 21							15 16 17 18 19 20 21						
18 19 20 21 22 23 24							22 23 R 25 X 27 E							22 23 24 25 26 < 28						
25 26 R 28 X 30 E														$ 30 E						

| April | | | | | | | May | | | | | | | June | | | | | | |
| Mo Tu We Th Fr Sa Su | | | | | | | Mo Tu We Th Fr Sa Su | | | | | | | Mo Tu We Th Fr Sa Su | | | | | | |

Depending on your system's configuration, different reports will be available to you. For example, if you have not configured the Human Resources module, you might not be able to execute all the Human Resources reports.

Take a minute to practice executing different reports from the General Report Selection Tree.

Report Attributes

To take a look at the attributes of a particular report in the General Report Selection Tree, select the report once using your mouse and then follow the menu path Edit, Node attributes. A window appears similar to the one shown in Figure 18.6, giving you some basic details about the report including the report type, technical name of the underlying executable program, report description, and variants (if any).

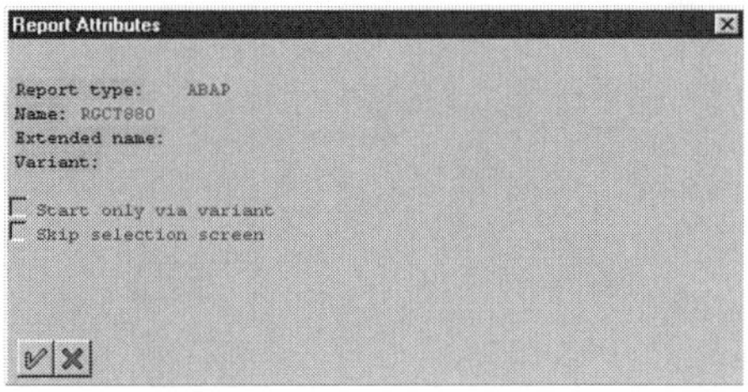

FIGURE 18.6

SAP's Report Attributes window gives you additional information about the selected report.

> **Report Attributes**   ☒
>
> Report type: ABAP
> Name: RGCT980
> Extended name:
> Variant:
>
> ☐ Start only via variant
> ☐ Skip selection screen
>
> ✓ ✗

Searching for Reports

The General Report Selection Tree has a search function in which you can enter search criteria and search for a report based on its name. From any starting point in the tree, use the menu path Edit, Find, Node and you will be presented with an SAP Find dialog box like the one shown in Figure 18.7. Enter your search criteria; for my example, I will enter the word `ledger`.

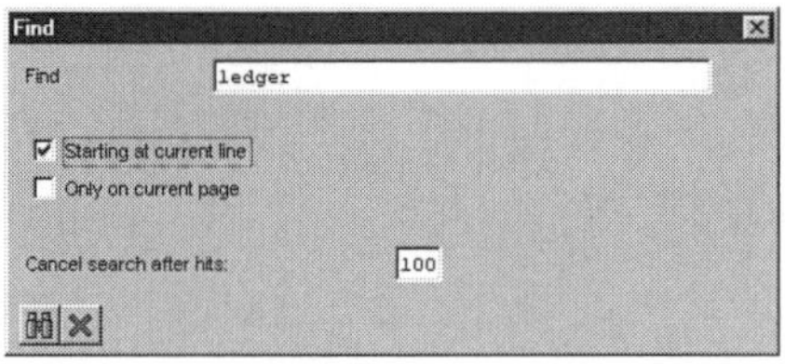

FIGURE 18.7

You are able to search for reports within SAP's General Report Selection Tree.

> **Find**   ☒
>
> Find   │ledger   │
>
> ☑ Starting at current line
> ☐ Only on current page
>
> Cancel search after hits: │100 │
>
> 🔍 ✗

SAP is a little finicky when it comes to searches. It is always a good idea to position your cursor at the top line of the report tree and expand all sub-trees (menu path Edit, Expand sub-tree) before searching, regardless of whether the Starting at current line check box is indicated.

After typing your search criteria in the Find box and selecting the Find button, you will receive a new Find window that displays the results of your search. The results include hot keys (sometimes referred to as *hypertext* in SAP documentation) so that you can jump directly to the report (see Figure 18.8). If there were no reports matching your search criteria, you will receive a message box saying, "Search unsuccessful—no hits found for your search criteria."

NEW TERM   The search results screen contains *hot keys* (sometimes referred to as hypertext in SAP documentation) shown as highlighted text, which link that text to the corresponding reports. When selected with your mouse, a hot key will take you directly to a report.

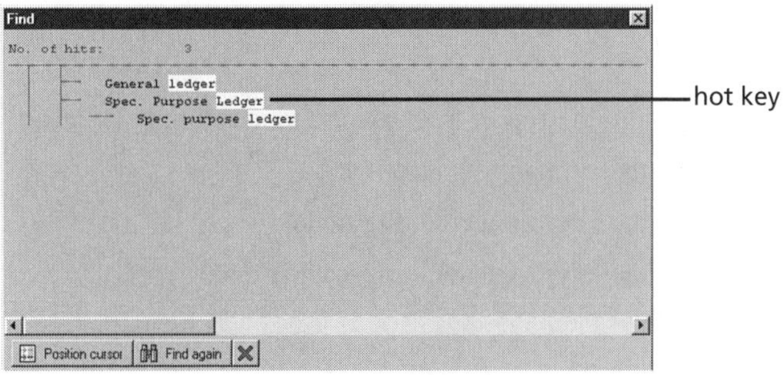

FIGURE 18.8

SAP's General Reporting Selection Search results will be presented in a window containing hot keys to link you to the reports that match your search criteria.

hot key

18

Selection Screens

As mentioned earlier, you will be presented with selection screens when you execute almost all SAP reports. The selection screens are quite useful in delimiting precisely which output you are hoping to yield. In some cases, the data that would be processed in a report is so large that the report output would be meaningless.

For example, if you wanted to generate a list of all open purchase orders in your SAP system, you can execute a report listing your company's purchase orders and indicate on the selection screen that you only want to yield orders with a status of open. In some cases though, each time you execute a report, you are looking for the same specific data. In this case, you would need to fill in the selection fields on the selection screen for the data you desire. To assist you in this task, SAP has a concept called variants.

Variants

A *variant* is a group of selection criteria values that has been saved. If you want to run a report with the same selection criteria each time, you can create a variant to save the data that you filled in on your selection screen. The next time you execute the report, you only need to enter the variant name; you do not need to re-enter the values in the selection criteria fields.

If you use variants, the selection screen for the report does not appear at all. The report can also be preset to execute with the variant automatically so that no data needs to be filled in at all. A report can have several different variants, with each variant retrieving different types of information. For example, a purchase order report might have one variant to retrieve all open purchase orders for your company and another variant for purchase orders for a specific vendor only.

Creating Variants

To demonstrate how variants work, return to the Payday Calendar report used earlier in the section "Executing Reports." Perform the following steps to return to the Payday Calendar report:

1. To return to the report tree, use the transaction code /nsart

2. Expand the Human Resources node

3. Expand the Payroll accounting node

4. Expand the Payroll accounting—USA node

5. Expand the Payday node

6. Expand the Payday calendar node

7. Double-click the Payday calendar report. You will see the selection screen that is displayed in Figure 18.4.

8. To save the selection criteria entered in this screen, select the Save button from the toolbar. The SAP Save as Variant screen appears, similar to the one shown in Figure 18.9.

9. On the Save As Variant screen, enter a variant name and description.

10. Select the Save button to return to the selection screen.

11. On the selection screen, change the values you have filled in and then execute the report.

12. From the report screen, use your green back arrow to return to the selection screen. Instead of manually filling in the original selection criteria, follow the menu path Goto, Variants, Get to see a window displaying the available variants saved for this report (see Figure 18.10).

13. Double-clicking your variant from the Variant Directory window populates your selection screen with your saved selection criteria.

FIGURE 18.9

*SAP's Save As
Variant screen allows
you to save your
selection criteria as a
variant.*

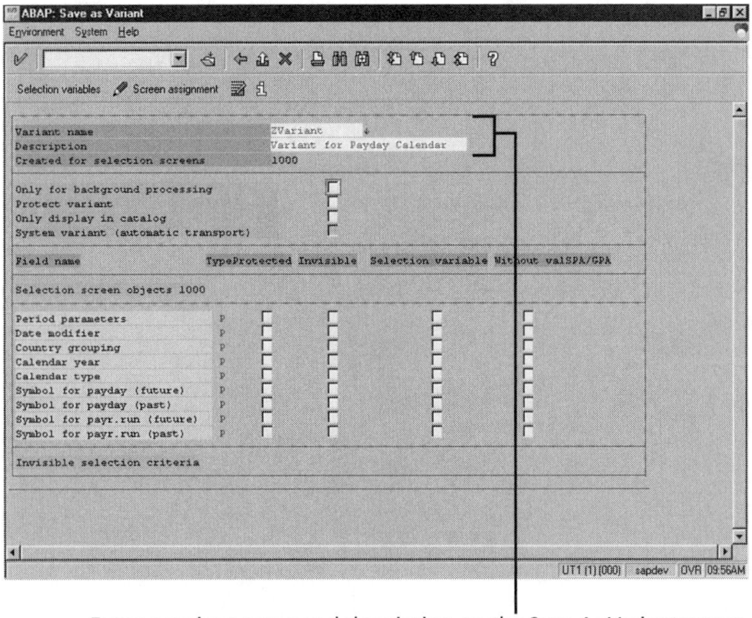

Enter a variant name and description on the Save As Variant screen

18

FIGURE 18.10

*Selecting Goto,
Variants, Get from
your reports selection
screen will bring you
to a Variant
Directory window for
your report.*

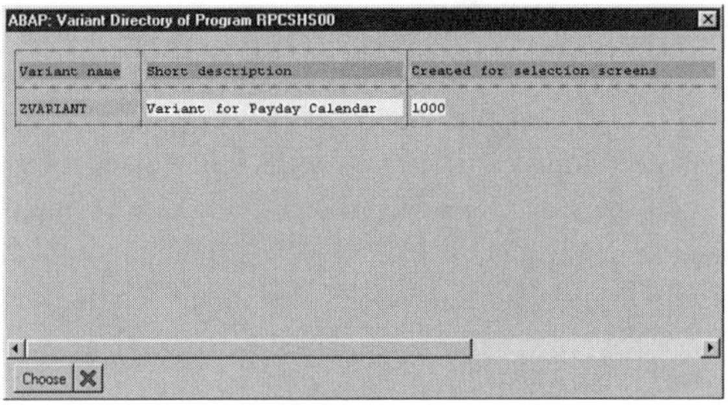

Variants are largely used for background execution of reports that occur behind the
scenes. You can schedule reports to run at certain times of the day, month, or year, and
you can schedule them to always execute with a variant.

Modifying Variants

From SAP's General Report Selection main screen, select a report that has variants
available for it and then follow the menu path Goto, Variants. This brings you to the
ABAP: Variants—Initial screen, similar to the one shown in Figure 18.11.

FIGURE **18.11**

The ABAP Variants initial screen can be accessed by selecting a report in the report tree and then following the menu path Goto, Variants.

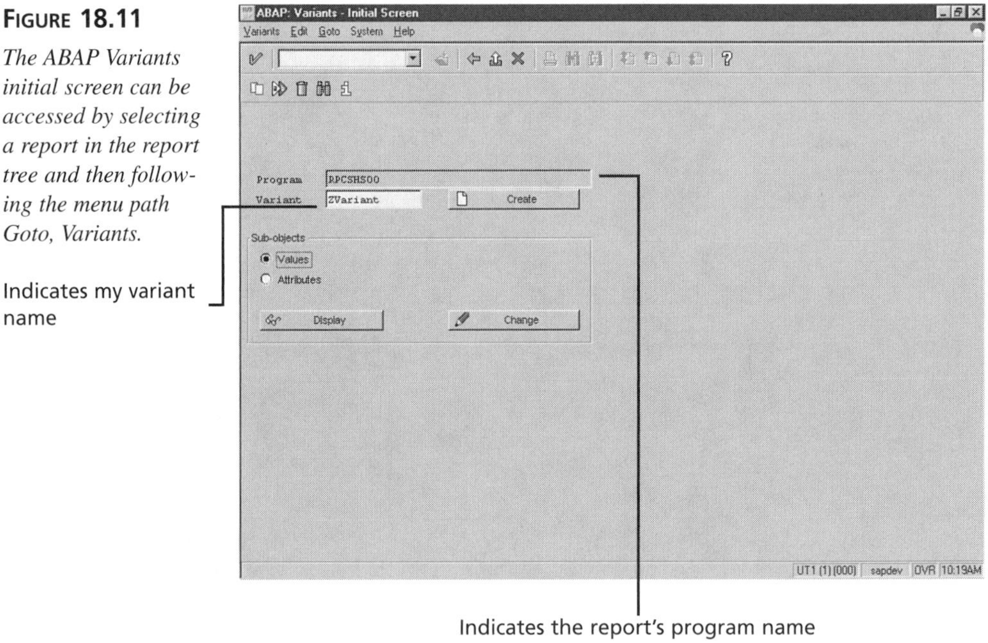

Indicates my variant name

Indicates the report's program name

From the ABAP: Variants—Initial screen, you can create new variants and modify existing variants. For example, you can enter the name of an existing variant and select the Values Sub-object and press the Change button. This brings you to the selection screen for the report, which allows you to modify the selection criteria for your variant. You can also select the Attributes Sub-object and press the change button, which brings you to the Save As Variant screen (shown in Figure 18.9) for the report, which allows you to modify the name, description, and attributes for your variant. On this screen, you can also specify additional variant criteria that is displayed in Table 18.1.

TABLE 18.1 ADDITIONAL VARIANT ATTRIBUTES

Variant	Attribute
Only for background processing	Reports can be generated in the background. Selecting this option specifies that the variant can only be executed in the background. Otherwise, if unselected, the variant can be run in the background or online.
Protect variant	If you select the field Protect variant, the variant can only be changed by the person who created or last modified it. This protects your variant from being modified by other people.

Variant	Attribute
Only display in catalog	If you select the field Only display in catalog, the variant name appears in the directory but not in the general input help.
System variant	This box is reserved for system variants (automatic transport).

Background Processing

Reports can be processed in the background and, more importantly, can be scheduled to run in the background at predefined intervals. For example, you can have a scheduled background job that prints a list of all the new invoices issued through your Purchasing application at the end of each business day. A background job specifies the ABAP report or external program that should be started, together with any variants for the report: start-time and printing specifications. The scheduling of jobs is a function of your System Administrator.

An advantage of background processing is that the report is started in the background by the R/3 system and has no influence on your interactive work with the R/3 system or the amount of resources allocated to you.

18

Lists

After generating a report in SAP, you can save the output as a list. On all report output screens, there are List options available that allow you to save the file in Office, a report tree, or to an external file. Saving the report as an external file is covered later in Hour 22, "Communicating with Microsoft Office." In that hour, I will discuss how you can work with your SAP data using the Microsoft Office Excel, Word, and Access applications.

Saving the list using the menu path List, Save, Office allows you to save the report output in a folder or email the output through SAP's email application. You also have the option of saving the generated list to a reporting tree.

It is important to note the distinction between a report and a list. A *report* generated at any time in the system contains real-time data at the time of generation. A *list* is saved output from a previously generated list and does not reflect the real-time data in your SAP R/3 system.

Summary

SAP has many reporting capabilities. This hour gives you an introduction to the basics of reporting in SAP, including the concepts of variants and background processing. One of the biggest concerns of using a new system is your ability to retrieve output from the system in a manner that is relatively easy to do and beneficial in format. Having all the data stored in your SAP system is good, but to be able to output that data into meaningful reports is crucial.

The information that you have learned this hour will be helpful in executing reports and creating variants for those reports. Instruction on creating your own custom reports is covered next in Hour 19, "ABAP Query Reporting."

Q&A

Q Are there external tools available for reporting in SAP?

A There are several products on the market that can be used for external reporting in SAP. Sample external reporting solutions include Argus, the Microsoft Office family of products (covered in Hour 22, "Communicating with Microsoft Office"), Oracle Data Browser, Monarch, Information Builders (FOCUS), Cognos's Impromptu, and Powerplay.

Q Can reports be made a part of SAP workflow?

A Reports can be made to integrate with business workflow in your SAP system. For example, you can have a report generated, saved as a list, and automatically sent to someone's inbox on a pre-determined schedule.

Q Is their an ideal way to determine if the canned reports in SAP can satisfy your reporting requirements?

A During the implementation process, it is a good idea to compile a list (including samples of each of the reports that your company currently generates) and perform a comparison between your current reports and the canned reports in SAP. In many cases, you will find that because of the functionality available in SAP, many of your hard copy reports may become obsolete. In other cases, many of your reports may already be combined in a single SAP canned report.

Workshop

The workshop is designed to help you anticipate possible questions, review what you've learned, and begin thinking ahead to putting your knowledge into practice. The answers to the quiz that follows can be found in Appendix A, "Answers."

Quiz

1. What reporting mechanism is used to pose one-time queries to the database?

2. Which type of SAP reporting tool requires the user to write code in the ABAP language in order to generate reports?

3. What is the menu path to view a report's attributes from the General Report Selection screen?

4. What is the menu path used to search for reports in the General Report Selection Tree?

5. Define the term variant.

6. What does it mean for you to "protect" a variant?

7. Name the big advantage to background processing.

Exercises

1. In the General Reporting Tree, search for a report named Product Group Planning Evaluation.

2. Create two new variants for the Payday calendar report and re-execute the report using each of the variants.

3. Search for and then retrieve the properties for the CO/FI Reconciliation in CCde Crcy report.

18

ABAP Query Reporting

The ABAP Query is a reporting tool that can be used by individuals with lit-tle to no technical experience. Unlike selecting reports from a report tree, with ABAP Query you create your own custom reports. Using ABAP Query requires that you become familiar with application areas, user groups, and functional areas. In this hour, I will cover these different topics and you will explore how to create custom reports using the R/3 ABAP Query.

Highlights of this hour include

- Learning how to create functional areas
- Exploring logical databases
- Creating custom queries
- Seeing the possibilities of advanced queries

The Structure of the ABAP Query

ABAP Queries are built upon the foundation of user groups and functional areas. The R/3 ABAP Query consists of four components:

- Maintain Queries (/nSQ01)
- Maintain Functional Areas (/nSQ02)
- Maintain User Groups (/nSQ03)
- Language Comparison (/nSQ07)

User groups contain a collection of SAP users who are grouped together. A user's assignment to a user group determines which queries he is allowed to execute and/or maintain. Functional areas determine which tables, or fields within a table, a query can reference. Functional areas are based on logical databases within SAP.

NEW TERM *SAP Logical database* refers to a special ABAP program that combines the contents of specific database tables.

A logical database allows you to select fields from multiple SAP R/3 database tables into your report. An overview of the relationship between these different elements is shown in Figure 19.1.

FIGURE 19.1

The ABAP Query consists of four components: queries, user groups, functional areas, and language comparisons.

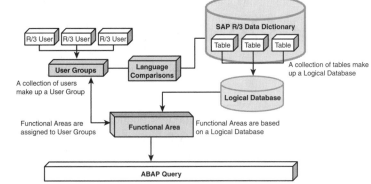

Application Areas

An *application area* contains your ABAP Query elements, queries, functional areas, and user groups. There are two distinct application areas in SAP: standard and global. In Hour 1, "Introduction to SAP," I discussed the concept of clients in SAP. I defined a client as a self-contained unit in an R/3 system with separate master records and its own set of tables. We use different clients in our SAP R/3 system to segregate our production data from our test and development data. Clients are an important concept in application areas.

Standard Application Areas

Standard application areas are client specific. The standard area is primarily designed for *ad-hoc* queries—that is, for queries that are created to fulfill a one-time demand and never used again. Queries created in the standard application area are not connected to the Workbench Organizer and are only available to the client that they were created in.

Global Application Areas

Queries designed in the global area are used throughout the entire system and are client independent. These queries are also intended for transport into other systems and are connected to the ABAP Workbench. All query objects delivered by SAP (starting from Release 4.0) can be identified by their prefix; see examples in Table 19.1.

TABLE 19.1   A SAMPLE OF SAP R/3 GLOBAL OBJECTS

User Groups	Name
Asset Manager	/SAPQUERY/AM
FI Accounts Receivable Evaluation	/SAPQUERY/FD
FI Accounts Payable Evaluation	/SAPQUERY/FK
FI General Ledger Evaluations	/SAPQUERY/FS
Human Resources	/SAPQUERY/HR
Functional Areas	**Name**
FI Accounts Payable Evaluations	/SAPQUERY/FIKD
FI Accounts Receivable Evaluations	/SAPQUERY/FIDD
FI General Ledger Evaluations	/SAPQUERY/FISD
FIAA—Address data	/SAPQUERY/AM11
FIAA—DEPRECIATION	/SAPQUERY/AM07
FIAA—Inventory information	/SAPQUERY/AM01
FIAA—LEASING	/SAPQUERY/AM04
FIAA—Real estate	/SAPQUERY/AM02
FIAA—Retirements	/SAPQUERY/AM09
FIAA—Vehicles	/SAPQUERY/AM03
FIAA—Period values from posting depreciation	/SAPQUERY/AM27
HR Personnel administration	/SAPQUERY/HR_ADM
HR Recruitment	/SAPQUERY/HR_APP

19

> User groups and functional areas can be assigned to any development class.
> Queries can only be assigned to transportable development classes if their
> corresponding user groups and functional areas are also assigned to trans-
> portable development classes.

User Groups

User groups are usually maintained by your system administrator. User groups are created on the Maintain User Groups screen, which can be found using the menu path
Tools, ABAP Workbench, Utilities, ABAP Query, User Groups, or by using transaction
code /nSQ03. Users who are working within the same application usually fall into the
same user group. For example, you can create a user group to store your purchasing
administrators and another group to store your receiving clerks.

Users can belong to multiple user groups and might, under certain circumstances, copy
and execute queries from other user groups (only if the functional area permissions are
the same). Any user within a user group has authority to execute queries that are assigned
to it, but only users with the appropriate authorization can modify queries or define new
ones. Users are not permitted to modify queries from other user groups. Although the
maintenance of user groups is usually a task for your system administrator, you will
learn how to create a sample user group here.

> Depending on your R/3 authorization privileges, you might need to request
> assistance from your system administrator in creating a test user group,
> functional area and query. It is also possible, if you are working with a
> newly installed SAP system, that you will receive a message saying convert
> objects first. If you receive this message, contact your system administrator.
> They will be required to perform a standard administration function to
> convert the objects before you can proceed.

Creating a New User Group

To create a new user group, perform the following steps:

1. Navigate to the Maintain User Group screen using the menu path Tools, ABAP
   Workbench, Utilities, ABAP Query, User groups, or by using transaction code
   /nSQ03.

2. Ensure that you are in the standard application area by following the menu path Environment, Application Areas, and selecting Standard area (client specific).

3. Type in the user group name that you will be creating, ZTEST, and select the Create button (see Figure 19.2).

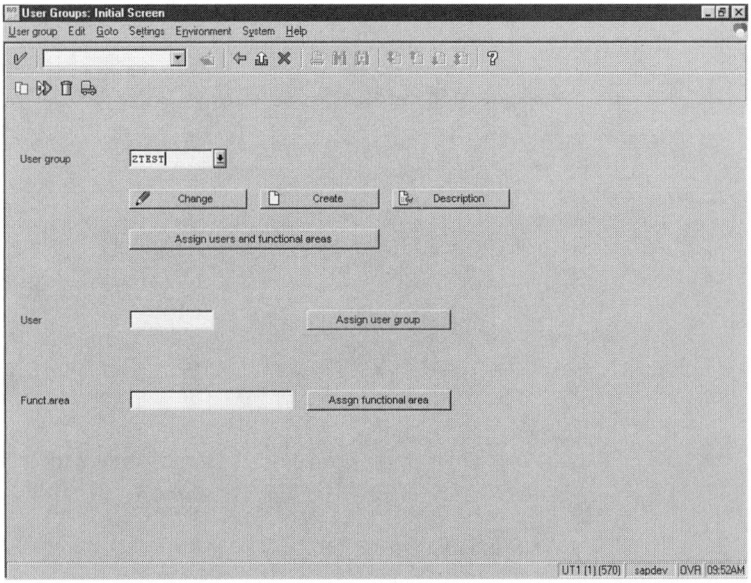

FIGURE 19.2

R/3 User Groups are created and modified using the Maintain Users Groups screen.

4. Type in a name for your user group on the User Group ZTEST: Create or Change screen as shown in Figure 19.3 and select the Save button.

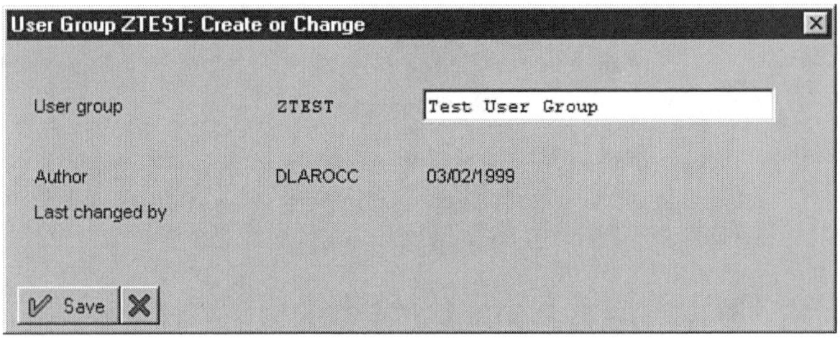

19

FIGURE 19.3

Enter the name for your user group in the User Group ZTEST: Create or Change screen.

5. A message will display in your R/3 Status bar saying User Group ZTEST saved.

6. Select the Assign Users and Functional Areas button. Type your User name into the first available box (see Figure 19.4).

FIGURE 19.4

*In your newly created
User Group, add
your User name.*

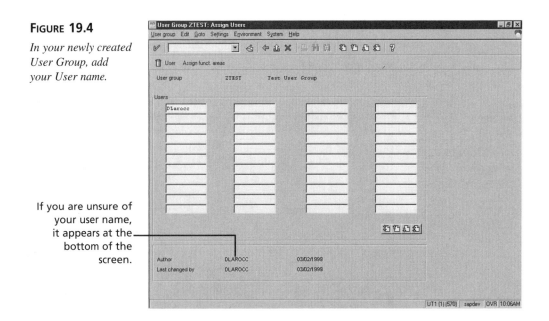

If you are unsure of
your user name,
it appears at the
bottom of the
screen.

7. Save the entry by selecting the Save button from the toolbar. A message will display in your R/3 Status bar saying User Group ZTEST saved.

Now that you have a user group created, your next step will be to create a functional area.

Functional Areas

Functional areas are also usually maintained by your R/3 system administrator. Functional areas are created on the Maintain Functional Areas screen, which can be found using the menu path Tools, ABAP Workbench, Utilities, ABAP Query, Functional Areas, or by using transaction code /nSQ02.

Functional areas provide special views of logical databases and determine which fields of a logical database can be evaluated in queries. As displayed in Figure 19.1, functional areas are assigned to user groups.

Creating a New Functional Area

To create a new functional area, perform the following steps:

1. Navigate to the Maintain Functional Areas screen using the menu path Tools, ABAP Workbench, Utilities, ABAP Query, Functional Areas, or use transaction code /nSQ02.

2. Ensure that you are in the standard application area by following the menu path Environment, Application Areas, and selecting Standard Area (client specific).

3. Type in the Functional Area name that you will be creating, ZTEST, and select the Create button (see Figure 19.5).

FIGURE 19.5

R/3 functional areas are created and modified using the Maintain Functional Areas Initial Screen.

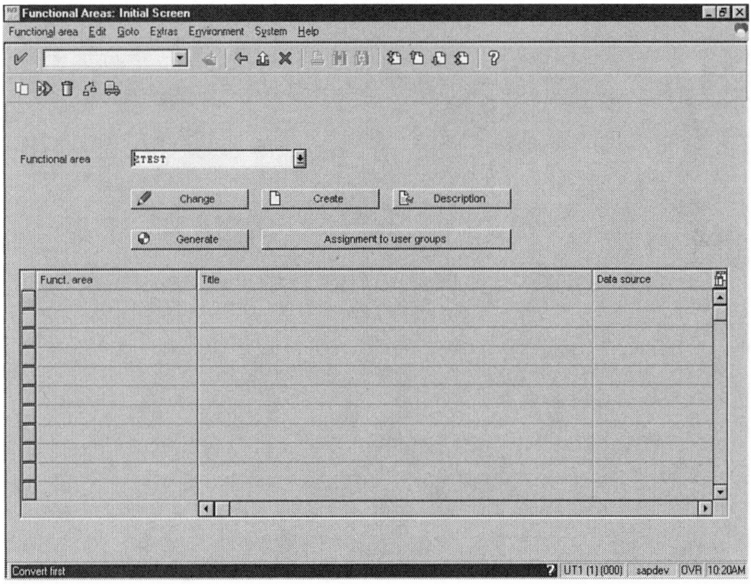

4. A Functional Area ZTEST: Title and Database screen will appear. On this screen, enter a name for your functional area and type F1S in the Logical database text box (see Figure 19.6).

19

To take a look at a list of available logical databases in your R/3 system, select the possible entries help button on the Logical Database field.

FIGURE **19.6**

Enter in a name and the logical database associated with your functional area in the Title and Database screen.

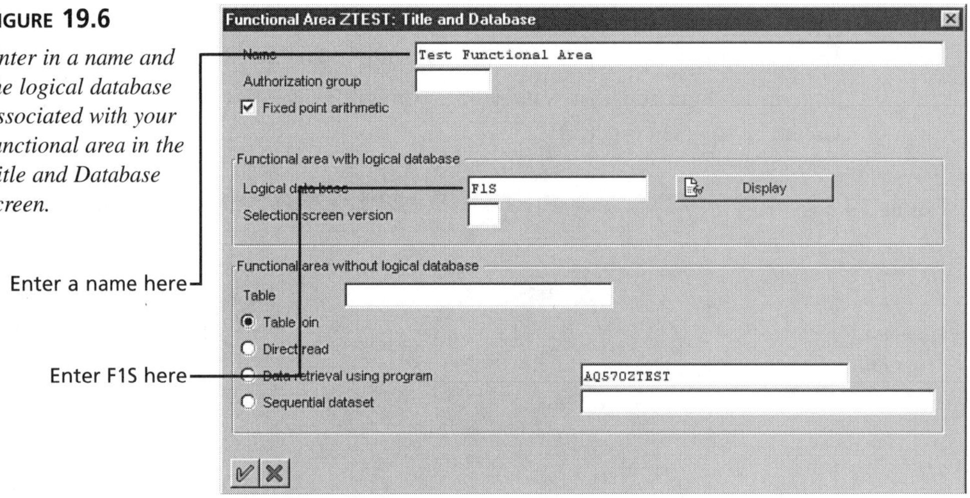

Enter a name here

Enter F1S here

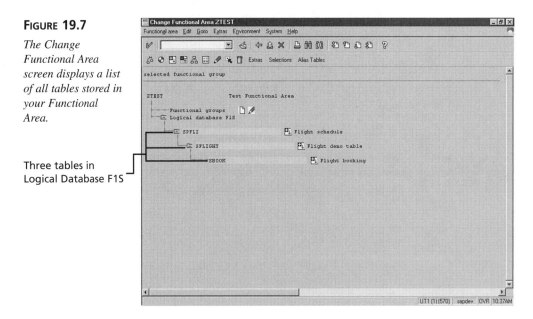

5. After entering in a name and the logical database, F1S, select the green check mark to continue.

6. You will be presented with a screen similar to the one shown in Figure 19.7, listing the tables stored in the Logical Database F1S.

FIGURE **19.7**

The Change Functional Area screen displays a list of all tables stored in your Functional Area.

Three tables in Logical Database F1S

7. The logical database F1S selected is a test logical database containing three test tables called SPFLI, SBOOK and SFLIGHT. To take a look at the fields in these tables, use the Expand Sub tree button listed next to each table name (see Figure 19.8).

FIGURE **19.8**

The Change Functional Area screen with expanded subnodes showing the fields available in each table.

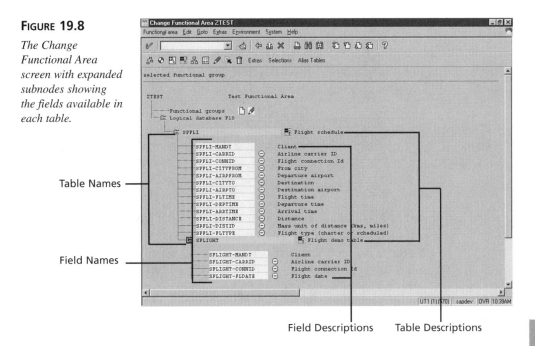

Table Names

Field Names

Field Descriptions   Table Descriptions

8. The next step would be to create functional groups within your functional area. Functional groups are where you place the fields that you want to be able to select from in your queries. Only the fields that you include in your functional groups will be available for field selection in your ABAP query. To the right of the line reading functional groups, select the white Create button, and a window will appear similar to the one shown in Figure 19.9.

9. Type in a FG of 01 and a Description of Test Group 1 (see Figure 19.9), and then select the green check mark Enter key.

10. Your newly created functional group will now appear at the top of the screen (see Figure 19.10).

19

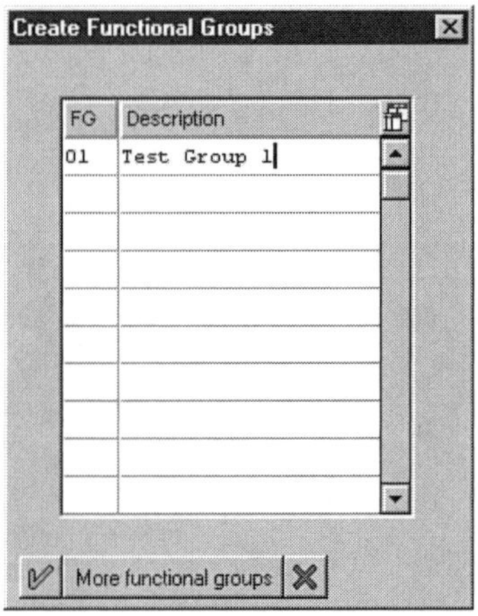

FIGURE **19.9**

*The Create
Functional Groups
window is used to
create functional
groups within your
functional area.*

11. Your selected functional group is also known as the *active functional group* (see Figure 10).

12. The next step is to add fields to your selected functional group. Fields are added by selecting the small circular dash in-between the field names and the field description. Selecting the small icon will change it from a dash to a plus sign with your Functional Group identifier (01) next to it (see Figure 19.11).

13. You can see the fields from each of the tables selected in your functional group by selecting the plus sign next to your functional group to expand the subnode (see Figure 19.12).

14. Now that you have added a couple of fields to your functional group, you need to save, generate, and exit your functional area. Select the Save button from the toolbar. A message will appear in the Status bar saying Functional Area ZTEST was saved.

Your functional group is the active functional group. If you had
multiple functional groups, only the selected one will appear here.

FIGURE 19.10

*Your new functional
group, 01 Test Group
1, will now appear at
the top of your
Maintain Functional
Areas window.*

Your functional
group

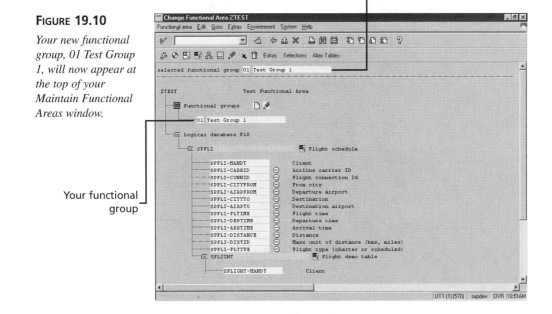

FIGURE 19.11

*Fields are added to
your functional group
by selecting the small
icon next to the field
name.*

Functional
group indicator

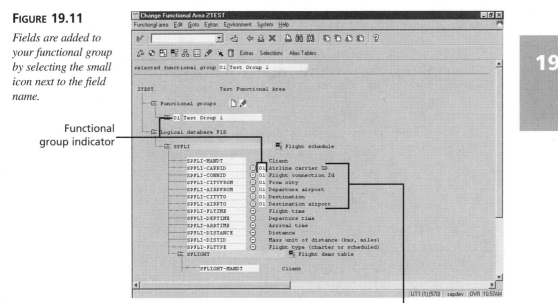

Selected fields for functional group 01 Test Group 1

19

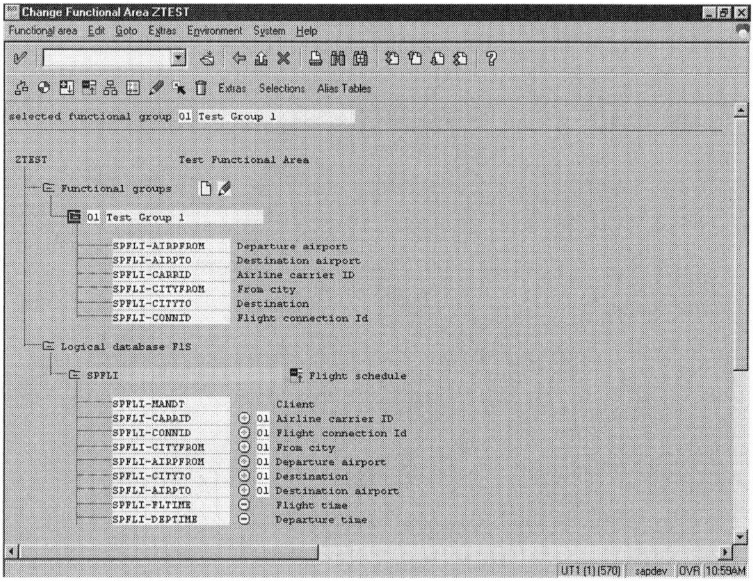

FIGURE 19.12

All selected fields now appear at the top of the screen listed under your functional group.

15. Next you need to generate the functional area by selecting the Generate button (red beach ball) from the toolbar. A message will appear in the Status bar saying Functional Area ZTEST generated.

16. The last step is to exit the Maintain Functional Areas screen by selecting the green back arrow.

Assigning the Functional Area to Your User Group

The first two steps in creating a custom report using ABAP Query have been accomplished. You have created a user group, and you have created a functional area. The last step before creating the query is to assign this functional area to your user group. This is an easy, three-step task:

1. From the Functional Areas: Initial Screen (transaction code /nSQ02), make sure your functional area ZTEST is present in the Functional Area text box and select the Assignment to User Groups button.

2. From the Functional Area ZTEST: Assign to User Groups Screen, highlight your user group name by selecting the gray button to the left of it, and then selecting the Save button.

3. A message will appear in the status bar saying Assignment of Functional Area ZTEST saved.

> Assignment of the functional area to a user group can also be maintained through the Maintain User Groups screen by selecting the Assign Funct. Areas button from the toolbar and selecting your Functional Area from a list.

ABAP Queries

The creation and maintenance of queries is managed through the Maintain Queries screen. The Maintain Queries screen can be found using the menu path Tools, ABAP Workbench, Utilities, ABAP Query, Queries, or by using transaction code /nSQ01.

Unlike user groups and functional areas, which are maintained by system administrators, depending on your company's population and distribution, ABAP queries are sometimes maintained by users. However, like user groups, only users with the appropriate authorizations can modify queries or create new ones.

> Security used to manage reports is available on a couple of different levels. Besides the user group segregation, there is also authorization group specifications. Security configurations are very customer specific; contact your systems administrator to learn more about your company's security.

19

Creating an ABAP Query

Ok, finally we are at the good stuff. Creating an ABAP query is a relatively elementary task now that we have made it through the technical preliminary steps:

1. Navigate to the Maintain Queries Initial screen using the menu path Tools, ABAP Workbench, Utilities, ABAP Query, Queries, or use transaction code /nSQ01.

2. The title bar will list the user group that you are currently in. For example, your screen should read, Query of User Group ZTEST: Initial Screen.

3. It is always a good idea to ensure that you are in the standard application area by following the menu path Environment, Application areas and selecting Standard area (client specific).

4. To ensure that you are in the correct user group, follow the menu path Edit, Other User Group and select your user group (ZTEST) from the list.

5. In the Query field, type in a name for the query you are creating, ZMYQUERY, and select the Create button (see Figure 19.13).

FIGURE 19.13

Queries are created using the Maintain Queries function, which can be accessed using transaction code /nSQ01.

On the main ABAP Query screen, the current user group is displayed.

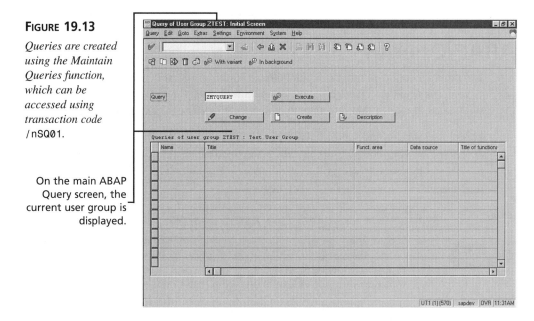

6. A Functional Areas of User group ZTEST window will appear listing all the available functional areas for your user group. Select the ZTEST functional area and the green check mark enter key to proceed.

7. You will next be presented with the Create Query Title Format screen, which allows you to save the basic formatting specifications for your query, including the name (title) and any notes you want to store for the query. For my example, I will only fill in the Title field (see Figure 19.14).

8. You might recognize the Further processing options on this screen from Hour 18, "R/3 Reporting Basics." The options listed here are the same as the options that appear on the selection screen for reports that you generate using the report tree in the R/3 Information System. After entering a title, select the Save button on the toolbar.

FIGURE **19.14**

The title, format, and processing options for your query are entered on the Create Query Title Format screen.

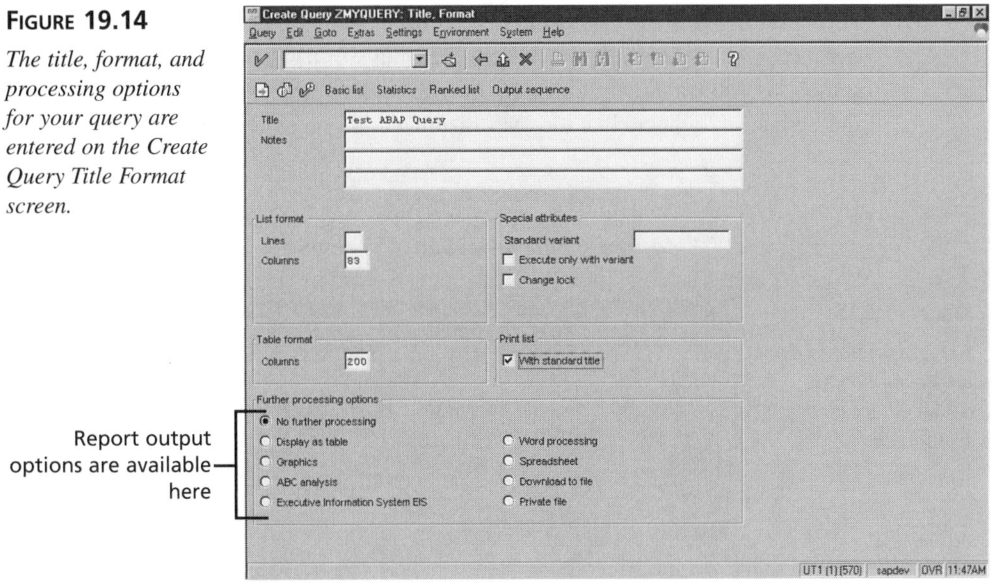

Report output options are available here

9. To navigate to the next screen in the ABAP Query creation process, select the Next Screen (white arrow) button from the application toolbar.

10. A screen will appear listing all the functional groups available for your functional area. You only created one functional group so that should be the only one to appear. If you had created multiple functional groups, you could select more than one on this screen. Select the functional group by placing a check mark in the box next to it. Select the Next Screen (white arrow) button from the application toolbar.

11. A Select Field screen will appear, giving you a list of all the available fields for your selected functional groups. In the example, only one functional group contains six fields. Select the fields by placing a check mark in the box next to each. Select the Next Screen (white arrow) button from the application toolbar to continue.

12. You will next be presented with the Selections Screen that allows you to specify which fields will appear on the selection screen for your report. This is the last screen in the sequence, and you are not required to fill in any information on this screen. Select the Basic List button from the application toolbar.

19

The Basic List button is available from the first screen in the sequence. If you want to jump directly to this screen, you can select it from the initial screen.

13. The Basic List screen shows you a list of the selected fields that you want to include for your report. For each field, you can specify the Line and Sequence number as you want them to appear on your report. Start by entering in the Line and Sequence numbers like the ones displayed in Figure 19.15.

Line corresponds to the line number the field will appear on in the report

Sequence determines the order the fields appear on for the line

FIGURE 19.15

Basic output options are defined on the ABAP Query Basic List screen.

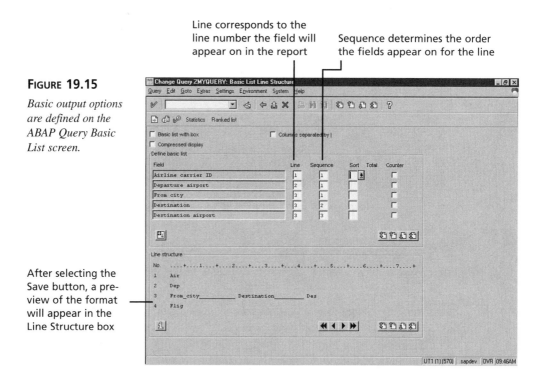

After selecting the Save button, a preview of the format will appear in the Line Structure box

14. Additional formatting options are available on the Basic List screen as well as on additional screens that can be accessed using the Next Screen (white arrow) button on the application toolbar. For this example, you will proceed directly to the report. Select the Execute button from the application toolbar.

15. You will be presented with the report's selection screen. The selection screen gives you an opportunity to specify any criteria for the output of your report. Select the Execute button again to display the report. Your report output should appear similar to Figure 19.16. (The output of the report corresponds to the specification entered in the basic list screen.)

FIGURE 19.16

Selecting the Execute button from your report's selection screen will execute your ABAP Query and display your report.

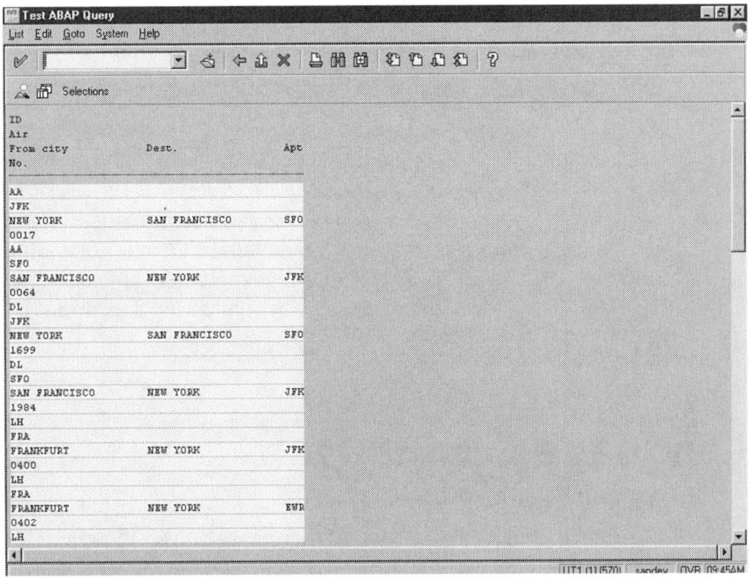

Advanced ABAP Queries

You have created a basic query using the ABAP Query tool. Before you start investigating the more advanced options available in ABAP Query, it would be a good idea to try creating a few queries using different functional areas (based on different logical databases). To do this, you will need to start from the section "Creating a New Functional Area" earlier this hour, and select a different logical database.

When you become familiar with the ABAP Query tool, you will want to try some of its more advanced options. To investigate some of the advanced options available for processing your queries, use the Next Screen (white arrow) button on the application toolbar from the Basic List Screen of the ABAP Query. Advanced options available for ABAP Queries include the following:

- *Grouping, sorting, and subtotaling*: You can group, sort, and subtotal your SAP data on to reports. For example, you can create a report listing all open purchase orders and their amounts grouped by vendor and location with sub totals.

- *Manipulating colors and texts*: You can manipulate the colors and text styles of the different data presented on reports. For example, your report can contain subtotals in yellow, group totals in green, and individual line items in boldface red text.

- *Custom headers and footers*: You can create custom headings and footers to be shown on each page of your reports. Your report can include the name of the report and the date and time it was created at the top of each printed page of the report.

- *Charts and graphics*: You can include graphics and create charts of your SAP data on reports. You can create a bar graph displaying the open items currently available in your warehouse in comparison to the items sold.

> You can also create calculated fields in your functional area to be used on reports. Calculated fields can be used to include variables that are not currently stored by SAP. Examples include a calculated field to store an invoice amount multiplied by a discount percentage or a calculated field to determine an employee's age by subtracting the current date from their date of birth.

Language Comparison

Defining queries, functional areas, and user groups involves the data entry of a great deal of text. A language comparison facility exists for all these text elements, which enables you to enter all the associated texts for a query or functional area in one or more different languages. You can then use that query or functional area in various logon languages.

This means that, for each text, there is an equivalent text in one (or more) other languages. The texts you see in your R/3 system are usually displayed in the logon language that you entered when logging on to SAP.

NEW TERM *The logon language* is the language that you enter on the logon screen when you log on to SAP. The interface and documentation are then displayed in that language.

The ABAP Query contains a language comparison component that allows you to store text and field labels in multiple languages in case there are users of your SAP system that will be reading your report. You perform this language comparison with the R/3 language comparison component.

Maintaining text elements is a useful tool if your SAP system is used in more than one country. For example if you create a report listing all open invoices and their date, you would have two column headings listing Date and Invoice Number at the top of your report. If you have system users who are logging on in Spanish, you can use the language comparison component to save the words Invoice Number and Date (translated to Spanish). If a user logs on to SAP in Spanish, the text labels for Invoice Number and Date will appear in Spanish when accessed, and users who logon in English will see the words presented in English.

Summary

In this hour, you have reviewed how to create user groups, functional areas, and ABAP queries in R/3. The skills learned in this hour might be the most meaningful to you as an end user because they will empower you with the skills to extract data from your R/3 system in a format that you design.

As you have seen, the reporting capabilities using ABAP Query are endless. Getting familiar with the technical aspects of creating and assigning user groups and functional areas is a big step in mastering report creation using the ABAP Query. Trial and error is usually the best method for getting accustomed to working with queries in SAP.

Q&A

Q Do users or system administrators generally regulate the creation of user groups, functional areas, and queries?

A The use of different tools in SAP largely depends on the customer. In general, user groups and functional areas are maintained by your company's technical users, although the creation of ABAP queries varies. In some organizations users see it as a great means of creating their own reports without seeking the assistance of the technical users. On the other hand, depending on your company's security configuration, the creation of ABAP queries may be restricted to technical users only.

Q Can ABAP queries be added to report trees for easy access.

A Any type of report, query, transaction, or program can be added to an SAP report tree. Hour 21, "Creating Custom Report Trees," introduces this concept.

19

Workshop

The workshop is designed to help you anticipate possible questions, review what you've learned, and begin thinking ahead to putting your knowledge into practice. The answers to the quiz that follows can be found in Appendix A, "Answers."

Quiz

1. What is the transaction code to access the Create Users screen?
2. What is the transaction code to access the Create Functional Areas screen?
3. What is the transaction code to access the Create ABAP Queries screen?
4. Are Global application areas client dependant or independent?
5. What are four different components of ABAP queries?

6. What does an application area include?

7. What are the two different application areas?

Exercises

1. Return to your functional area ZTEST, and add a new functional group, 02 Test group 2, and add a few fields to it.

2. Create a new user group in the standard area called ZTEST2.

3. Create a new functional area in the standard area ZTEST2.

4. Within the functional area ZTEST2, add a couple of functional groups and generate the functional area.

5. Assign the functional area ZTEST2 to the user group ZTEST2.

6. Create a new ABAP Query in the standard area called ZMYQUERY2 using the functional area ZTEST2.

Hour **20**

Ad Hoc Query Reporting (HR Module)

SAP R/3's Ad Hoc Query reporting tool enables you to request specific data in the form of a report or table from your Human Resources module. You can use the Ad Hoc Query to answer a simple question, such as how many employees earn more than $100,000.00, or to create a report to print or download.

The Ad Hoc Query tool produces output that is more user friendly than the ABAP Query, and it requires less SAP experience. In the next hour, you will learn how to create ad hoc queries using the Ad Hoc Query tool in the R/3 Human Resources module.

Highlights of this hour include

- Creating a functional area using a Human Resources logical database
- Creating reports using the Ad Hoc Query

- Discovering additional processing available for your Ad Hoc Query output

> Before proceeding with this chapter, you need to understand several concepts covered in Hour 19, "ABAP Query Reporting," including application areas, user groups, and functional areas, because the Ad Hoc Query tool is based on the very same concepts as the ABAP Query.

Understanding the Ad Hoc Query

In the R/3 Ad Hoc Query, the user interface for selecting fields is designed to be user friendly and enables you to have immediate access to your data from all areas of Personnel Management. Output created using the Ad Hoc Query tool can be saved as a query or to a list or download file. The Ad Hoc Query is designed so that a user can pose questions to the SAP system and receive immediate results. Sample questions that can be posed using the Ad Hoc Query include

- How many employees are over the age of 50?
- What percentage of employees are in cost center 400?
- How many employees in position 50001234 from department 100 earn salaries less than those of employees in position 50001776 in department 200, excluding employees that make less than $50,000.00?

As you will soon see, the Ad Hoc Query is a very helpful tool that can be used by your functional users to retrieve important, comprehensive information in a quick and easy fashion. To navigate to the main screen of the Ad Hoc Query, follow the menu path Human Resources, Information System, Ad Hoc Query, or use transaction code /nPQAH. The main screen of the Ad Hoc Query appears in Figure 20.1.

Like ABAP queries, ad hoc queries are built on the foundation of application areas, user groups, and functional areas. In Hour 19, you created a functional area based on the test logical database F1S, which corresponds to SAP's test system. To work with the ABAP Query tool, you must create a new functional area using a Human Resources logical database.

Human Resources Infotypes

In Hour 11, "SAP Human Resources," I covered the concept of R/3 infotypes in great detail. Because the Ad Hoc Query is a human resources reporting tool, it is based on the concept of infotypes. During the creation of a functional area, you have to select infotypes that you want to be able to report from.

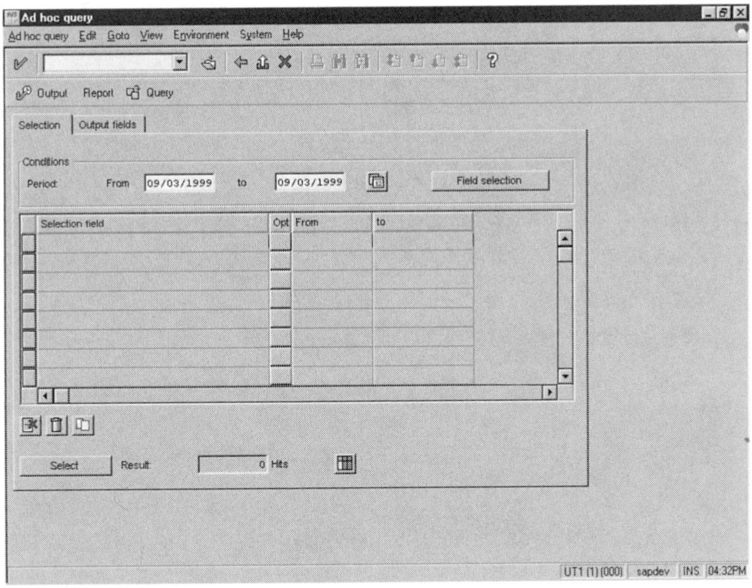

FIGURE **20.1**

The Ad Hoc Query reporting tool allows you to request output from your Human Resources module.

FIGURE **20.1**

The Ad Hoc Query reporting tool allows you to request output from your Human Resources module.

An *infotype*, as you might recall, is a screen in your Human Resources application that stores particular information about an employee, such as payroll data or personnel data. A sample infotype is shown in Figure 20.2. Table 20.1 lists sample human resources infotypes.

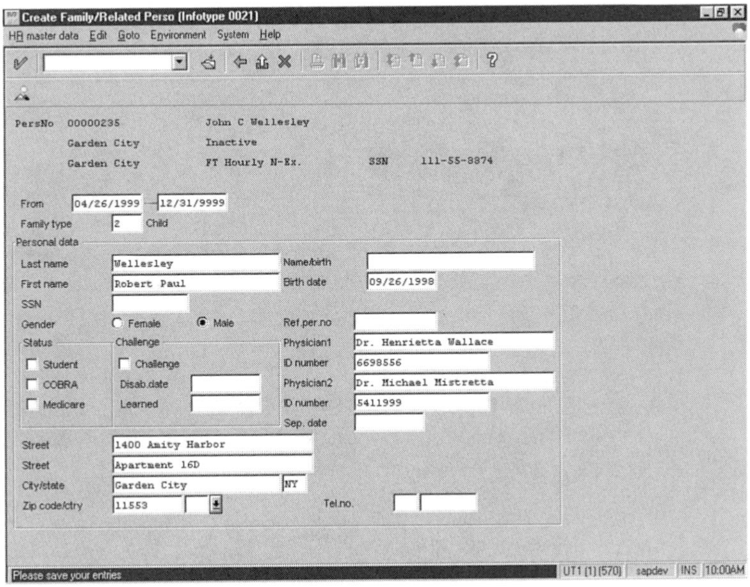

FIGURE **20.2**

Infotype 0021 stores an employees' family member information.

20

TABLE 20.1 SAMPLE SAP HUMAN RESOURCES INFOTYPES

Infotype Number	Description
0000	Actions
0001	Organizational Assignment
0002	Personal Data
0003	Payroll Status
0004	Challenge
0005	Leave Entitlement
0006	Addresses
0007	Planned Working Time
0008	Basic Pay
0009	Bank Details
0010	Capital Formation
2001	Absences
2002	Activity Alloc. (Att)
2003	Substitutions
2004	Availability
2005	Overtime
2006	Absence Quotas
2007	Attendance Quotas
2010	Cost Allocation (EE Rem.Info)
2011	Time Events

Creating a Functional Area Using a Human Resources Logical Database

Because the Ad Hoc Query tool is designed for the Human Resources module, you have to create a functional area based on a logical database from the Human Resources module. The steps (which are similar to the steps used in Hour 19 for creating a functional area) are as follows:

1. Navigate to the Maintain Functional Areas screen using the menu path Tools, ABAP Workbench, Utilities, ABAP Query, Functional Areas, or use transaction code /nSQ02.

2. Ensure that you are in the standard application area by following the menu path Environment, Application Areas, and selecting Standard Area (client-specific).

3. Type in the Functional Area name you will be creating (ZHRTEST) and click the Create button.

4. A Functional Area ZHRTEST: Title and Database screen will appear. On this screen, enter a name for your functional area, and type PNP for the logical database (see Figure 20.3).

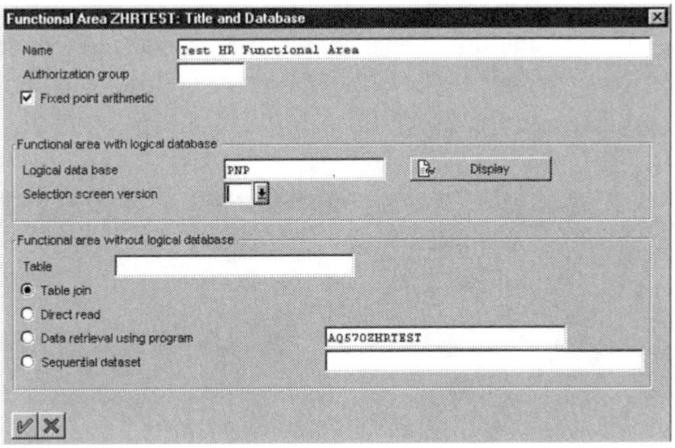

FIGURE 20.3

Enter the name and logical database associated with your functional area in the Functional Area ZHRTEST: *Title and Database screen.*

5. After entering a name and the logical database, click the green check mark to continue.

6. You will be presented with a selection screen similar to the one in Figure 20.4.

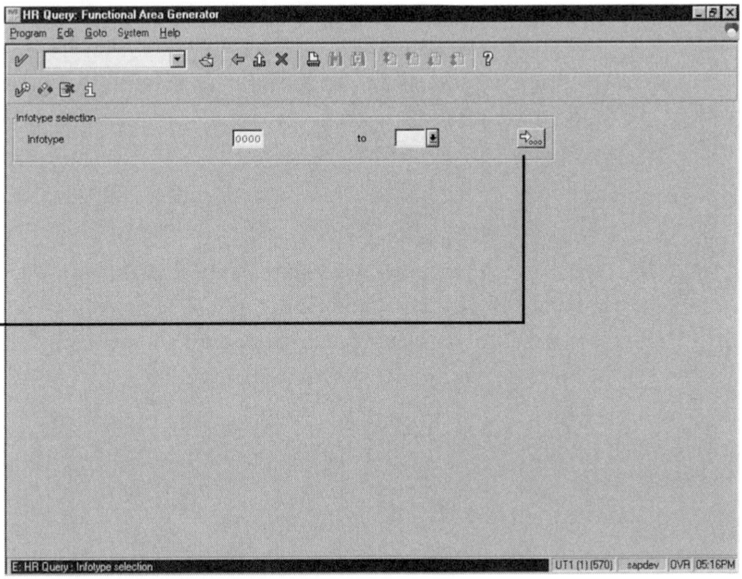

FIGURE 20.4

You select the infotypes to be included in your functional area from the Human Resources Query: Functional Area Generator screen.

The Additional Selections button

20

7. On this selection screen, you must specify a selection of infotypes you would like to include in your functional area. You can have a maximum of 95 infotypes in your functional area. On this main screen, you can select a range from and to a certain infotype number, or you can select the additional selections button, (indicated in Figure 20.4) to specify additional infotypes, as shown in Figure 20.5.

> For the additional selections button to work, you must enter an initial info-type number in the first box before clicking the additional selections button.

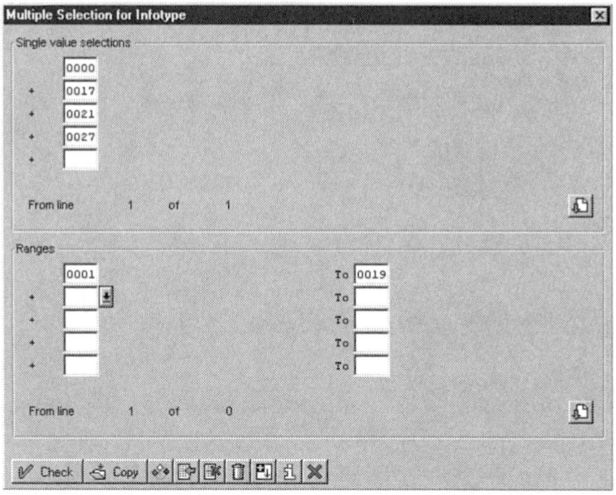

FIGURE 20.5

If you want to select individual infotypes rather than use only a from-and-to range, click the additional selections button to bring up the Multiple Selections for Infotype window.

8. After entering in your selections, such as the ones in Figure 20.5, click the Copy button to return to the selection screen. Your additional selections button now appears green.

9. Click the execute button from the application toolbar to proceed to the functional area screen.

10. The Change Functional Area screen appears, similar to the one shown in Hour 19 (in Figure 19.10), but with one exception: When you are working with human resources infotypes, functional groups are automatically created for you based on the infotype number, as shown in Figure 20.6.

FIGURE 20.6

When you are creating functional areas based on infotypes, the creation of functional groups is automated, based on the infotype number.

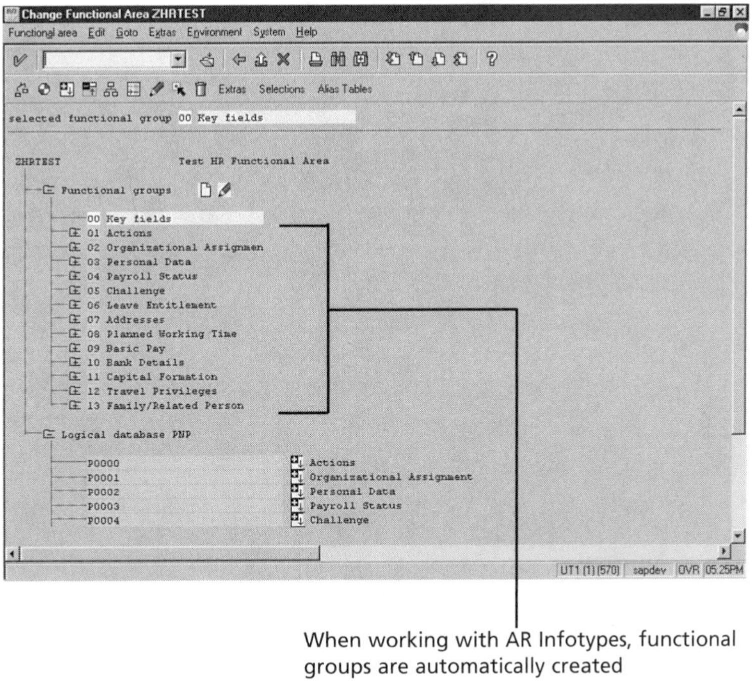

When working with AR Infotypes, functional
groups are automatically created

11. Expand functional group 01 Actions, and you will see that all the fields that appear
on the infotype are included in the functional group (see Figure 20.7).

> When the functional groups are automatically generated by the SAP system,
> they are assigned sequenced numbers that no longer correspond to the
> infotype.

12. Although functional groups are automatically created, you can also add your own.
(Follow the steps in Hour 19, starting at step 8 of " Creating a New Functional
Area".)

13. If you do not want to create your own functional groups, you can add fields to the
00 Key Fields group, which is empty by default. As you did when adding fields to
your functional groups, you must first double-click the Key Fields functional group
so that it appears as the selected (active) functional group at the top of your screen.

14. Then, navigate to the bottom of the screen where the actual infotypes are listed,
and expand the first listed infotype by clicking the expand subnode icon, as shown
in Figure 20.8.

20

FIGURE 20.7

Each functional group in your functional area contains each of the fields that are in that infotype.

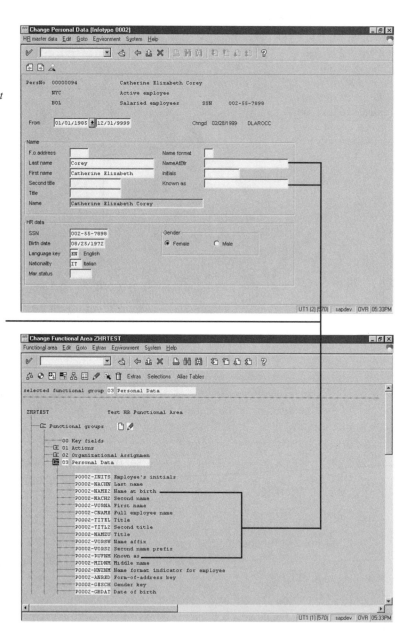

The fields correspond to the fields on the infotype.

Be sure that you are on an actual infotype and not a functional group.

00 Key Fields is the selected functional group.

FIGURE 20.8

Add fields to the 00 Key Fields functional group by selecting them from the info- types listed at the bottom of the func- tional area.

Functional groups

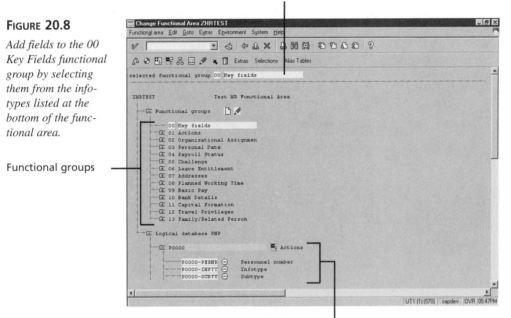

Infotypes with fields

15. Select the fields indicated in Figure 20.9 to be included in the 00 Key Fields functional group.

16. The next step is to save, generate, and exit your functional area. Click the Save button from the toolbar. A message will appear in the status bar saying `Functional Area ZHRTEST was saved`.

17. Next, you have to generate the functional area by clicking the generate button (the red beach ball) on the toolbar. A message will appear in the status bar saying `Functional Area ZHRTEST generated`.

20

If you did not add any fields to the Key Fields functional group, you would receive a warning dialog box after clicking the generate button, saying that there is an empty functional group.

18. The last step is to exit the Maintain Functional Areas screen by clicking the green back arrow.

FIGURE 20.9

Select fields to be included in the 00 Key Fields functional group by clicking the icon (-) indicator next to the field name.

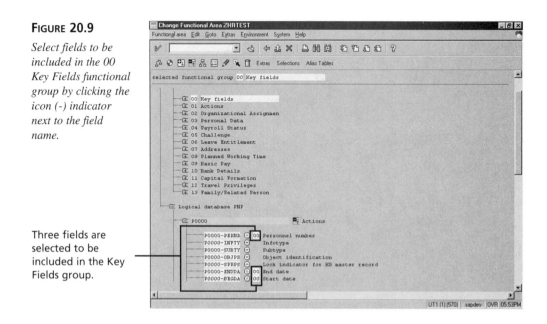

Three fields are selected to be included in the Key Fields group.

Assigning the Functional Area to Your User Group

You will recall that after you created your functional area in Hour 19 for your ABAP Query, you had to assign it to a user group. Because you already created a user group in Hour 19, you only have to assign this functional area to it.

1. From the Functional Areas: Initial Screen (transaction code /nSQ02), make sure that your functional ZHRTEST is present in the Functional Area box, and click the assignment to user groups button.

2. From the Functional Area ZTEST: Assign to User Groups Screen, highlight your user group name (ZTEST) by clicking the gray button to the left of it, and then click the save button.

3. A message will appear in the status bar saying Assignment of Functional Area ZHRTEST saved.

Assignment of the functional area to a user group can also be maintained through the Maintain User Groups screen by clicking the assign functional areas button from the toolbar and selecting your functional area from a list.

Creating an Ad Hoc Query

Now that the basics are out of the way, you have a user group and a functional area assigned to that user group, and you can create an R/3 ad hoc query.

> Keep in mind that you have to create a functional area only one time to use it for all your reports. New functional groups can be added in existing functional areas, but additional infotypes cannot be added to an existing functional area. You can create additional functional areas if you want to include more infotypes.

Perform the following steps:

1. Navigate to the Ad Hoc Query screen by using the menu path Human Resources, Information System, Ad hoc query, or by using transaction code /nPQAH.

2. Ensure that you are in the standard application area by following the menu path Environment, Other work areas, and selecting Standard area (client-specific) by double-clicking it.

3. You should ensure that you are within the correct user group. To do so, follow the menu path Environment, Other user groups, and select ZTEST from the selection window by double-clicking it.

4. You should ensure that you are within the correct functional area. To do so, follow the menu path Environment, Other functional area, and select ZHRTEST from the selection window by double-clicking it.

5. Now that you are in the right place at the right time, click the Field selection button in the main Ad Hoc Query screen.

6. The Ad Hoc Query screen will appear (see Figure 20.10).

7. Expand the first functional group 00 Key Fields subnode—by clicking the plus sign (+) to the left of it—to see the three fields you added to it, shown in Figure 20.11.

8. To the left of each field name are two check boxes. The top of the screen indicates that the box on the left is for selection and the box on the right is for display. Placing a check in the Selection field includes the field on the query's selection screen when you execute the report. Placing a check in the Display box includes the field in the output of your report (not all fields are available for both). Select a few fields for selection and display (see Figure 20.12).

20

FIGURE 20.10

Field selection from the Ad Hoc Query is designed to be very user friendly.

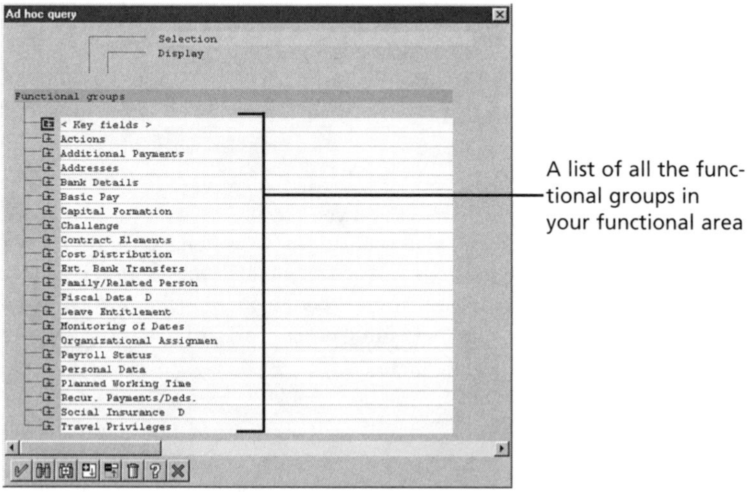

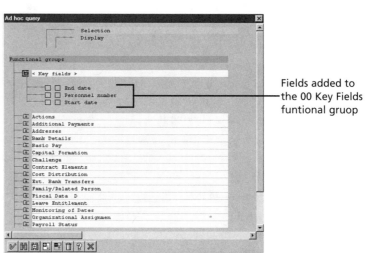

A list of all the func-tional groups in your functional area

FIGURE 20.11

Fields added earlier to the functional group 00 Key Fields appear in the Ad Hoc Query screen.

Fields added to the 00 Key Fields funtional gruop

> If you are unsure of what a field is by just reading the description, select the display check box, and press the F1 function key on your keyboard for a description of the field's contents.

9. After selecting your fields, click the green check mark enter key to return to the Ad Hoc Query main screen. Any fields that you marked to be included on the selection screen will appear on the Selection tab of the Ad Hoc Query screen (see Figure 20.13).

FIGURE 20.12

Fields in your functional groups can be marked for inclusion on the query's selection screen, for actual output in the report, or both.

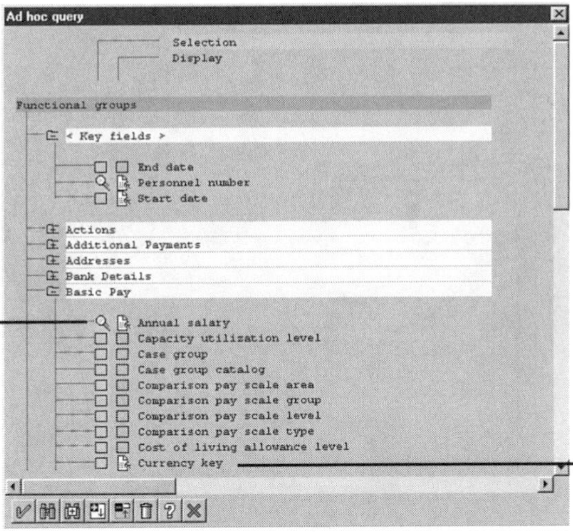

Field selected for selection and display

Field selected for display (output) only

FIGURE 20.13

Fields marked for selection appear on the Selection tab in the grid of your Ad Hoc Query screen.

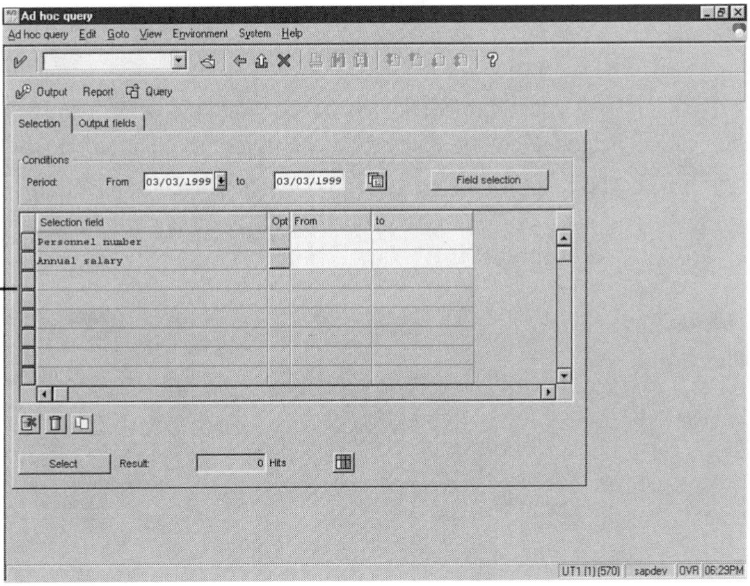

Fields selected for selection appear in the Selection tab.

20

10. Any fields that you marked for display will appear on the Output Fields tab of the Ad Hoc Query screen (see Figure 20.14).

11. You use the Selection tab like a selection screen in all other areas of reporting to further delineate the data you want to see in your output. For this example, you will not specify any selection criteria.

FIGURE 20.14

Fields marked for display appear on the Output Fields tab in the grid of your Ad Hoc Query screen.

Fields selected for display appear in the Output Fields tab.

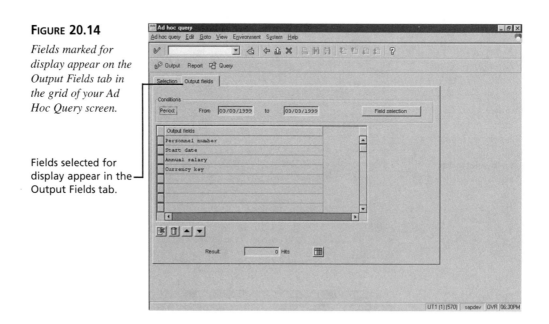

12. Save your ad hoc query by clicking the Save button from the toolbar, and then execute your ad hoc query by clicking the Execute button from the application toolbar.

13. The executed ad hoc query will be displayed in a table form similar to the format of a spreadsheet. All fields marked for output will be included in the ad hoc query (see Figure 20.15).

FIGURE 20.15

The ad hoc query displays your output in table form.

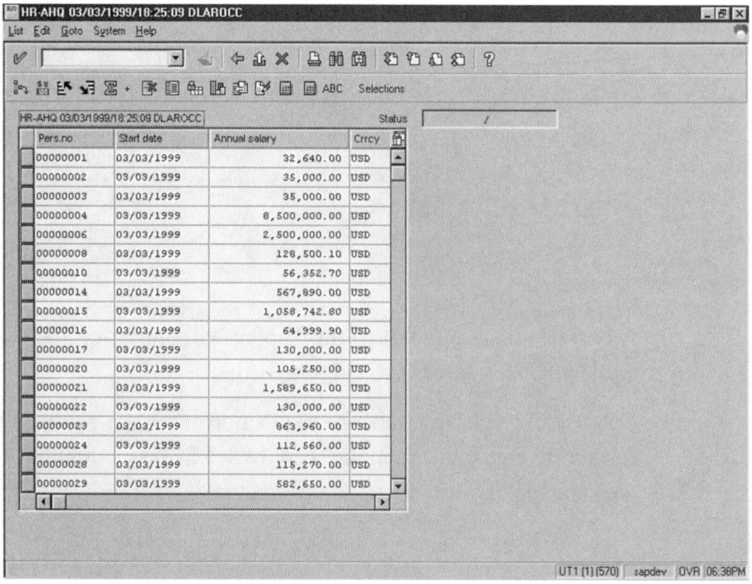

Specifying Criteria in Your Ad Hoc Query

The main purpose of the Ad Hoc Query tool is to pose questions to your database—it's a way to receive fast answers to questions about your human resources information. Now, add some selection criteria to your ad hoc query:

1. Use the green back button to return to the Ad Hoc Query screen.

2. Select the Selection tab.

3. Click the small gray OPT button to the right of the Annual Salary field to display your selection options (see Figure 20.16).

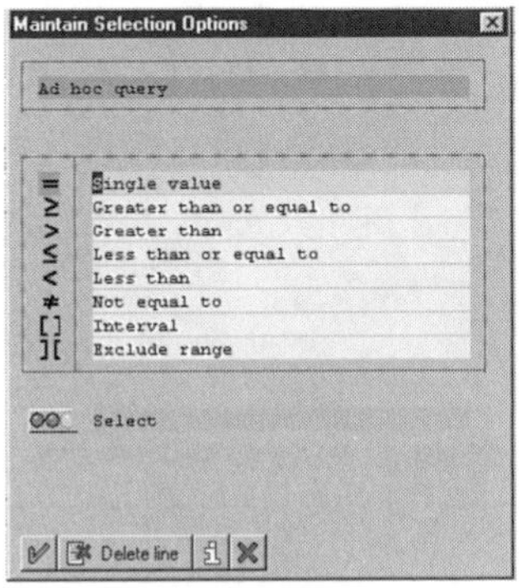

FIGURE 20.16

The Ad Hoc Query Maintain Selection Options dialog box allows you to select a delineator for your selection criteria.

3. Select the less than indicator (<) and then the green check mark to continue.

4. You will return to the Selection tab. Enter in the number 100,000.00 and then select the execute button from the application toolbar (see Figure 20.17).

5. Your Ad Hoc Query output will display only those salaries that are less than 100.000.00 (see Figure 20.18).

6. From your Ad Hoc Query screen, you can save your query by selecting the Save button from the toolbar. A Query dialog box will appear, where you have to fill in a query name and description. Save your query, giving it the name ZAHQUERY and a description of My Ad Hoc Query Showing Salaries Less Than $100,000.00.

20

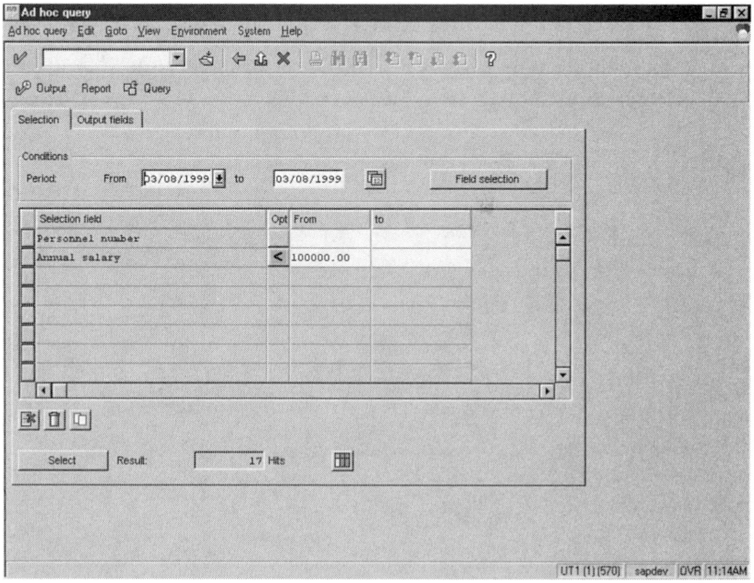

FIGURE 20.17

Specifying criteria in the Selection tab of the Ad Hoc Query allows you to delineate exactly the output you want to receive.

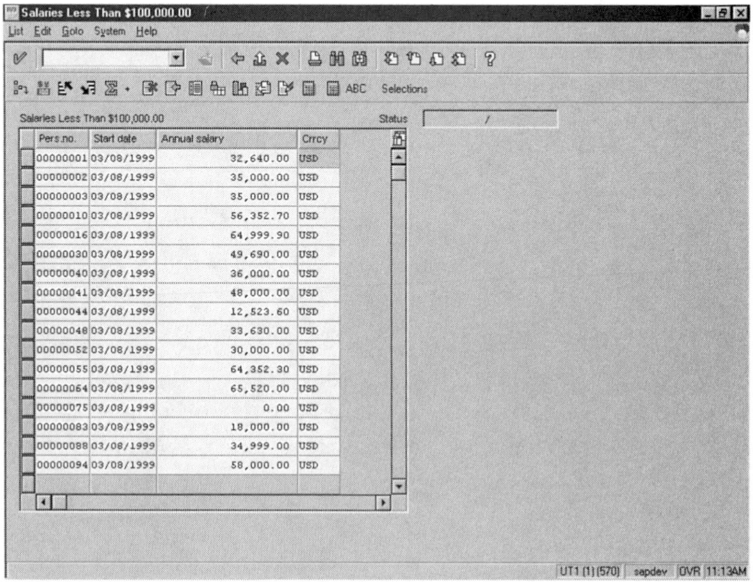

FIGURE 20.18

The Ad Hoc Query displays your output in table form. Only salaries matching selection criteria appear.

Take a minute to practice using the Selection tab to produce different results. Try the various selection options available on the OPT Selection Options dialog box. Also, try entering selection criteria for multiple fields.

Opening Existing Ad Hoc Queries

From your Ad Hoc Query screen, you can open existing queries:

1. Choose Ad hoc query, and select Query.

2. Select a query from the list of queries, shown in Figure 20.19.

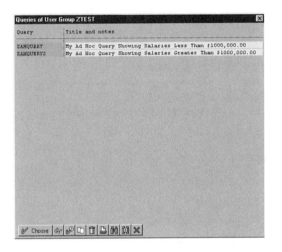

If you have not created any additional queries for this functional area, you will receive a message in the status bar saying "No queries found."

Advanced Reporting with the Ad Hoc Query

The Ad Hoc Query is a handy tool used to generate crude queries from your Human Resources module. It is a valuable tool when you want a quick tabulation of all employees' salaries or, by using the selection screen, to retrieve a list of employees who match search criteria. The Ad Hoc Query toolbar shown in Figure 20.20 contains functions to assist you in further processing your data.

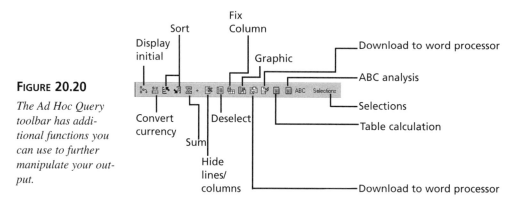

FIGURE 20.20

The Ad Hoc Query toolbar has additional functions you can use to further manipulate your output.

Additional functionality available on your toolbar includes

- Currency conversions
- Sums and totals
- Sorting
- Graphics generation
- Easy download options
- Expert mode options (increased report complexity)

Summary

In the past hour, I have reviewed how to create ad hoc queries in the Human Resources Information System in R/3. If you will be working with the Human Resources module of SAP, the skills you learned in this hour will be priceless. You no longer have to rely on the systems personnel to generate data from the system.

Using this simple tool, you can pose questions to the database and yield the output you want in just minutes. You also have the ability to perform further analysis of the data within the query or by saving or downloading the report to a local spreadsheet. As I recommended with the ABAP Query, your best bet is to work with the Ad Hoc Query, trying various infotypes and testing the more advanced options available on the output screen. It is through this trial and error that you will become accustomed to working with the Ad Hoc Query and your SAP data.

Q&A

Q Can you create your own functional groups in your functional area when working with human resources infotypes?

A You can create your own functional groups, and the R/3 system automatically generates functional groups for you, based on infotype.

Q If you create calculated fields in your functional area, will these appear in the Ad Hoc Query?

A Any fields in your functional area will be available in your Ad Hoc Query.

Q Does security restrict access in Ad Hoc Query reporting?

A There are several ways that security can influence the availability of infotypes in Ad Hoc Query reporting. Like ABAP Query reporting, security depends on your company's security configuration.

Workshop

The workshop is designed to help you anticipate possible questions, review what you've learned, and begin thinking ahead to putting your knowledge into practice. The answers to the quiz that follows can be found in Appendix A, "Answers."

Quiz

1. What is the transaction code to access the Ad Hoc Query main screen?
2. What must you always do after creating or modifying a functional area?
3. What is the menu path to open existing ad hoc queries?
4. In what R/3 application modules is the Ad Hoc Query available?
5. What is the name of the functional group that is automatically created for you when you create a new functional area in Human Resources?
6. What button do you have to click in order to select additional infotypes when creating a functional area?

Exercises

1. Create a new ad hoc query called ZAHQUERY2 displaying all employees and their annual salaries.
2. Restrict the output of the ZAHQUERY2 using the OPT button to display only employees whose annual salaries are greater than, or equal to, 50,000.
3. Save your ZAHQUERY2 query as a list. (See Hour 18, " Reporting Basics," for assistance if needed.)

20

HOUR **21**

Creating Custom Report Trees

In the earlier lessons, you learned how to create custom reports in R/3. The next step is to display them and make them available for execution for a single location by creating your own custom report trees. In Hour 18, "R/3 Reporting Basics," I introduce the General Report Selection tree. In this hour, you will learn how to create a report tree structure of your own.

Highlights of this hour include

- Creating a custom report tree
- Adding your own ABAP query reports to your report tree
- Adding transaction codes to your report tree

Understanding Report Trees

Navigating between reports from the General Report Selection tree makes it easy for you to find and execute the reports you need. Report trees can be navigated using the expand and collapse node buttons reviewed in Table 9.1

in Hour 9, "The SAP Implementation Guide." Having the ability to segregate, group, and classify your custom reports in an R/3 report tree provides the same ease of use. The Report Tree: Initial Screen used for creating report trees can be found by using transaction code /nSERP (see Figure 21.1).

FIGURE 21.1

Custom report trees are created in the Report Tree: Initial Screen window.

Possible entries help
button

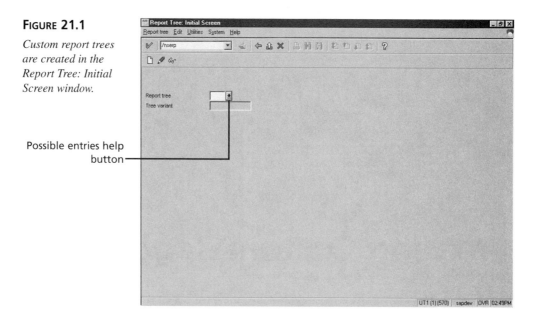

Clicking the possible entries help button in the Report Tree field will bring up a list of report trees available in the client you are logged in to. A sample of the report trees that come preinstalled with your SAP R/3 system is presented in Table 21.1.

TABLE 21.1 SAMPLE R/3 REPORT TREES

Report Tree	Description
PC07	Actual Costing/Material Ledger
HRPA	Administration
FIA1	Asset Accounting Infosystem
FMCB	Cash Budget Management
TRTC	Cash Management
VI16	CO Third Party Management
FILC	Consolidation
VI11	Contracts

Report Tree	Description
VI07	Controlling/Settlements
VICP	Correspondence
RKS1	Cost Center Accounting
FIAR	Customers
TRTR	Derivatives
EIS	Executive Information System
PS93	Finances
TRTV	Foreign Exchange
FMCA	Funds Management
VI02	Funds Overview
FIGL	General Ledger
HR00	Human Resources
IMFA	Investment Management
VI04	Journal Entry Reports
TRTD	Loans
PC3	Make-To-Order Production
TRTM	Market Risk Management
VI10	Master Data
TRTG	Money Market
PC2A	Order-Related Production
OPA1	Overhead Orders
PCIA	Process Manufacturing
PC06	Product Cost By Order
PC03	Product Cost By Period
PC04	Product Cost By Sales Order
PC	Product Cost Controlling
PC8	Product Costing
PCA1	Profit Center Accounting
COPA	Profitability Analysis
PS01	Project Information System
VI08	Real Estate Information System
PC4	Repetitive Manufacturing
SDAL	Sales Activity: Address Reports

21

continues

TABLE 21.1 CONTINUED

Report Tree	Description
TRTW	Securities
FISL	Special Purpose Ledger
PS97	Summarization: Revenues
VI15	Taxes
HR21	Time Management
HR22	Tools
TRMA	Treasury Management
FIAP	Vendors

Some of the report tree descriptions are ones you might recognize. For example, the Project Information System contains all the reports included in the Project Information System. Depending on your system configuration, many of these reports might be of no use to you.

Reports that you yourself create using the ABAP Query might be of most relevance to you, and it is these reports that you will want to include in your custom report tree. Two transaction codes are associated with report trees.

Transaction Code	Function
/nSERP	Create and maintain report trees.
/nSARP	Display report trees.

You will toggle back and forth between these two views of your report tree during the creation process.

Creating a Custom Report Tree

To create a custom report tree, perform the following steps:

1. Use transaction code /nSERP to access the Report Tree: Initial Screen.
2. Create a new session, and start a new task at the same time by using the transaction code /oSARP. You will now have two open sessions. Return to the first session by clicking it from the Windows taskbar or by using the keyboard combination Alt+Tab.
3. On the Report Tree: Initial Screen, type the report tree name, ZTRE, and click the white Create button on the application toolbar.

Remember to check which session you are in by looking at the bottom-right side of your SAP window. The session number appears in brackets to the left of your client number. Sessions are discussed in Hour 2, " SAP Basics."

4. A very basic Change Report Tree screen will appear with your report tree, ZTRE, listed at the top (see Figure 21.2).

FIGURE 21.2

The modifications made to your report tree are made on the Change Report Tree screen.

The Change Report Tree screen contains only your report tree name.

Session 1

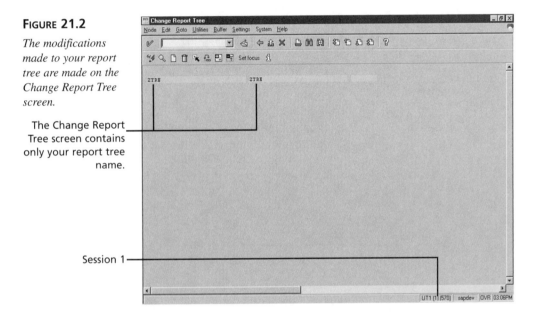

5. By default, the description of your report tree will be the same as its name. Your first priority is to change the name. Select the report tree by highlighting it with your cursor, and follow the menu path Node, Change Node Text.

6. A Rename Node Texts box will appear. Enter a new description for your report tree, and click the green check mark enter key to continue (see Figure 21.3).

FIGURE 21.3

By default, the description of your report tree will be the same as the report tree name.

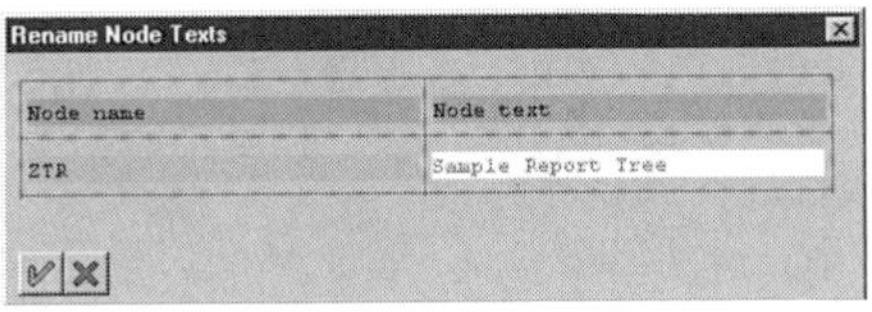

21

7. The new description should now appear on the Change Report Tree screen.

8. Click the Save button on the toolbar.

9. Navigate back (toggle) to your second session. Type your report tree name, ZTRE, in the report tree, and click the display (glasses) button on the application toolbar. Your report tree should appear similar to the one shown in Figure 21.4.

FIGURE 21.4

In the Display Report Tree screen, you can view your newly created report tree.

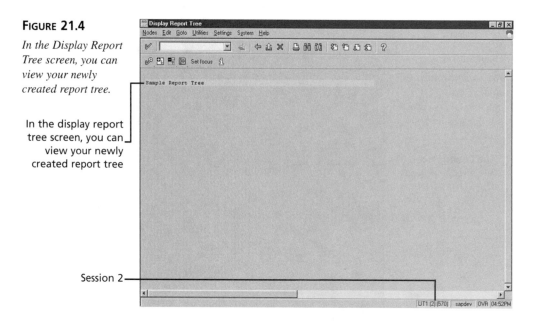

In the display report
tree screen, you can
view your newly
created report tree

Session 2

Adding Nodes and Subnodes to Your Report Tree

Now that you have created a report tree you will want to add reports to it. If you want to group these reports together by different categories you will need to create nodes and subnodes. These nodes will allow for classification of your reports. For example all of your employee reports can be grouped together in a Human Resources node and all of your open purchase orders can be grouped together in a Financials node. To create nodes, perform the following steps:

1. Toggle back to the Change Report Tree screen, in session 1. The next step is to create nodes under your report tree where you can segregate your reports. Place your cursor on the report tree, and click the white Create button on the application toolbar.

2. The Create Node window will appear. Enter nodes for your report tree by typing them in the Create Node window, shown in Figure 21.5.

FIGURE 21.5

Create nodes for your report tree in the Create Node window.

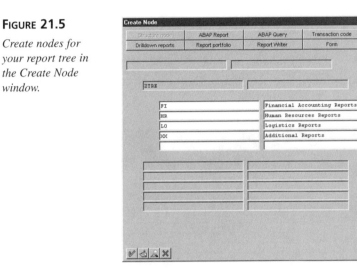

3. Click the Save button and then the green check key to return to the Change Report Tree screen, which should now list each of your nodes.

4. Click the Save button on the toolbar. Toggle to session 2 and enter the transaction code /nSARP. Type your report tree name, ZTRE, and click the display button on the application toolbar. Your report tree should now appear similar to the one shown in Figure 21.6.

FIGURE 21.6

Toggling back and forth between the Change and Display Report Tree screens enables you to see how the report tree will appear to the end user in the Display Report Tree screen.

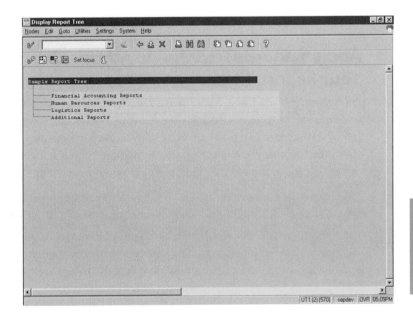

21

5. Toggle back to session 1. Within the node you just created, you might want to create subnodes to further classify your reports. Place your cursor on the Human Resources node, and then click the white Create button on the application toolbar.

6. The Create Node window will now appear. Enter two subnodes for your Human Resources node (see Figure 21.7).

7. Click the Save button and then the green check key to return to the Change Report Tree screen, which should now list each of your subnodes (see Figure 21.8).

Adding an ABAP Query or Ad Hoc Query Report to Your Report Tree

After you create your own ABAP and ad hoc queries you may want to have a single source to access these reports instead of having to navigate to the ABAP Query or Ad Hoc Query screens to retrieve them. If you add these reports to your custom reports to your reporting tree you can have a single location from which you can execute multiple reports. To add reports to the report tree, perform the following steps:

1. Now that you have set up the structure, you can add your first report to the tree. Select the XX Additional Reports node, and then click the white Create button.

2. The familiar Create Node window appears. Here, you can select reports to be added to your report tree. This time, you will turn your attention to the buttons on the top of the Create Node window. Click the button for ABAP Query.

FIGURE 21.8

Viewing your report tree in the Change Report Tree screen, rather than the Report Tree Display screen, allows you to see the object names, in addition to the descriptions.

Object name

Object description

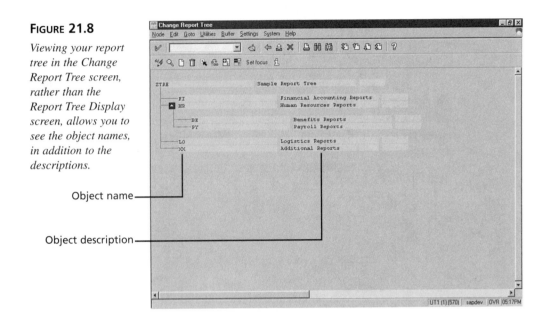

3. In Hour 19, "ABAP Query Reporting," you created a user group and an ABAP query. Select the User Group ZTEST and the ABAP Query ZMYQUERY here (if you select the possible entries help, you should see your ABAP Query report and your Ad Hoc Query report listed), shown in Figure 21.9.

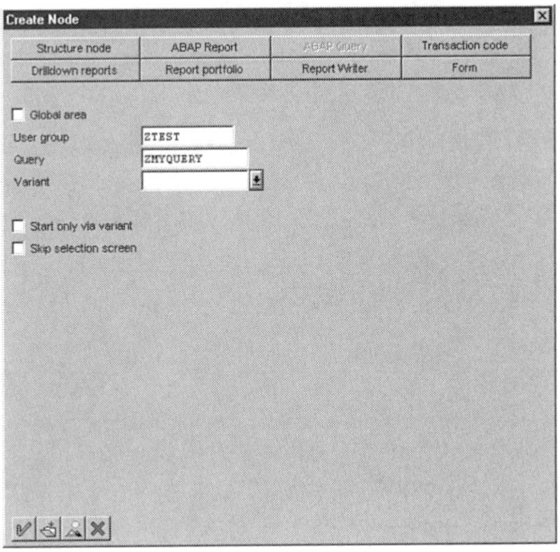

FIGURE 21.9

You can add an ABAP Query report to your report tree by entering in the user group and ABAP query name for your report on the Create Node screen.

21

4. Click the Save button and then the green check key to return to the Change Report Tree screen. Your added report will *not* be visible from this screen. You have to view your report tree from the Display Report screen.

5. Click the Save button on the toolbar. Toggle to session 2 and enter the transaction code /nSARP. Type your report tree name, ZTRE, and click the display button on the application toolbar. Your report tree should now include your report (see Figure 21.10).

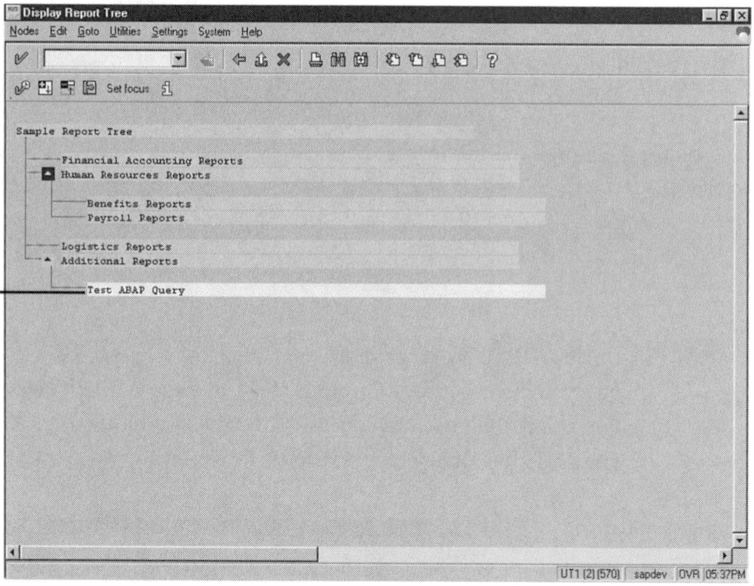

FIGURE 21.10

Your ABAP query can be executed directly from the Display Report Tree screen.

Your executable report has been added to the report tree.

6. To execute your report, select your report and then click the execute button on the application toolbar (or double-click the report name).

7. The selection screen for the report will appear. Click the execute button again to execute the report. Depending on the data stored in your test system, your report might appear slightly different from the one shown in Figure 21.11.

On the Change Nodes screen, you can also specify your ABAP query to run with a variant, thus skipping the selection screen. Variants are covered in Hour 18 "R/3 Reporting Basis."

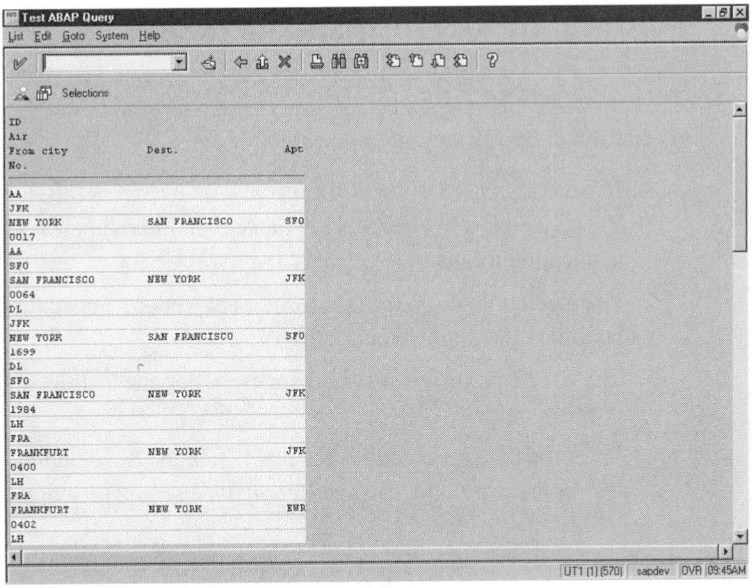

FIGURE 21.11

The ABAP Query report executed from the report tree will function the same as if you had executed it from the ABAP Query screen.

8. Toggle back to session 1, the Change Report Tree screen. If you want to view or execute your report from here, double-click the node above it (XX Additional Reports), and the reports listed under that node will appear on a new Change Nodes screen (see Figure 21.12).

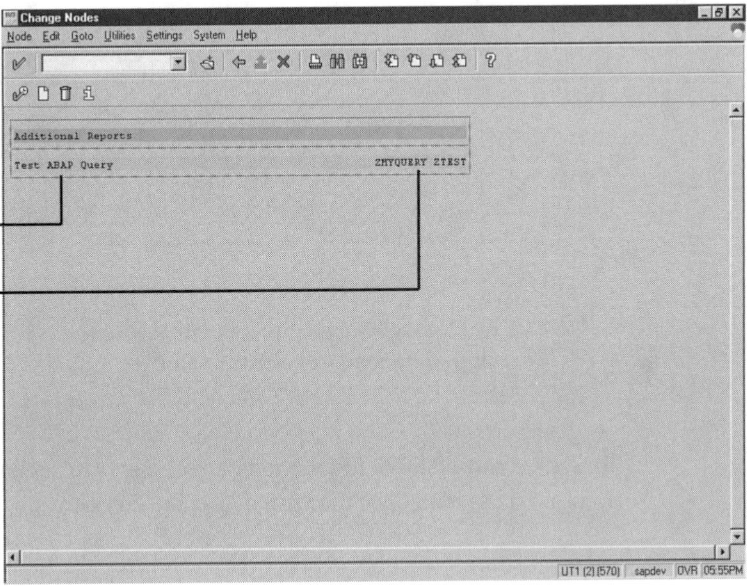

FIGURE 21.12

On the Change Nodes screen, your ABAP query appears with its name and description.

ABAP query description

ABAP query name

21

Adding an SAP Transaction Code to Your Report Tree

Using your SAP report tree as a navigation tool can be very handy. Not only can you
execute ABAP Query reports, but you can also navigate directly to SAP screens (via
transaction codes) from your report tree.

1. In session 1, use transaction code /nSERP to access the Report Tree: Initial Screen.
   Type the report tree name, ZTRE, and click the red pencil change button on the
   application toolbar.

2. Place your cursor on the XX Additional Reports node, and click the white Create
   button on the application toolbar.

3. The Create Node window will appear. Click the Transaction Code button at the top
   of this window.

4. Enter the transaction code ME24, and click the Save button and then the green check
   mark to return to the Change Report Tree screen (see Figure 21.13).

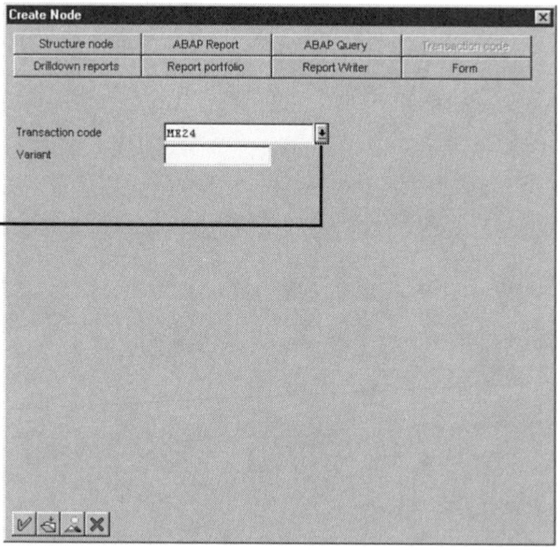

FIGURE 21.13

*SAP screens can be
called directly from
your report tree.*

To see a list of all
available transaction
codes, select the
possible entries help
button.

Create Node			
Structure node	ABAP Report	ABAP Query	Transaction code
Drilldown reports	Report portfolio	Report Writer	Form

| Transaction code | ME24 |
| Variant | |

As with the ABAP Query, on the Change Nodes screen, you can specify your
transaction code to run with a variant.

5. To test the new addition to your report tree, toggle to session 2 and use the transaction code /nSARP to open the Display Report Tree screen.

6. Type your report tree name, ZTRE, and click the display button on the application toolbar. Expand the XX Additional Fields node, and your transaction code should appear (see Figure 21.14).

FIGURE 21.14

Transaction codes added to your report tree appear with their SAP title bar as the description.

Transaction code
SM24

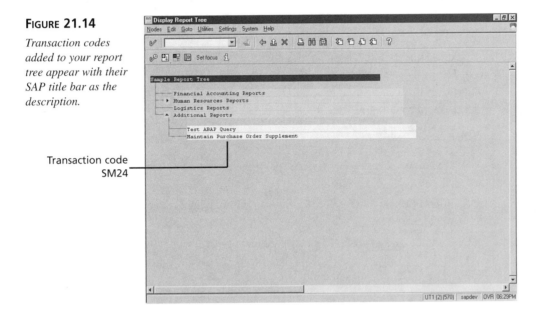

7. Double-clicking the object or selecting it and then clicking the execute button on the application toolbar will bring you directly to the SAP screen SM24, Maintain Purchase Order Supplement.

Report Tree Security

You can also assign authorizations for each node in a report tree. When a user attempts to display a node in the report tree, the system checks whether he or she has the appropriate authorizations. If not, the user is unable to access the objects within the node. The security authorizations used for your report tree depend on your R/3 system security configuration.

No two companies are the same and your security configuration can be based on many different variables. As mentioned in earlier chapters your security is configured by your system administrators. A basic introduction to security concepts was covered in Hour 14, "System Administration."

21

Summary

As with the ABAP Query and the Ad Hoc Query, the best way to master creating custom report trees is to practice[md]through trial and error. Additionally, more advanced options are available for customizing your SAP R/3 report trees. As you can see on the Create Node screen, there are additional buttons you can use to add objects to your report tree.

As you become a more advanced user, these configurations will be more available to you. The skills you have learned in the past hour will well equip you to create your own report trees that can be used as a comprehensive functional tool for executing your reports and navigating in your R/3 system.

Q&A

Q If you create a report tree in a particular client will it be available in all clients?

A Report trees are client dependant, they will only be available in the client that they were created in.

Q Can you add other SAP canned reports to your reporting tree?

A You can add any programs to your SAP tree just by knowing the program name of the report.

Workshop

The workshop is designed to help you anticipate possible questions, review what you've learned, and begin thinking ahead about putting your knowledge into practice. The answers to the quiz that follows can be found in Appendix A, "Answers."

Quiz

1. What are the steps necessary to create nodes or subnodes in your report tree?
2. What are the steps necessary to add ABAP queries, ad hoc queries, or transaction codes to your report tree?
3. If you want to execute a report directly from your report tree and skip the selection screen for that report, what information must you include in the Create Node window for that report?
4. What is the transaction code to Display report trees?
5. What is the transaction code to change modify or create report trees?
6. What is the menu path to edit the description of your report tree?

Exercises

1. Add the ad hoc query ZAHQUERY2 created in Hour 20 to your reporting tree.

2. Retrieve the program name for the Payday Calendar Report (discussed in Hour 18) and add it to your report tree (see the Report Attributes section of Hour 18 for help).

3. Add the transaction code for the main SAP screen to your reporting tree.

21

Hour **22**

Communicating with Microsoft Office

Using object linking and embedding (OLE), a concept introduced in Hour
13, "Basis Overview," you can output your SAP data into a Microsoft application. Output created in SAP can provide you with all the necessary information, but sometimes you might prefer to use an external reporting tool
such as Microsoft Access to perform additional analysis on your R/3 data.
Microsoft Access is an ideal tool to assist you in further manipulation of
your SAP data or for comparison with additional data not stored in SAP.

Another useful tool is Microsoft Excel, which you can use to create
advanced charts of your data. Creating form letters, mailing labels, and mail
merges is easy using an SAP link to Microsoft Word. In this hour, you will
take a look at utilizing these external reporting tools to enhance the benefit
you receive from SAP.

Highlights of this hour include

- Using SAP with Microsoft Access
- Using SAP with Microsoft Excel
- Creating a Microsoft Word form letter mail merge

You can find convenient, step-by-step quick references for exporting to Microsoft Word, Excel, and Access at the end of this lesson.

The Architecture of R/3 Desktop Office Integration

In Hour 13, I introduced the topic of *object linking and embedding (OLE)*. You use OLE to integrate PC applications with the SAP R/3 system. OLE is the technology for transferring and sharing information among applications.

Integration allows you to take data out of your SAP system and place it in to another system with its format and integrity intact. For example SAP tables can be viewed as a series of columns and rows. Using OLE these columns and rows could be transferred to Microsoft Excel and still appear as a series of columns and rows. Having this data in Microsoft Excel it may be easier to work with and more options for working with the data may be available here than in SAP.

The R/3 system is designed so that you can integrate with any OLE-compatible application. Sample OLE-compatible applications include

- Microsoft Office
- Corel Office
- Star Office
- Lotus Smart Suite
- Visio

Exporting SAP to Microsoft Excel

Microsoft Excel is a popular spreadsheet program used to analyze and manipulate data. It can be used to efficiently calculate, sort, chart, analyze and present text and numbers. Although SAP has the ability to perform many of these functions, Microsoft Excel provides a user-friendly format and helpful tools to assist you in the process.

22

Many companies use external reporting systems with their SAP systems (again using that OLE compatibility) and many companies rely on SAP's reporting capabilities (which was discussed earlier in Hour 18, "Reporting Basics"). Regardless of which reporting tools your company decides on, using Microsoft Excel as an additional tool for reporting on your SAP data is fast, easy and produces great looking output.

Exporting Lists to Microsoft Excel

To get your SAP data into Microsoft Excel, you can employ several methods. The most basic method involves the System List function. As you learned in Hour 2, "SAP Basics," the System option on the menu bar is available from all system screens. Another option from this menu allows you to save lists displayed on your SAP screen. Now you will give this function a try:

1. Navigate to the main reporting screen, which you looked at in Hour 18. Using the menu path Information Systems, General Report Selection or transaction code /nSART, navigate to the SAP main reporting screen. It will appear similar to the screen in Figure 22.1. This screen displays a list of available reports that come preinstalled with SAP and is a good example of a list in SAP. It will be your example of how to use the System List function to export objects into Microsoft Excel.

FIGURE 22.1

SAP's General Report Selection screen can be used to execute many of SAP's standard reports.

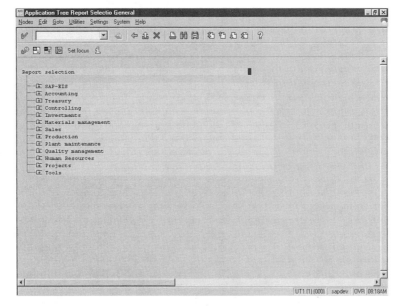

NEW TERM   An *SAP list* refers to any listing of objects on a screen.

2. Follow the menu path System, List, Save, Local File, shown in Figure 22.2. This
   will open a dialog box similar to the one shown in Figure 22.3.

FIGURE 22.2

*SAP's System List
function can be
accessed from any
SAP screen where a
list is displayed.*

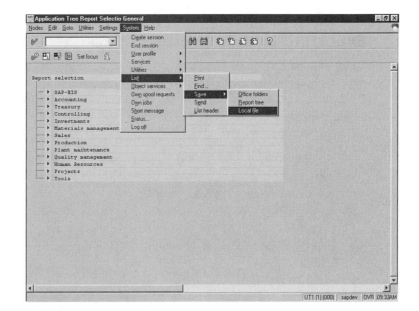

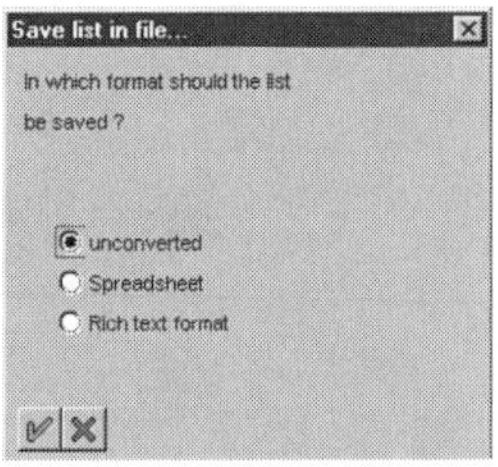

FIGURE 22.3

*SAP's Save List in
File dialog box
allows you to select
the desired format for
download.*

3. This dialog box provides you with three layout options for output. To export this
   list to Microsoft Excel, select the Spreadsheet radio button, and then click the
   green check mark enter button. You will then be prompted with the Transfer List to
   a Local File dialog box, shown in Figure 22.4.

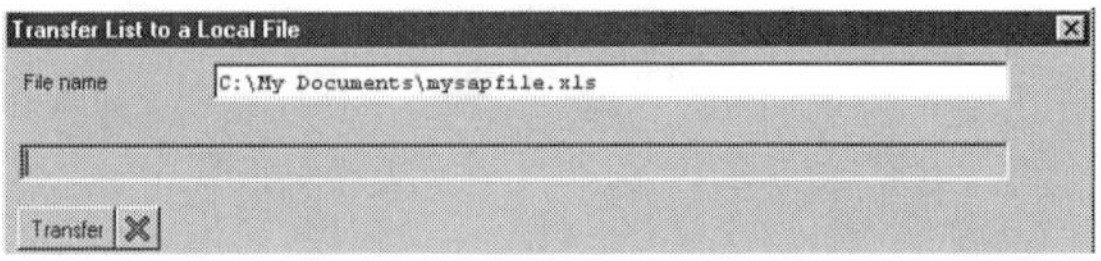

FIGURE 22.4

*SAP's Transfer List
to a Local File dialog
box allows you to
store the file on your
hard drive.*

4. The path in your dialog box may be different from the one in Figure 22.4. When the dialog box first appears it will contain a path corresponding to the directory where your SAPGUI is installed. It is a good idea to change the path where you want to store your Microsoft Excel file to a location you are more familiar with. To do this, click the possible entries help (down arrow) to the right of the File Name box. It will open a Windows Save As box that allows you to select a new location and name for your file.

5. Using the Save As box, navigate to a more familiar location, such as your C:\My Documents directory. Type in a filename for your file, using the extension .xls to associate it as a Microsoft Excel spreadsheet. Figure 22.5 gives an example.

FIGURE 22.5

Select a location that you are familiar with for placing your SAP download file.

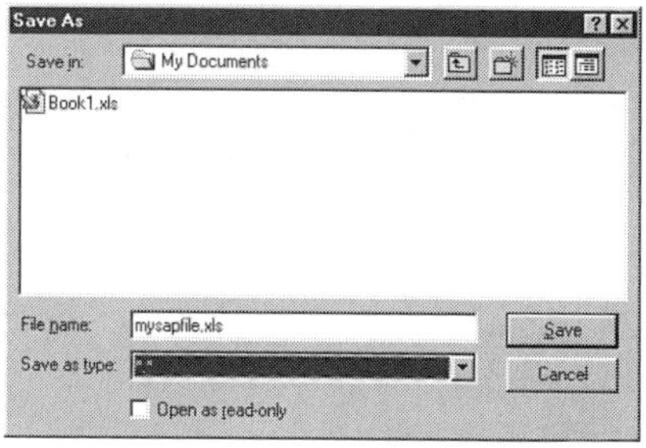

6. After you enter your filename, click Save. This will return you to the Transfer List to a Local File dialog box (refer to Figure 22.4), which will then display your new location and filename.

7. Click Transfer. After the file is transferred, you will see a message appear in the status bar saying Bytes Transferred.

8. To take a look at your new spreadsheet, launch your Microsoft Excel application. On the Microsoft Excel menubar select the menu path File, Open, and navigate to your saved file location (see Figure 22.6 for an example).

FIGURE 22.6

The Microsoft Excel Open dialog box showing the C:\My Documents directory and the mysapfile.xls filename.

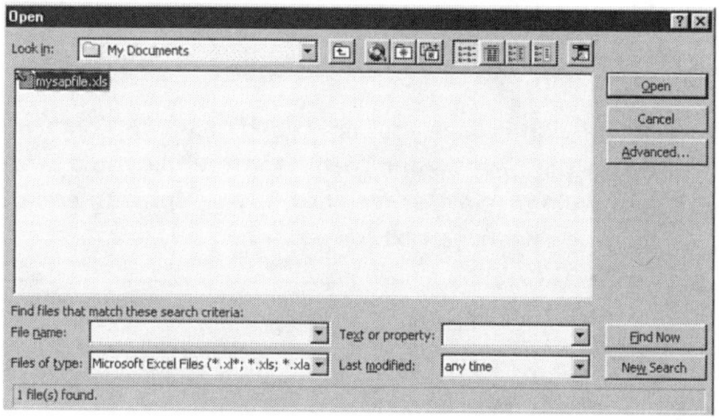

9. Click the Open button from the Microsoft Excel Open dialog box. Next, you will be presented with the Text Import Wizard, shown in Figure 22.7. You can use this Microsoft Excel tool to assist you in importing data with different formats into Excel.

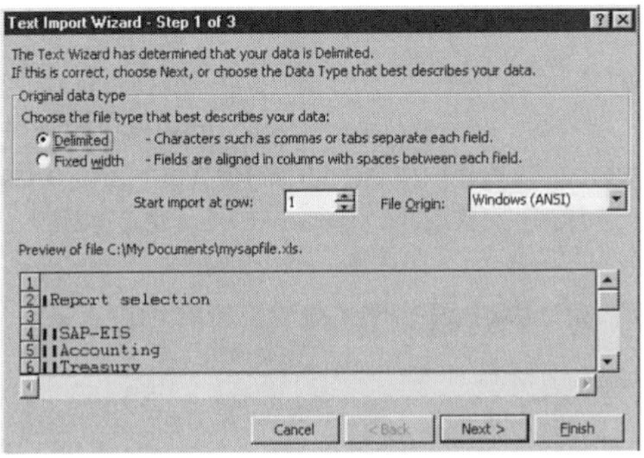

FIGURE 22.7

The Microsoft Excel Text Import Wizard assists in the export of data.

The type of SAP list and the way the format of your SAP data appears on your SAP screen will affect how your data is converted into another OLE-compliant application. Trial and error is the best tool for deciding how SAP lists appear best in your OLE-compliant applications.

10. When you use the Microsoft Excel Text Import Wizard, it's usually a good idea to accept its default selections for your imported file. To do this, click the Next button in the dialog box until you reach the last step of the import.

11. At the last step in the import, the Next button is no longer available, and you have to click the Finish button. Click Finish import your SAP list into your Microsoft Excel worksheet (see Figure 22.8).

12. Compare the format of your list in Microsoft Excel (in Figure 22.9) with its format in SAP (Figure 22.1).

If you wish to save your downloaded SAP list in Microsoft Excel be sure to select File, Save As and then select the Microsoft Excel Workbook (*.xls) option in the Save as type box or your spreadsheet; otherwise, by default it may be saved in a text format.

FIGURE 22.8

Your imported list now appears within a Microsoft Excel spreadsheet.

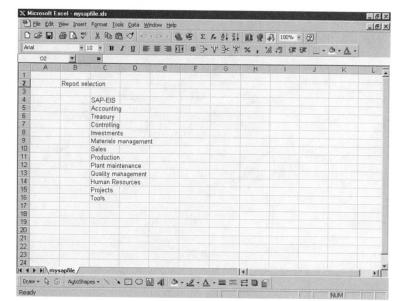

Exporting ABAP Query Reports to Microsoft Excel

In Hour 19, "ABAP Query Reporting," you learned how to create reports using the ABAP Query tool. These reports can also be exported to Microsoft Excel, as follows:

1. Execute an existing ABAP Query (you can use the one created in Hour 19) On the selection screen for ABAP queries is a section titled Program Selections, shown in Figure 22.9.

2. The options listed on the selection screen allow you to designate the type of output you want for your report. As noted earlier, trial and error will determine which format works best for different reports. For a basic transfer to a Microsoft Excel spreadsheet, I find that the most seamless transfer results when you select the Display as Table radio button from the selection screen (see Figure 22.9); to output your data into a spreadsheet format in SAP, see Figure 22.10.

FIGURE 22.9

Exporting file options can be found on almost all report selection screens

Exporting file options for your ABAP query report

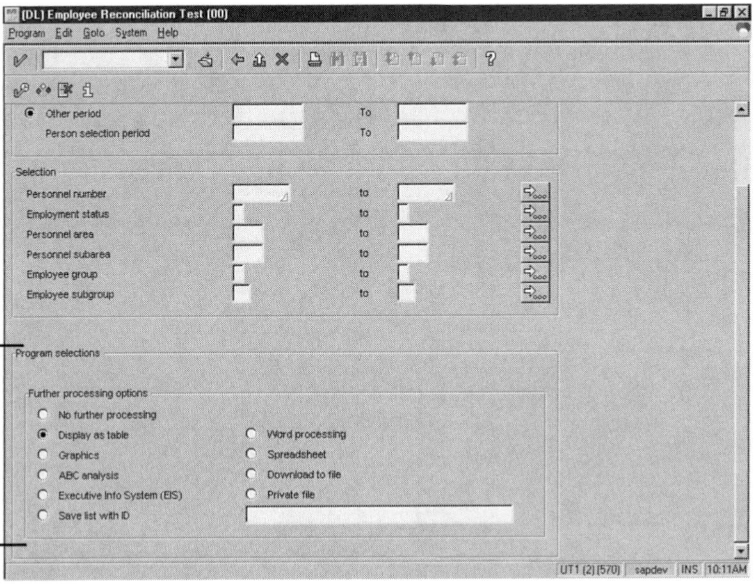

FIGURE 22.10

Selecting the Display as table radio button on the selection screen outputs the ABAP query in table form in SAP.

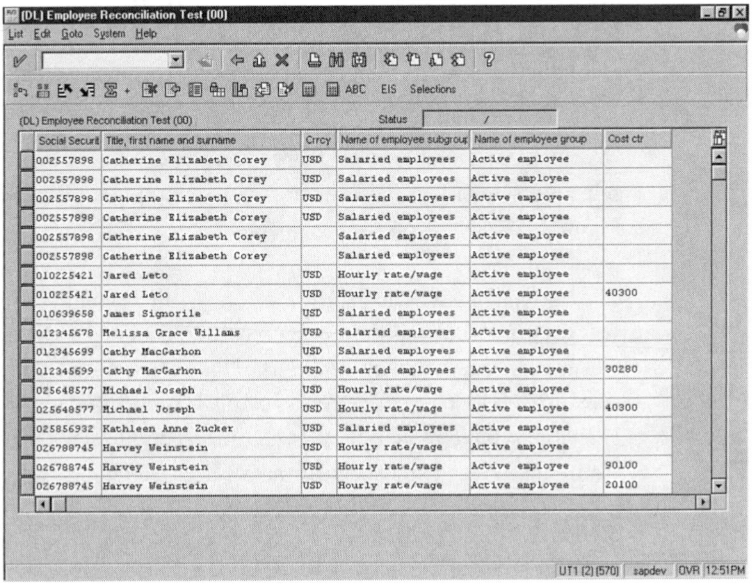

If you want to bypass the generation of the report on your SAP screen, you can select the Download to File radio button (see Figure 22.9) in Program Selections.

3. From this table display view, you can select the List, Download to File menu path to download this table into Microsoft Excel, as you did in the preceding example. (For assistance, refer to the quick reference at the end of this lesson.) A Save As box will appear, similar to the one shown earlier. The only difference is that this one allows you to select the download file format from a list box,) be sure to select the spreadsheet option (wks). This will output your table into Microsoft Excel.

4. When complete, navigate to Microsoft Excel to see your output (see Figure 22.11).

FIGURE 22.11

Your Microsoft Excel spreadsheet containing your SAP ABAP Query data will appear the same as the data appeared in the SAP ABAP query output.

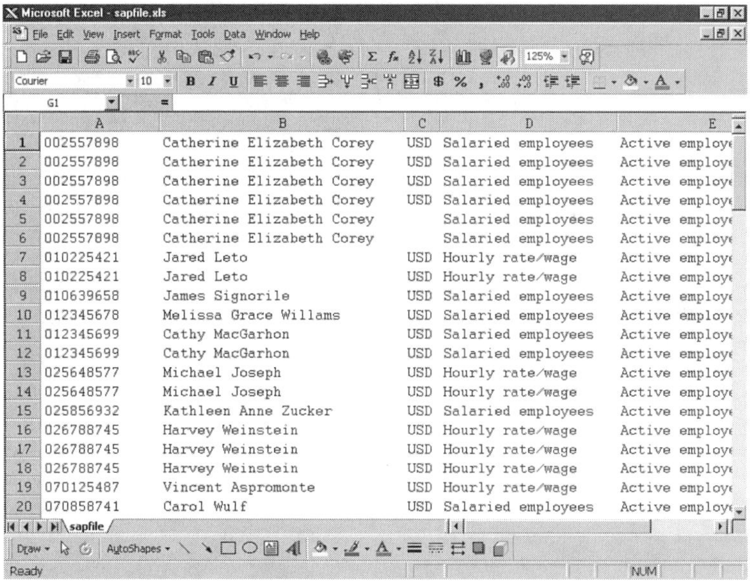

	A	B	C	D	E
1	002557898	Catherine Elizabeth Corey	USD	Salaried employees	Active employe
2	002557898	Catherine Elizabeth Corey	USD	Salaried employees	Active employe
3	002557898	Catherine Elizabeth Corey	USD	Salaried employees	Active employe
4	002557898	Catherine Elizabeth Corey	USD	Salaried employees	Active employe
5	002557898	Catherine Elizabeth Corey		Salaried employees	Active employe
6	002557898	Catherine Elizabeth Corey		Salaried employees	Active employe
7	010225421	Jared Leto	USD	Hourly rate/wage	Active employe
8	010225421	Jared Leto	USD	Hourly rate/wage	Active employe
9	010639658	James Signorile	USD	Salaried employees	Active employe
10	012345678	Melissa Grace Willams	USD	Salaried employees	Active employe
11	012345699	Cathy MacGarhon	USD	Salaried employees	Active employe
12	012345699	Cathy MacGarhon	USD	Salaried employees	Active employe
13	025648577	Michael Joseph	USD	Hourly rate/wage	Active employe
14	025648577	Michael Joseph	USD	Hourly rate/wage	Active employe
15	025856932	Kathleen Anne Zucker	USD	Salaried employees	Active employe
16	026788745	Harvey Weinstein	USD	Hourly rate/wage	Active employe
17	026788745	Harvey Weinstein	USD	Hourly rate/wage	Active employe
18	026788745	Harvey Weinstein	USD	Hourly rate/wage	Active employe
19	070125487	Vincent Aspromonte	USD	Hourly rate/wage	Active employe
20	070858741	Carol Wulf	USD	Salaried employees	Active employe

5. Return to your SAP ABAP Query output screen displaying your table. Another available option from the SAP ABAP Query screen is to select the calculator button on the toolbar to open the Export List Object to XXL dialog box, or the MS Excel settings dialog box shown in Figure 22.12.

6. Depending on the type of data in SAP one of the two dialog boxes will appear providing you with additional options for downloading your ABAP query file to Microsoft Excel.

FIGURE 22.12

*From the ABAP
Query screen you can
select the calculator
button to retrieve a
dialog box for pro-
cessing your SAP
data in Microsoft
Excel.*

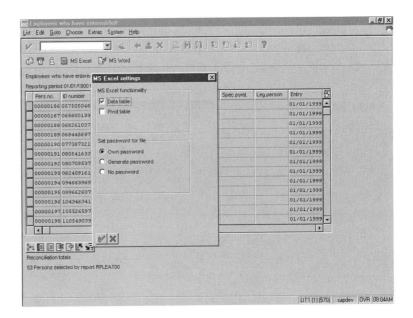

You can use the same method detailed above to download ad hoc queries,
covered in Hour 20, "Ad Hoc Query Reporting (HR Module)" to Microsoft
Excel.

Creating SAP Form Letters in Microsoft Word

SAP has a great interface for creating form letters using Microsoft Word. This tool has
endless possibilities for your company. For an example, you are going to output SAP
Human Resources employee data into Microsoft Word so that you can create a form
letter to all employees.

1. You begin at the ABAP Query reporting screen (ABAP Query reporting is covered in Hour 19). Select a query to execute (you can use the ABAP query you created in Hour 19).

2. On the selection screen use the Display as Table option and then execute your report. Your output will appear similar to that in Figure 22.10.

3. Rather than output this file to Microsoft Excel, select the menu path List, Word Processing. This will open the Word Processor Settings dialog box shown in Figure 22.13.

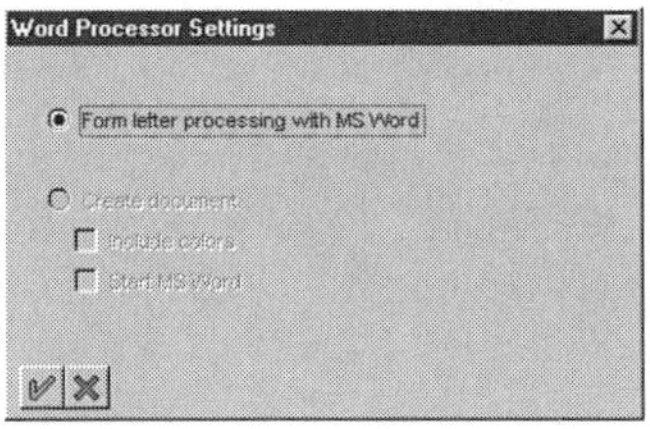

FIGURE 22.13

SAP's Word Processor Settings dialog boxes allow you to download your SAP data into Microsoft Word.

4. Click the Enter key to continue. You will then be prompted with the MS Word Settings dialog box, shown in Figure 22.14.

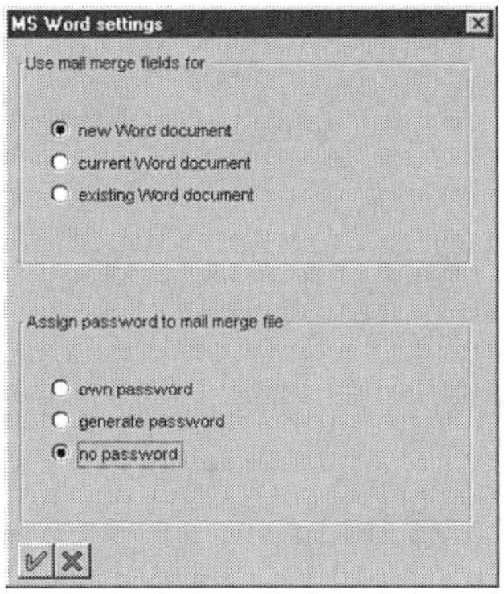

FIGURE 22.14

SAP's MS Word Settings dialog box allows you to designate a password for your document in case you are working with sensitive data.

5. This dialog box presents you with some options regarding your Microsoft Word document. You can designate whether you want to create a new Word document, use a current Word document (which means a word document you presently have open on your system), or use an existing Word document (one that you have saved on your computer). It also allows you to designate whether this Microsoft Word file will contain a password. For the example, you will create a new Microsoft Word document without a password. Clicking the green check mark enter key will

begin the merge between SAP and Microsoft Word. Upon execution, SAP will open Microsoft Word and create a new document (see Figure 22.15).

FIGURE 22.15

A Microsoft Word application will launch with a new document named Document1.

The mail merge toolbar containing a link to your SAP fields

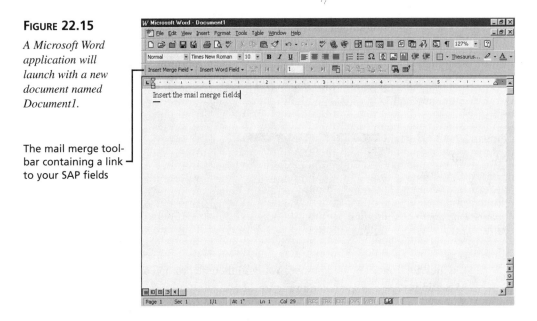

6. An important thing to note is that your Microsoft Word application will now contain a new mail merge toolbar, as indicated in Figure 22.15, which gives you the ability to insert your SAP fields into your Microsoft Word form letter. In Microsoft Word, press the Enter key to bring you to a new line, and then select the Insert Merge Field button on the toolbar. In the drop-down list, shown in Figure 22.16, you will see all the SAP fields contained in your ABAP query.

7. Select the Insert Merge Field button on the toolbar, and then select one of your SAP fields. It will appear in brackets in your Microsoft Word document. Press Enter, and insert another SAP field. Type some text into your Microsoft Word document, and then insert another SAP field (see Figure 22.17).

8. To preview the output of your form letter, click the ABC (view merged data) button from the mail merge toolbar, shown in Figure 22.18.

9. Use the record selection buttons on the mail merge toolbar to view the various records.

FIGURE 22.16

The Microsoft Word Insert Merge Fields button contains the names of your SAP fields from your ABAP query.

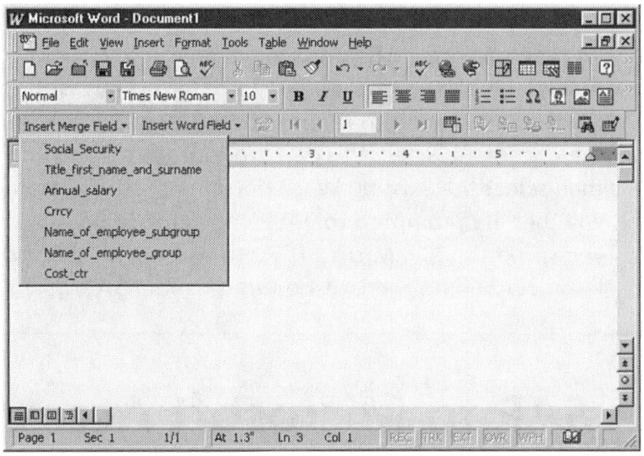

FIGURE 22.17

Your Microsoft Word form letter contains the SAP fields from your ABAP Query that you inserted in addition to any text you typed.

SAP fields appear in brackets.

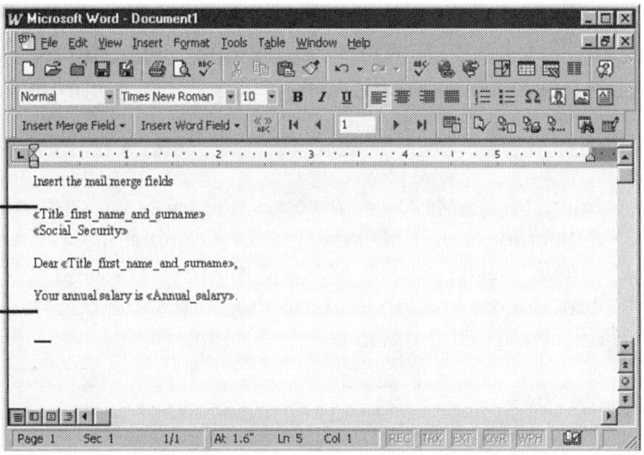

FIGURE 22.18

A sample Microsoft Word form letter containing the SAP fields from your ABAP Query, in view merged data view.

Actual SAP data

View merged data button

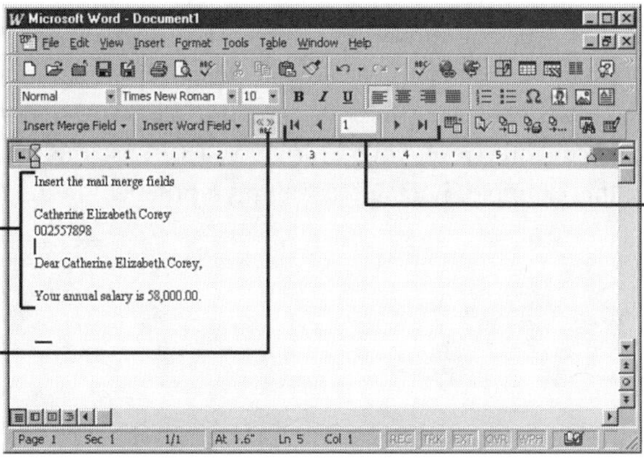

Record selectors

You can save your Microsoft Word merge document for repeated use. Next time you wish to use the same form letter (but with the latest data from SAP), you will need to reopen the ABAP query that serves as the source of the document, select the List, Word processing option from the menu, and then select the existing Word document radio button (see Figure 22.14). You will then be prompted to enter the name of your Word document where you saved the file. Microsoft Word will launch displaying your existing form letter containing the latest data from your SAP system.

Exporting SAP to Microsoft Access

I have reviewed how to export SAP data to Microsoft Excel, which can be useful for performing further manipulation of the data or for creating reports and graphs. Exporting the data to Microsoft Word is a great tool for creating form letters. Exporting data to a Microsoft Access database is useful, also, as a general reporting tool.

Exporting to Microsoft Access is helpful as well when you want to compare data among multiple systems. For example, if your company stores your vendor master data in SAP and it also stores vendor master data in a non-SAP application, you can use Microsoft Access as a tool to compare the consistency of the two sources of information.

The initial steps to export data into Microsoft Access are the same as the steps to download a file into Microsoft Excel, see sections, Exporting Lists to Microsoft Excel and Exporting ABAP Query Reports to Microsoft Excel. In both instances, using either the System List function method or the ABAP Query report, a file will be created on your system with an .xls extension. In the "Exporting Lists to Microsoft Excel" section, you created a file and stored it on your C drive. You will use this same file for the Access example. In this example, I created a file (mysapfile.xls) in the C:\ My Documents directory.

> Depending on your Microsoft configuration, you might have to perform a few extra steps here:
>
> 1. Launch Microsoft Excel, and open the spreadsheet you worked on earlier.
> 2. In Excel, use the menu path File, Save As to save this file.
> 3. In the Save As window, in the Save as Type box, make sure that the file is saved as a Microsoft Excel Worksheet and not any other format.

Importing SAP in to Microsoft Access

Once the download file from SAP has been created on your system, you will need to import this file in to Microsoft Access:

1. Launch Microsoft Access on your system. You will first be presented with a window similar to the one in Figure 22.19.

FIGURE 22.19

The launch screen of Microsoft Access.

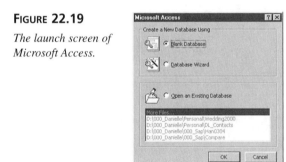

2. From this initial window, select the Blank Database option, and then click OK. You will be prompted to create a name and to select a location for your database. In this example, I selected the C:\My Documents directory and named the database MySap.mdb, as shown in Figure 22.20.

3. Click the Create button; you will see the main Microsoft Access window, which appears in Figure 22.21.

4. To bring the SAP data into Microsoft Access, use the Microsoft Access menu path File, Get External Data, Import. You will be prompted with a window similar to the one shown in Figure 22.22. This is where you have to input the location and file-name of the output file you saved earlier. By default, the Files of Type box lists `Microsoft Access (*.mdb)`. You have to change this to Microsoft Excel.

Figure 22.20

The Microsoft Access File New Database window prompts you to create a new database file.

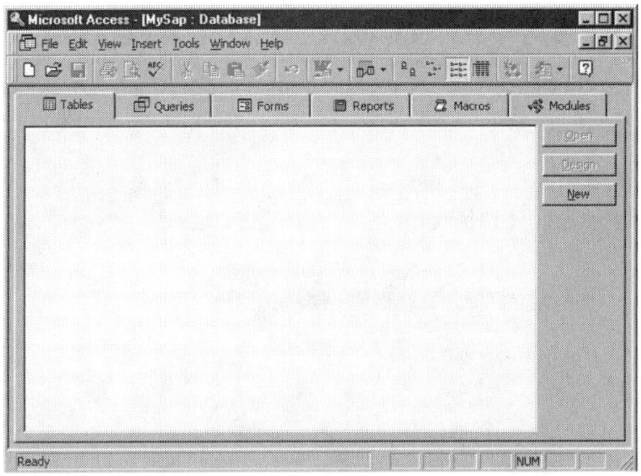

Figure 22.21

The Microsoft Access database main window shows a tab view of the different database elements.

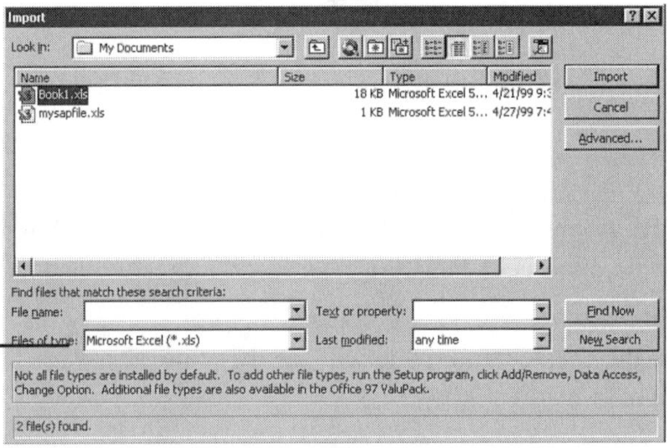

Figure 22.22

Select your file location in the Microsoft Access Import window.

Be sure to change the Files of type box to indicate Microsoft Excel.

5. After changing the Files of type box and selecting your file, click Import. Just as in the Microsoft Excel import, in Access you are presented with an Import Spreadsheet Wizard similar to the one shown in Figure 22.23.

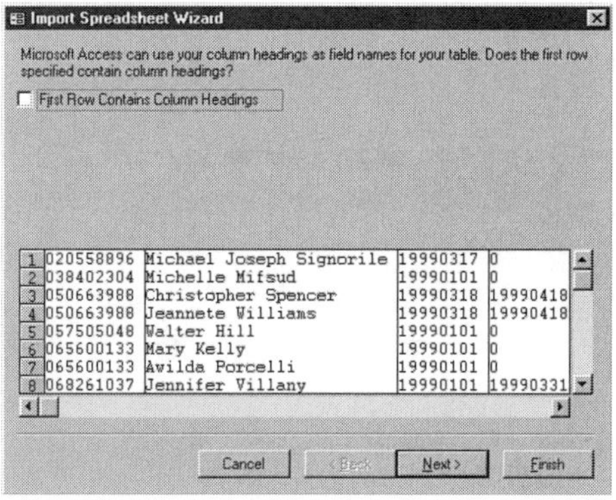

FIGURE 22.23

The Microsoft Access Import Spreadsheet Wizard assists you in importing your file.

6. On the first screen of the Import Spreadsheet Wizard, click the Next button to continue. On the second screen, it asks whether you want to create a new table or add the data to an existing table. To create a new Access database table containing your SAP data, click Next. The next window, shown in Figure 22.24, will give you an opportunity to name each of your fields.

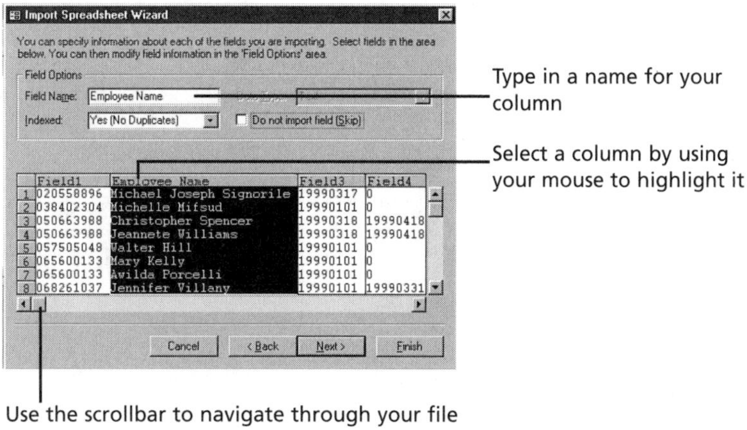

FIGURE 22.24

Microsoft Access Import Spreadsheet Wizard field allows for individual field specification.

Type in a name for your column

Select a column by using your mouse to highlight it

Use the scrollbar to navigate through your file

7. By selecting each column (using your mouse to highlight each column), you can type in a field name for each. After you have named all your fields, click Next.

8. The next screen allows you to assign a unique identifying number for each of your records, to be used as a primary key (primary keys are discussed in Hour 3, "Database Basics"). Click the Next button to continue.

9. The last screen asks you to provide a name for your table. Type in My SAP Table and click Finish. Microsoft Access will then present you with a confirmation

window, shown in Figure 22.25, saying that your data has been successfully imported.

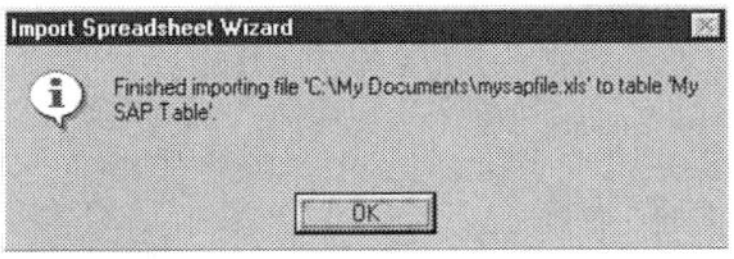

FIGURE 22.25

The Microsoft Access confirmation window announces that data was successfully imported.

10. Click OK in the confirmation window; you will be returned to the Microsoft Access main window, and your new table will be listed under the Table tab.

11. To take a look at your table, select it and then click the Open button. Your SAP list will then appear as a Microsoft Access table (see Figure 22.26).

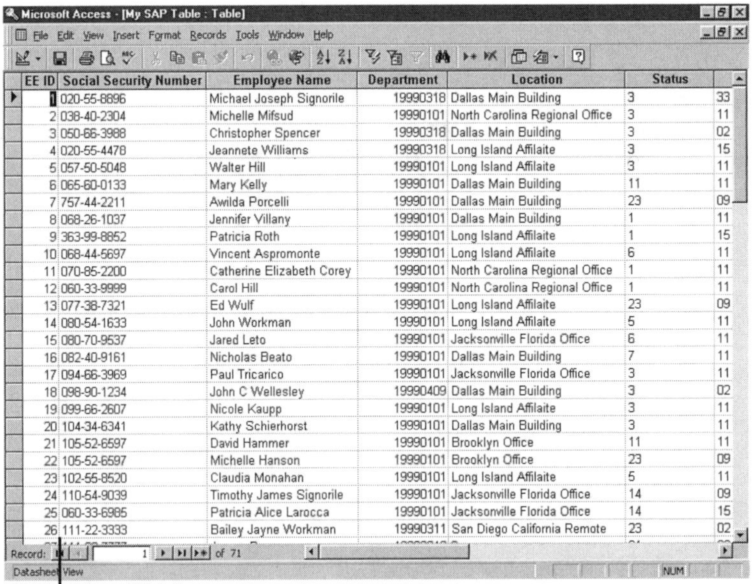

FIGURE 22.26

Your SAP data now appears in a Microsoft Access database table.

Your SAP file now appears in an Access table with an additional primary key field.

This may seem a few steps longer than exporting an SAP file to Microsoft Excel. However, Microsoft Access is a very popular reporting tool used by a large number of SAP customers as their main reporting tool. The reason for its popularity is that

Microsoft Access has report wizards that give a step-by-step, easy way for individuals with little-to-no Microsoft Access skills to create advanced, comprehensive reports. Now you will create one sample report using a Microsoft Access Report Wizard.

The Microsoft Access Report Wizard

Creating reports in Microsoft Access is easy using a tool called the Microsoft Access Report Wizard. The use of reports wizards simplifies the layout process of your fields by visually stepping you through a series of questions about the type of report that you want to create. The wizard walks you through the step-by–step creation of a report, while behind the scenes Access is formatting, grouping and sorting your report based on selections you make.

Instead of having to create a report from scratch, Microsoft Access contains many standard report formats that you can use for the output of your data. Microsoft Access is a widely used reporting tool for SAP because it delivers many preset reporting formats for different types of reports including tabular and columnar reports, mail-merge reports and mailing labels. Reports created using the Microsoft Access Report Wizard can also be customized to fit your needs. To use the Report Wizard, perform the following steps:

1 In the main Microsoft Access database window, click the Reports tab. (If you are still viewing your table, close it by using the menu path File, Close.)

2. In the Reports tab, click the New button to launch the Microsoft Access Report Wizard (see Figure 22.27).

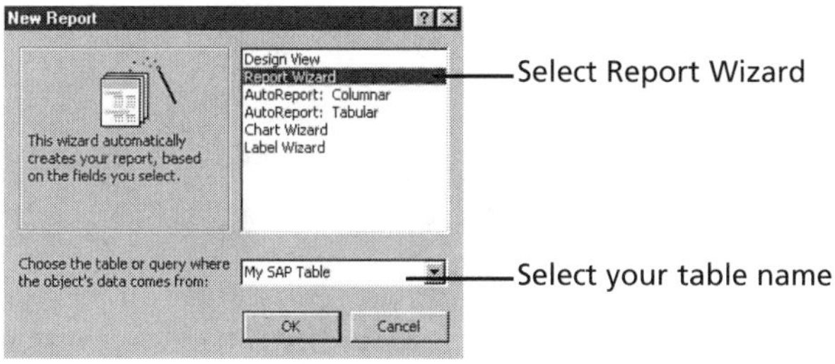

FIGURE 22.27

The Microsoft Access Report Wizard is used for the easy creation of Access reports.

Select Report Wizard

Select your table name

3. On this screen, select the Report Wizard option in the top box and your table name in the second box. Click OK to proceed.

4. Next, you are presented with a field selection screen. From this screen, you can select which fields will be output to your report. Select a field by highlighting it with your mouse, and use the Next button to include it in the report. In the example, I selected the Social Security Number and Employee Name fields, as shown in Figure 22.28.

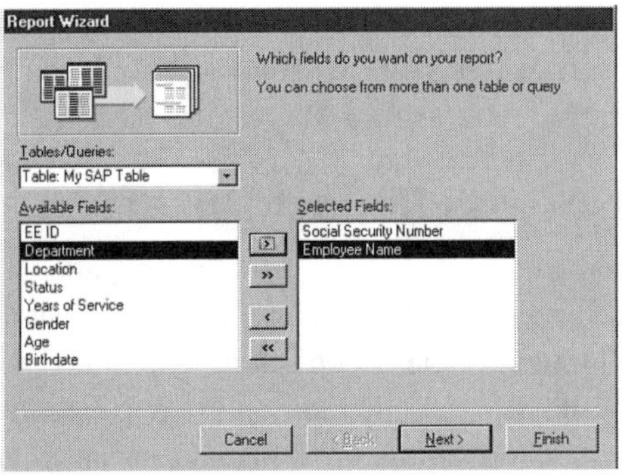

FIGURE 22.28

The Microsoft Access Report Wizard field selection window allows you to specify which fields you would like to include on your report output.

5. After you click Next, the Report Wizard will ask whether you want to add any grouping levels to your report. This is a helpful step when you are creating a report in which you want to group and subtotal by multiple criteria. For this example, you don't need grouping or subtotaling, so click the Next button to continue.

6. The next screen allows you to identify sorting criteria. In the example, shown in Figure 22.29, I have sorted according to Employee Name.

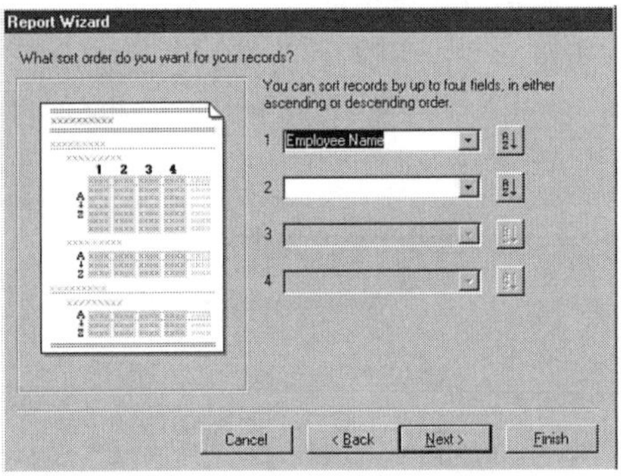

FIGURE 22.29

The Microsoft Access Report Wizard allows you to select multiple sorting criteria.

7. The Report Wizard allows you to specify formatting criteria. The orientation of the report (portrait or landscape) and the layout of the report (columnar, tabular, or justified) are designated on this screen. After making a selection, click Next.

8. You can choose from a selection of predefined formats for your report. After making a selection, click Next.

9. The last step asks you to type in a name for your report. Type one in, and click Finish to complete the creation of your report. Your new Microsoft Access report will be saved with that name in your database.

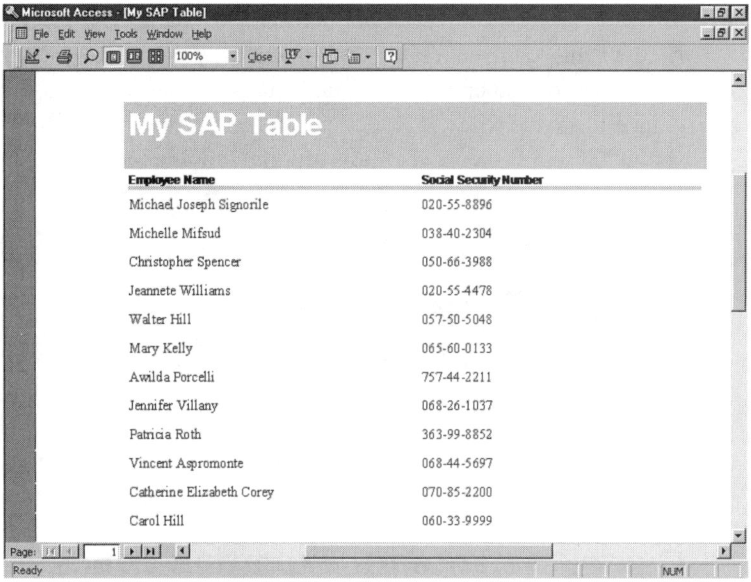

FIGURE 22.30

The Microsoft Access Report Wizard completes by displaying the new report of your SAP data.

Microsoft Access - [My SAP Table]

File Edit View Tools Window Help

100%   Close

My SAP Table

Employee Name	Social Security Number
Michael Joseph Signorile	020-55-8896
Michelle Mifsud	038-40-2304
Christopher Spencer	050-66-3988
Jeannete Williams	020-55-4478
Walter Hill	057-50-5048
Mary Kelly	065-60-0133
Awilda Porcelli	757-44-2211
Jennifer Villany	068-26-1037
Patricia Roth	363-99-8852
Vincent Aspromonte	068-44-5697
Catherine Elizabeth Corey	070-85-2200
Carol Hill	060-33-9999

Page: 1

Ready   NUM

You can save your Microsoft Access database for repeated use. Any reports that you create will be saved in the database file. Next time you wish to use the database (but with the latest data from SAP), you will need to follow the steps outlined in the "Quick Reference for Exporting ABAP Query Reports to Access" or the "Quick Reference for Exporting SAP Lists to Access" at the end of this hour. Next you will need to follow the steps outlined in the "Importing SAP to Microsoft Access" section of this hour.

When you launch Microsoft Access be sure to open your existing database and when you are using the Import Spreadsheet Wizard (see Figure 22.23) you can select to append your records to your existing Access table or create a new one.

Advanced Microsoft Access users can write a macro that will automatically retrieve the latest SAP download file and import it in to your existing Microsoft Access table replacing the old data and thus automating the Microsoft Access process. For more information on this function search the Microsoft Access help for "automate importing."

In addition advanced SAP, ABAP programmers can write a program that will automatically generate a file that can be used for download, thus automating the SAP process.

Microsoft Access is a great reporting tool that enables users with minimal Microsoft Access skills to create reports. Using Access, you can also include graphics in your reports, or you can create graphs and charts of your SAP data. If you take a few minutes to investigate the types of reports you can create using Microsoft Access, I'm sure that you will discover the value of this reporting tool for SAP.

Quick References for Exporting SAP Data to Microsoft Office

Once you get going in SAP and begin to unleash the power of reporting in SAP you may want to revisit these downloading options so that you can work with your SAP data in Microsoft office. The "Quick Reference for Exporting Data to Microsoft Office" section gives you an overview of each of the processes. For a more detailed review of the integration between SAP and Microsoft Office, return to the beginning of this hour.

Quick Reference for Exporting Lists to Microsoft Excel

The following is a recap of the steps required to use the System List function to export SAP lists to Microsoft Excel. See the section "Exporting Lists to Microsoft Excel" earlier in this hour for more information.

1. Navigate to the SAP screen containing the list you want to output.
2. Follow the menu path System, List, Save, Local File.
3. Use the possible entries help button (down arrow) to change the location and filename for your new file.
4. Click the Transfer button.
5. Launch Microsoft Excel and open the file.

Quick Reference for Exporting ABAP Query Reports to Excel

The following is a recap of the steps required to output ABAP Query reports to Microsoft Excel. See the section "Exporting ABAP Query Reports to Microsoft Excel" earlier this hour for more information.

1. Execute the SAP ABAP Query report that contains the data that you want to include in your report.
2. On the selection screen, select the Display as Table option, and execute the report.
3. Select the List, Download to File menu option.

22

4. Use the possible entries help button (down arrow) to change the location and filename for your new file.

5. Click the Transfer button.

6. Launch Microsoft Excel and open the file.

Quick Reference for Creating Form Letters with Microsoft Word

The following is a recap of the steps required to create SAP form letters using Microsoft Word. See the section "Creating SAP Form Letters in Microsoft Word" earlier in this hour for more information.

1. Execute the SAP ABAP Query report that contains the data that you want to include in your report.

2. On the selection screen, select the Display as Table option, and execute the report.

3. Select the List, Word Processing menu option.

4. Click the Enter button on the Word Processing Settings dialog box.

5. Select your required options from the MS Word Settings dialog box, and then click the enter button.

6. Type your document, and insert merge fields using the Insert Merge Field button on the Microsoft Word mail merge toolbar.

7. Use the ABC view merged data button to review your document and the record selection buttons to navigate between records.

Quick Reference for Exporting Lists to Microsoft Access

The following is a recap of the steps required to use the System List function to export SAP lists into Microsoft Access. The initial steps of this process are the same for downloading files to Microsoft Excel, see the section "Exporting Lists to Microsoft Excel" for additional information. See the section "Importing SAP in to Microsoft Access" earlier this hour for more information on getting the data in to Access.

1. Navigate to the SAP screen containing the list you want to output.

2. Follow the menu path System, List, Save, Local File.

3. Use the possible entries help button (down arrow) to change the location and filename for your new file.

4. Click the Transfer button.

5. Open your file in Microsoft Excel, and use the menu path File, Save As to save it as a Microsoft Excel worksheet. Close Excel.

6. Launch Microsoft Access and create a new database.

7. Use the menu path File, Get External Data, Import, and select your Microsoft Excel file to import the file in to Microsoft Access using the Import Spreadsheet Wizard.

Quick Reference for Exporting ABAP Query Reports to Access

The following is an explanation of the steps required to output an ABAP Query report to Microsoft Access. The initial steps of this process are the same for downloading files to Microsoft Excel, see the section "Exporting ABAP Query Reports to Microsoft Excel" earlier this hour for more information. For more information about importing the file into Microsoft Access see the section, "Importing SAP in to Microsoft Access."

1. Execute the SAP ABAP Query report that contains the data that you want to include in your report.

2. On the selection screen, select the Display as Table option, and execute the report.

3. Select the List, Download to File menu option.

4. Use the possible entries help button (down arrow) to change the location and file-name for your new file.

5. Click the Transfer button.

6. Open your file in Microsoft Excel, and use the menu path File, Save As to save it as a Microsoft Excel worksheet. Close Excel.

7. Launch Microsoft Access and create a new database.

8. Use the menu path File, Get External Data, Import, and select your Microsoft Excel file to import the file in to Microsoft Access using the Import Spreadsheet Wizard.

Summary

Many tools on the market are designed to assist you in creating reports of your SAP data. This lesson gives you a look at how Microsoft Excel, Word, and Access can used for that purpose.

The reporting functionality offered by SAP (see Hour 18) might not be sufficient to satisfy your companies needs. In many cases, external systems are used for reporting. Using the Microsoft Office family of products is one avenue where you can easily create the reports you need without advanced technical knowledge and without the help of an SAP technical professional.

Microsoft Excel is an ideal tool used to create advanced charts, pivot tables and reports involving advanced calculations of your SAP data. Microsoft Word is ideal for creating merged form letters and mailing labels. An advantage of using Microsoft Access as a reporting tool for SAP is that you can use it as a comparison tool for data that is stored outside of SAP. This is useful if you want to compare data among multiple systems. You can use Microsoft Access as a tool to compare the consistency of the two sources of information. The skills learned in this hour will prove very valuable in working with your SAP data.

Q&A

Q Instead of using the reporting tools provided by SAP can custom reports be created from scratch in SAP?

A Custom reports can be created from scratch in all SAP applications. These reports (or programs as they would be called in SAP) would be written in the ABAP language by an advanced ABAP programmer. Some companies create many customized reports and others rely on customized reports only when absolutely necessary.

Q If SAP data is output to a Microsoft Excel spreadsheet and then the spreadsheet is edited is it possible to get that data back in to SAP.

A The easy answer is yes, but it is no easy task. This would require the skills of an advanced ABAP programmer who could write a program that would upload the data in to SAP.

Workshop

The workshop is designed to help you anticipate possible questions, review what you've learned, and begin thinking ahead about putting your knowledge into practice. The answers to the quiz that follows can be found in Appendix A, "Answers."

Quiz

1. Name two methods you can use to create output files to be imported into Microsoft Excel.

2. Which type of interface do you use to communicate with Microsoft Office?

3. Which Microsoft application do you use to create form letters?

4. What does the term *OLE* mean?

5. Name some additional OLE-compatible applications?

Exercises

1. Create a file using the System List function and open the file in Microsoft Excel.

2. Create a new Microsoft Word form letter using an existing Microsoft Word document.

PART VI

SAP R/3 Help

Hour

Hour 23

Help Overview

SAP's Help system is designed to assist you in retrieving information about your SAP system. Right off the bat, I will indicate that the SAP Help system is not designed like any other Help system that you might have used in other applications, such as Microsoft Windows. Unlike the SAP system itself, the design, structure, and functionality of the Help system is not a comprehensive, logical application. The Help application is a collection of diverse components that each fulfill a function, but act together more like a Rube Goldberg machine than a system.

Highlights of this hour include

- Navigating the R/3 Help menu
- Obtaining context-sensitive help
- Taking a look at the HTML Help Viewer

R/3 System Online Documentation

The SAP Help referred to as the Online Documentation for your R/3 system is contained on a separate CD-ROM that you receive with your SAP products. You can also obtain additional copies of the CD-ROM by attending SAP-sponsored training courses. The language for your R/3 Help is specified on the CD-ROM, as is the version number. The version number for your Help CD-ROM should correspond to the version of your SAP GUI.

The Online Documentation CD-ROM contains documentation for the R/3 system in two different formats:

- Standard HTML
- Compressed HTML

The Online Documentation in Standard HTML format is to be viewed with a standard Web browser like Microsoft Internet Explorer or Netscape. The Compressed HTML format is designed to be viewed with a Microsoft HTML Help Viewer that can be used for Windows NT 4.0 or Windows 95-compatible systems.

The configuration of your SAP Online Documentation is managed by your systems administrator. If you access the Online Documentation via a browser, the HTML files are accessed via a Web server or a file server. If you access the Online Documentation via the Microsoft HTML Help Viewer directly off the CD-ROM, it is referred to as viewing the help offline.

> The Microsoft HTML Help Viewer is included on the Online Documentation CD-ROM. Instructions for installing the Help Viewer are contained in a readme.txt file on the CD-ROM, although the instructions are over fifteen pages long and not very clear. It is a good idea to seek the assistance of your SAP system administrator for the installation.

The R/3 Help Menu

From any screen in your R/3 system, you can access the Help menu. The functions of the Help menu are outlined in Table 23.1.

TABLE 23.1 HELP MENU FUNCTIONS

Menu Item	Function
Extended Help	Selecting Extended help launches your R/3 Online Documentation and presents you with the context-sensitive help for your work with the components of your R/3 system.
R/3 Library	Selecting the R/3 Library launches your R/3 Online Documentation and presents you with the main menu.

Menu Item	Function
Glossary	Selecting the Glossary launches your R/3 Online Documentation and presents you with the Glossary main screen.
Release Notes	Selecting Release Notes launches your R/3 Online Documentation (or an SAP dialog window) and presents you with the section pertaining to release information for your R/3 system.
Getting Started	Selecting the Glossary launches your R/3 Online documentation and presents you with the R/3 Getting Started Guide.
Settings	Selecting Settings provides you with a dialog box where you can define how you want your field help displayed.
Help on Help	Selecting Help on Help launches your R/3 Online Documentation and presents you with the R/3 Getting Started Guide.

Navigating in the R/3 Online Documentation Using A Browser

The main screen of the Online Help will appear similar to the one shown in Figure 23.1.

FIGURE 23.1

SAP R/3's Online Help main screen can be accessed from the R/3 main screen by selecting the menu path Help, Extended help.

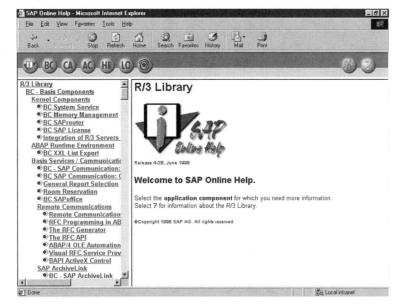

The top of the Help screen, shown in Figure 23.2, indicates the R/3 toolbar.

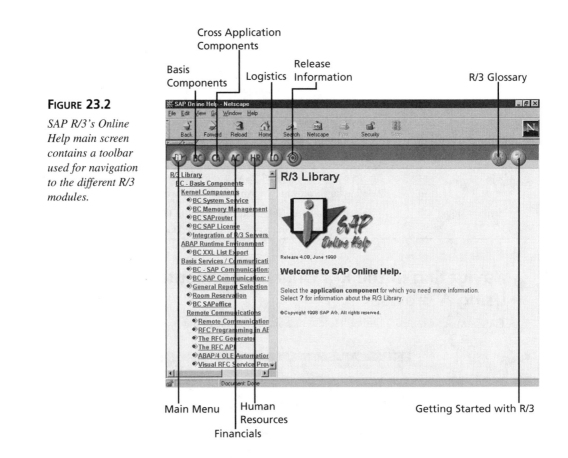

FIGURE 23.2

SAP R/3's Online Help main screen contains a toolbar used for navigation to the different R/3 modules.

Viewing the R/3 Online Documentation using a browser works in the same fashion as browsing on the Internet. Using the buttons on the R/3 toolbar shown in Figure 23.2, you can navigate to the different areas of the R/3 help. You can also use the navigational buttons on the browser's toolbar to navigate back and forth and print your R/3 Online Documentation. Test out your Help by selecting the second list item BC—Basis Components in the left frame of the browser window. The selected topic should now appear in the right side of your window (see Figure 23.3).

In some instances, selecting a list topic in the left frame will repaint your browser window, remove the main menu, and display a new submenu. Select the list item BC—System Service to launch a new menu (see Figure 23.4).

You can also select links in the right window to navigate to additional items in the Online Documentation. These links are usually underlined words.

FIGURE 23.3

Viewing the R/3 Online Documentation using a browser will display a list of topics in the left frame and the detail on the topic in the right frame of the browser window.

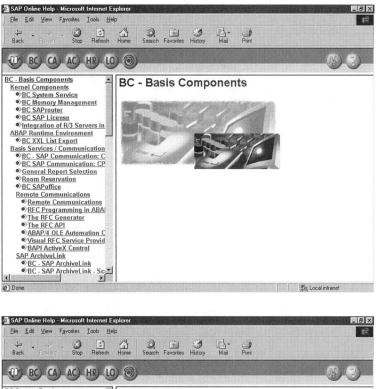

FIGURE 23.4

Selecting certain list items in the item list in the left frame will repaint your browser screen with a new submenu.

The BC System Service submenu now appears in the left frame.

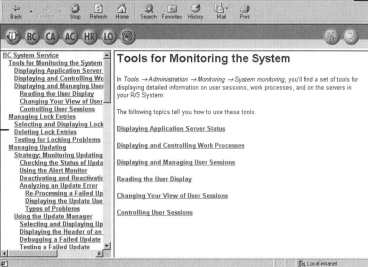

If you are unsure whether text in the right frame of the Online Help is a link, place your cursor over the text. If your cursor changes from an arrow to a hand pointer, the text is a link.

Select the first link in the right frame of your Help window to navigate to that topic. In my screen, it is Displaying Application Server Status (see Figure 23.5).

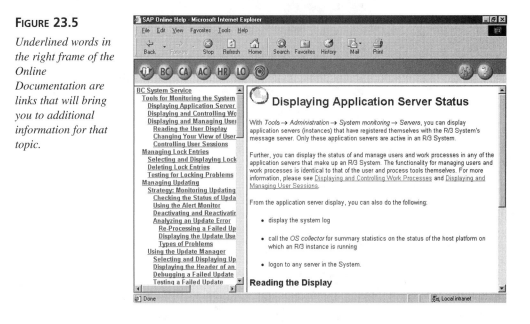

Now that you have traveled deep into the Online Documentation, you might want to return to previous screens or the main menu screen. Using the Back arrow on your browser's toolbar returns you to previous screens. To jump directly to the main menu of list items in the left frame, select the main menu button from the R/3 toolbar (see Figure 23.2).

The pictures used in the preceding examples were taken using the Microsoft Internet Explorer Web browser. SAP recommends the use of the Microsoft Internet Explorer, although the Netscape Navigator browser will provide the same functionality.

Navigating in the R/3 Online Documentation Using the HTML Help Viewer

The standard installation of Help is usually on a browser. Viewing the Online Documentation using the HTML Help Viewer is often used as an offline tool when you are not connected to your R/3 SAP system. The format of this help is similar to accessing the help using a browser (see Figure 23.6).

> The installation of the HTML Help Viewer is done on your local PC and a shortcut is provided to access the Online Documentation in the Programs menu of your Windows Start menu. The Online Documentation CD-ROM needs to be inserted in your CD-ROM drive in order for you to access the Help. It is also possible to install the entire CD-ROM onto your hard drive. This method will consume a large portion of your systems resources and is not recommended.

23

FIGURE 23.6

Viewing the Online Documentation using the HTML Help Viewer is usually done offline.

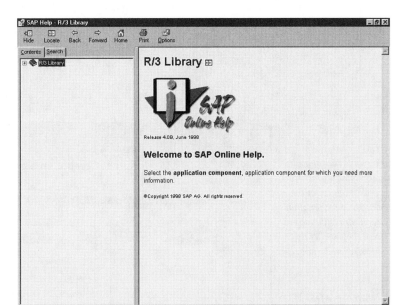

Navigation buttons like the ones on typical browser screens appear at the top of the Help application. The R/3 toolbar buttons representing the different modules that were present when viewing the Help through a browser are not available here. Instead, the Help is displayed in a tree structure in the left frame of the Help Viewer window. As in SAP, you can expand the different nodes by clicking on the + sign indicated to the left of a list item. Expand the R/3 library item to see a list of nodes. You will notice that the list is comparable to the R/3 toolbar shown in the browser (see Figure 23.7).

Selecting subnodes from within an application launches a new HTML Help Viewer window containing a submenu of items (see Figure 23.8).

FIGURE 23.7

The HTML Help Viewer is structured in a tree diagram.

Items listed here match the R/3 tool-bar shown in Figure 23.2.

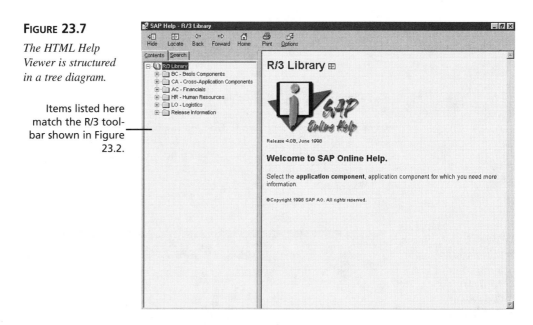

FIGURE 23.8

The HTML Help Viewer creates multiple windows during your navigation in the Help rather than repainting the current window as the browser view does.

With the HTML Help Viewer, new windows are created.

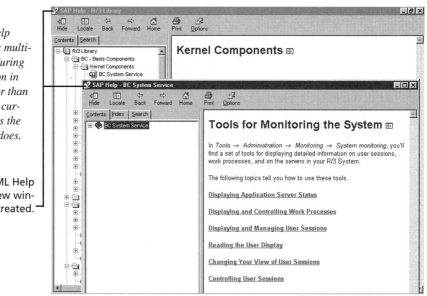

Multiple windows will be created during navigation. Unlike viewing using a browser, the Back button will return you to the previous screen for that window only. You can select the Home button from the top of any window to return to the main screen.

Release Notes

Release Notes are available from within your R/3 system or in the Online Documentation under the Release Notes option. Release Notes provide you with a list of modifications and additions to your R/3 system since prior releases. This includes functionality and conceptual changes.

To view Release Notes in a tree structure from within your R/3 system, select the menu path Help, Release Notes. Release Notes can also be viewed from the Online Documentation by selecting the Release Notes button from the R/3 toolbar.

23

Searching For The Help You Need

When working in SAP, you will often need to retrieve help. You might need conceptual help in order to better comprehend subject matter; definition help, to help you understand an SAP term; or general help, when you are completely at a loss. There are a couple of different methods that can be used to obtain help in your R/3 system.

Unlike help systems that you might be familiar with from other PC applications, such as Microsoft Office, SAP Online Documentation does not have an easy one-two-three for-mat for retrieving help. You need to be familiar with the different methods of retrieving help, which depend on

- Where you are in the system
- The type of help you are looking for
- Your Online Documentation configuration

The Search and Index Functions in the HTML Help Viewer

The Search Tab in the HTML Help Viewer is used to allow you to search for words and strings on the SAP R/3 Online Documentation CD-ROM. To perform a search, enter your search criteria, and then select the List Topics button. Online Help will scan the CD-ROM looking for all occurrences of the search criteria and list them in the left frame.

You can select any item in the left frame, and then select the Display button to display the help in the right frame. When entering search criteria, you need to be very specific; otherwise, the search will yield all help topics that contain your words.

There are many complaints about the functionality of the Search feature in the Microsoft HTML Help Viewer. Many joke that regardless of the search criteria you enter you will always retrieve a "No Topics Found" response. More effective than the Search tab is the

Index tab in the HTML Help Viewer. The Index tab is not available on the main HTML Help Viewer window. It only becomes available when you select a list item from the main menu that in turn launches a second window (see Figure 23.8). Entering your criteria into the field on the Index tab will yield a list of related topics and is a more efficient method of searching for help in the HTML Help Viewer.

Retrieving Topic-Specific Help

When processing in your R/3 system, you will encounter screens and functions about which you have questions. Rather than launching the Help and trying to search for the information you need, select the menu path Help, Extended Help from the screen that you have questions about. Your Online Documentation application will launch with topic-specific help related to the SAP screen that you were processing in. To see the functionality of topic-specific help, perform the following steps:

1. Use transaction code nPS01to navigate to the R/3 Project Information System.

2. Follow the menu path Help, Extended Help to launch the Online Documentation. Instead of opening to the main menu, help related to the R/3 Project Information System will be launched (see Figure 23.9).

FIGURE 23.9

You can retrieve topic-specific help by navigating to the screen that contains the topic and choosing the menu path Help, Extended Help from the menu bar.

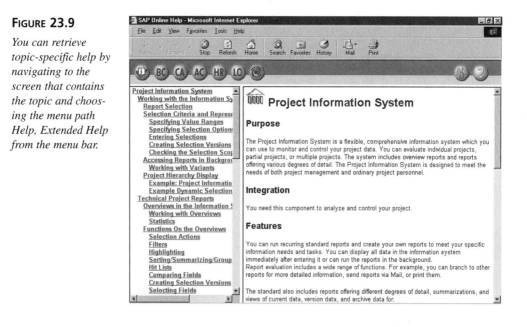

Retrieving Field-Specific Help

SAP also contains Help information that is embedded into the SAP R/3 application. You can retrieve field-specific help by performing the following steps:

1. Use transaction code nME21 to navigate to the Create Purchase Order: Initial screen.

2. Position your cursor in the Vendor field and press F1 (see Figure 23.10).

FIGURE 23.10

Field-specific help can be obtained by positioning your cursor in an SAP field and pressing F1.

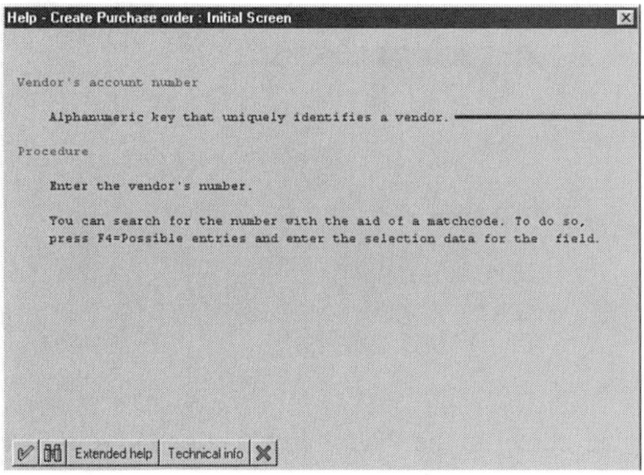

Field-specific help contains hypertext, which can be used to navigate to additional Help topics.

As indicated in Figure 23.10, field-specific help contains hypertext that can lead you to additional help topics within SAP (see Figure 23.11). Hypertext is usually shaded with a background color for identification.

FIGURE 23.11

Selecting the Vendor hypertext launches a second window with additional information.

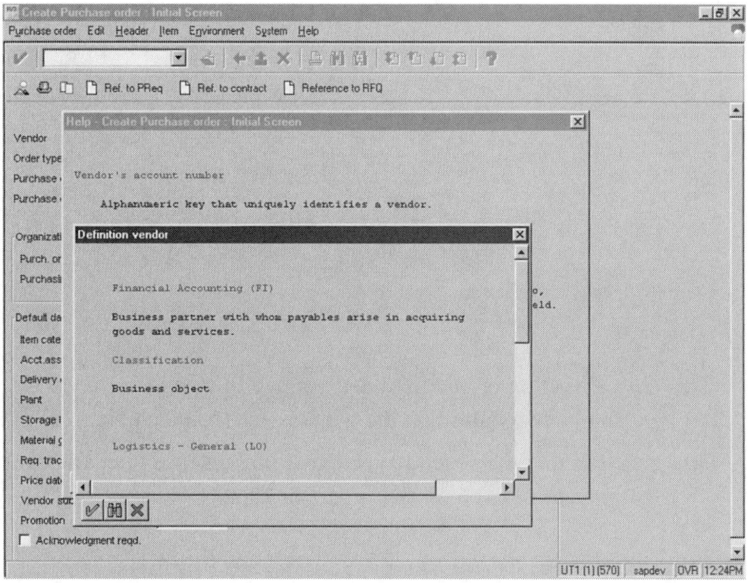

Retrieving Extended Help for a Field

When you press F1 to retrieve field-specific information, sometimes there is a button available for you to request additional information from the R/3 Online Documentation. Follow these steps:

1. From the main SAP window, follow the menu path Human Resources, Payroll to bring up a dialog box similar to the one shown in Figure 23.12.

FIGURE 23.12

Field-specific help can be obtained by positioning your cursor in an SAP field on any SAP screen, including dialog boxes, and pressing F1.

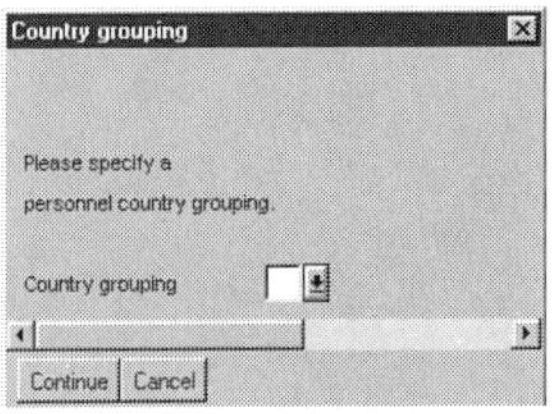

2. Position your cursor in the Payroll area field and press F1 to launch the field-specific help (see Figure 23.13).

FIGURE 23.13

Extended Help is available on some SAP field-specific help windows.

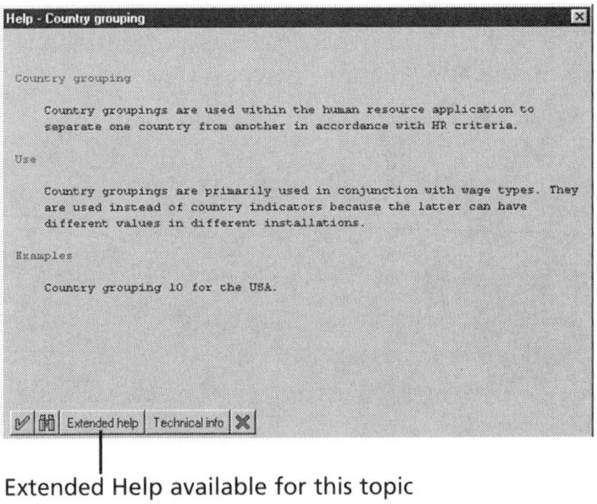

Extended Help available for this topic

3. Depending on the field that you are in when you select the field-specific help, there might be a button on the window for Extended Help, as in Figure 23.13.

4. Selecting the Extended Help button launches your Online Documentation containing additional information on the topic.

Searching in the Field-Specific Help

When you select field-specific help, you are presented with a window containing information related to your selection. Depending on the amount of data presented in that window, it might be helpful for you to search the data for a particular term or keyword. This functionality is available by performing the following steps:

1. From the main SAP window, follow the menu path Human Resources, Payroll to bring up a dialog box similar to the one you saw in Figure 23.12.

2. Place your cursor in the Country grouping field and press F1.

3. Select the Find button (represented by the binoculars icon) to bring up a Find dialog box (see Figure 23.14).

FIGURE 23.14

Using the Find button, you can search for specific keywords in the Help window.

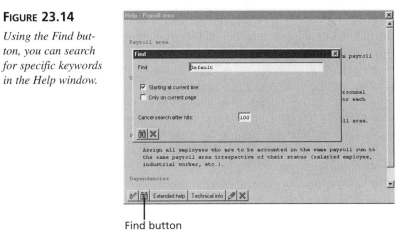

Find button

4. Enter a word that you want to search for and select the Find button.

5. If the word is found, a new Find window appears, indicating the number of matches (hits) for your search criteria (see Figure 23.15). It also provides the list of matches as hot keys you can select to automatically navigate to that line.

6. Selecting the hypertext returns you to the initial help window at the line of help that contains your search criteria.

Field-Specific Help Settings

You can customize the way your field-specific help functions by modifying the Settings option. Follow the menu path Help, Settings, which presents the Help—Settings dialog box, as shown in Figure 23.16.

FIGURE 23.15

If any words in the Help text match your search criteria, they will be presented in a second Find window.

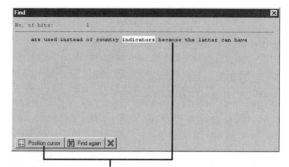

Placing your cursor on any other text and then selecting the Position Cursor button brings you directly to that line in the text.

FIGURE 23.16

You can modify the display of your field-specific help by changing the settings in the Help—Settings dialog box.

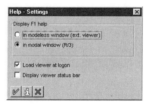

The first two radio buttons are used to specify whether you want your field-specific help presented in an R/3 window (shown in Figure 23.13) or displayed in the HTML Help Viewer. The Load viewer at Logon check box specifies that the F1 Help Viewer with modeless window is to be loaded and put on the desktop as an iconized application when you log on to the R/3 system. The Display Viewer Status Bar specifies that the status bar of the F1 Help Viewer is to be displayed.

The R/3 Glossary

The R/3 Glossary contains a few hundred SAP terms. Each entry contains a definition and, in some cases, additional information about the topic. Because the Glossary is relatively limited and does not contain all SAP terms, it is a good idea to also search for the word using the Index tab in the Microsoft HTML Help Viewer as discussed in "The Search and Index Functions in the HTML Help Viewer" section earlier in this hour.

Glossary Browser View

The R/3 Glossary can be accessed by selecting the Glossary button from the R/3 toolbar. The alphabet appears at the top of the screen from which you can select the letter of the word you want to define. All words contained in the R/3 Glossary beginning with that letter will appear listed in the left frame of the browser window. Selecting a word in the left frame displays its definition in the right frame.

Glossary HTML Help View

The R/3 Glossary functions a little differently in the HTML Help Viewer. Here, you would need to use the Search and Index tabs as discussed in "The Search and Index Functions in the HTML Help Viewer" section earlier in this hour to obtain the definitions of SAP terms.

This method is not as useful when looking for simple definitions of SAP terms because the search will return all text listings that contain your word.

Problems With SAP R/3 Help

As mentioned earlier in the hour, the Online Documentation available in SAP has limited capabilities. For those of us accustomed to the elaborate help applications offered by Microsoft Office and other common desktop applications, SAP help cannot compare.

Comparing the Online Documentation to a Rube Goldberg machine at the introduction of this hour is an accurate description. For all the functionality and capabilities of SAP, its help application appears to be a complicated combination of functionality that does not in the end provide the necessary output. Some of its shortcomings are outlined in the following sections.

Limited Searching Capabilities

As indicated earlier, you have the ability to search in the R/3 HTML Help Viewer. The limited searching capabilities discussed here refer to Online Documentation. Those of us used to the Help capabilities included with Microsoft applications have become accustomed to searching and retrieving data in Help based on full-text descriptions or partial descriptions. These capabilities, although presented as options in some of the SAP Help, do not work the way that you might think.

You cannot search for additional information on a concept in the Browser view of the Online Documentation. Searching is also not possible in the list of menu items in the left frame of the Help viewed in a browser. Regardless of the number of times your search criteria exists, it will always indicate that your search item is not found. If you want to search for a text string, you need to access the R/3 HTML Help Viewer Index tab.

German Conversions

The SAP R/3 Help application, like the training materials provided at SAP-offered training courses, is first written in German and then translated to English. Because of this method, much is lost in the translation. In addition, in many places the translation process is not yet complete, and some screens will appear with words and definitions in German. In some cases, you will be presented with text saying "Not available in this language," and in other cases, your Help will appear in German.

Version Inconsistencies

The Help application also is not in sync with your SAP version number. For example, some functionality and concepts that existed in 3.X versions of SAP were replaced with new concepts and functionality in 4.X, but are not covered in the 4.X Help. In many cases, the 4.X Help corresponds to 3.X concepts and module naming conventions that no longer exist in R/3 4.X. As you can imagine, this causes a lot of confusion for users.

The most troubling problem with this discrepancy is that the menu paths provided in the Help refer to paths that no longer exist in the 4.X version of your SAP system. A good example of this would be the SAP 4.0B Help for Creating a User Menu, shown in Figure 23.17.

FIGURE 23.17

The instructions for Creating a User Menu in SAP R/3's Online Help correspond to menu paths and functionality from version 3.0, which no longer exist in version 4.0.

Screen print presented in the Online Documentation corresponds to the way the screens appeared in version 3.X and not 4.X.

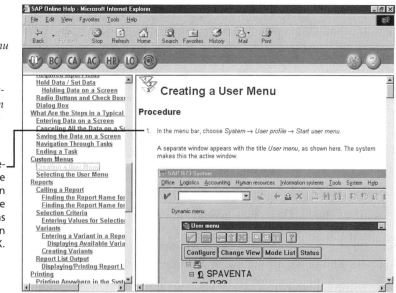

In the 4.0B Online Help, step 1 for Creating a User Menu says to follow the menu path System, User Profile, Start User Menu. If you try to find this menu path in your 4.0B system, you will have a problem (see Figure 23.18). In fact, this functionality has been significantly modified in version 4.0, although there is no mention of it in the Help.

FIGURE 23.18

Menu paths that existed in version 3.0 of R/3 and no longer exist in version 4.0 of R/3 are still listed in the 4.0 Help application.

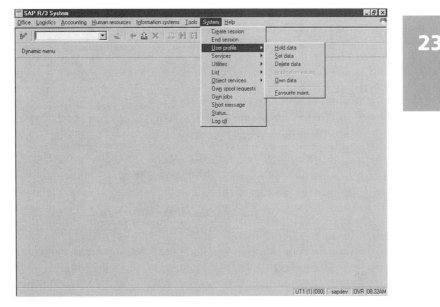

23

Training Materials

When you attend an SAP Training course, in most instances, you will be presented with a notebook binder containing your training materials. The standard documentation provided is in the format of a Microsoft PowerPoint Presentation. This means that each page of the notebook contains a large screen print followed by a few bullet points of information.

The bullet points usually only scratch the surface of a concept. Although the concept might be discussed and instructed at length in the class, the training materials serve as a poor reference for the topic. In addition, as with the documentation available in the Help, sometimes the translation process is not yet complete and some pages of your English documentation might still be in German. In other cases, some of your 4.0 documentation might still contain 3.0 concepts and menu paths.

Summary

In the past hour, you have learned how to obtain help in your R/3 system. You should now feel comfortable navigating through the Online Documentation in SAP and also retrieving context and field-sensitive help in SAP. Although the design of the R/3 system and its modules is truly comprehensive, and SAP is the leader at enterprise solution software, the SAP Help application is really behind the times in its design and functionality. Because of this, there is a wealth of outside information available for SAP R/3 users. Examples are covered in Chapter 24, "Additional SAP Resources."

Q&A

Q What are the minimum system requirements for viewing the Help Online Documentation?

A The minimum system requirements for viewing the Help Online Documentation are the installation of Microsoft Internet Explorer version 3.02 (or Netscape 3.0) or higher and the HTML Help, version 1.1.

Q If, after the installation of the Microsoft HTML Help Viewer, a shortcut is not available from your programs menu, how do you add it?

A To insert a menu item into your Microsoft Windows program menu to access the Microsoft HTML Help Viewer, run the installation script HH40B-DE.inf located in the HTMLHELP\HelpDATA\En\ directory of the Online Documentation CD-ROM.

Q Are full help text searches available in the Web browser view?

A Full help text searches are available in the Web browser view only with help type "PlainHtmlHttp" and not with help type "PlainHtmlFile." Contact your system administrator for additional information on the installation of your SAP Online Documentation.

Workshop

The workshop is designed to help you anticipate possible questions, review what you've learned, and begin thinking ahead to putting your knowledge into practice. The answers to the quiz that follows can be found in Appendix A, "Answers."

Quiz

1. What is the menu path used to see Release Notes within the R/3 application?
2. How can you obtain field-specific help?
3. How can you obtain context-specific help?

4. What is the R/3 menu path used to navigate to the Online Documentation Getting Started guide?

5. Where do you change the settings for how you want your SAP field help to appear?

6. How do you distinguish links in the browser view of your R/3 Online Documentation?

Exercises

1. Navigate to transaction code nFMP0 and request Field Specific Help on the FM area field.

2. Navigate to transaction code nCRC0 and retrieve Context Sensitive Help for the Resources screen.

3. Using the Microsoft HTML Help Viewer, use the Index tab to search for the term Invoice.

4. Launch the Getting Started Guide from the main SAP window.

5. Navigate to the Release Notes for release 4.0B from the main SAP window.

23

Hour **24**

Additional SAP Resources

Although SAP is the fourth largest software vendor in the world and the market leader in Enterprise applications software, unlike with Microsoft, there is not an overabundance of resources available to the user. For example, if you wanted to retrieve additional help and information on the Microsoft Excel application, there are hundreds of up-to-date books available on the market, in addition to probably more than a handful of experts available within your company. With SAP, it's not that easy.

As mentioned in Hour 23, "Help Overview," the instructional documentation provided by SAP is in the format of Microsoft PowerPoint Presentations with large screen prints and few bullet points. There are books present on the market, but the availability of current version reference materials is slim.

This hour I will discuss additional SAP resources available to users and developers to retrieve additional information about their SAP R/3 systems.

Highlights of this hour include

- Introduce the concept of SAP Newsgroups
- See a list of helpful SAP Web sites
- Take a look at some professional resources
- Browse available employment resources

Professional Resources

There is a wealth of professional resources available for SAP users to take advantage of to get the most from their SAP systems. Because of the size of SAP's customer base, there is a strong need for resources for all areas of SAP business. A couple of the prominent professional resources are outlined below.

America's SAP User's Group (ASUG)

In almost every facet of business, it is always helpful to network with people who are trying to meet similar goals. SAP is no exception. An organization, America's SAP Users Group—known as ASUG—is an independent, not-for-profit organization of SAP customer companies and eligible third-party vendors and consultants (see Figure 24.1).

FIGURE 24.1

ASUG is an independent, not-for-profit organization of SAP customer companies and eligible third-party vendors and consultants.

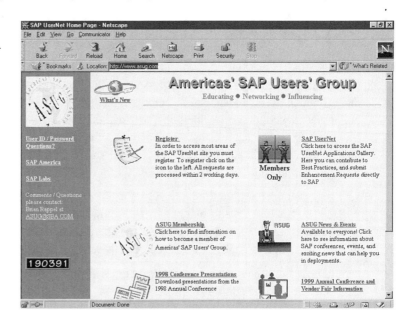

ASUG's goals of educating members, facilitating networking among colleagues and SAP representatives, and influencing SAP's global product and service direction forms the foundation of all that ASUG does. ASUG provides a forum for members to communicate mutual concerns to SAP, influence software development, exchange ideas and best practices, and establish future priorities. ASUG is dedicated to the advancement, understanding, and productive use of SAP products.

Founded in 1990, ASUG began immediately following the SAPPHIRE conference in Orlando, Florida, as a group of 15 participants. One year later, ASUG was officially incorporated. At the end of 1996, the organization had grown to over 450 member companies, representing both R/2 and R/3 installations in North, Central, and South America. Also in 1996, ASUG expanded its customer-only membership to include third parties (vendors and consultants) under a new Associate Membership category. By the close of 1998, the organization was 950 corporate memberships strong, with more than 12,000 participants. Installation Member and Associate Member companies participate both locally and nationally through various ASUG groups, geographic chapters, and ASUG's annual conferences.

ASUG provides its members with direct access to peer resources, serving as the definitive communication link among SAP customers. The organization takes a focused approach to problem solving that is beneficial to users and developers alike. User participation is very important because staying cutting edge requires the input and strong voice that represents the collective wisdom of the SAP user community. Joining ASUG allows a member company to learn from the shared experiences of other users, forging solutions to common user challenges and influencing and shaping SAP's product development.

ASUG maintains more than 950 corporate memberships that encompass the more than 12,000 individuals who participate in ASUG functions throughout the year. Paralleling the success of SAP in North and South America, the Users' Group's membership base continues to grow dramatically. To obtain more information about Americas' SAP Users' Group, use the following contact information:

Americas' SAP Users' Group
401 North Michigan Avenue
MC: 2200-1
Chicago, IL 60611-4267
Phone: 312.321.5142
FAX: 312.245.1081
Email: ASUG@SBA.COM
www.asug.com

SAP Technical Journal

The SAP Technical Journal is a hard copy journal aimed at SAP developers. The journal that users receive in the mail is designed to provide the solid advice, resources, and technical information SAP developers (SAP users involved with the technical side of SAP) need to make critical development decisions and build and maintain the best R/3 applications possible. Within the pages of SAP Technical Journal, you'll find technology tutorials, reviews of new products and options, technical tips, case studies, integration and systems management advice, and best-practice code samples.

In addition to solid technical advice, SAP Technical Journal will include user group information, book reviews, product walk-throughs, and the latest news from SAP developers: all the resources and information you need to stay abreast of the most current developments in the SAP community. For information about the SAP Technical Journal, visit `www.saptechjournal.com` or call (650) 358-9500.

Books

Many books are available on the market today for SAP. Using online bookstores like Barnesandnoble.com and amazon.com you can search for SAP-related books to see the latest of what is available on the market today. Like this book, there are several books focusing on SAP in general. One such book is the following:

Sharpe, Simon. *Sams Teach Yourself SAP R/3 in 10 Minutes*. Indianapolis: Sams Publishing, 1999.

This handy guide focuses on the end-user by covering general tasks including basic navigation skills, working with master data, and running reports. With Timesaving Tips, Plain English definitions, Panic Button advice and easy-to-follow tutorials that can be completed in 10 minutes or less, users can get productive immediately.

There are also books designed as an overall reference of the capabilities of SAP which serve as a complete guide to SAP, with a thorough overview of each module and how they work together. An example of one such book is the following:

ASAP World Consultancy, et al. *Special Edition Using SAP R/3, Third Edition*. Indianapolis: Que Corp., 1998.

There are also many books available that address the technical side of SAP. Throughout this book we have learned that the language behind-the-scenes in SAP is called ABAP. There are several books on the market that assist a technical user in learning the complex language of ABAP:

Barrett, Dennis. *SAP's ABAP/4 Command Reference*. Indianapolis: Que Corp., 1997.

Greenwood, Ken. *Sams Teach Yourself ABAP/4 in 21 Days*. Indianapolis: Sams Publishing, 1999.

After selecting SAP as your vendor of choice, you will require assistance in the implementation of this advanced system. There are several books available to assist you in addressing your implementation concerns. One such book is the following:

Hiquet, Stanley D., Conley, Canitano and Associates, Inc. *SAP R/3 Implementation Guide: A Manager's Guide to Understanding SAP*. Indianapolis: Macmillan Technical Publishing, 1998.

There are also several books that focus on the specific modules in SAP. These books are designed to assist the user in the configuration and use of a particular module:

ASAP World Consultancy, et al. *Administering SAP R/3: The FI-Financial Accounting and CO-Controlling Modules*. Indianapolis: Que Corp., 1998.

24

ASAP World Consultancy, et al. *Administering SAP R/3: The HR-Human Resources Module*. Indianapolis: Que Corp., 1999.

ASAP World Consultancy, et al. *Administering SAP R/3: The MM-Materials Management Module*. Indianapolis: Que Corp., 1997.

ASAP World Consultancy, et al. *Administering SAP R/3: The SD-Sales and Distribution Module*. Indianapolis: Que Corp., 1998.

Internet Resources

Many SAP Internet resources are available for you to communicate, as well as share ideas about your SAP system, with SAP professionals and other users. The Internet is a great way to get connected and to see what is available. Searching the Internet for SAP sites is easy, and you will find that the amount of information available is overwhelming. A sample of these resources follows.

SAP Fans

SAP Fans, located on the Internet at `www.sapfans.com`, is an ideal source of SAP information. SAP Fans is designed as a forum to exchange ideas with other SAP customers working with SAP R/3 and R/2 systems. This Web site includes Discussion Forums that provide you with the opportunity to post questions, comments, and experiences about your SAP system, and retrieve responses from other SAP users. Discussion forums include

Logistics

Implementation Issues

Business Warehouse

Educational Services/Training

Basis

Third-Party Products

Human Resources

Financials

Industry Solutions

Job Postings/Resumes

Interfaces

Internet Solutions Digest

Using the discussion forums, you can post a question or problem that you are having with your R/3 system (see Figure 24.2).

FIGURE 24.2

In the SAP Fans' discussion forum, you can post comments or questions or respond to other users' comments or questions.

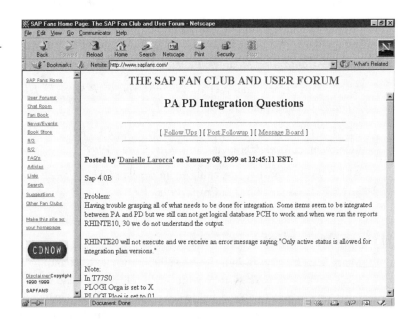

Other SAP Fans users will see your posting and respond with possible solutions (see Figure 24.3).

The network of contacts that you will gain with whom you can share similar experiences will be invaluable. SAP Fans is also an ideal source for SAP news, events, products, books, SAP chat, and employment opportunities. Using SAP Fans, you can gain exposure to the SAP market and other SAP fans around the world.

FIGURE 24.3

The SAP Fans' discussion forum is an ideal source for answers to your SAP questions.

My posting

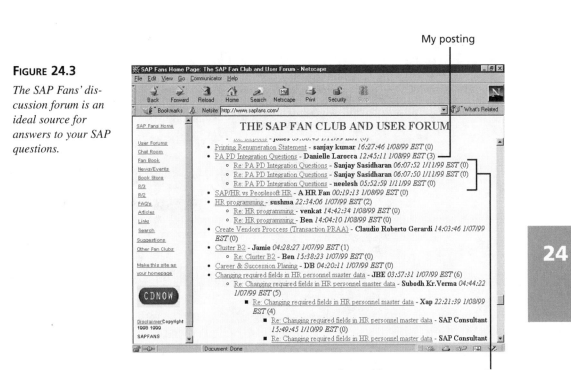

Response postings with answers to my question

ERPcentral

ERPcentral is the Internet Enterprise Resource Planning portal, featuring information on the ERP leaders, SAP, PeopleSoft, Oracle and Baan with forums, news, events, investing e-commerce, and more related to ERP (see Figure 24.4). ERPcentral is a good source to retrieve information on the best practices used in the different industries as part of their SAP postings forum. Visit ERPcentral at www.erpcentral.com.

SAP Labs

SAP Labs, Inc. (formerly SAP Technology, Inc.) develops cutting-edge software and add-ons for SAP R/3 systems. They are an extension of the R/3 system development group located in Walldorf, Germany. Since February, the PlanetSAP Solution Center has been making positive contributions to the SAP community through the showcasing of new products and technology.

Their Web site intends to improve its accessibility so that salespeople and management can make online requests to use PlanetSAP, as well as introduce all SAP employees to the mission of the Solution Center. As a world-class facility, they have a vision to take their customer's business to the next level by making their technology work for your business. Visit SAP Labs at www.saplabs.com.

FIGURE 24.4

ERPcentral is an all-in-one source of Enterprise Resource Planning.

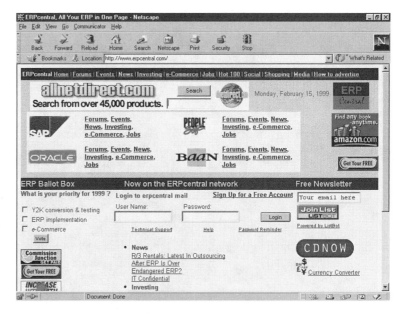

FIGURE 24.5

SAP Labs, Inc. is personally overseen by SAP AG co-founder Hasso Plattner.

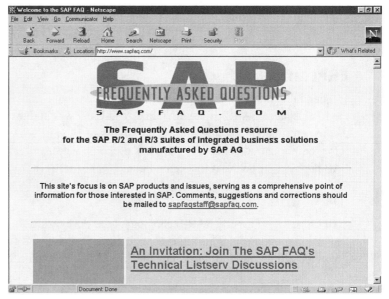

SAP FAQ

The SAP FAQ originated in 1994 as a Web-based adjunct to the de.alt.sap-r3 Usenet discussion forum from Germany's University of Oldenberg, a pioneering SAP academic installation site (see Figure 24.6). As a longstanding, not-for-profit, technology-specific resource, the SAP FAQ has earned and maintained a position of global credibility and respect. Its objective is to serve as a comprehensive point of information about SAP for those who work with SAP, companies that are implementing SAP, students, and those who are looking into SAP as a potential ERP solution or career option.

FIGURE 24.6

SAP FAQ is the Frequently Asked Questions resource for the SAP R/2 and R/3 suites of integrated business solutions manufac-tured by SAP AG.

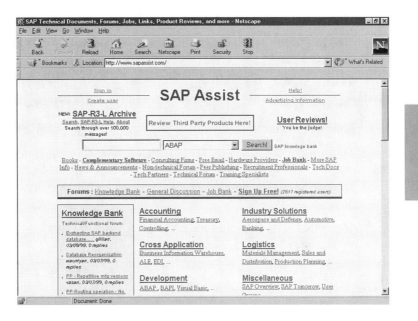

FAQ Technical Listserv Discussions

The SAP FAQ's "by subscription" discussion forums combine the value of global partici-pation with the ease and convenience of email. The SAP FAQ's discussion lists are designed to be used as a kind of cafeteria-style, modular system in which subscribers are encouraged to discuss topic-related issues in detail, ask questions, share expertise, and exchange ideas. From general, core module-related discussions, to industry-specific dia-logue, subscribers can select a customized combination of discussions that fit very specifically into their areas of interest and expertise.

To participate, you subscribe to an SAP FAQ discussion forum via email, specifying a certain topic or topics. Discussion topics are available for Human Resources, EDI, R/3 Security, and so on. A discussion forum even exists for SAP-specific humor. Then you will receive postings in your email inbox regarding the topics you specified. You can also send postings that will in turn be received in the inbox of all users who subscribed to the newsgroup.

This type of automated communication between users facilitates the expedient resolution of problems and the increased awareness of features and functions within your SAP R/3 system. For more information about the SAP FAQ, visit `www.sapfaq.com`. Sample SAP FAQ discussion groups are as follows:

AEROSPACE & DEFENSE: Special Interest Group Discussion List

AUTOMOTIVE: Special Interest Group Discussion List

BANKING: Special Interest Group Discussion List

BASIS: Special Interest Group Discussion

BUSINESS INFORMATION WARE-HOUSE: Special Interest Group Discussion

BUSINESS TO BUSINESS PRO-CUREMENT: Special Interest Group Discussion

BUSINESS INTELLIGENCE: Special Interest Group Discussion

CHANGE MANAGEMENT: Special Interest Group Discussion

CHEMICALS: Special Interest Group Discussion List

CONSULTANT EDUCATION & TRAINING: Special Interest Group Discussion

CONSUMER PRODUCTS: Special Interest Group Discussion List

CUSTOMER RELATIONSHIP MAN-AGEMENT: Special Interest Group Discussion

DEVELOPMENT: Special Interest Group Discussion

EDI/EC/WORKFLOW: Special Interest Group Discussion

END USER TRAINING: Special Interest Group Discussion

ENGINEERING & CONSTRUCTION: Special Interest Group Discussion List

EUROPEAN ECONOMY/ECONOMIC UNION: Special Interest Group Discussion

FINANCIALS: Special Interest Group Discussion

HEALTHCARE: Special Interest Group Discussion List

HIGH TECH: Special Interest Group Discussion List

HUMAN RESOURCES: Special Interest Group Discussion

HUMOR & TRIVIA: Special Interest Group Discussion

IMPLEMENTATION ISSUES: Special Interest Group Discussion

INSURANCE: Special Interest Group Discussion List

INTERFACES: Special Interest Group Discussion

INTERNET SOLUTIONS: Special Interest Group Discussion

LOGISTICS: Special Interest Group Discussion

MEDIA: Special Interest Group Discussion List

METAL, PAPER & WOOD: Special Interest Group Discussion List

MID-SIZED BUSINESS: Special Interest Group Discussion

NON-TECHNICAL: Special Interest Group Discussion

OIL & GAS: Special Interest Group Discussion List

PHARMACEUTICALS: Special Interest Group Discussion List

POST-IMPLEMENTATION SUPPORT ISSUES: Special Interest Group Discussion

PUBLIC SECTOR: Special Interest Group Discussion List

R/2 GENERAL: Special Interest Group Discussion

REAL ESTATE: Special Interest Group Discussion List

RETAIL: Special Interest Group Discussion List

SALES FORCE AUTOMATION: Special Interest Group Discussion

SECURITY: Special Interest Group Discussion

SERVICE PROVIDER: Special Interest Group Discussion List

SUPPLY CHAIN MANAGEMENT: Special Interest Group Discussion

TELECOMMUNICATIONS: Special Interest Group Discussion List

TOOLS AND TECHNOLOGY: Special Interest Group Discussion

TRANSPORTATION: Special Interest Group Discussion List

UTILITIES: Special Interest Group Discussion List

Y2K: Special Interest Group Discussion

SAP R/3 Mailing List and Searchable Archive

The SAP-R3-L list is for discussion of SAP R/3's technical and non-technical software. MIT hosts and administers the list that works in the same fashion as the FAQ Email Discussion forum mentioned previously. The SAP R/3 Mailing List Searchable Archive gives you the forum to search through all postings to retrieve information about any SAP topic.

What I particularly appreciate about this list and Web site is that recruitment, product, and service advertisements are not permitted. This list promotes strictly SAP business and in my opinion is one of the best tools available in gaining help and contacts with which to share SAP concerns and experiences.

The Searchable Archive can be found at www.documentation.com/saplist/ saplist.htm, and for any questions about the SAP-R3-L list, you can write to the list owners at the email address, SAP-R3-L-request@MITVMA.MIT.EDU.

SAP Assist

The SAP Assist Web site is an online service providing tools and information to SAP practitioners to assist them in making informed decisions and completing their daily activities (see Figure 24.7). Like all ERP Assist Web sites, the SAP Assist Web site combines a functionally organized database of information and the benefits of global communication capabilities to bring useful information to user's fingertips.

FIGURE 24.7

To complement the most comprehensive and organized listing of SAP third-party vendors, Sap Assist also includes a review process for products and services.

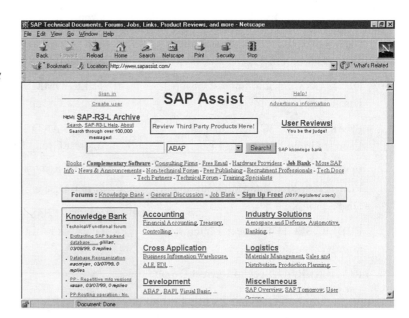

Some of the helpful resources found on the SAP Assist Web site include a Knowledge Bank where you can search for SAP-related information, a General Discussion Forum, a Job Bank, and a searchable archive of SAP information. For more information about SAP Assist, visit www.sapassist.com.

Employment Opportunities

One of the first things you will notice when you begin an SAP project, regardless of the role you play, is that you will suddenly be launched into a new employment stratosphere. Your email inbox and voice mail box will be bombarded with messages from recruiters offering to double your present salary. Not that this is a bad thing; however, you need to be prepared for it.

SAP knowledge is the hot skill to have right now, and a wealth of positions are available for people with the right skills. This would include functional as well as technical skills. Possessing in-depth knowledge on how to configure and set up a module is just as valuable as being able to write ABAP code and programs. A large amount of Web sites are devoted to providing you with employment opportunities. A sample of these Web sites is provided in the next section.

SAP Club

The mission of SAP Club is to effectively and efficiently provide accurate, up-to-date information in the SAP arena. This includes an Online Career Opportunities Center for employers and job seekers. Other features of SAP Club include chat rooms and discussion forums using WebBoard technology, a comprehensive list of SAP-related Hotlinks on the Web, concrete SAP technical papers written by industry experts, implementation experience from consultants who have worked on SAP projects, and free email to anyone who registers (see Figure 24.8).

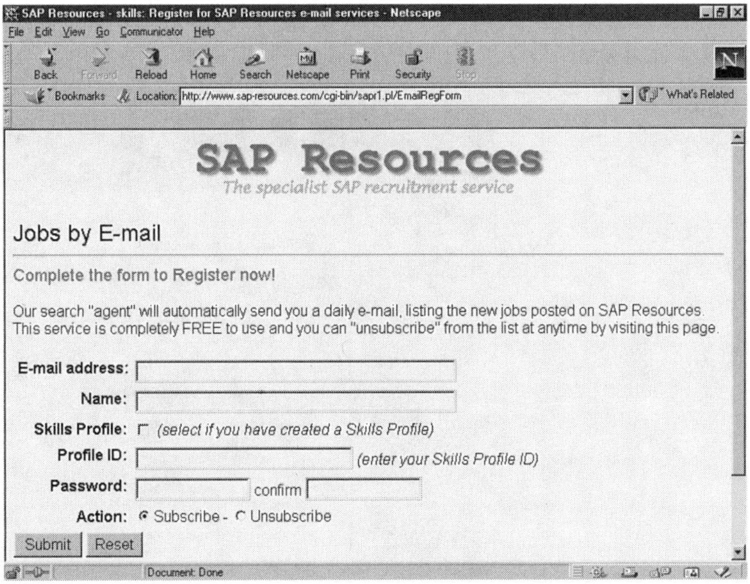

24

FIGURE 24.8

SAP Club is a good source of information on technical papers written by industry executives in the SAP arena.

SAP Club also includes a Book Watch, which is updated with the latest SAP-related books. For more information about SAP Club, visit www.sapclub.com.

SAP Resources

SAP Resources is a Web-based recruitment service focused solely on the SAP market place and designed to make identifying the best SAP opportunities easier. SAP Resources allows you to approach the tasks of finding an SAP opportunity in different ways and provides the following services:

The Jobs Database, which is constantly being added to, includes details of some of the hottest SAP positions currently available. Just enter some relevant keywords to perform a search.

The Skills Profile Service is aimed at professionals who know that some of the best opportunities are never advertised and wish to make their skill details available to the widest audience possible. It's simple to create and activate your skills profile and to be contacted by recruiters handling the hottest SAP opportunities. All levels of experience are always in demand. Check out the full details at the Professionals Information page.

Lastly, the Jobs-by-Email service provides subscribers with a daily Email message listing the latest jobs posted to SAP Resources(see Figure 24.9). For more information about SAP Resources, visit `www.SAP-Resources.com`.

FIGURE 24.9

All services offered on SAP Resources are free of charge.

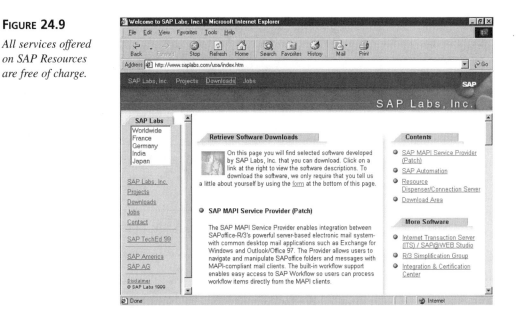

Summary

This hour, you have taken a look at some of the additional resources available for your use to gain the most out of your SAP system. As time goes on, more and more books will be available on SAP for your use as a reference to turn to with SAP questions. In addition, the number of Internet resources grows each day. Take advantage of these resources to get the most out of your SAP system.

Through your use of the R/3 system, the resources defined here, and the skills you learned in the past 24 hours, you will be a true "Sapper." Welcome to the world of SAP, and I hope that you have enjoyed the past 24 hours.

Q&A

Q What things should you keep in mind when shopping for SAP books?

A One of the most important things to keep in mind when looking for SAP books is the version number that the book is written under. Major changes are evident between versions 3.X., 4.0, and 4.5 in SAP. If you find an SAP book written earlier than 1999, it is likely written on an early version of 3.0 and may not be applicable for your 4.0 system.

Q How can you get more information about participating in an SAP email discussion group?

A You can learn more about participating in an email discussion group by sending an email to sapforuminfo@sapfaq.com.

Q How can you keep up-to-date with the latest SAP information available on the internet?

A It is a good idea to use an internet search site like www.yahoo.com or www.hotbot.com to search for new SAP sites on a periodic basis to keep up-to-date with the latest SAP information available.

24

APPENDIX A

Answers

Hour 1 Quiz

1. What does SAP stand for?

2. Name a few of the industries that SAP offers comprehensive solutions for.

3. Describe a client/server environment.

4. Define the SAP term *dispatcher*.

5. What are the three distinct servers that comprise the R/3 system architecture?

6. What is the main benefit of SAP's integration?

7. Describe an important benefit to the design of a relational database management system (RDBMS).

8. A logical unit of work (LUW) is not complete until what action is accomplished?

Answers to Quiz for Hour 1

1. SAP stands for Systems, Applications, and Products in Data Processing.

2. SAP offers comprehensive industry solutions including SAP Aerospace & Defense, SAP Automotive, SAP Banking, SAP Chemicals, SAP Consumer Products, SAP Engineering & Construction, SAP Healthcare, SAP High Tech, SAP Insurance, SAP Media, SAP Mill Products, SAP Oil & Gas, SAP Pharmaceuticals, SAP Public Sector Real Estate, SAP Retail, SAP Service Provider, SAP Telecommunications & Transportation, and SAP Utilities.

3. A client/server environment is one in which the client (an individual PC or workstation) is requesting information (via a connection) of the supplying machine, known as the server. The communication and interchange of data between the requesting and supplying machine is known as a client/server relationship.

4. A dispatcher allows SAP to communicate with the presentation server by managing the information exchange between the SAPGUI and the work processes.

5. The presentation server, application server, and database server constitute SAP's distributed R/3 system. The presentation server displays the SAP R/3 window, also known as the SAPGUI, and is the system that users, such as you, will be entering data into. The application server manages the SAP administrative functions including background processing and spool requests for the printer. The database server houses all the data stored and is comprised of a database composed of multiple tables and structures.

6. Although there are many benefits to SAP's integrated design, the most important is the communication of modules among the business environment.

7. The most important element in the design of a relational database management system (RDBMS) is that it eliminates redundancy.

8. An R/3 logical unit of work contains all the dialog steps of a transaction, concluding with the update to the SAP database.

Hour 2 Quiz

1. What is the maximum number of sessions that you can have open at one time in SAP?

2. What is the transaction code to the Users Overview screen?

3. If you are on any screen in the SAP system EXCEPT the main screen, what two-digit code must you enter before entering a transaction code so that you can navigate using the command field?

4. What two items on the Menu bar are constant on all SAP screens?

5. What is one of the most important benefits of using multiple sessions in SAP?

6. What three items are required in order for you to log on to the SAP system?

7. What is the menu path to create a new session in SAP (without using the command field)?

Answers to Quiz for Hour 2

1. Users can have a maximum of nine sessions open at one time in SAP, although this number might be reduced by your system administrator during configuration.

2. The transaction code for the Users Overview screen is SM04.

3. If you are navigating using the command field in SAP from any screen other than the initial screen, you must enter a /N (N for New) before the transaction code or an /O (O for Open new session).

4. The System and Help options are constant on the menu bar of all SAP screens.

5. Using multiple sessions in SAP allows you to begin and complete multiple tasks at once without losing your place in a current task.

6. You will need a user name, password, and client number.

7. The menu path to create a new session without using a transaction code in the command field is System, Create Session from the menu bar.

A

Hour 3 Quiz

1. What is a database?

2. A database is composed of what three components?

3. What kind of database contains two-dimensional relationships between its tables?

4. What kind of key in a database table requires unique values in each field?

5. What is the field or fields used to link a primary key field in another table called?

6. What causes a check key violation?

7. What is used in a database to speed up the retrieval of records?

Answers to Quiz for Hour 3

1. A database is a container used to store, retrieve, process, and present data.

2. A database is composed of tables, columns (called fields), and rows (called records or data).

3. An RDBMS or Relational Database Management System is a connection of multiple tables connected through relationships.

4. A primary key in a database table is composed of one or more fields that make a record in that table unique.

5. A foreign key is a field or fields that is used to link a primary key field in another table.

6. If a value is entered in a field that does not match an entry in that field's check table, you will receive a check table violation.

7. A Database index is used to enhance the time it takes to retrieve records from a database table.

Hour 4 Quiz

1. What is the name of the beach ball looking item in the top right side of your SAP window?

2. What should you always do before changing a setting in the Customizing Display Window?

3. How do you change the SAP system setting from Overwrite mode to Insert mode?

4. How do you access the SAP R/3 Customize Display options window?

5. Where would you change the setting, if you would like your SAP error messages to display in a pop-up window (dialog box)?

6. How many different color choices do you have for changing the colors in lists?

Answers to Quiz for Hour 4

1. The beach ball–looking item used to change system settings is called the SAP Interface menu.

2. Before making any changes in the Customizing Window Display window, you should always write down what the current settings are in case you need to restore to the default.

3. Selecting the Insert button on your keyboard will change the SAP system setting from Overwrite to Insert mode and vice versa.

4. Single left-click on the Interface Menu in the top right-hand corner of your SAP window and then select options.

5. On the General tab in the Customizing window, you would need to select the Dialog Box at Error Message check box.

6. The List Colors dialog box contains 21 color choices for changing the colors in lists.

Hour 5 Quiz

1. What is the transaction code for the main SAP screen?

2. What Windows application can you launch to paste and save SAP screen prints in?

3. What check box on the SAP Print List Screen would you select if you do not want your spool request saved in the SAP system for the duration of the retention period?

4. To select SAP menu paths using your keyboard instead of your mouse, you first need to select what function key?

5. How do you find the transaction code from any screen in the SAP system?

6. How do you access the history list?

7. What is the Retention Period used for on the Print Screen List window?

Answers to Quiz for Hour 5

1. The transaction code for the main SAP screen is S000.

2. Microsoft Windows Paintbrush application can be used to paste and then save or print SAP screen prints.

3. You would select the Delete After Print check box on the Print Screen List window in order for your spool request not to be saved by the SAP system.

4. The F10 function key activates the menu bar so that you can navigate through the menu paths using only your keyboard.

5. Using the menu path System, Status, you can find the transaction code for the current screen listed in the transaction box.

6. The history list of all transaction codes processed since you logged in can be accessed by selecting the down arrow on the right-hand side of the command field.

7. The Retention Period determines how many days a spool request is to remain in the spool system before it is deleted.

Hour 6 Quiz

1. How do you check your entries on a screen?
2. Is it the Hold Data or Set Data option that allows you to overwrite the default entry in an input field?
3. What item on an SAP screen that contains a SAP Tree do you need to select in order to expand the tree?
4. What is the name of a window that pops up to give you more information or supplies you with feedback on your current task?
5. When looking at a screen, what determines how many characters you can enter in an input field?
6. How do change your system setting to toggle between Insert and Overwrite mode?
7. To display a list of available entries for an input field that is linked to a database table you need to do what?
8. What type of fields contain a question mark?

Answers to Quiz for Hour 6

1. The Enter key on your keyboard or the green check mark on your Windows toolbar can be used to check the entries made on an SAP screen.
2. The Hold Data feature allows you to overwrite the default value that you have set for an input field.
3. To expand a SAP tree structure, you use the (+) sign located to the left of the desired line.
4. A dialog box appears to a user to provide messages or specific information about a current task.
5. The length of an input field determines how many characters you can enter in the field.
6. Using the Insert key on your Windows keyboard you can toggle between Insert and Overwrite mode.
7. The possible Entries help button (down arrow on the right side of an input field) can be used to display valid entries for that input field.
8. Required input fields display a question mark in the SAP system.

Hour 7 Quiz

1. How many levels of SAP training are available?
2. What level of SAP R/3 training does not require any perquisites?
3. What is the difference between a functional and a technical analyst on your Project Team?
4. What is one of the most important factors contributing to the success of your SAP R/3 implementation?
5. What is the highest level of structure in your Project Team hierarchy?

Answers to Quiz for Hour 7

1. There are three levels of SAP training: Level 1 focusing on awareness, Level 2 concentrating on readiness, and Level 3 focusing on proficiency.
2. Level 1 training classes are designed as an introduction and do not require any prerequisite courses.
3. A Functional Analyst focuses on your SAP business process. Functional Analysts are not technical people but work in the functional end of the business: Human Resources Managers, Shipping Clerks, and so on. Technical Analysts are IT professionals who are bringing a technical savvy to the Project Team because of their computer and technical experience.
4. Your selected SAP R/3 Project Team is one of the most important factors that contributes to the success of your SAP R/3 implementation.
5. The project manager or lead manages the project followed by the highest level in the structure, the Executive Steering Committee.

A

Hour 8 Quiz

1. What does knowledge transfer in Phase 3 of the AcceleratedSAP solution refer to?
2. Which implementation solution option delivers all the SAP configuration hardware, database, and software pre-configured right out of the box?
3. What operating systems will the Ready-to-Run R/3 solution run under?
4. What are the five consecutive phases of the AcceleratedSAP Roadmap?
5. What is the AcceleratedSAP Project Estimator used for?
6. How many different levels are offered of the SAP training courses?

Answers to Quiz for Hour 8

1. Knowledge transfer applies to the transference of SAP know-how from one individual to another.

2. The Ready-to-Run R/3 solution is "project ready" from the day that the Ready-to-Run system is delivered.

3. The Ready-to-Run R/3 solution will run under Microsoft Windows NT and IBM AS/400, and there is also a UNIX solution available from Sun Microsystems.

4. The five consecutive phases of the AcceleratedSAP Roadmap are Project Preparation, Business Blueprint, Realization, Final Preparation, and Go Live.

5. The Project Estimator guides your team though a series of predefined questions, and conducts interviews with relevant company representatives to assist in deriving the necessary information for the implementation.

6. There are three levels: Level 1, 2, and 3 offered of the SAP training courses.

Hour 9 Quiz

1. What is the difference between an Optional and a Mandatory activity in the IMG?

2. What is the difference between Critical and Non-Critical activities in the IMG?

3. Which view of the IMG contains only the relevant documentation for the SAP components that your company is implementing?

4. What does the icon symbol of the hand indicate?

5. What are three different project views of the IMG?

6. What model displays the structure of your R/3 implementation projects?

7. What is the transaction code to launch the IMG?

Answers to Quiz for Hour 9

1. IMG activities designated as Mandatory are customizing steps that you are required to perform because SAP does not deliver standard default settings. Optional activities are configurations steps that are not required because SAP does deliver initial default settings.

2. IMG activities designated as Critical are crucial in the SAP implementation and might have far reaching implications in your SAP system. Non-Critical activities do not have far reaching implications and are not considered crucial steps in the configuration.

3. The SAP Project Implementation Guide contains only the customizing steps necessary for the application components that your company is implementing.

4. The hand icon displayed in the IMG indicates that there are Release Notes available for that particular activity.

5. The Reference, Enterprise, and Project IMGs are the three different project views available for the IMG.

6. The R/3 Procedure Model is a graphical representation of your implementation.

7. The transaction code /nSPRO can be used to launch the initial screen of the IMG.

Hour 10 Quiz

1. Which Financials submodule is designed to support your company in creating budgets?

2. Which Financials sub module provides the functions necessary for effective and accurate internal cost accounting management?

3. What are the four components of the Treasury sub module?

4. What are the six components of the Financials module?

5. In the Financials module, what subcomponent serves as a complete record of all your company's business transactions?

6. In which component can automatic transference of depreciation values for appropriation requests and investment measures be made?

7. How does SAP define the term profit center?

Answers to Quiz for Hour 10

1. The Funds Management component is designed to support your company in creating budgets.

2. The Controlling sub module provides the functions necessary for effective and accurate internal cost accounting management.

3. The four components of the Treasury sub module include: Cash Management, Treasury Management, Market Risk Management, and Funds Management.

4. The six components of the Financials module include: Financial Accounting, Controlling, Investment Management, Treasury Cash Management, Enterprise Controlling, and Real Estate.

5. The General Ledger Accounting subcomponent serves as a complete record of all your company's business transactions.

6. Automatic transference of depreciation values for appropriation requests and investment measures be made in the Investment Management, Depreciation Forecast component.

7. The SAP term profit center refers to a management-oriented organizational unit used for internal controlling purposes.

Hour 11 Quiz

1. Define the SAP term *Actions*.

2. Knowing that SAP infotypes are named according to number range specifications, what category would infotype 0001 Organizational Assignment fall under?

3. What is the main benefit from the Human Resources, Recruitment component?

4. The Human Resources module is divided into what two submodules?

5. Define the SAP term *infotype*.

6. What are two methods that can be used for R/3 Employee Self-Service?

7. What is the name of the graphical tool that can be used when generating reports in R/3 Human Resources?

Answers to Quiz for Hour 11

1. When a series of R/3 infotypes are bundled together, they are called Actions.

2. Infotype 0001 Organizational Assignment belongs to the range 0000-0999 for Personnel Administration (PA) data.

3. The main benefit from the Human Resources, Recruitment component is its automation.

4. The Human Resources module is divided into Personnel Administration and Personnel Planning and Development.

5. An infotype is a carrier of system-controlling characteristics, such as attributes or time constraints, and so on.

6. The two methods that can be used for R/3 Employee Self Service are Web-based technology and interactive voice response functionality.

7. The graphical tool that can be used to generate reports in R/3 Human resources is called Structural Graphics and is part of the Human Resources Information System (HRIS).

Hour 12 Quiz

1. Name the components available in the Materials Management submodule.

2. Name the components available in Quality Management submodule?

3. What are the eight components of the Logistics module?

4. The focus of the Production Planning and Control component is to contribute solutions for what three areas?

5. Describe the types of data available to facilitate sales and marketing activity in the Sales and Distribution submodule.

6. What component of the Production Planning submodule is used for creating realistic and consistent planning figures to forecast future sales?

7. What are the three main benefits that you will derive from your Materials Management submodule?

Answers to Quiz for Hour 12

1. The components available in the Materials Management submodule include Inventory Management, Warehouse Management, Purchasing, Invoice Verification, Materials Planning, and Purchasing Information System.

2. The components available in the Quality Management submodule include Quality Planning, Quality Inspections, Quality Control, Quality Notifications, Quality Certificates, Test Equipment Management, and Quality Management Information System.

3. Sales and Distribution, Production Planning, Materials Management, Quality Management, Plant Maintenance, Logistics Information System, Project System, and Product Data Management are the eight Components of the Logistics module

4. The focus of the Production Planning and Control submodule is to contribute solutions for production planning, execution, and control.

5. Data on products, marketing strategies, sales calls, pricing, and sales leads can be accessed at any time to facilitate sales and marketing activity in the Sales and Distribution submodule.

6. Sales and Operations Planning is used for creating realistic and consistent planning figures to forecast future sales.

7. Three main benefits that you will derive from your Materials Management submodule are time, money, and resources.

A

Hour 13 Quiz

1. Which type of interface do Internet communications usually communicate with?
2. Which type of interface would be used to communicate with Microsoft Office?
3. What are the three different types of data transmitted through Application Link Enabling (ALE)?
4. What are two different types of update processes?
5. What does the term middleware represent?
6. What is a CPI-C?
7. What are the four different areas of rules that govern CPI-C communications protocol?

Answers to Quiz for Hour 13

1. The most popular interface form used for Internet applications is EDI. EDI is the electronic exchange of structured data between environments that use different hardware, software, and communication services.
2. Object linking and embedding (OLE) is used to integrate PC applications with the SAP R/3 system. OLE is the technology for transferring and sharing information among applications like Microsoft Office.
3. The three different types of data transmitted through ALE are control and customizing data, master data, and transaction data.
4. The two different types of update processes are synchronous and asynchronous processes.
5. Middleware is the layer of software that functions as a conversion or translation layer between two different layers.
6. A Common Program Interface Communication (CPI-C) facilitates the communication (talking back and forth) and the processing of applications and programs within the R/3 system.
7. Session start-up, session control, communication, and session termination are the four different areas of rules for CPI-C.

Hour 14 Quiz

1. Name three items that a user master record contains.
2. What is the name of the profile that gives you authorization access to everything in the SAP R/3 system?

3. What is the name of the SAP tool that helps administrators to create user profiles based on standards?

4. What does the acronym CCMS stand for?

5. What is the menu path to reach the SAP Servers System Monitoring Screen?

6. Define an SAP instance.

7. Where are user authorizations stored in your R/3 system?

Answers to Quiz for Hour 14

1. Any of the following examples can be found on your user master record: user name, assigned client, user password, company address, user type, start menu, logon language, personal printer configuration, time zone, activity group authorizations, expiration date, default parameter settings.

2. The SAP_ALL authorization profile gives users access to everything in your SAP R/3 system.

3. The R/3 Profile Generator assists in the implementation of your company's security and it is based on the concept of authorization objects, authorizations, and authorization profiles.

4. The acronym CCMS stands for SAP's Computing Center Management System used for monitoring your SAP system.

5. The SAP Servers System Monitoring screen can be reached by following the menu path Tools, Administration, Monitor, System Monitoring, Servers or by using the transaction code /nSM51.

6. An instance in the R/3 system is an administrative unit, which groups together R/3 system components that provide one or more services.

7. The user authorizations are stored in the master record of each user.

Hour 15 Quiz

1. What is the transaction code for the General Table Display function?

2. Define the term structure.

3. Name the three components for defining data in the R/3 Data Dictionary.

4. What are SAP selection screens used for?

5. Are pooled tables associated with a one-to-one relationship or a one-to many relationship?

6. What is a major distinction between cluster tables and pooled tables in the R/3 Data Dictionary?

7. What type of tables contain a one-to-one relationship with tables in the R/3 database?

Answers to Quiz for Hour 15

1. Transaction code /nSE16 can be used to access the General Table Display function of the R/3 Data Dictionary.

2. A structure is a group of internal fields that logically belong together.

3. The three components for defining data in the R/3 Data Dictionary are tables, domains, and data elements.

4. Selection screens are used to specify criteria for the output that will appear.

5. Pooled tables contain a one-to-many relationship.

6. One major distinction between cluster tables and pooled tables is that table pools hold a large number of tables and table clusters hold only a handful of tables.

7. Transparent tables contain a one-to-one relationship with tables in the database.

Hour 16 Quiz

1. ABAP Dictionary objects are broken down into what three components?

2. Environment objects are composed of what three subcomponents?

3. Which button on the Repository Information System application toolbar would you use to search or find?

4. What is the Find button on the menu bar used for?

5. Describe what the R/3 Repository Information System is used for.

6. Give an example of the types of queries you can request in the R/3 Repository Information System.

7. The Repository Information System displays a hierarchical list of the four different types of objects in the R/3 system. What are they?

Answers to Quiz for Hour 16

1. ABAP Dictionary objects are broken down into basic objects, other objects, and fields.

2. Environment objects are composed of development coordination, authorizations, and automatic tests.

3. The three components for defining data in the R/3 Data Dictionary are tables, domains, and data elements.

4. The Find button (which looks like a pair of binoculars) is used to search for objects in the R/3 Repository Information System.

5. The Repository Information System is an R/3 tool designed to assist you in retrieving information on the objects in your R/3 ABAP/4 Dictionary.

6. In the Repository Browser, you can search by objects attributes, research relationships between tables, do data review, and query the R/3 system for modified objects.

7. Modeling objects, ABAP Dictionary objects, programming objects, and environment objects comprise the four different types of SAP objects in the Repository Information System.

Hour 17 Quiz

1. What are the two different modes of the R/3 Screen Painter?

2. What are dynpros?

3. Give two example of items considered as part of screen elements.

4. The programming code behind your screen that makes it work is called what?

5. On which screen do you maintain the ABAP Dictionary fields for your screen?

6. What are the four components of a GUI Status in the R/3 Menu Painter?

7. How could you view a list of all the title bars for each of the screens contained in your program?

Answers to Quiz for Hour 17

1. The two different modes of the R/3 Screen Painter include the Alphanumeric and the Graphical Screen Painter.

2. In German, SAP refers to screens as dynpros.

3. Screen Layouts consist of the items on your screen with which the user interacts, such as check boxes and radio buttons.

4. The programming code behind your screen that makes it work is called the flow logic.

5. The Field List screen is where you maintain the ABAP Dictionary fields or program fields for your screen.

6. The four components of a GUI Status in the R/3 Menu Painter include the menu bar, standard toolbar, application toolbar, and function key setting.

7. Using the R/3 Menu Painter and selecting the Title List subobject, you can view all the title bars for each of the screens contained in your program.

Hour 18 Quiz

1. What reporting mechanism is used to pose one-time queries to the database?

2. Which type of SAP reporting tool requires the user to write code in the ABAP language in order to generate reports?

3. What is the menu path to view a report's attributes from the General Report Selection screen?

4. What is the menu path used to search for reports in the General Report Selection Tree?

5. Define the term *variant*.

6. What does it mean for you to "protect" a variant?

7. Name the big advantage to background processing.

Answers to Quiz for Hour 18

1. The Ad Hoc Query (HR Module) reporting mechanism is used to pose one-time queries to the database.

2. ABAP List Processing requires the user to write code in the ABAP language in order to generate reports.

3. To take a look at the attributes of a particular report in the General Report Selection Tree, select the report and then follow the menu path Edit, Node attributes.

4. The menu path used to search for reports in the General Report Selection is Edit, Find, Node.

5. A variant is a group of selection criteria values that has been saved.

6. A variant is "protected" if the variant can only be changed by the person who created it or last updated it.

7. An advantage of background processing is that the report is started in the background by the R/3 system and has no influence on your interactive work with the R/3 System or the amount of resources allocated to you.

Hour 19 Quiz

1. What is the transaction code to access the Create Users screen?
2. What is the transaction code to access the Create Functional Areas screen?
3. What is the transaction code to access the Create ABAP Queries screen?
4. Are Global application areas client dependant or independent?
5. What are four different components of ABAP queries?
6. What does an application area include?
7. What are the two different application areas?

Answers to Quiz for Hour 19

1. The transaction code to access the Create Users screen is /nSQ03.
2. The transaction code to access the Create Functional Areas screen is /nSQ02.
3. The transaction code to access the Create ABAP Queries screen is /nSQ01.
4. Queries designed in the global area are used throughout the entire system and are client-independent.
5. The four different components of ABAP queries are maintain queries, maintain user groups, maintain functional areas, and language comparisons.
6. An application area includes ABAP Query elements, queries, functional areas, and user groups.
7. The two different application areas in R/3 are standard and global.

A

Hour 20 Quiz

1. What is the transaction code to access the Ad Hoc Query main screen?
2. What must you always do after creating or modifying a functional area?
3. What is the menu path to open existing ad hoc queries?
4. In what R/3 application modules is the Ad Hoc Query available?
5. What is the name of the functional group that is automatically created for you when you create a new functional area in Human Resources?

6. What button do you have to click in order to select additional infotypes when creating a functional area?

Answers to Quiz for Hour 20

1. The transaction code to access the create users screen is /nPQAH.

2. After creating or modifying a functional area, you must save and generate it.

3. The menu path to open existing Ad Hoc Queries is Ad Hoc Query, Queries.

4. The Ad Hoc Query tool is only available in the R/3 Human Resources module.

5. The 00 Key Fields functional group is the name of the functional group that is automatically created when you create a new functional area in Human Resources.

6. The button you have to select in order to request additional infotypes when creating a functional area is the additional selections button.

Hour 21 Quiz

1. What are the steps necessary to create nodes or subnodes in your report tree?

2. What are the steps necessary to add ABAP queries, ad hoc queries, or transaction codes to your report tree?

3. If you want to execute a report directly from your report tree and skip the selection screen for that report, what information must you include in the Create Node window for that report?

4 What is the transaction code to display report trees?

5 What is the transaction code to change modify or create report trees?

6 What is the menu path to edit the description of your report tree?

Answers to Quiz for Hour 21

1. To create nodes or subnodes in your report tree, select your report tree, and then click the white Create button on the application toolbar.

2. Select your report tree, and then click the white Create button on the application toolbar to add transaction codes to a report tree.

3. If you wish to execute a report and skip the selection screen, you would use a variant for the report.

4. The transaction code to Display report trees is /nSARP.

5. The transaction code to change modify or create report trees is /nSERP.

6. The menu path to edit the description of your report tree is Node, Change Node Text.

Hour 22 Quiz

1. Name two methods you can use to create output files to be imported into Microsoft Excel.

2. Which type of interface do you use to communicate with Microsoft Office?

3. Which Microsoft application do you use to create form letters?

4. What does the term *OLE* mean?

5. Name some additional OLE-compatible applications.

Answers to Quiz for Hour 22

1. The System list function method and the export method from ABAP Query are the two methods you can use to create output files to be used in Microsoft Excel.

2. Object linking and embedding is used to integrate PC applications with the SAP R/3 system.

3. Microsoft Word can be used to create form letters using your SAP data.

4. *OLE* means object linking and embedding. OLE is the technology for transferring and sharing information among applications.

5. Some additional OLE-compatible applications include: Microsoft Office, Corel Office, Star Office, Lotus Smart Suite, and Visio.

A

Hour 23 Quiz

1. What is the menu path used to see Release Notes within the R/3 application?

2. How can you obtain Field-Specific Help?

3. How can you obtain context-specific help?

4. What is the R/3 menu path used to navigate to the Online Documentation Getting Started guide?

5. Where do you change the settings for how you want your SAP field help to appear?

6. How do you distinguish links in the browser view of your R/3 Online Documentation?

Answers to Quiz for Hour 23

1. The menu path used to see Release Notes within the R/3 application is Help, Release notes.

2. Field-Specific Help can be obtained by navigating to the field and pressing the F1 key.

3. Context-specific help can be obtained by navigating to a screen that is relative to your subject and using the menu path Help, Extended Help.

4. The R/3 menu path used to navigate to the Online Documentation Getting Started guide is Help, Getting Started.

5. To change the settings for how you want your SAP field help to appear, follow the menu path Help, Settings.

6. Links in the browser view of your R/3 Online Documentation are underlined.

APPENDIX B

SAP R/3 Financials Sample Standard Reports

SAP's Financials module includes an impressive collection of canned reports that can be executed through the general report tree or through the different submodules and component Information Systems within the Financials module. Execution of each report will bring you to a selection screen where you can further specify exactly which data you were hoping to see. This allows you to use the same report for different purposes.

Reports and lists generated in your R/3 system can be downloaded to different formats including Microsoft Word, Excel, Access, and HTML. The following are examples of standard reports that are available in the SAP R/3 Financials module.

Financial Accounting

Account Assignment Manual

Account Balances

Account Directory Company Code

Asset List By Asset Class

Asset List By Asset Number

Asset List By Asset Super Number

Asset List By Business Area

Asset List By Cost Center

Asset List By Location

Asset List By Plant

Asset List By Worklist

Bal. Sheet/P+L From Cos Ledger

Balance Audit Trail

Balance Lists

Balance Sheet/P+L

Bank Statement

Bill Of Exchange List

Cash Flow

Chart Of Accounts Directory

Display Utility For Audit File

Duplicate Invoice Numbers

Extended Bill Of Exchange Information

Fiscal Year Version—Local Currency Year-To-Date

Fiscal Year Version—Transaction Currency

Fiscal Year Version—Transaction Currency Year-To-Date

Forced Update Of Audit File

G/L Account Balances

G/L Line Items

Line Items Extract

Local Currency Period Version

Posting Date Daily Version

Recurring Entry Original Docs

Spec. Purpose Ledger Summary Record Display

Structured Account Balances

Update Of Audit File

Value Date Daily Version

Vendor Balances In Local Currency

Vendor Due Date Forecast

Vendor Open Items

Vendor Payment History With Open Item Analysis

Controlling

Actual/2 Plan Versions

Actual Comparison Report

Actual Costing/Material Ledger

Actual In 2 Timeframes

Actual Line Items

Actual Quarterly Comparison

Actual/Plan Comparison By Accts.

Area List Plan/Actual

Balance Sheet Items

Co Documents: Actual Costs

Co Plan Documents

Cost Elements: Master Data Report

Costs For Intangible Goods And Services

FI Doc. Breakdown By Payb/RecvDrilldown Claims

FI Doc. Breakdown By Payb/RecvDrilldown Payables

Forecasting

Line Item Report: Periodic Asset Transfer

Line Item Report: Periodic Creditor Transfer

Line Item Report: Periodic Debitor Transfer

Line Item Report: Periodic Materials Transfer

Master Data List Internal Orders

Orders: Line Items Actual

Orders: Line Items Commitments

Orders: Plan Line Items

P/A Comp. Of Profit Center Group

P/A Comp. Of Profit Center Group (Origin)

Pctr: Plan/Actual Comparison

Plan In 2 Timeframes

Plan Line Items

Plan Quarterly Comparison

Plan/Actual Comparison With Partner Profit Center

Plan/Actual Current Period+Cumulative+Annual Total

Planned/Actual Comparison

Planned/Actual Comparison By Origin

Planned/Actual Comparison In Local Currency

Product Cost By Order

Product Cost By Period

Product Cost By Sales Order

Product Cost Planning

Profitability Report

St. Key Figures: Master Data Report

Investment Management

Acquisitions By Invest. Reason

Assigned Funds Per Summarization Version

Avail. Investmt Measure Budget

Available Budget In Prog. By Budg. Categ.

Available Meas. Budget By Org. Units

Available Meas. Budget By Resp. Person

Budget Availability In Program

Budget Available For Measures

Budget Distribution To Measures

Budget For Measures By Org. Unit

Budget For Measures/Committed Funds

Depreciation Forecast From Order Planning

Depreciation Forecast From Program Planning

Depreciation Forecast From Project Planning

Depreciation Forecast Total Dep. (Plan. Inv. + Curr.)

Depreciation Simulation Capital Investment Program

Depreciation Simulation Investment Projects

Depreciation Simulation Planned Investment And Assets

Distrib. Of Budg. To Meas. By Budg. Categ.

Distrib. Of Plan To Meas. By Budg. Categ.

Display Plan Inv. Prog. Position

List Of Origins Of Asset Charges

B

Measure Budget/Downpayments/Assignd. Val.

Overall/Annual Budget In Measures

Overall/Annual Budget In Program

Overall/Annual Plan From Measures

Overall/Annual Plan In Program

Plan From Measures/Appropriation Request

Plan In Program, Approp. Req., Measures

Plan/Budget Comparison In Program

Prog. Budg./ Standard Investment Reasons

Program Budget/Committed Funds

Proof Of Origin By Cost Elements

Request Plan/Assigned

Request Plan/Budget For Measures

Request Plan: Investments/Expenses

Treasury

Cash Position

Commitment Items Alphabetical List

Commitment Items Assignment To G/L Accounts

Commitment Items Hierarchy Graphics

Commitment/Actual By Doc. No.

Commitment/Actual By Fin. Com.

Commitment/Actual/Inventory

Liquidity Forecast

Planned/Actual Comparison

Enterprise Controlling

Changes In Hidden Reserves

Changes In Investee Equity

CM: Region/Business Area/Product Group

Company Code: Concl. Prv. Yr Comp In G/L

Company Code: Fin. Statement Prv. Yr LC

Company Code: Success Struct. Pr. Yr LC

Company: Prev. Year Comp. In Local Curr.

Comparison: Current Year/Previous Year

Division Comparison

Elimination Of IC Profit: Inventory Management Companies

Equity Holdings Adjustments For Associated Companies

Equity Structure Of Investee Companies

Group: Year/Previous Year In Group Curr.

Overview Company Codes: Key Figs GC

Percentage

Plan/Actual Comparison

Print Asset Transfers

Quarterly Comp.: Customer Group/Division

Quarterly Comparison: State List

Quarterly Comparison: Product Group List

Ranking List By Customer Group

Value Development In In Group Currency

Value Development In Local Currency

B

Real Estate

Actual—Period Comparison

Actual Yearly Comparison

Actual/Apportionment Unit

Actual/Area Unit

Actual/Commitments/Plan/Variance

Actual: Year Overview

Allocation Per Tenant

By Cost Elements Actual—Period Comparison

By Cost Elements Actual Yearly Comparison

By Cost Elements Actual—Year Overview

By Cost Elements Periods—Actual

By Management Contracts Actual—Period Comparison

By Management Contracts Actual Yearly Comparison

By Management Contracts Actual—Year Overview

By Management Contracts Periods—Actual

Changes To Option Rates

Changes To Rental Units And Agreements

Commitments—Period Comparison

Commitments—Year Overview

Commitments—Yearly Comparison

Credit/ Receivables

Cumulative Values Actual Line Items

Deadline Monitoring

Distribution Of Settlement Result

Input Tax Distribution

Itemization Of Settlement Units

Option Rates BE/PR/BU

Overview Of External Heating Costs

Payroll Result

Periods—Actual

Periods—Commitments

Periods—Plan

Plan—Period Comparison

Plan—Year Overview

Plan—Yearly Comparison

Posting Log For Settlement

Premium Reserve Fund List—Real Estate

Settlement By Cost Elements

Settlement By Line Items

Settlement By Settlement Units

Transaction Control

B

APPENDIX C

SAP R/3 Human Resources Sample Standard Reports

SAP's Human Resources module includes a large collection of standard reports that can be executed through the report tree in the Human Resources Information System. Execution of each report will bring you to a selection screen where you can further specify exactly which data you were hoping to see. This allows you to use the same report for different purposes.

For example you can use the Employee Directory report to create an employee directory for all employees in a certain location, of a certain nationality, age, or gender all by modifying the selection criteria on the selection screen. Different selection criteria for reports can be saved as variants and the reports can be executed with the variants so that you do not need to fill in the selection screen.

Reports and lists generated in your R/3 system can be downloaded to different formats including Microsoft Word, Excel, Access, and HTML. The

Human Resources report tree also contains a report entitled Flexible Employee Data, which allows you to custom build your own report (similar to the Ad Hoc Query tool discussed in Hour 20) with an easy point-and-click functionality. The following standard reports are available in the SAP R/3 Human Resources module.

Human Resources Administration

Assignment to Wage Level

Birthday List

Defaults for Pay Scale Reclassification

Education and Training

Employee Directory

Employee Groups and Subgroups

Employee History

Employees According to Seniority and Age

Employees with Powers of Attorney

Family Members

Flexible Employee Data

Grade Time-Related Statistical Evaluations

Grievance Summary

Group Value for Appraisal Evaluation

HR Master Data Sheet

Key Plans for Education Types

Label Printout with Country-Specific Address Editing

List of Employee Numbers

List of Maternity and FMLA Data

Log of Report Starts

New Hire/Terminated Employees

Salary According to Seniority

Service Anniversaries

Staffing Changes

Staffing Level Development

Telephone Directory

Time Spent in Job

Vehicle List

Organizational Management

Authorities and Resources of Positions and Workplaces Throughout an Organizational Structure

Employee Development Data

HR Cost Planning Budget Scenario

Job & Position Task Description by Percentages

Job and Position Descriptions

Job Descriptions with Tasks, Requirements, and Career Paths

Job Directory with Coordinating Position Details

Organizational Assignments

Organizational Plan/Display

Organizational Structure Existing Intervals

Organizational Unit and Position Reporting Structure

Organizational Unit and Position Staff Functions

Planned Labor Costs

Position Staffing Schedule/Assignments

Status Overview per Organizational Type

Suitable Evaluation Paths

Task Catalog

Task Characterizations

C

Vacant/Obsolete Positions

Work Center Restrictions/Health Exams per Organizational Unit

Recruitment

Applicant Selection

Applicant Statistics

Applicants by Action

Applicants by Name

Applicant's Education and Training

Applications

Evaluate Recruitment Instruments

Job Advertisements

Maintain Vacancy Assignments

Vacancies

Vacancy Assignments

Variable Applicant List

Employee Development

Career Maintenance

Career Planning

Change Qualifications Catalog

Change Training Plan Catalog

Create Appraisal

Display Appraisals Catalog

Display Profile

Display Qualifications Catalog

Display Training Plan Catalog

Display/Change Appraisal Model Catalog

Edit Appraisals Catalog

Edit Career Items (graphic)

Edit Qualifications Catalog

Evaluate Careers

Expired Qualifications

Find Appraisals

Graphical Training Plan Maintenance

Individual Training Plan

List of Alternative Qualifications

Match up Positions with Holders for an Organizational Unit

Profile Matchup

Profiles

Qualification Profile: Mass Data Maintenance

Search for Employees who Participated in a Training Plan

Search for Employees who Participated in Parts of a Training Plan

Search Person to Qualification

Succession Planning

Training Plan Catalog

Training Plan History

Compensation Management

Assignment to Wage Level

Comp-Ratio Analysis

Display Pay Scale Groups

Planned Labor Costs

Salary According to Seniority

C

Salary Structure List

Training and Event Management

Attendee Reports

Appraisals

Attendance and Sales Statistics

Attendance Statistics

Attendee Bookings

Attendee List

Attendees for Rebooking

Attendee's Qualifications

Attendee's Training History

Budget Comparison

Cancellation List

Cancellation List per Attendee

Employee List

Pre-bookings per Attendee

Pre-bookings per Course

Prerequisites for Attendance

Training Resource Reports

Available/Reserved Resources

Graphical Resource Reservation

Material Requirements per Course

Resource Equipment

Resource List per Course

Resource Reservation

Resource Reservation Statistics

Resources Not Yet Assigned per Course

Resources Type

Training Course Reports

Appraisals

Course Brochure

Course Dates

Course Demand

Course Hierarchy by Group and Type

Course Prices

Course Schedule

Travel Management

Employees with Exceeded Trip Days

Overview of Trips with Detail Selection

Trip Cost Reporting by Period

Trip Statistics—Cost Assignment

Trip Statistics—Trip Framework Data/Trip Totals

Trip Statistics—Trip Receipts

Statistic Manager

Overview of Planned Trips

Trip Itinerary

Overview of Imported Credit Card Accounting Runs

Overview of Existing Credit Card Documents

Payroll

Wage Type Reporting

Assignment of Wage

Benefits Administration
Benefits Administration Reports
Eligible Employees

Employee Participation

Eligibility Change

Vesting Percentage

Benefit Changes

Employee Demographics

Change of General Benefits Data

Benefits Choice Analysis

Dependents List

Health Insurance Portability Accountability Act (HIPAA)

COBRA Administration Reports

401 Non-Discrimination Testing

Form 5500 Reporting

Workers' Compensation by State and Department

Premium Reports
Health Premiums

Insurance Premiums

Savings Premiums

Spending Premiums

Miscellaneous Premiums

Utility Reports
Currency Conversion in a Benefit Area

Plan Cost Summary

Check Actual Working Hours

C

Time Management

Time Evaluation

Cumulated Time Evaluation Results

Time Leveling

Time Management: Error Processing

Time Recording Overview List

Time-related Statistical Evaluations

Time Spent in Each Pay Scale Area/Type/Group/Level

Working Time From Time and Incentive Wage Earners

Attendance and Absences

Frequency of Attendance and Absences

Graphical View of Absence/Attendance

Leave Deduction Check

Leave Obligation Report

Leave Overview

Prerequisites for Attendance

Time Balances

Time Statement Form

Shift and Workforce Planning

Display Personal Timetable

Display Target Requirement in Weekly Overview

Overview of Daily Work Schedules

Personal Shift Plan

Planned Labor Costs

Staffing Changes Per Employee

Staffing Schedule

Target Requirement in Daily Overview

Personnel Work Schedule

Regulatory Reports

The following regulatory reports are ordinarily not accessed through the General Reporting Tree. These reports can be accessed through the ABAP Editor (transaction code /nSE38) by entering their program names listed in parentheses next to each report name.

OSHA - 101 Report (RPSOSHU2)

OSHA - 200 Report (RPSOSHU1)

Vets - 100 Report (RPSVETU0)

EEO-1 (Equal Employment Opportunity) Report USA (RPSEEOU1)

AAP: Movement Analysis USA (RPSAAPU0)

AAP: Turnover Analysis USA (RPSAAPU1)

AAP: Workforce Distribution USA (RPSAAPU2)

Date Monitoring (RPPTRM00)

C

Appendix D

SAP R/3 Logistics Sample Standard Reports

SAP's Logistics module includes a large selection of standard reports that can be executed through the general report tree, or through the different submodules and component Information Systems within the Logistics module. Execution of each report brings you to a selection screen where you can further specify exactly which data you want to see. This allows you to use the same report for different purposes.

Reports and lists generated in your R/3 system can be downloaded to different formats, including Microsoft Word, Excel, Access, and HTML. The following are examples of standard reports that are available in the SAP R/3 Logistics module.

Sales and Distribution

Call Up List of Price Groups

Call Up Material/Matprcgroup List

Call Up Price List W. Stepped Display

Customer Credit Memos—Selec.

Customer Returns, Selection

Customer, Inv. Sales—Selection

Customer, Inc. Orders—Selection

Delivery Notes List

Display Backorders

Display Blocked Orders

Display Customer (Centrally)

Display Material

Employee—Credit Memos, Selec.

Employee—Inv. Sales, Selection

Employee—Returns, Selection

Employee, Inc. Orders Selection

List of Incomplete Documents

List of Inquiries

List of Quotations

List of Sales Orders

Material Credit Memos, Selec.

Process Billing Due List

Process Delivery Due List

Sales Org. Returns, Selection

Salesorg. Inc. Orders Selection

Salesorg. Credit Memos Selection

Salesorg. Invoiced Sales, Selec.

Production Planning and Control

Amounts Work Center Analysis Selection

Cap. Planning, Work Center Load

Capac. Planning, Work Center Backlog

Capac. Planning, Work Center Orders

Capac. Planning, Work Center Pool

Capacity Planning: Overload at Wkcnt

Capacity Where-Used

Deadlines Work Center Analysis Selection

Lead Times Work Center Analysis Selection

Material Analysis Selection

Material Usage Analysis: Selection

Operation Analysis Selection

Product Cost Analysis: Selection

Product Group Planning Evaluation

PRT: Where-Used Lists

PRT: Usage of Document in Orders

PRT: Usage of Material in Orders

PRT: Usage of PRT Master in Orders

Sales and Operations Planning

Single Display Mrp List

Work Center Assignment to Cost Ctr

Work Center Capacities

Work Center Hierarchy

Work Center List

Materials Management

Analysis of Order Values

Lng-Term Plg Mat. Gr. Analysis

Long-Term Plg Mat. Analysis

Long-Term Plg Vend. Analysis

D

Outl. Agreements by Acct. Assignment

Outl. Agreements by Req. Tracking No.

Outline Agreements by Agreement No.

Outline Agreements by Material

Outline Agreements by Material Group

Outline Agreements by Vendor

POS by Requirement Tracking Number

Purch. Orders by Account Assignment

Purch. Transactions by Tracking No.

Purchase Orders by Material

Purchase Orders by Material Group

Purchase Orders by PO Number

Purchase Orders by Vendor

Purchase Orders for Supplying Plant

Purchasing Reporting

RFQs by Collective Number

RFQs by Material

RFQs by Material Group

RFQs by Requirement Tracking Number

RFQs by RFQ Number

RFQs by Vendor

WM: Material Flow—Selection

WM: Material Plcmt/Removal: Selection

WM: Movement Types—Selection

WMS: Flow of Quantities Selection

WMS: Stck Placemt.+Remov. Selection

Quality Management

Cust. Analysis Expense

Cust. Analysis Level/Disp.

Cust. Analysis Lot Counter

Cust. Analysis Q Score

Cust. Analysis Quant. Overview

Cust. Analysis Quantities

Cust. Analysis, Lot Overview

Customer Anal. Overview Q Not.

Customer Analysis Item Q Not.

Customer Analysis Items QF

Display Quality Score Time Line

General Results for Customer

General Results for Material

General Results for Vendor

Mat. Analysis Items QF

Mat. Analysis Overview Q Not.

Material Analysis—Effort

Material Analysis—Quantities

Material Analysis—Lot Overview

Matl Analysis—Level & Disp.

Matl Analysis—Lot Numbers

Matl Analysis—Qty Overview

Matl Analysis—Quality Score

Matl. Analysis—Q Notif. Item

Quant. Results for Material

Quant. Results for Vendor

Quantitative Results for Cust.

Vendor Analysis—Level & Disp.

Vendor Analysis—Effort

Vendor Analysis—Lot Numbers

Vendor Analysis—Qty Overview

Vendor Analysis—Quantities

Vendor Analysis Lot Overview

Vendor Analysis Quality Score

D

Plant Maintenance

Breakdown Analysis

Display Equipment

Display Equipment List

Display Functional Location

Display Maintenance Item

Display Maintenance Plan

Display Object Network

Display PM Notification

Display PM Order Confirmation

Display PM Orders

Display Strategies

Equipment Structure

Equipment: Mean Time Between Repair

Functional Location Structure

Functloc: Mean Time Between Repair

Graphical Scheduling Overview

Location Analysis

Manufacturer Analysis

Obj. Statistic Analysis

Object Class Analysis

Object Damage Analysis

Package Order

Planner Group Analysis

Project System

Actual Contribution Margin

Budget/Actual/Commitment

Budget/Actual/Variance

Cap. Planning, Work Center Load

Missing Parts List

Multi-Level Order Report

Outl. Agreements By Acct. Assignment

Overview: Costs/Revenue/Expenditure/Income

Overview: Project Hierarchies

Plan/Actual/Commitment

Plan/Actual/Variance

Planned Contribution Margin

Profit/Loss Results

Project Result and Stock

Purch. Orders by Account Assignment

Purchase Orders for Project

Purchase Requisitions for Project

Requisitions by Account Assignment

Reservations by Account Assignment

Revenues Hierarchical Actual Contribution Margin

Revenues Hierarchical Plan/Actual/Variance

Revenues Hierarchical Planned Contribution Margin

Sobj: Actual/Commitment/Available

Sobj: Plan/Actual

Stock/Requirements List

D

INDEX